Listening In

Listening In

The First Decade of Canadian Broadcasting, 1922–1932

MARY VIPOND

McGill-Queen's University Press
Montreal & Kingston • London • Buffalo

© McGill-Queen's University Press 1992
ISBN 0-7735-0917-8

Legal deposit fourth quarter 1992
Bibliothèque nationale du Québec

Printed in the United States of America
on acid-free paper

This book has been published with the help of a grant
from the Social Science Federation of Canada, using
funds provided by the Social Sciences and Humanities
Research Council of Canada. Funding has also been
received from Concordia University.

Canadian Cataloguing in Publication Data

Vipond, Mary, 1943–
   Listening in: the first decade of Canadian broadcasting,
   1922–1932
   Includes bibliographical references and index.
   ISBN 0-7735-0917-8
   1. Broadcasting – Canada. 2. Broadcasting policy –
   Canada. 3. Broadcasting – Law and legislation –
   Canada. I. Title.
   PN1991.3.C3A96 1992   384.54 0971   C92-090382-7

Typeset in 10/12 New Baskerville by
Nancy Poirier Typesetting Ltd., Ottawa.

For My Family

Contents

Tables

Acknowledgments

The publication of this book would not have been possible without the assistance and support of archivists, librarians, colleagues, students, friends, and family.

At the top of the list of those I would like to thank are the archivists and librarians at the National Archives in Ottawa and the Vanier Library at Concordia University, who have been unfailingly knowledgeable and pleasant. For encouragement, and for listening, I am grateful as well to Howard Fink, Bill Hubbard, John Jackson, Ron Rudin, Leona Senez, and Dorothy and Reid Vipond. I also gained much from the opportunity to present various aspects of my work to students and colleagues at the Association for the Study of Canadian Radio and Television, the Centre for Broadcasting Studies at Concordia, the School of Journalism at Carleton University, and the history departments at Brock, Concordia, and Trent universities. My thanks also go to Irene Spry of Ottawa for permission to quote from the Graham Spry Papers and to the manuscript's two assessors for their helpful suggestions. Once again I appreciated the care, patience, and good humour that Curtis Fahey brought to the editing task.

Finally, special thanks to Bill, Peter, and Catherine Butler for their love and comfort, and for putting up with my absences, both physical and mental.

Introduction

Countless times during the seven years I have been working on this book, I have been asked about my research subject. When I replied, "The early years of Canadian broadcasting," the response was almost invariably, "Oh yes, the history of the CBC." No, I explained (I hope patiently), *before* the CBC – the more than ten years of broadcasting in Canada before the Canadian Radio Broadcasting Commission (CRBC), the predecessor to the Canadian Broadcasting Corporation, was created in the spring of 1932.

The assumption made by my interlocutors is not surprising. The first years of broadcasting in Canada have never been systematically examined and indeed have been almost forgotten. While full scholarly histories of early broadcasting in the United States and Great Britain were published in the 1960s,[1] in Canada the book that has so far served as the definitive history of Canadian radio – Frank Peers's *The Politics of Canadian Broadcasting, 1920–1951* – covers the period up to 1932 in 104 pages, of which only 34 deal with the growth of the medium before 1929, when the Royal Commission on Radio Broadcasting (the Aird commission) made its momentous recommendation that a national company be created to control all Canadian broadcasting facilities.[2]

This point is not intended as a condemnation of Peers's work. As the title of his volume makes clear, it was never intended to be a fully rounded study but rather to emphasize political debate and public-policy decisions about broadcasting, especially the CBC, over a considerable span of years. Nevertheless, the fact that Peers chose this focus is instructive. Canadians have always been America-watchers. We have assumed – not incorrectly – that what is unique about Canada in North American broadcasting is the presence of a government-owned national broadcasting organization, the CBC. We have therefore proceeded to the corollary assumption that what is *interesting* about Canadian broadcasting is the CBC. Consequently, private broadcasting, including the period before 1932 when there was little else, has been neglected by serious scholars despite the fact that private stations have always attracted the majority of listeners.[3]

Even on those occasions when the decade of the twenties is discussed in the historical literature, disproportionate emphasis is placed on the chain of stations set up by Canadian National Railways, indeed sometimes to the exclusion of all other topics.[4] The assumption behind this approach is, of course, the same: because these stations were purchased by the CRBC in 1933 and are thus in a certain sense the forerunners of the CBC, they must, it seems, be the most important factor in the broadcasting of the 1920s. As we shall see, however, this was far from true.

There are other reasons as well for the emphasis on public-policy and public-ownership issues in the previous historiography. Canadian scholars have been intensely interested in the regulation of radio and television (again, at least in part, because of the preoccupation with the question of the American cultural presence). In the absence of legislation specifically to regulate broadcasting in the 1920s, it has been assumed that none occurred. The decade is thus again dismissed as insignificant. This is also, however, a false perception; radio was indeed regulated in Canada in the 1920s, by the Radio Branch of the Department of Marine and Fisheries – although to what effect does need close examination.

My bias is somewhat different. It seems to me (an inveterate listener to CBC radio, by the way) that it is vitally important to study the "total" history of Canadian broadcasting, not just those aspects that make it different from what happens south of the border.[5] We have today in Canada what is usually described as a "mixed" public and private broadcasting system. Typically, historians have argued that this was a sort of compromise between the British and the American ways of doing things; while public ownership à la the BBC was attractive to many Canadians, especially English-Canadian nationalists, it was necessary to allow private enterprise also to remain in the field as a concession to the realities of the North American market-place. Yet those scholars who have argued in this manner have concentrated their attention on one side of the balance, on the publicly owned broadcaster, and have neglected to look at the other. Or, when they have done so, private-broadcasting interests have been the villains of the piece. Thus, for example, most of what has been written about the conditions of Canadian broadcasting in 1929 when the Aird commission reported – or in 1932 when the Radio Broadcasting Act set up the CRBC – has been rather uncritically derived from sources preserved by the proponents of public broadcasting, most notably the Canadian Radio League (CRL).

The public-policy decisions taken in the early 1930s *were* very important, and they have shaped the direction of Canadian broadcasting to the present day. But we cannot understand them fully unless we also know how the Canadian radio industry developed in the 1920s and how it reached the point that the government decided that changes were essential. The CRBC and later the CBC were not created in a vacuum. The fact that broadcasting had been pioneered by private entrepreneurs for ten years previously and the various successes and failures of that period substantially affected the way these public organizations were formed and therefore the way they subsequently operated.

My intention in this work, then, is to examine the development of Canadian radio broadcasting in all possible dimensions from its beginnings until the passage of the Radio Broadcasting Act of 1932. Over the course of those years, a rapid and dynamic evolutionary process occurred. Technology, culture, economics, and politics all interacted in the birth and early development of what was simultaneously a new industry and a new cultural endeavour. In his stimulating study *Media and the American Mind*, Daniel J. Czitrom argues that each modern communications medium is "a matrix of institutional development, popular responses and cultural content that ought to be understood as a product of dialectical tensions, of opposing forces and tendencies clashing and evolving over time ..."[6] complex interrelationships not only between but within the categories of institutions, audience, and content determined the directions in which radio broadcasting developed. Each choice made, and its timing, had an incremental effect upon the next.

Essentially, radio involves a triangular relationship among broadcasters, manufacturers of equipment, and audiences/customers. In the very early 1920s, this worked relatively straightforwardly, as broadcasting was initiated by manufacturers for the purpose of selling receiving sets. This linkage was subject to many pressures, however. Before long other organizations began to broadcast. Consumers began to ask for radios that were easier to operate and of better quality both in a technical and a programming sense. This demand strained under-financed broadcasters and resulted among other things in the practice of networking. Another solution to the problem of subsidizing good broadcasting was to bring advertisers into the equation; once that occurred the primary transaction involved broadcasters selling audiences to advertisers, with the programming acting as a sort of "loss leader." Indeed by the early 1930s some advertisers were producing the programs themselves to ensure that they served this purpose as effectively as possible. Meanwhile the government, itself beset by many conflicting pressures, played a role as well; as the licenser of the broadcasters, it had the power to make rules about both advertising and program content, to impose technical-quality standards, and above all to determine who could broadcast. Over the decade, transmission and reception equipment and programming became increasingly sophisticated, the improvements being driven by the demands of the various parties in the relationship. As broadcasting became more costly, however, survival in a competitive North American market became more difficult; by the end of the period (and in the context of the Great Depression) broadcasters, manufacturers, and government all agreed that some method of allocating listeners' dollars to help pay the capital, network, and programming costs of coast-to-coast Canadian broadcasting was essential to its continuance.

None of the parties involved came to broadcasting with a *tabula rasa.* While radio was a new medium, it did not develop in isolation from the rest of society but rather within a context of earlier technologies and business structures and previously established social, political, and cultural formations. In turn, however, it changed some of those structures and priorities. The new medium was shaped by society and in turn reshaped it. For the 1920s, nevertheless, the main emphasis rests on the former. Two-thirds of Canadian homes still did not own receivers at the end of the period being examined here, so although many practices had been established, the full impact of radio on Canadian life remained undetermined in 1932.

In Canada as well, to a greater extent than any other country, the development of broadcasting was affected by the lead taken by a neighbouring country to whose technology and programming many Canadians had access. This fact simultaneously spurred and hampered Canadian broadcasters; they were pressed to improve their services to the level being offered by American stations but at the same time they possessed fewer resources, in part because American corporations owned much of the Canadian electrical-manufacturing industry. Again, this was a prime motivation in the call for more government involvement in Canadian broadcasting by 1932.

Out of this tangle of pressures and counter-pressures, Canadian radio had evolved by 1932 from being a toy for mechanically inclined boys and men to a major cultural force whose impact, it was clear, would become even greater in the future. The directions that evolution had taken were not pre-determined or predictable in 1920; they were the result of an ongoing process by no means at an end in 1932. There was no inevitability about it, although certain near-immutable factors such as contiguity with the United States and general public acceptance of a liberal free-enterprise ideology certainly narrowed the margins of manoeuvre. The industry grew by fits and starts over the course of the 1920s and few knew (although many predicted) what lay ahead. There were many ups and downs, much confusion, but also much excitement, as all those involved in broadcasting, from the big corporate manufacturers to the Radio Branch bureaucrats, from the pioneer broadcasters to the ordinary listeners, had a strong sense that they were participating in a new era in history.

While not the first mass medium in twentieth-century Canada, radio was uniquely important because of the choices ultimately made about its ownership and regulatory structure. Not only did it become the focal point for a major nationalist campaign in the early 1930s but the eventual result of that debate was a step toward public ownership, a measure unprecedented in Canadian cultural policy. Nevertheless, despite the creation of the CRBC and CBC, many of the political, financial, and cultural questions that confronted Canadians concerned about broadcasting in the 1920s remain with us today.

In order to describe and explain most effectively the evolution of Canadian radio broadcasting in its first decade, this book is divided into three approximately equal parts. The first four chapters survey the beginnings of broadcasting; the growth of the listening audience, the radio-manufacturing industry, and the broadcasting business; the financing of radio; and the evolution of programming. The four middle chapters discuss in detail how broadcasting was regulated by the Radio Branch of the Department of Marine and Fisheries during the 1920s. The final three chapters examine in the context of this background the debates and policy decisions taken from the time the Aird commission was set up in 1928 to the passage of the Radio Broadcasting Act in May 1932.

PART ONE

1 The Beginnings of Radio Broadcasting in Canada

On 20 May 1920, the members of the illustrious Royal Society of Canada gathered in the ballroom of the Chateau Laurier Hotel in Ottawa to hear a concert performance featuring vocalist Dorothy Lutton. The unusual feature of the event was that Miss Lutton was singing in a small room in the factory of the Marconi Wireless Telegraph Company of Canada over one hundred miles away in Montreal and her voice was being transmitted to Ottawa through the air, without wires.[1] This specially arranged demonstration was, some scholars argue, the first regularly scheduled radio broadcast ever, and gives XWA, the Marconi experimental radio station, the distinction of being the first broadcasting station in the world.[2] Whatever the strength of that claim, many Canadians first became aware of radio broadcasting through reading press reports of this remarkable concert.

Although the concept of broadcasting, literally the sending out of radio signals to a "random, anonymous, and potentially unlimited audience,"[3] was new in 1920, radio (or wireless telephony as it was first known) was the descendant of earlier devices for electronic communication, the telegraph, the telephone, and the wireless telegraph. Long before broadcasting began, the institutional, legal, technological, and economic structures within which it would develop had been formed. To understand fully that context, it is necessary to glance back briefly at these earlier inventions in modern electronic communications.

The American Samuel Morse invented the first practical electromagnetic telegraph in 1838 and opened the first line between Baltimore and Washington in 1844. Within two years the first Canadian telegraph company, the Toronto, Hamilton, Niagara and St Catharines Electro-Magnetic

Telegraphy Company, had set up wires and begun commercial operations. Telegraph lines multiplied rapidly and quickly became essential to the
railway and newspaper businesses, as well as a great boon to many other
commercial concerns. Canada and the United States were virtually the only
nations in the world that left the development of this major new means
of communication to private enterprise.[4] (Although telegraphy began in the
private sector in Britain, the Post Office took over the domestic telegraph
system in 1869 in the interests of cheap and reliable service.) In the two
North American countries, ownership not only remained private but
became increasingly concentrated; by the end of the nineteenth century
Western Union dominated the us market, while the Great North Western
Telegraph Company, tied to Western Union both physically and financially,
along with the smaller Canadian Pacific Railway Telegraphs controlled the
Canadian.[5]

While Canadian telegraph companies were privately owned, governments both chartered and regulated them. The first Canadian legislation to regulate telegraphs was the Electric Telegraph Companies Act of
Upper Canada, passed in 1852.[6] This early law provided for a limited
amount of supervision of the operations of the private telegraph companies,
for example regarding where lines could be constructed, and allowed
the crown to take over a line and require the service of its operators at any
time on a temporary basis or, on two months' notice, to assume permanent
possession. An act passed after Confederation in 1881 asserted some
federal-government responsibility over the telegraph companies by placing
the Department of Public Works in charge of administering an oath of
secrecy to their employees.[7] With the telegraph, then, an important institutional precedent was established in allowing a communications medium
to remain in private hands, minimally regulated.[8]

By 1850 the technology existed to lay telegraph cables under small
bodies of water and by the end of the 1860s a trans-Atlantic cable was in
operation. Again, cables were developed by private enterprise in the
United States and Canada; in Britain as well, overseas cables remained in
the private sector. In 1875 the Canadian Parliament passed a marine
electric telegraph act dealing with a number of details concerning the
construction and maintenance by private firms of underwater telegraph
cables. This act placed the supervision of cable companies in the hands of
the federal Department of Marine and Fisheries.[9]

Once the scientific principles behind the transmission of electrical
impulses by wire were understood and applied, it was not long before inventors and scientists succeeded in transmitting sounds – voices. Most noteworthy in this respect was the work of Alexander Graham Bell, culminating
in the invention of the telephone in 1874.[10] Bell gave his father, Professor
A. Melville Bell, 75 per cent of the Canadian patent rights to his invention

in 1877, but, unable to raise sufficient capital to form a Canadian company, Bell senior sold his rights in 1879 to the National Bell Telephone Company of Boston (later to become American Bell, and in 1885 to be transformed into an umbrella company, American Telephone and Telegraph, or AT&T). National Bell sent Charles F. Sise to Montreal to found the Bell Telephone Company of Canada in 1880. Under Sise's direction for the next thirty-five years, Bell Canada (to use its current name) aggressively expanded to dominate much of the Canadian telephone market.[11] In Britain and the United States as well, private enterprise, especially the Bell interests, developed the telephone; in Britain, however, the system was taken over by the Post Office in 1912.[12]

Canadian legislation supervising telegraph companies specifically excluded telephones;[13] like their predecessors, however, telephone companies could be chartered provincially or, if they were deemed to be "to the general advantage of Canada," federally. The Bell Telephone Company of Canada was from its inception, at its own request, federally incorporated.[14] In 1906, after a lengthy House of Commons inquiry into issues of monopoly and rates, the Board of Railway Commissioners was given the power to regulate telephone rates, but Bell managed to fight off the threat of public ownership at this time.[15]

In Canada, then, both the telegraph and the telephone were developed in the private sector. Owing to the nature of their business and their technology, especially because large-scale interconnection of lines was essential, both industries have often been viewed as "natural monopolies," although a lot of hard work by astute businessmen as well as supportive governmental interventions also went into the achievement of near-monopoly status by Bell, Great North Western, and CP Telegraphs by 1900.[16] While no systematic study of either industry in Canada has been written, it is clear that, of the three basic options of relatively free private enterprise, closely regulated private enterprise, or government ownership, the Canadian federal government opted for the first in the communications field in the nineteenth century. What regulatory legislation existed was relatively insignificant before 1905 and even after that still assumed that economic criteria rather than "the public interest" should prevail.[17] This policy remained a precedent for attitudes and practice even after the circumstances were somewhat altered with the development of wireless telegraphy and telephony and despite the acceptance of more stringent regulation and even government ownership in some other public utilities.

The scientific principles and technological advances lying behind the transmission of dots and dashes and later of voices *without wires* differed considerably from those using wires, and were first developed primarily by individuals and firms not centrally involved in the telegraph or telephone business.[18] As a result, much of the early history of commercial wireless concerned competition with the previously established technologies. The greatest entrepreneur of wireless telegraphy was the Italian Guglielmo Marconi, who, building upon the research of James Clerk Maxwell and Heinrich Hertz, developed and promoted the wireless telegraph from the mid-1890s on.[19] Unable to get financing in Italy, Marconi moved to England, where he and his backers set up the Wireless Telegraphy and Signal Company in 1897 (after 1900 to be known as Marconi's Wireless Telegraph Company) and soon established subsidiary companies in a number of other countries.

In May 1901, the Canadian government ordered two wireless stations from the Marconi Company which it erected at Belle Isle, Newfoundland, and Chateau Bay, Labrador, because the cable connecting these two points was vulnerable to ice damage. These stations, which went into operation in late 1901, were, it seems, the first wireless installations in Canada.[20] More spectacularly, on 12 December 1901, the first successful transoceanic wireless message, sent from Poldhu, Cornwall, was received by Marconi and his assistants on Signal Hill at St John's, Newfoundland. On 1 November 1902, the Marconi Wireless Telegraph Company of Canada (hereafter called Canadian Marconi, the name it officially adopted in 1925) was registered as an Ontario company, and a dominion charter was granted in August 1903. The principal assets of the new Canadian company were the Canadian and Newfoundland rights to all patents of British Marconi.

The primary activity of the Marconi group of companies was the erection and operation of wireless-telegraph stations on ships and coastal shores for navigational and commercial purposes.[21] This function reflected the most obvious advantage of wireless telegraphy, the liberation of communications from dependence on wire networks. Marconi wished to set up a permanent transmitting and receiving station in Newfoundland but was prevented from doing so by the Anglo-American Telegraph Company, which had the monopoly in Newfoundland for receiving cabled trans-Atlantic messages. On his way to New York to find an American location for his station, Marconi disembarked at North Sydney, Nova Scotia, where he was apparently met by Alexander Johnston, the owner and editor of the Sydney *Record*, the local Liberal MP and a man who already realized "the tremendous possibilities of wireless communication."[22] Johnston, according at least to one version of the story, convinced Marconi to set up his main North American station at Glace Bay, primarily by using his political contacts to persuade the Canadian government to foot the bill up to $80,000.[23] Again by this action a precedent was established: while the government was willing to finance the station in the interests of cheaper communication with Europe, it preferred to leave ownership and operation in the private hands of the Marconi firm.[24] Johnston we shall hear of again, for coincidentally he was to serve as the deputy minister of Marine and Fisheries throughout the 1920s and thus be one of the chief architects of early Canadian broadcasting policy.

The Glace Bay wireless station and a similar station at Clifden, Ireland, were ready for full commercial operations by February 1908, although wire links from Clifden to London and Glace Bay to Montreal and New York remained unsatisfactory until about 1912.[25] In the meantime Canadian Marconi also contracted with the Canadian government to build coastal wireless-telegraph stations for ship-to-shore communications in the interests of marine safety; while these stations (fifteen were erected by 1907) were owned and subsidized by the Canadian government, they were leased to Canadian Marconi and operated by Marconi employees, with the company keeping the tolls collected.[26]

A third activity of the Marconi companies was the manufacture of wireless apparatus. Initially, this was concentrated at the main plant in Chelmsford, England, but smaller factories were also built by the subsidiary companies. In 1909 a Canadian manufacturing operation to meet local needs commenced with the opening of a workshop on Delorimier Ave in Montreal.[27]

In 1904 the British government passed a wireless telegraph act, which provided that all those transmitting or receiving wireless signals must be licensed by the Post Office. (As mentioned earlier, the Post Office already operated all wire-telegraph lines in Britain, and was soon to take over telephones as well.) While wireless was left in the private sector, the licensing requirement was introduced on the grounds that the authorities must be in a position to prevent unauthorized information from leaving the country, to prevent interference with naval communications, and to enforce any international wireless agreements Britain might make.[28] Soon after its passage, the Colonial Office forwarded a copy of the act to the Canadian government with the recommendation that similar legislation be prepared in the dominion on the grounds that "if private persons or companies are left at liberty to establish Wireless Telegraph installations, without having to obtain a license, such installations may interfere with one another, and with the working of any installations that the Government might think fit hereafter to establish ..."[29] The Canadian government took the advice.

Canada's 1905 Wireless Telegraphy Act was virtually identical to the British one, with the important difference that it made the Department of Marine and Fisheries, rather than the Post Office, the licensing body.[30] This followed the Canadian precedent of placing both cable jurisdiction and the fisheries-signals service in that department; in Canada, the Post Office was never involved in regulating electronic communications. By the 1905 act, the minister of Marine and Fisheries was given the authority to determine the form, period, terms, conditions, and restrictions pertaining to licences to operate wireless transmitting and receiving devices, and penalties for the operation of unlicensed apparatus were prescribed. It may be noted that there seems to have been no consideration in 1905 as to whether wireless licensing was a federal or a provincial responsibility; the federal government simply took charge.[31] Almost immediately after the passage of the act, the Wireless Telegraphy Branch (later called the Radiotelegraph or Radio Branch) was set up within the Department of Marine and Fisheries.[32] In 1910 C.P. Edwards, a young Englishman who had come to Canada in 1905 to work at a Marconi coastal station, was appointed to head the branch. We shall hear a great deal more of Edwards, who was to remain director until 1936.

By the time the Wireless Telegraphy Act of 1905 was passed, however, the concerns it addressed were on the verge of being superseded by the arrival of wireless telephony or radio. The Marconi system of wireless telegraphy had used radio waves generated by a series of sparks jumping across a gap. This was not suitable for voice transmission because the interruptions made speech unintelligible; what was needed was a more powerful transmitting instrument that could send continuous waves with the voice superimposed or modulated on them. For detection or reception of the waves, Marconi used a coherer, a device that was temperamental and slow. Both to establish the commercial future of wireless telegraphy and to move into radio telephony, therefore, it was clear by the early twentieth century that improved technology was necessary both for transmission and reception.[33] Between 1900 and 1914 a number of different means of generating continuous waves were explored, including the arc transmitter invented by Duddell in Britain and Poulsen in Denmark and adopted by the US Navy in 1913 and the high-frequency alternator developed by E.F Alexanderson in the General Electric laboratory. The real breakthrough, however, came with Dr Lee de Forest's 1907 patenting of the audion, "one of the pivotal inventions of the twentieth century."[34] The audion or triode was similar to an earlier two-element tube patented by Ambrose Fleming in England in 1905, but with a grid added between the two electrodes. Initially viewed only as a more sensitive detector, the audion really came into its own after 1912, when discovery of its great powers of amplification made it clear that in the future this tube would be central to the apparatus for both transmitting and receiving by wireless telephony.[35]

Most authorities credit the first wireless transmission of speech to Reginald Fessenden, a Canadian from Quebec's Eastern Townships. While an employee of the National Electric Signalling Company, Fessenden broadcast speech and music using an Alexanderson alternator on Christmas Eve, 1906, from Brant Rock, Massachusetts, which was picked up by shipboard radio operators on their telegraph receivers.[36] During the next few years Lee de Forest, one of America's most innovative engineers in this field, broadcast music on several occasions from a transmitter in New York City. Radio telephony reached the practical stage for moderate distances using an arc transmitter in 1913–14; the first long-distance transmission was made by AT&T engineers between Arlington, Virginia, and Paris in 1915.

Although individual inventors began the research into radio, because of the expense of experimentation and especially of patent protection, development of the new technology was soon taken over by large companies already well established in the electrical or communications fields. In North America, General Electric, AT&T, and American Marconi dominated in research and development by 1914. Among them they also controlled the patents central to radio's future: Marconi the Fleming diode, AT&T de Forest's audion, and General Electric the powerful alternator. At this early stage, the big companies were not necessarily as interested in developing wireless telephony as a communications system as they were in commercial use of its various parts and in gaining control of competing technologies. To cite just the most famous example, AT&T snapped up rights to the audion between 1913 and 1917 and spent a great deal of money improving it, not because the company foresaw itself moving into radio as a commercial endeavour but because the audion was useful in the amplification of voices on long-distance telephone lines, because radio might be a useful extension of wired networks in remote areas, and because control of the audion patent would give the corporation a bargaining lever in future developments in the whole field.[37] So it was to prove.

The rapid growth and improvement of wireless telegraphy, increasing appreciation of its uses for navigational safety, an international radiotelegraphy agreement (the London Convention) signed by Britain and the colonies in 1912, and the advent of wireless telephony prompted the Canadian government to draft legislation more comprehensive than the 1905 act to cover the wireless field. The most important provision of the Radiotelegraph Act of 1913 at the time was the requirement (in line with the resolutions of the international convention) that virtually all passenger steamers plying Canadian ports, whatever their registry, must possess radiotelegraph apparatus and a qualified operator.[38] The act also required that all radiotelegraph operators in Canada be British subjects and that they sign a declaration of secrecy.

More important for our purposes were the sections that became directly relevant to the growth of broadcasting, as this 1913 act remained the legislative basis for regulation of radio until the Radio Broadcasting Act of 1932. The defining clause was 2(b), which read: 'Radiotelegraph' includes any wireless system for conveying electric signals or messages including radio-telephones." Apparently it was not the original intention of the drafters of the Canadian bill to add radiotelephony to its compass; copies of the documentation show that the word was pencilled in at the second draft, the handwriting being that of C.P. Edwards. An unsigned memo, apparently also from Edwards, justified bringing radio under the provisions of the act because "the electric waves that are used in wireless telephony are identical with those used in wireless telegraphy, and a wireless telephone station is capable of interfering with a wireless telegraph station or visa [*sic*] versa."[39] Edwards's intervention was not only technically correct but far-sighted. The inclusion of radiotelephony in the act was to give the federal government considerable authority over the development of all aspects of radio, including broadcasting, well into the 1920s.

The Canadian legislation of 1913 (like that of 1905) specified that no person could "establish any radiotelegraph station or install or work any radiotelegraph apparatus in any place in Canada ... except under and in accordance with a license granted in that behalf by the Minister." It gave the minister power to make regulations with respect to classes of licences, the form and manner of applications for licences, "the conditions and restrictions to which the ... licenses shall ... be subject," and the authority to inspect the radiotelegraph stations. The Governor in Council was given the power to set licence fees, make censorship regulations in time of war or emergency, and accede to international radiotelegraph conventions. Provisions were also made for finding and seizing unlicensed apparatus, and penalties for violations of any part of the act were laid out. Thus, although designed primarily for the regulation of the wireless-telegraph business, especially its marine applications, because it included jurisdiction over radio telephony the act gave the federal government a firm legal footing on which to build radio regulation and sufficient discretionary power to guide the fast-changing radio field until 1932.

The Radio Branch had originally been created within the Department of Marine and Fisheries but by the time of this 1913 legislation it had been transferred to the new Department of the Naval Service, where it was to remain until 1922.[40] The most important activity of the branch in the years following 1913 was, in the words of its annual report, "to provide facilities for communication with ships at sea and thus assist in their navigation and the safeguarding of the lives of the people they carry ..."[41] Many of the steadily growing number of shore stations on the east coast as well as all of those on the west coast were both owned and operated by the Radio Branch; by 1920 there were sixteen of these. A number of other stations (thirty-one by 1920), as already mentioned, were owned by the government but built and operated by Canadian Marconi on a long-term lease basis. In connection with marine navigation, it was also the branch's responsibility to license shipboard stations and to examine all operators for competency. Permanent inspectors were located at key ports for this purpose.

The Radio Branch also licensed and supervised commercial, experimental, and amateur users of wireless apparatus. At this early stage, the principal commercial uses foreseen for wireless approximated those already developed for wired telegraph and telephone. It was generally assumed that wireless would be used for point-to-point communication from one specific location to another, either as a "private" service for the internal communications of a single company (for example, for messages between a head office and a remote field location), or as a "public" service, that is, for the use of the general public in sending messages for a fee. Wireless, it seemed obvious, would be most useful in those areas where geographical features or low-population density made the erection of lines impracticable. There was, however, one great drawback to wireless as a means of business or personal communication: the messages transmitted could not be kept private but on the contrary were accessible to anyone with a receiver tuned to the appropriate wavelength.[42] When sending telegraphically, the use of codes could somewhat alleviate this problem, but for the wireless telephone, which had the great advantage of being simpler to use, there seemed to be no solution to the danger that competitors might eavesdrop. Thus, although wireless had certain obvious benefits as a means of commercial communication, there was also a major obstacle inhibiting the full development of the technology for this purpose alone.

Nevertheless, a few Canadian firms took out licences for the use of wireless transmitters and receivers in their private operations before and during the First World War. According to government records, the first private commercial licences were issued in the fiscal year that ended 31 March 1912 to Goodyear Tire and Rubber Company for stations at Toronto and Bowmanville (for communication between the head office and the factory) and to Canadian Explosives of Montreal for a station at Bowen Island, British Columbia, (for communication between the eighty-six men at the factory in Howe Sound and the government coastal station at Point Grey, from which messages could travel to the head office by conventional telegram).[43] Thereafter several lumber and oil companies in Alberta and British Columbia also obtained licences for private commercial stations, presumably also for communication with field operations. All of these were telegraph stations, operating in telegraph code. In the 1914–15 fiscal year sixteen private commercial licences were issued in Canada, but this dropped to four in 1915–16 and to three in each of the two subsequent years.[44]

As we have already seen, Canadian Marconi operated a trans-Atlantic commercial-message service from its Glace Bay transmitter, for which it held a public commercial licence. After 1915 two more public commercial licences were issued to Universal Radio Syndicate for stations in New Brunswick and Cape Breton but these do not seem to have ever become operational.[45] During the 1914–15 fiscal year, Canadian Marconi opened a test room in its Montreal factory, for which it obtained an experimental licence with the call letters XWA. During the First World War all the above classes of stations were allowed to continue to operate, although under tighter secrecy rules.[46] A number of experimental licences were also issued to army camps (as early as 1909) and to four radiotelegraphy-training schools set up to fill the heavy wartime demand for trained shipboard operators.[47]

Well before the war, however, wireless use had also spread in a very different direction. Although high-powered and long-distance telegraphic and telephonic communication without wires necessitated increasingly complex apparatus, simple transmitters and receivers were relatively easy and inexpensive to build, especially following the discovery that adequate reception could be achieved by touching a thin wire to certain mineral crystals. Beginning around 1907, magazines such as *Popular Mechanics* and *Scientific American* printed diagrams and instructions to guide those interested in constructing their own wireless sets. A fraternity mainly of teenage boys and young men, the amateurs, began to listen in to ships' calls and to communicate with one another in telegraphic code, constantly tinkering with their equipment and making imaginative use of scavenged or mail-ordered parts.[48] In the fiscal year ending 31 March 1911, the Radio Branch issued an experimental licence to Frank Vaughan of Saint John, New Brunswick, Canada's first licensed amateur. (Eighteen years later, in 1929, Vaughan, by then an engineer and the manager of the electrical engineering firm Vaughan Electric, would appear before the Aird commission's hearings in Saint John to argue for a private broadcasting station for his home town.[49]) By the time the war began and all amateur licences were cancelled for the duration for security reasons, there were ninety-five amateurs in Canada, sixteen of them licensed for receiving only, concentrated along the waterways in the Maritimes and central Ontario, in Montreal (including the École Polytechnique and many individuals with French names), and on the west coast, especially in Victoria.[50] When the war ended, amateur licensing was resumed by Order in Council PC 888 on 5 May 1919, and within a year 281 amateurs were on the government's books. These now included many, especially airmen, who had been trained in wireless technique during the war and who kept it up as a hobby after demobilization.[51] A number of wireless clubs sprang up in which veterans, teenagers, engineering students, professors, and other interested "hams" gathered to exchange technical and experimental information. One, the Winnipeg Radio Club, founded in March 1919, had as its secretary young University of Manitoba student Graham Spry, who ten years later was to return to his interest in radio with significant consequences for the history of Canadian broadcasting.[52]

Recent historians of radio in both Britain and the United States have remarked upon how decades of neglect have hidden the important role of the amateurs in popularizing radio in its first years.[53] The same may be said for Canada. By the end of 1920 there were nearly six hundred licensed amateurs in Canada; they formed the nucleus both of the first broadcasting audience, helping to popularize radio by spreading news of its delights and marvels, and of the first experts, teaching many of those interested only in listening in (soon to be known as broadcast listeners or bcls to distinguish them from the hams) to build and operate their new equipment. They worked in radio shops, factories, and radio stations too, providing their expertise to early retailers, manufacturers, and broadcasters. They were an essential ingredient in the mix necessary for the take-off of broadcasting as a popular medium in 1921.

By the end of the fiscal year 1920–21, then, the year broadcasting began and our story commences, there were 610 licensed radio-telegraph stations in Canada: six public commercial, twelve private commercial, eleven experimental and 581 amateur experimental, as well of course as the ship and shore stations concerned with marine navigation. All these stations were operated by individuals capable of transmitting and/or receiving Continental code, the variant on the Morse code used for international radiotelegraphy. With some tinkering, all the receivers in use could be converted to hear voices. As early as July 1914, twenty-year-old amateur Edward S. Brooks of New Westminster, British Columbia, applied for a licence to experiment "with a wireless telephone," and he was undoubtedly not alone.[54] Successful telephonic transmission, however, as already explained, required continuous wave rather than the old-fashioned spark apparatus, and to the end of 1920 only XWA, the Marconi test room in Montreal, was seriously experimenting with that new technology (although the Canadian Independent Telephone Company of Toronto also received a licence to do so in August 1920).[55]

There remains one piece of the puzzle to put into place. Most of the inventions central to effective wireless telephony had been made by 1915, and the United States already dominated research and development in the field. The great American corporations had, however, got themselves into a hopeless muddle of patent suits and counter-suits such that no one company could make much commercial progress because none controlled enough of the necessary rights.[56] At the urging of Navy officials, when the United States entered the war a patent truce was declared. With conflicts temporarily set aside and military and naval purposes made the top priority, great and nearly final strides were taken to perfect radiotelephony.

Most essential for future commercial development, in addition to the creation of a cadre of trained operators, was the wartime development of mass-production techniques for standardized sets and tubes.[57]

The next important step in North America was taken in November 1919, when, under nationalist and protectionist pressure from the US Navy and the federal government, American Marconi sold out to a new company, the Radio Corporation of America (RCA), controlled by General Electric. By mid-1920 GE, RCA, and AT&T had signed a cross-licensing agreement that put all their patents into a single pool, to be joined two years later by those of Westinghouse. This arrangement ended the manufacturing stalemate caused by the patent split.

Still, it would not be too great an exaggeration to say that even at this point radio remained a technology in search of an industry.[58] There certainly were military and commercial uses for point-to-point wireless-telephone stations, with enough potential to make the negotiation of complex patent deals and continued research expenditures worthwhile, but those possibilities were nothing compared with what broadcasting was to bring. Already, however, GE, Westinghouse, and AT&T formed an "invincible triumvirate in the field of communications and electrical manufacturing" in the United States and, via their subsidiaries, in Canada, and it was evident that henceforth their role in determining the direction in which the technology would develop would be crucial.[59]

Prior to 1920, the concept of broadcasting existed only in daydreams, most notably those of inventor Lee de Forest, who as early as 1907 had predicted that in years to come opera, news, and "even advertising" would be sent out over the wireless telephone, and of David Sarnoff, who as a young American Marconi employee in 1915 had written of the day when there might be a "radio music box" in every home.[60] But most of those in the industry, even after the war, continued to think of radio telephony solely as a means of military, business, and maritime communication. It was the amateurs and experimenters who pointed the way to the future.

The story of the beginning of broadcasting in the United States has been told often. Although there has been considerable controversy over the years as to which station was the first to broadcast, all agree that one of the main contenders for the honour is KDKA Pittsburgh.[61] Whether the very first station or not, KDKA's birth is best documented, and is worth briefly recounting for its explicit revelation of some key aspects of what commercial broadcasting, as distinct from private point-to-point radio communication, was to mean.

During the war the Westinghouse Electric Company had been doing radio-research work for the British government and in this connection had licences for two experimental stations, one in its plant in East Pittsburgh, the other at the home of Dr Frank Conrad, the company's assistant chief engineer.[62] When the war ended and amateur licensing was re-established, Dr Conrad and his sons amused themselves talking to hams in the area from their home set and, when they tired of that, began playing records into the microphone, mentioning the name of the store that supplied the records. By September 1920 they had attracted enough attention that a local department store ran an advertisement for radio apparatus "for those who desired to listen to the Conrad programs."[63] A Westinghouse vice-president, Harry P. Davis, who had been on the lookout for ways to recoup the company's investment in radio research, noticed the ad and began to contemplate the manufacturing spin-offs possible from transmitting entertainment on the air. In other words, he was one of the first to consider the possibility, as he put it later, "that the efforts that were being made to develop radio telephony as a confidential means of communication were wrong, and that instead its field was really one of wide publicity, in fact, the only means of collective communication ever devised."[64] More specifically, he realized that broadcasting had the potential to stimulate both receiver sales and goodwill for the Westinghouse firm.[65] Davis set some employees to work constructing a little transmitter on the roof of the tallest plant building, which was licensed as KDKA on 27 October 1920. The station began its broadcasting schedule with the results of the 2 November 1920 presidential election and continued mounting regular programming (one hour per night at first) from that day on.

The KDKA story shows that the birth of broadcasting was not so much a technological as a marketing innovation. Neither Conrad nor Davis performed any technical feat impossible for many others at the time; what they did, however, was to recognize a market opportunity for a large corporation seeking to utilize previously developed technology to its best advantage. The future directions of American broadcasting were suggested from the beginning.

The first broadcasting in Canada developed in a similar manner.[66] At the end of the war, the Marconi company in Britain had realized that it must move into radiotelephony or be left behind in the communications field. By 1919 speech was being transmitted on an experimental basis from Clifden to Glace Bay.[67] In March 1919, the executive committee of the Canadian Marconi board noted that good results were being obtained in these telephonic experiments and that an aerial was being erected at the Montreal factory to facilitate more testing by the experimental station XWA.[68] In September the executive committee authorized the expenditure of $5000 on two wireless-telephone sets ordered from the English company, to be used for demonstrations and as models for manufacturing such sets in Canada.[69]

Late in 1919 or early in 1920, Canadian Marconi employees in Montreal began using at least one of these sets for demonstrations to business firms and government officials, attempting to persuade them of the utility of the system for their communication needs, especially in remote northern areas. Displays of this type were also given in Toronto in April 1920 and in Winnipeg and Portage la Prairie in May. On 20 May, as we have already seen, the first widely reported radio presentation occurred, the special concert for the Royal Society, arranged by Professor A.S. Eve of McGill's physics department as part of a display of wartime inventions. C.P. Edwards of the Radio Branch, by the way (now a lieutenant-commander after his wartime naval service), was the Ottawa operator for this transmission, which seems to have been the first Canadian instance of the use of an entertainment program for demonstration purposes. Many more soon followed. In September 1920, Fred Barrow and D.R.P. (Darby) Coats of Canadian Marconi showed off the equipment at the Canadian National Exhibition in Toronto, broadcasting from the railway building to the horticultural building and displaying crystal sets and other amateur equipment for sale.[70] Several similar demonstrations were given in and around Montreal in the fall of 1920 and the spring of 1921, and regular testing continued at the factory using the 1200 metre wavelength. On Christmas Eve, 1920, Santa Claus even came to XWA, although, as Darby Coats admitted in an unpublished manuscript relating his experiences in early Canadian radio, very few heard Santa's "Ho ho ho" because listeners were not alerted in advance in the press.[71]

The significance of all this activity was that two important factors were beginning to come together. As Coats explained it:

Radio programs began with the addition of music to speech at the microphone. To begin with, the terse sentences of the engineers, thrilling as they were to experimenters, had little interest to the public, to whom we were trying to sell receiving sets. The engineers, too, ran out of breath and grew tired of repeating the alphabet and saying "ninety-nine". Probably personal convenience persuaded them to do less talking and fill in the intervals while testing, by playing phonograph records. In the interests of economy the company refrained from buying a phonograph. Instead, they asked the proprietor of a music store on Ste. Catherine West to lend them an instrument and records in return for suitable acknowledgments on the air. Thus, I suppose, the first "sponsored" programs from Canada went into the hitherto undefiled ether around Montreal.[72]

As Montrealers learned by such demonstrations that voices and music could be drawn out of the "air", sales of radio equipment were stimulated. Content for awhile to hear the odd record being played or the voice at the factory engaged in testing, people soon asked if there might be some periods each week in which they could be sure of hearing something other than code signals from amateur and commercial stations. So regular evening broadcasts were established on Tuesdays and later on additional evenings as the demand increased.[73]

Thus by the end of 1920 those in charge of the experiments at XWA, like their counterparts at Westinghouse in Pittsburgh, were already thinking of broadcasting as a means of selling receiving apparatus to listeners. Canadian Marconi's interest in this market had already been shown by its opening of a small shop on McGill College Ave.

Several different versions of the gradual transformation of XWA from an experimenter in radio telephony to a regular broadcaster (with the call letters CFCF) exist. Donald Bankart in 1926 ascribed the original idea of broadcasting in order to sell radio apparatus to Max Smith (Smyth), a Canadian Marconi employee, in January 1920. Sandy Stewart has written more recently that voice-transmission experiments began in December 1918 (which is unlikely) and credits A.J. (A.H.) Morse, the managing director, for gambling on producing receiving sets. Donald Godfrey, in the fullest examination of the subject, has suggested that "all records agree that speech and music were programmed by 1919" but also cautions that "the gradual expansion of CFCF's initial service into a continuous pattern of programming, intended for the public, took approximately two years."[74] It is worth noting that in 1928 the manager of CFCF himself wrote to the Radio Branch in Ottawa with the ingenuous query, "With the knowledge that we are the pioneer Broadcasting Station in the World we would consider it a very great favour if you would kindly let us know the date of our first broadcast." To this he received the reply: "We have not the exact details of this on our files, but find that test programmes were carried out by your Company in Montreal during the winter evenings of 1919, and regular organized programs were commenced in December, 1920, by your Experimental Station, 'XWA' on a wavelength of 1200 metres." [75]

While the precise date on which XWA/CFCF began regular broadcasting may be impossible to determine, it is clear that interest in its activities grew quickly. In the summer of 1921 Canadian Marconi launched a little magazine, *Canadian Wireless*, edited by Coats, to "inform its readers of general progress in broadcasting and serve as a medium for radio 'Hams' and others interested in wireless as a hobby to report their activities and exchange ideas."[76] In August 1921, by arrangement with the Montreal *Standard*, the results of the Dempsey-Carpentier fight were broadcast; the fight was also aired in Toronto on the experimental transmitter Canadian Marconi had now set up there. That fall, Layton Bros. music store in Montreal began advertising the Marconi concerts "being demonstrated daily."[77] In January 1922 the company received permission to extend its wireless programs to 8 to 10 p.m. every night of the week except Sunday.[78]

Gradually, not only in Montreal but across Canada, over the winter of 1921–22, radio became more and more widely known to the general public and the "radio craze" began. Continuing Marconi-sponsored demonstrations in Toronto, Halifax, and Montreal and similar displays organized by old wireless hands and amateurs in various other cities helped spark interest in radio as the latest miracle of the modern world. Crowds gathered to hear faint, tinny sounds coming over rudimentary loud-speakers and marvelled. Demonstrations in theatres and cinemas before and after the regular show gave many their first experience of the new medium.[79] In September 1921 a program was broadcast from the down-town Toronto Marconi facilities to the main bandstand at the CNE daily from noon to 1 p.m., where it was heard by large crowds over loudspeakers. Eaton's department store in Toronto set up a radio-apparatus depart-ment in the fall of 1921 and constructed a small transmitter to broadcast programs every afternoon for salesmen's demonstrations. By November the Marconi test station was apparently broadcasting every Tuesday evening in Toronto and Canadian Independent Telephone was airing concerts Monday and Thursday evenings, as well as the occasional lecture.[80] The results of the December 1921 federal election were broadcast in at least four Canadian cities – Montreal, Toronto, Vancouver, and Saint John.[81] By this time concert programs were also available from a number of American sta-tions for an hour or two each night for those whose receivers could pick them up.

Above all, in this period the press discovered radio, advertised it, and pro-moted it. By the late spring of 1922 no regular newspaper reader could fail to be aware of the new scientific wonder. Darby Coats was just one of many working in radio in its first days who believed that the role of the press in the development of broadcasting was central:

Looking backward to those days, I can never help feeling grateful to the Press for the assistance they rendered in bringing broadcasting to the notice of the public ... The support of newspapers was vital to the success of our efforts just as soon as the experimental speech transmissions were augmented by the odd musical number and provided something more interesting though still not highly entertaining. One might broadcast for months or years, but until people were supplied with "ears to hear" one's efforts would be wasted on the desert air. Somehow, the general pub-lic had to be told about it ... The newspapers kept close track of us. For better or worse, they spread the news into the homes of their readers. They co-operated with us in promotional stunts, and in innumerable ways the Press helped the cause along, so that you who enjoy the broadcasting and we in the radio profession can thank the enterprising Press for helping the infant broadcasting through the measles and the mumps ...[82]

Canadians of that period read American newspapers and magazines in large numbers as well, and similar attention being paid to the even more rapid strides of broadcasting south of the border had a spillover effect in Canada.[83] (In the United States, the Department of Commerce began issu-ing licences for broadcasting at the beginning of 1921. By the end of that year twenty-eight had been issued; by July 1922, 458.[84])

In the first rush of enthusiasm, many Canadian newspapers set up their own broadcasting stations. One was the Toronto *Star*. In February 1922 a young features editor at the *Star*, Main Johnson, got the idea that a broadcasting station might be just the boost the paper needed in its vigorous circulation battles in the Toronto market. Joseph Atkinson, the owner, and J.R. Bone, managing editor, were sufficiently persuaded that they sent Johnson to Detroit to see WWJ, the Detroit *News* station, in operation and another employee, Basil Lake, to Pittsburgh to check out equipment, costs, and programming at KDKA. On their return, Johnson's recommendation that the *Star* commence broadcasting was accepted and negotiations with the Canadian Independent Telephone Company to provide the physical plant began immediately. The *Star* was suddenly in a hurry, because both the *Telegram* and *Globe* were showing signs of interest in similar projects.[85]

On 28 March 1922, with great fanfare, the *Star* began its broadcasting service.[86] Eleven hundred "serious, considerable people of consequence" were present for the concert of light classics and popular songs at the Masonic Hall; meanwhile "youth, experimenting, questioning youth, was away sitting in the upper rooms of the city with receivers on its ears listening."[87] Telegrams, telephone calls, and letters poured in to the *Star* from amateurs who had been able to receive the program as far as 150 miles away.

On 29 March, the *Star* began publishing the daily broadcasting schedules of WGY Schenectady, WJZ Newark, WBZ Springfield, Massachusetts, and WWJ Detroit. The newspaper's own station (CFCA) began regular daily service on 10 April 1922. On that same day, there appeared a letter to the editor from Major W. Arthur Steel of the Royal Canadian Corps of Signals, who in 1932 was to become one of the first three members of the Canadian Radio Broadcasting Commission. "We are very glad to see that a Canadian firm is taking up the matter of concert broadcasting," he wrote. "We appreciate what our American cousins are doing, but at the same time hate to see Canada getting too far behind in this branch of radio."[88] But such intimations of future nationalist concerns were rare in the spring of 1922. Rather, a sense of wonder prevailed. Even the somewhat curmudgeonly journalist Hector Charlesworth, never one to lack suspicion of anything newfangled, enthused about the "daily miracles" of radio that had come upon Canadians "like a thief in the night."[89] Ten years later Charlesworth became the first chairman of the CRBC.

Interest in establishing broadcasting stations sprang up almost simultaneously in most major Canadian centres during the winter and spring of 1922. As Coats put it, "The story of early broadcasting in Canada is not one respecting a concerted effort, but a multiplicity of independent efforts, similar sometimes by coincidence."[90] In March 1922 officials at the Radio Branch of the Department of the Naval Service decided that a new category of licences for "private commercial broadcasting" should be created for these stations, which had hitherto been operating on experimental licences. Licensing specifically for broadcasting began on 1 April 1922; the stations were given call letters in the range between CFA and CKZ which had been assigned to British dependencies by international radiotelegraphic authorities. By the end of the month twenty-one such licences had been allotted, as shown in Table 1 on the following page.[91]

It will be observed that, of these twenty-one licences, six were granted to electrical manufacturers (four to Marconi, one to Bell Canada's manufacturing arm, Northern Electric, and one to the Canadian Independent Telephone Company), two to department stores, eight to newspapers, and the remainder to two prairie men, Lynn V. Salton, who was involved in the electrical business, and G.M. Bell, an insurance broker on his way to becoming a newspaper magnate.

During the rest of the year the station-building spree continued and the general pattern of ownership remained the same. By September 1922, there were forty-seven broadcasting stations licensed in Canada, by December fifty-eight. A number of these never in fact commenced operations, but some survived throughout the twenties, and a few still operate under the same call letters today.

The Radio Branch officials seem to have believed that Canadian geographic and economic conditions allowed for indefinite expansion in the number of broadcasting stations and, as far as can be ascertained, granted licences to all who applied.[92] This paralleled the practice of American officials at the time but was in marked contrast to the contemporaneous British decision to restrict licensing severely until future needs were more evident.[93] It is not clear whether the Canadian authorities made a conscious choice to grant licences to all comers or whether they just followed the path of least resistance. Nevertheless, the precedents established in the telegraph, telephone, and cable industries held true; despite the greater regulatory authority afforded by the Radiotelegraph Act, private enterprise was left to set the pace and direction of development for this new electronic medium. The implications were enormous. As a result of this decision made in the very first days of broadcasting, the Canadian broadcasting system was set almost irretrievably on a course of private competitive broadcasting similar to that in the United States.

Meanwhile, fascinated Canadians scrambled to buy the parts to put together simple crystal sets which could, with the use of headphones, receive stations up to twenty or twenty-five miles away or even further under optimum conditions. Those with more skill and more money were soon venturing into purchasing tube sets and parts with which they could hear more distant American stations. In the rush, parts became hard to get. Most of them were imported from the United States either by mail order

Table 1
Licensed broadcasting stations, April 1922

Name	Wavelength	Call Signal
MONTREAL		
Marconi	440 metres	CFCF
Dupuis Frères	420 metres	CJBC
Northern Electric	410 metres	CHYC
TORONTO		
Independent Telephone	450 metres	CKCE
Marconi	440 metres	CHCB
Evening Telegram	430 metres	CJSC
Globe	420 metres	CHCZ
T. Eaton	410 metres	CJCD
Star	400 metres	CFCA
WINNIPEG		
George Melrose Bell	430 metres	CHCF
Lynn V. Salton	420 metres	CKZC
Manitoba Free Press	410 metres	CJCG
Tribune	400 metres	CJNC
REGINA		
George Melrose Bell	420 metres	CKCK
CALGARY		
George Melrose Bell	430 metres	CFAC
VANCOUVER		
Marconi	440 metres	CFCB
George Melrose Bell	430 metres	CHCA
Vancouver Sun	420 metres	CJCE
Vancouver Province	410 metres	CKCD
Vancouver World	400 metres	CFYC
HALIFAX		
Marconi	440 metres	CFCE

or through retailers; some also came from England and a small number were manufactured in Canadian electrical plants. The very occasional complete receiving set was available but patent and manufacturing difficulties still interfered with large-scale distribution of such receivers.[94] Thus the majority of radio fans at this stage were, of necessity, those both interested in and capable of constructing their own sets. In January 1922 a new category of licences for receiving only was created. Henceforth those interested only in broadcast listening could simply purchase a licence for $1; it was no longer necessary to prove one's competence to operate in code, to be a British subject, or to swear an oath of secrecy to have a radio-receiving licence in Canada. By the end of June 1922 there were 2588 Canadians with radios licensed for reception only; by the end of the fiscal year, 31 March 1923, there were 9954.[95]

By the summer of 1922 many newspapers, even those that did not run their own stations, were carrying radio columns with information about programs and about construction and reception problems. A number of magazines catering both to the traditional amateurs and to the growing number of the new class of broadcast listeners came into existence. These little magazines, among them *Radio, Wireless and Aviation News, The Radio Bug,* and *Radio News of Canada,* as well as others such as *Radio Broadcast* from the United States, published programming and technical information in varying proportions; they were soon supplemented as well by how-to books and manuals.[96] In April 1922 a writer in one of these radio magazines was bold enough to declare (albeit somewhat prematurely) that "radio has passed its term of probation, it has received the popular approval and now takes its place, not as a luxury, but as a necessity in the advancement of civilization."[97]

Supervising this remarkable spurt of growth of a brand new industry was the Radio Branch, which was transferred on 1 July 1922 in connection with the abolition of the Department of the Naval Service back to the Department of Marine and Fisheries.[98] At the time of the transfer, radio officials found themselves not only performing their traditional tasks relating to marine navigation and licensing but suddenly coping with the unprecedented new demands of broadcasters and listeners. Soon they were to find broadcasting regulation and policy formation taking up most of their time and causing most of their headaches but also affording continuing excitement and fascination. The broadcasting era had dawned.[99]

Journalists and other élite commentators greeted the new age with great anticipation. Virtually every article about the potential of radio in the early 1920s was laden with such superlatives as "miraculous," "the birth of a new world," or "the greatest discovery of the twentieth century."[100] A sense of awe and excitement pervaded the commentary – awe at this new sign of man's mastery over nature and excitement about the uses to which the new medium might be put. "Time and space," intoned one expert, were "finally yielding to victory."[101] One recurrent theme was that radio was one of the beneficial by-products of the war and as such helped to counterbalance the many "trials and tribulations" the conflict had also engendered. The invention of radio was yet another proof that, despite the setback of the war, the twentieth century was laden with possibilities, that through modern science, progress toward a more perfect world would continue.[102]

Not unexpectedly, the most frequently voiced hopes concerned the role radio would play in a country of Canada's large size and scattered population.[103] Very typical of the immediate post-war period was the worry that east and west seemed to be drifting apart; radio was greeted enthusiastically as a means of counteracting that tendency to separation. Similarly, journalists expressed the belief that dangerous class antagonisms would be alleviated by this most "democratic" of all media. Now the finest artists would be accessible to all without charge; every Canadian would be broadened, elevated, educated. "There are no class distinctions in the air!" exclaimed one editor, oblivious to the very real sense in which he and others like him were already viewing radio as a medium by which bourgeois values could be instilled in the masses.[104] Nevertheless, the major emphasis throughout was of community, of "human fellowship" and "comradeship," of what Marshall McLuhan would many years later term the "global village."[105]

This sort of rhetoric was not unique to Canada, to this period, or to this medium, of course. The telegraph was welcomed with similar hopes in the United States in the mid-nineteenth century. In Canada, from the earliest days of railways (especially the CPR) the technology of modern systems of communication has been viewed by many observers as central to the Canadian attempt to create a nation; the nationalists who were to call for a publicly owned coast-to-coast radio network in the early 1930s reiterated the same theme. Indeed, it may be argued that the idea of communication – and the celebration of the technology of communication – has always been central to both the material and the mythological definition of Canada.[106]

Not only did the commentators of the 1920s expect radio to play a central role in binding the country together (the difficulty in including francophone Canadians by means of an oral medium was little discussed) but they assumed that radio would provide special solace for the isolated and the lonely. Although there was occasional mention of the sick and shut-in who would benefit from radio, much more emphasis was placed on those who lived in rural areas. "Radio [will] assist Canada to people the country districts, and take away that sense of loneliness that has been felt by the settlers of earlier days," wrote the editor of *Radio News of Canada* in 1923.[107] Again, this sanguine conviction highlighted a particular concern of the élite in the 1920s – the drift to the city. These journalistic observers foresaw an essentially utilitarian role for radio; it would help keep "them" – especially recent immigrants – down on the farm.[108] Housebound women as well, the commentators were certain, would find companionship in radio; it would alleviate their sense of isolation and consequent "restlessness."[109] In the evenings radio would also perform the enormously useful task of keeping young people, especially teenaged boys, off the streets. As one very early advertisement for radio equipment put it: "Mr. Canadian Father, think it over! A few dollars on one side of the balance. *Your* boy's good character and future on the other. What is it worth to YOU?"[110]

In general, then, radio was very quickly perceived by those who reflected on it as an instrument that would contribute to stability, especially in the home. A Canadian radio magazine quoted with approval a New York clergyman's sermon extolling radio as a "God-sent agency to restore and keep intact the family circle and the home life of our city that was being torn apart by so many other diversions."[111] As Elton Johnson wrote in *MacLean's* in 1924: "Radio does not destroy, but builds up the happiness of the home. Radio is an indoor entertainment which can be, and is, enjoyed by the women-folk and the children equally with the man of the house. Reduction in cost, improvement in clarity and tone and simplification in operation are the three features which are converting family after family, as families, into enthusiastic groups of radio fans ... That radio will have an important influence in moulding and changing Canadian home life will be admitted."[112]

All of these hopes and dreams, it may be seen, were fundamentally conservative in their cast. The journalists rejoicing in the potential of the wonderful new medium in fact predicted uses for it that would reinforce the most traditional values of Canadian society: family, home, farm, and national community. Radio was welcomed for both its entertainment and its ideological potential for maintaining stability in a troubled age.[113] That radio was viewed as a new means of accomplishing old tasks is not surprising. It may be argued, indeed, that all new technology is initially integrated into society, not only imaginatively but also politically and economically, in very conservative ways, to serve existing ends rather than to challenge and change them.

Only a few of the early commentators expressed any fears or hesitations about what radio might bring, and even these cautions were not so much about permanent dangers as about temporary problems – reception difficulties, over-technical equipment, exaggerated claims.[114] In Britain, according to Asa Briggs, early alarms were sounded that radio might lead to habits of passivity and a decline in reading.[115] Few in Canada expressed such fears publicly. Nor was there much serious discussion before 1928 on questions of censorship, ownership, control, or regulation. On the contrary, although it was admitted that the real future of radio could not yet be discerned, the new medium was welcomed unquestioningly as the successor to the phonograph, the automobile, and the movies; a novelty now, it would soon be a necessity in every home.[116] With the manufacturers, the amateurs, and the broadcasters, the overheated rhetoric of Canadian journalists created an atmosphere of uncritical acceptance of the new medium. Some of what was anticipated came to pass, some did not. But in the meantime, until its precise social role had been determined, radio symbolized and embodied the hopes of the post-war generation.

Broadcasting became a widely popular phenomenon in a short period of time as the result of a conjunction of circumstances. The "boom" of 1921–22 was largely contrived by manufacturers and retailers aware of a potential market for radio apparatus and by newspaper publishers and journalists in search of new and happy stories. The hitherto-unprecedented number of trained men being released from the armed forces available to act as technical experts, listeners, and popularizers was also important to the take-off, as were the phonograph companies and department and electrical stores that quickly became sponsors and broadcasters. The process was only minimally controlled by the Radio Branch of the Department of Marine and Fisheries, which limited its concerns to checking the transmission apparatus of the various private broadcasters and assigning them wavelengths. Over the course of the next decade, Canadian broadcasting was to be gradually transformed into a sophisticated industry in its own right. Our examination of that transformation will begin with a look at the development of the Canadian radio-manufacturing industry, the changing size and distribution of the listening audience, and the nature and financing of the broadcasting stations.

2 Manufacturers, Listeners, and Broadcasters

Broadcasting involves three interdependent parties: the manufacturer, the broadcaster, and the listener, who provide three interdependent services: equipment, programming, and consumption. The evolving inter-relationship among these parties and their functions determined the rather uneven patterns in the growth and spread of broadcasting in its first decade. Fuelling the process was a double-pronged drive for markets: the manufacturers trying to sell a new product to as many customers as possible, and the broadcasters endeavouring to attract as many listeners as they could.

As outlined in Chapter 1, broadcasting in North America was initiated by the interaction between manufacturers searching for a new market for transmitting and receiving equipment and amateur wireless operators pursuing an enjoyable hobby, the latter group soon supplemented by less technically oriented individuals seeking entertainment. At first it was the manufacturers who provided the third element in the triangle, the broadcast programming, for without programs few receivers would be sold. As the decade passed, manufacturers added many improvements to their radio equipment (both transmitters and receivers) to attract more purchasers. Some of them, particularly in the United States, also continued to provide high-quality programming; the failure of manufacturers to interest themselves similarly in Canadian broadcasting had important repercussions. In both countries, other individuals and organizations began broadcasting as well. Like the manufacturers, they were interested in enlarging the number of listeners as rapidly as possible, either to create goodwill or publicity for their own firms or, later, to attract advertisers to help cover the rising costs of broadcasting as a self-sustaining business enterprise. Listeners demanded higher technical quality and better programming, thus in turn spurring a continuing series of improvements in both set manufacturing and broadcasting, with consequent spiralling costs. An editorial in *Radio News of Canada* in 1925 highlighted this triangular relationship: "If we can stimulate a greater interest in radio, we shall be able to have better programmes and more of them. This will, in turn, mean a greater interest on the part of the buying public and will encourage the engineers and manufacturers to make greater efforts in perfecting the apparatus used both in transmission and reception."[1] This chapter will examine in detail the growth of the Canadian radio-manufacturing industry and the spread of radio listening and radio broadcasting in Canada in the 1920s. The analysis will continue in the following chapter with a look at the financing of broadcasting, the role of advertising, and the beginning of the networks.

Developments in Canadian radio manufacturing in the 1920s were almost entirely derivative from the situation in the United States. When the war ended, in a nationalistically inspired move to prevent American Marconi from re-establishing its dominance in the American communications field, General Electric bought out its assets and transferred them to a new company called the Radio Corporation of America, with which it then signed a licensing agreement dividing up roles between the two firms, with GE as the manufacturer and RCA the communications and sales arm. All the essential radio patents were not under the control of GE-RCA, however, so in 1920 a cross-licensing agreement was worked out with AT&T-Western Electric to pool patents and further subdivide spheres of operation in the electrical-communications area.[2] Later the United Fruit Company and Westinghouse were also brought into the pool in an arrangement placing RCA under the ownership of the other four corporations. By the end of 1921, not only had all the important US patents been pooled but the interests of the various parties had been united by their joint ownership of RCA, a company initially created explicitly to represent US interests in the international communications field but now also increasingly important as the central player in the rapidly expanding domestic broadcasting business.

These arrangements had considerable impact on Canada. With the first Marconi-GE deal, it became necessary for British Marconi and General Electric to sort out the relations of their subsidiaries in other countries. Canadian Marconi was effectively controlled by British Marconi; while Canadian General Electric was not a subsidiary of GE, it was closely affiliated with it in that it had exclusive right to GE patents in Canada. After more than a year of negotiations among all the parties, an agreement was signed in 1921 whereby CGE and British Marconi became joint owners of Canadian Marconi and the Canadian patent rights of the two firms were pooled.[3] Although the ownership arrangement fell apart before long, the two companies remained affiliated in a cross-licensing agreement and in 1922 they also set up a jointly-owned company to manufacture radio tubes in Canada, the Radio Valve Company.[4] Simultaneously negotiations were begun among other subsidiary organizations to recreate in Canada the larger pool already in existence in the United States. (Westinghouse of Canada was a subsidiary of the US firm; AT&T owned 23 per cent of Bell Canada's stock at this time, and Western Electric 43 per cent of Northern Electric. In 1923 General Electric also acquired a controlling interest in CGE.)[5] In March 1923 Canadian General Electric, Canadian Marconi, Westinghouse of Canada, Bell Canada, Northern Electric, and International Western Electric (a subsidiary of Western Electric) signed the Canadian Radio License Agreement, which effectively pooled all important Canadian radio patents and assigned fields of interest.[6] For our purposes here, the principal feature was the allocation of manufacturing rights to Canadian Marconi, CGE, and Canadian Westinghouse.

From the beginning, the firms involved in the patent pool were sensitive that it might be viewed as monopolistic or price-fixing.[7] While to a certain extent competition did continue (for example, the three companies competed in manufacturing radio sets), from a larger perspective the group as a whole from 1923 on monopolized the radio-equipment industry in Canada by virtue of its control of all important existing patents and its ability to acquire any others developed or bought by its members' corporate affiliates in Britain and the United States. Additionally, their combined strength and wealth put the signatories of the agreement in a virtually unbeatable position if and when litigation with rival patent holders arose.[8]

In the United States battles soon developed among the interests involved in RCA, with the Telephone Group (AT&T and Western Electric), and the Radio Group (GE and Westinghouse) vying over the general orientation of the company and more specifically over how the new markets created by broadcasting should be shared. There were few immediate repercussions in Canada, however, mainly because the Canadian arrangement was simply a cross-licensing agreement and did not involve common ownership of a communications company such as RCA, thus obviating quarrels over policy and also reducing public suspicion about the existence of a "radio trust."[9]

Nevertheless, the Canadian cross-licensing agreement soon needed attention and revision. While the members of the group controlled all the major patents necessary for production of receiving sets using tubes, a number of small manufacturers were also in the marketplace. The patent situation was very complex, partly because a radio set involves so many components and circuits and also because original inventors had sometimes retained personal rights when they had sold their patents to the corporations. Legal rights were thus often unclear and, in the context of an over-heated market unable to supply demand, many small companies set up manufacturing and assembly operations. Some of these were prosecuted by the pool members but generally there was a tendency before 1926 to delay in pressing charges. What became the most important instance in Canada involved rights for personal and amateur manufacturing that Lee de Forest had retained when he sold his audion patent to AT&T between 1913 and 1917. Beginning in 1922, de Forest began to manufacture under these reserved rights and authorized others to do the same. In Canada, some of these rights were acquired by the Canadian Independent Telephone Company and when it dissolved were purchased by A.S. Rogers, who formed Standard Radio Manufacturing.[10] Standard Radio was also the parent company of Rogers Radio, which had purchased Canadian patent rights to a type of vacuum tube necessary for electrically powered sets from F.S. McCullough, an employee of Westinghouse in Philadelphia. E.S. (Ted) Rogers, the son of A.S., and the radio buff behind these companies, carried out laboratory work to make McCullough's tubes commercially practicable and in August 1925 the Rogers' company began manufacturing its famous batteryless radios. It also established CFRB Toronto in 1927 as the first broadcasting station transmitting by electrical power. (In 1929, the company's name was changed to Rogers-Majestic after it began distributing the Majestic products of the American Grigsby-Grunow Company in Canada.)

The patent position of Standard Radio was just strong enough that the members of the licensing pool feared that litigation against it was risky, or at the very least potentially costly and protracted.[11] Rather than go to court, the two groups negotiated. The result was the creation of Canadian Radio Patents Ltd (CRPL) in November 1926, owned by the four major members of the previous pool plus (with a smaller share) Standard Radio. CRPL existed solely for the purpose of issuing licences to other Canadian radio firms to manufacture sets using the patents controlled by the signatories (the value of the patents was subsequently calculated for tax purposes at $2.5 million).[12] This move to issue licences to others in exchange for royalty payments was primarily motivated, it seems, by the need to supply the fast-growing market without alienating consumers and by the profit potential and legal and administrative efficiency involved in joint licensing. The five shareholding members of CRPL of course continued to have the right to manufacture themselves, royalty-free. These five companies (along with RCA Victor, which was also included in the non-royalty group after RCA bought out Victor Records in 1929) manufactured about 43 per cent of the sets sold in Canada between 1928 and 1932, with 55 per cent of the sales value.[13] Although by 1930 the three original manufacturers, Canadian Marconi, Canadian Westinghouse, and CGE, supplied only about 15 per cent of the domestic market and were losing money on their set-manufacturing operations, the slack was taken up when sales generally fell off in 1932 and the non-royalty-paying manufacturers as a group surged to a 55 per cent share of the market (58 per cent of sales value).[14]

It should be noted that the CRPL arrangement did not involve radio tubes. While the 1923 cross-licensing agreement among the original firms had included tube patents, and that remained in effect, these rights were not extended to Standard Radio or to other firms, a situation not resolved until the mid-1930s with the creation of Thermionics, a licensing agency parallel to CRPL. It is also significant that the oligopolistic arrangements prevailing in radio manufacturing in North America were not paralleled in Great Britain, where Marconi, the leader, was forced by a compulsory licensing provision to share its patents with virtually all comers. The result was quite different ownership patterns in radio manufacturing and – in part consequently – in broadcasting.[15]

CRPL's standard licensing agreement called for licensees to pay royalties at the rate of 10 per cent of the manufacturer's selling price of the chassis (minus batteries, tubes, and speakers) plus $5 or $10 on cabinets, with a minimum payment of $10,000 annually regardless of the number of sets produced.[16] The latter provision undoubtedly had the effect of discouraging the smallest manufacturers. Additionally, at initial licensing many manufacturers were asked to pay a sum of money "in settlement of past infringements." By 1932 CRPL had collected $233,359 in past and $2,193,146 in current royalties.[17] All told, about twenty firms were licensed by CRPL to manufacture radios in Canada by mid-1931, most of them American subsidiaries. Apparently almost all applications were granted before 1930 but after that a number of interested American and British manufacturers were refused licences.[18] Many of the licensed firms did not survive the Depression but CRPL nevertheless seems to have remained a profitable venture for the patent holders.

CRPL enforced its position by shouldering the cost of attacking alleged infringers of its shareholders' patents. Indeed, legal costs were the company's largest expense.[19] Most of these suits paralleled similar cases by the parent companies in the United States; the patent allies won every one.[20] As one observer wrote: "The financial power and resources of the group are so great that few rival companies could hope to stand the strain of prolonged litigation. It is cheaper to pay royalties than to contest such a vast array of major and minor patents."[21]

In mid-1930 an application was made under the Combines Investigation Act alleging that a combine reducing competition and keeping prices unreasonably high existed in the manufacture and sale of radio sets and tubes in Canada, along the lines of a similar combine charged against RCA in the United States and being prosecuted at the time under the Sherman Act. The case was handed over to Professor K.W. Taylor of McMaster University for investigation. Taylor's report, submitted a year later, reached some interesting conclusions. First, he said, the comparison between CRPL and RCA was, strictly speaking, not sound, because CRPL was solely a licence-granting and royalty-collecting agency, whereas RCA also manufactured, sold, broadcast, and supplied technical data to its licensees. On the other hand, Taylor wrote, a "fairly good analogy" did exist if one compared RCA not just to CRPL but to "the general situation in Canada observed by reading together the Canadian Radio Licence Agreement and all the facts connected with the formation and operation of Canadian Radio Patents, Ltd."[22] More specifically, Taylor exonerated the many firms licensed by CRPL because there was plenty of evidence that they competed with one another actively. Nevertheless, he concluded that there *was* a combine composed of CGE, Canadian Marconi, Canadian Westinghouse, Northern Electric, Rogers-Majestic, and CRPL which "has operated and is likely to operate against the interest of the public" in the radio-receiving-set business because of its complete domination of the industry by means of its patent monopoly. These firms, Taylor charged, had used their control to prevent and lessen competition and to levy "onerous" royalties on other firms. Moreover, he pointed to the complete monopoly over tube manufacture held by the signatories of the 1923 cross-licensing agreement and to the "unreasonably high" prices consequently charged for tubes.

Taylor's report was eventually handed over to the minister of labour, who concluded that "the combine in the manufacture and sale of radio tubes is the only combine proved by the evidence."[23] In order to take action under the provisions of the act, he submitted the matter to the attorney-general for Ontario, who in turn referred the file to Mr Justice Armour, crown attorney for the County of York. In the end the prosecution was dropped at Armour's recommendation, on the grounds, among "other matters," that tube prices had fallen since the investigation began and that public complaints had eased.[24] (Ironically, the case against the parent firms in the United States succeeded and by a consent decree in late November 1932 GE and Westinghouse divested themselves of RCA stock – AT&T had done so some years earlier – and all the corporations signed new non-exclusive patent-pooling agreements.[25])

Students of the early days of the American radio industry have pointed out that patents were used by the large corporations in the early 1920s primarily as bargaining chips.[26] Given that each of the major corporations involved had an important patent position by 1920, competition would have retarded the growth of the industry immeasurably. Instead patent rights were used as instruments to negotiate mutual cooperation with monopoly control for the whole group as the final goal. Cross-licensing agreements and the creation of RCA were means to this end, as was litigation against patent infringers.

In the Canadian case, the patent rights involved were derivative from American parent companies, except in the cases of Marconi (with a British parent) and Rogers-Majestic (Canadian-owned).[27] The basic problem from the manufacturers' viewpoint was the same, however: how to replace unproductive competition with mutually advantageous cooperation leading to control of the market. The means used differed from those in the United States in that CRPL, with a more limited mandate and somewhat different ownership, replaced RCA as the licensing and royalty-collecting agency. Nevertheless, it remained by far the most powerful force in the Canadian radio industry. While there was very little public outcry about CRPL's monopoly position in Canada before 1932, those in the industry were well aware that it constituted the means by which Canadian radio manufacturing was centrally controlled by a small oligopoly which was in turn to a significant extent subordinate to the American "radio trust." This fact, when taken together with the broadcasting might of these same manufacturers in the United States, was to prove an important and emotional aspect of the argument for publicly owned radio in Canada in 1932.

The actual manufacture of radio sets, parts, and tubes in Canada occurred within the framework of the patent arrangements just described. Little statistical evidence about the industry has survived from the period before 1927, but what there is suggests that it got off the ground very slowly. Until about 1925 parts outsold complete sets and the Canadian market was supplied primarily by imports until 1927. According to a CRPL publication, 61 per cent of the receivers sold in Canada in 1927 were imported.[28] By 1930 this proportion had dropped to 36 per cent, and it continued to decline after that as imports were restricted – to 11 per cent in 1931 and 0.4 per cent in 1932.[29] These figures are deceptive, however, for the rising domestic manufacture they imply was in fact occurring for the most part in branch plants and constituted to a considerable extent simply the assembly of American-made parts.

The first major Canadian set manufacturers were Canadian Marconi, CGE, and Canadian Westinghouse. The former firm, along with Northern Electric, also dominated transmitter production. By the end of the decade, under CRPL licensing, a number of other companies were in the market as well. Table 2 gives the number of sets sold by the major firms between 1928 and 1932.[30]

The totals given in Table 2 are for numbers of sets *sold* (over-production was an ongoing problem) and they do not include all the figures for CGE, one of the major producers, which either would not or could not submit them.[31] The same year these numbers were gathered, the Dominion

Table 2
Number of sets sold by Canadian manufacturers, 1928–32

Company	1928	1929	1930	1931	1932
Rogers	18,500	30,600	29,500	32,900	19,200
RCA Victor	9,900	23,800	18,000	30,700	19,300
Philco	2,000	13,000	35,200	53,000	16,000
CGE	n.a.	n.a.	n.a.	17,100	12,800
Marconi	5,900	4,900	7,000	14,300	9,000
Stewart-Warner	n.a.	n.a.	n.a.	n.a.	6,600
Westinghouse	14,000	20,400	14,900	13,400	9,500
Northern	nil	nil	nil	7,600	5,900
Mohawk	2,200	3,300	5,700	4,200	2,000
Total	52,500	96,000	110,300	173,200	100,300

Bureau of Statistics reported the totals given in Table 3 for complete receiving sets *produced* in Canada.[32]

Whichever set of figures one uses, clearly substantial growth occurred in the Canadian set-manufacturing industry between 1925 and 1931, followed by a sharp drop in 1932. The firm-by-firm breakdown shows, however, that most of the production was by subsidiaries of foreign companies (only Rogers-Majestic of those on the list was Canadian-owned). While no more detailed data seems to be available, it was claimed in 1932 that 60.1 per cent of the capital invested in Canadian radio manufacturing was American, 33.8 per cent Canadian, 4.8 per cent British, and 1.3 per cent other.[33] Moreover, as mentioned above, a substantial proportion of Canadian manufacturing consisted of the assembly of imported parts; even Rogers-Majestic followed this practice. Professor Taylor produced the figures given in Table 4 for 1929 and 1930.[34]

For these two years, only 38 per cent and 37 per cent respectively of radios sold in Canada were wholly Canadian made. In both years slightly more than 50 per cent were either imported complete or assembled here from all-foreign parts. The implication of these figures is, of course, that Canadian radio receivers were essentially the same as American. Almost all the research and development was done by or for the US parent firms, although minor design modifications were made in some Canadian plants to adapt to special Canadian circumstances such as more long-distance listening. This limited, as we shall see in chapter 7, the ability of the Canadian government to make independent regulatory decisions with respect to frequency assignment in particular.

Generally, then, the Canadian radio-manufacturing industry grew substantially before 1932, to the point that it employed many thousands of people in supplying the bulk of the domestic market. Most of the production,

Table 3
Complete receiving sets produced in Canada, 1925–32

Year	Number	Year	Number
1925	48,531	1929	150,050
1926	42,430	1930	170,082
1927	47,500	1931	291,711
1928	81,032	1932	121,468

however, occurred in non-Canadian-owned plants concentrated in Toronto, Hamilton, and Montreal, and much of it involved the assembly of imported parts. Moreover, through the agency of Canadian Radio Patents, the industry was tightly controlled by a small group of firms of which only one – the minor shareholder – was Canadian-owned. In the triangular relationship among manufacturers, listeners, and broadcasters essential to the growth of the Canadian radio broadcasting industry, one of the three sides – manufacturing – was not Canadian, a fact that was to have a significant weakening effect on the whole structure.

THE RAPID GROWTH OF RADIO LISTENING in Canada in the 1920s is quickly illustrated with radio-set ownership data. The most explicit statistics come from the records of the Department of Marine and Fisheries and show the number of receiving-set licences issued in each province in each fiscal year (1 April to 31 March).[35] As can be seen from Table 5, over the course of eleven years the number of licences issued annually increased from virtually none to almost 600,000. While each year there were more radios licensed than in the previous one, the growth rate was not steady. The small increment between 1927–28 and 1928–29 may be particularly noted, and especially the actual decline in licences issued in Quebec in that year. Nevertheless, the overall pattern is one of remarkable expansion in a short span of years.[36]

These figures reflect licence, not set, ownership. For a variety of reasons – lack of accessibility, ignorance, forgetfulness, not to mention deliberate evasion – many Canadians who owned a receiving set did not comply with the regulation that each year they must purchase a $1 licence for it. Contemporary evidence suggests that from 20 to 40 per cent of radio owners in Canada did not hold valid licences.[37] Even using the minimum figure, therefore, one should probably add one-fifth more to the totals presented in Table 5 to get a true picture of Canadian set ownership in the twenties.[38]

These gross figures also disguise many changes in radio listening. The decade's evolution had three main phases. In the first, from 1922 to

Table 4
Number of sets sold in Canada, by composition, 1929 and 1930

| | 1929 | | 1930 | |
	No. Sold	% of Total	No. Sold	% of Total
Wholly made in Canada	74,312	38	83,775	37
Partly made in Canada, partly assembled from foreign parts	20,286	11	25,140	11
Wholly assembled from foreign parts	54,551	28	36,798	16
Chassis imported complete	44,957	23	79,688	36
Total	194,086	100	225,399	100

approximately 1926, listening in began as a novelty indulged in mainly by men and boys with some technical facility but quite quickly became a family-entertainment activity utilizing factory-made sets. Many fans first listened in on a crystal set consisting of little more than a tuning coil, a crystal detector, and a pair of earphones connected to an outside antenna. While these sets could be purchased complete for about $40, mostly they were put together from bits and pieces of scrounged parts and cost very little. Their range was limited to five to twenty-five miles because they did not amplify the signals received; neither could they distinguish signals transmitted on narrowly separated frequencies or be effectively attached to loudspeakers for group listening.

Because the free-wheeling policies of American and Canadian authorities allowed hundreds of broadcasting stations to be set up on the continent within a very short period, thus making long-distance listening both feasible and fascinating, the demand for more discriminating and powerful receivers soon accelerated. RCA as early as 1922 advertised a one-tube set for $65 to $100 and a three-tube set for $150 to $300 but these did not become widely used until the mid-twenties. When a three-tube regenerative receiver was hooked up to a loudspeaker, several persons could listen in together to stations up to one hundred miles away. The listening was not particularly easy, however. While these sets were quite selective, tuning required the manipulation of several controls and much squealing and distortion occurred. Moreover, many hours of work could go into "repairing broken wires, testing batteries, matching tubes, tightening connections, [and] cleaning dust and corrosion from the vital parts of [the] equipment."[39] Manufacturers were well aware that the radio industry would not grow substantially until more listener-oriented products were developed

Table 5
Receiving licences issued 1921–32 (fiscal years 1 April–31 March)

	1921–22¹	1922–23	1923–24	1924–25	1925–26	1926–27	1927–28	1928–29	1929–30	1930–31	1931–32	1931C²
PEI	17	27	138	163	202	289	587	757	985	1,270	1,189	3,022
NS	45	314	970	2,772	3,288	4,998	7,106	8,587	13,379	16,942	21,109	25,393
NB	20	105	430	1,240	2,612	2,968	4,475	6,285	8,783	11,829	13,256	15,537
Que.	197	3,018	9,250	18,211	21,141	39,207	51,347	49,751	71,757	96,999	127,804	148,873
Ont.	635	3,532	11,677	41,347	60,110	102,504	125,012	145,263	211,775	260,359	285,048	362,303
Man.	71	632	1,722	6,553	14,503	18,005	19,288	20,450	26,370	33,265	35,262	44,518
Sask.	42	562	2,655	9,303	15,944	22,238	26,635	27,358	32,906	34,152	31,487	54,845
Alta.	24	448	1,994	5,843	7,152	10,588	14,936	14,957	21,456	24,493	27,481	43,926
BC	172	1,316	2,769	6,049	9,494	14,776	18,561	23,407	35,998	43,644	55,534	65,029
Yukon	[3]	[NR]	–	12	23	31	14	[111]	[148]	[147]	[188]	70
NWT	–	–	4	3	17	46	94	–	–	–	–	NR
Canada	1,226	9,954	31,609	91,996	134,486	215,650	268,055	296,926	423,557	523,100	598,358	763,446

¹ Amateur station
² Sets reported to census takers 1 June 1931

– more attractive, easier to tune, more selective, and with better tone and greater volume. As one radio columnist put it in 1924: "The ultimate radio set will be so simple that any member of the household can operate it. This must come before the great purpose of radio is accomplished. Radio entertainment must be for the masses; not for the technically-versed minority. The ultimate radio set will be less complicated than a phonograph ... It will be the principal instrument of entertainment in all our homes."[40] On the transmitting side, it became more and more important to be able to send stronger and more consistent signals and to hold them closely to the assigned wavelength, thus necessitating increasingly powerful tubes and better controls.

The second phase, encompassing the years 1926 to 1929, was marked by growing factory production, sophistication, simplification, and power in receiving sets. More selective superheterodyne receivers were introduced into the North American market in 1927 and 1928. By 1929 dials were clearly illuminated and calibrated, single-control tuning was standard, and built-in loop antennas had replaced outside aerials.[41] Finally, and perhaps most important, by 1929 electrically operated sets were widely marketed, eliminating the need for messy, costly, and unsightly batteries. Along with these advances, however, came prices that made radio ownership prohibitive for many. While it is difficult to determine the "average" price of a receiver in this period because the range was so great, by 1929 the newer models with five or six tubes, a good loudspeaker, indoor antenna, simplified controls, and attractive cabinet cost between $175 and $325, batteries not included. The first electric sets on the market were similarly priced. The combination of high prices, consumer caution in the face of rapid innovation, and dissatisfaction with reception because of both atmospheric conditions and regulatory problems resulted in the slowdown in industry growth noticeable in the licence figures in Table 5. Thus, while the refinements of the late 1920s moved radio from the basement or attic to the living-room, the market went through a considerable shake-out.

After 1929, however, the slump ended – at least briefly. The most important factor was engineering improvements that enabled the introduction in late 1930 of good-quality midget-table models at much lower prices. According to somewhat incomplete figures collected a decade later, the average list price of sets sold in Canada in 1929 was $121; by 1931 this had dropped to $58 and the number of sets sold had risen correspondingly.[42] To put it another way, in 1930 about 30 per cent of the electrical receiving sets sold in Canada cost less than $136, while 70 per cent cost more. The following year, the figures were exactly opposite: 70 per cent cost less than $136 and 30 per cent more.[43] So despite the onset of the Depression, radio sales spiralled in 1930 and 1931 before dropping off sharply into the mid-thirties. In general, by the early 1930s, after a number of fits and starts typical of a new industry based on new technology, a substantial number of Canadian homes had radio receivers that were relatively easy to purchase, use, and maintain, and capable of providing good-quality in-home entertainment.

The figures in Table 5 reporting provincial totals for licence purchases provide us with only very general information about radio diffusion in Canada as a whole, but they are all we have for the 1920s. At the time of the 1931 census, however, a special attempt was made to collect more systematic data on Canadian radio ownership. Although these figures relate only to the situation as of 1 June 1931, they are quite complete and precise and illustrate the trends developing through the twenties. In the published version of the 1931 census the number of households that reported owning a radio, broken down by province, rural or urban residence, and by major centres, was presented. Additional material collected and distributed in a supplementary bulletin also gave a detailed breakdown of radios reported per 1000 population by province, by county or census division, by city, town, and village, and for urban and rural (farm and non-farm) dwellers.[44]

One obvious discrepancy is that 763,446 Canadians reported owning a radio to the census takers in June 1931[45] (see Table 5), while during the 1931–32 fiscal year, which encompassed that date, only 598,358 purchased licences. This confirms the estimates from observers in the twenties that many sets (here an average of 22 per cent) were unlicensed.[46] Table 6 illustrates the disparity, province by province, between the number of radios licensed in 1931–32 and those reported by the census.

More important, the detailed breakdown of sets per 1000 population presented in Table 7[47] demonstrates that there were large variations in ownership among the provinces. While in June 1931 the rate of ownership for Canada as a whole was 74.32 per 1000 and the Ontario rate was 106.16 per 1000, in Prince Edward Island it was only 34.98 per 1000. Perhaps the most striking difference is between the two largest provinces; by 1931 Ontario had a substantially larger proportion of licensed sets than Quebec, 106.16 per 1000 versus 52.35 per 1000. (In comparison, the ownership rate in Denmark was 119.5 per 1000, in the United States 98.4 per 1000, in Sweden 78.9 per 1000, and in Great Britain 77.5 per 1000. These were the only countries with higher ownership rates than Canada's in 1932.[48])

The principal factor affecting radio ownership in 1931 seems to have been urban versus rural residence. The 1931 census analysis delineated the situation graphically. In Canada's rural areas, the ownership rate was 45.78 per 1000, while in the urban areas it was more than twice that, or 98.87 per 1000. On farms, the rate was 36.09 per 1000, while in the largest cities, with populations over 30,000, it was 107.71 per 1000. This situation corresponds with both the British and the American ones at the same time.[49] It also explains much of the difference among the provinces; for the most part, the provinces with the highest proportion of rural dwellers

Table 6
Sets licensed in 1931–32 compared with sets reported in 1931 census

Province/ Territory	1931–32 Licences	1931 Census	% Licensed
PEI	1,189	3,022	39.3
NS	21,109	25,393	83.1
NB	13,256	15,537	85.3
Que.	127,804	148,873	85.8
Ont.	285,048	362,303	78.7
Man.	35,262	44,518	79.2
Sask.	31,487	54,845	57.4
Alta.	27,481	43,926	62.6
BC	55,534	65,029	85.4
Yukon	[188]	70	–
NWT	–	n.r.	–
Canada	598,358	763,446	78.4

had the lowest rates of set ownership. The people least likely in all of Canada to own a radio in 1931 were Quebec farmers (10.07 per 1000); those most likely were residents of Ontario cities of over 30,000 (138.86 per 1000).[50] Rural/urban residence was not the sole explanatory factor, however. For example, a resident of rural Ontario was still more likely to own a radio than an urban Prince Edward Islander. A resident of Quebec City, the sixth largest city in Canada, but with an ownership rate of only 64 per 1000, was less likely to own one than a resident of tiny Swift Current, Saskatchewan (88 per 1000), or Ingersoll, Ontario (142 per 1000), or rural British Columbia (74 per 1000).[51]

There are a number of explanations for these variations. One suggestion has been that the "innate conservatism" of rural dwellers led them to resist radio as a faddish urban intrusion.[52] While this proposition may appeal, it is not easy to measure. It might be mentioned, however, that rural residents have by and large been quite happy to subscribe to such "new-fangled" inventions as electricity, telephones, and automobiles just as soon as they are perceived to have sufficient utility in relation to their cost. The usefulness of radio as an information and entertainment medium was no less in the country than in the city. More concrete explanations must be sought for the phenomenon.

Another possibility relates to the care and servicing necessary for early receivers. Batteries had to be recharged and tubes replaced frequently, at some expense. While a farmer would likely possess a battery charger for use with other equipment, if he did not a trip into town to the garage would be necessary to recharge the radio battery. Or in the summer months the bat-

Table 7
Radio sets per 1000 population according to class of locality, 1931

| PROV. | RURAL | | | URBAN | | | | | TOTAL |
	On farms	Not on farms	Total Rural	More than 30,000	5–30,000	1–5,000	Less than 1,000	Total Urban	POPU-LATION
PEI	25.00	32.78	26.46	–	65.85	60.76	57.15	63.28	34.98
NS	26.04	41.86	32.07	87.52	64.59	69.98	77.73	72.03	50.12
NB	14.42	37.61	22.79	82.99	68.87	64.08	80.59	72.90	38.62
Que.	10.07	24.64	14.41	83.94	72.39	54.59	49.55	74.54	52.35
Ont.	50.98	97.90	70.30	138.86	120.41	116.71	104.00	129.01	106.16
Man.	38.35	68.87	48.67	87.21	79.73	70.93	77.75	83.94	64.59
Sask.	48.94	45.51	48.57	87.66	85.58	83.48	82.44	84.87	60.02
Alta.	46.09	53.82	47.49	82.84	86.76	79.28	79.43	82.03	60.64
BC	50.93	81.47	74.26	118.77	91.95	90.80	88.76	111.16	95.24
Yukon	–	15.65	15.33	–	–	–	19.12	16.55	
Canada	36.09	65.67	45.78	107.71	95.76	83.28	75.26	98.87	74.32

tery might be needed for other farm uses, leaving the radio idle.[53] Even more problematic would be the cost of tubes to those with little cash to spare. After 1927, as electrically operated sets began to take over the market, rural areas were at a very considerable disadvantage because of the lag in rural electrification.[54]

Another possibility is that urban dwellers were wealthier. Although the necessary evidence for a breakdown of set owners according to their wealth does not exist, all the anecdotal accounts suggest that ownership spread most quickly among the better off. While simple crystal sets could be purchased cheaply, they were also of limited value as a permanent fixture. As we have seen, more elaborate receivers could cost $200, $300, or more, and upkeep costs ran to about $30 a year.[55] The average Canadian wage-earner at that time had an annual income of $927; clearly, only those considerably above average were buying these receivers.[56] Comparisons of average urban wages do show that there was some connection between income and set ownership, but the correlation is not perfect.[57] For example, while some relatively low-wage cities such as Oshawa, Brantford, and Guelph had quite high ownership rates, some with high wages, such as Ottawa and Moncton, were below average.[58] Consequently, while it seems that income had a bearing on whether a city dweller owned a radio or not, it was not the sole determining factor. One may presume the same to be true for rural dwellers. As well, while the fairly intensive 1933 American study done for the President's Research Committee on Recent Social Trends concluded that "concentration of wealth and radio ownership are linked," it also found that some metropolitan areas "where wealth was not a factor" had very high ownership rates.[59] Canadian radio historian T.J. Allard suggests in fact that in large cities such as Toronto, where the wealthy already had a host of concerts, theatres, and so on to entertain them, it was the poorer citizens who turned to radio first.[60] The direct link between wealth and radio ownership in Canada in 1931 remains unproven.

Finally, and probably most important in explaining lower rates of radio ownership in rural areas, was the matter of access to good programming – good both technically and in terms of content. The US Social Trends survey concluded after analyzing all the factors involved: "Where programs are good and reception is clear, there is inducement to ownership."[61] Here the rural areas suffered their greatest disability. Most Canadian stations before 1932 were based in the major urban areas and broadcast with relatively weak signals. The lack of good rural reception indeed was one of the concerns impelling the formation of the Aird commission in 1928 and its recommendation that the Canadian government establish a national chain of high-power stations. Although it is true, as some have argued,[62] that even quite weak transmitters could be heard over wide areas in the early days because of the low levels of general electrical interference, nevertheless there were many rural districts with unsatisfactory reception from Canadian stations, as innumerable contemporary comments attest.[63] In 1928 the Radio Branch produced a map showing by colour-coded circles the coverage areas of Canadian stations by day and night. (Radio signals travel both by "ground" and "sky" waves; the latter, reflecting off the ionosphere only after sunset, extend much further.) According to this map, most of southern Canada except for the area between Sault Ste Marie and the Lakehead could receive Canadian stations at night. In the daytime, some districts could hear the stations of several centres, while others (including the territory between the New Brunswick/Quebec border and Moncton, the Rocky Mountains, and anywhere more than fifty miles north of Edmonton or south of Calgary) had no daytime reception.[64] Residents in some of these areas could tune in to strong American stations at night, but that reception was often made less than ideal by fading and atmospheric disturbances because of the long distances involved. For better reception, more powerful and more expensive receivers were required, exacerbating the economic disadvantage rural residents already suffered. As time passed, listeners became more discriminating and less willing to tolerate constant problems with static, so the lack of good local reception became more, rather than less, a factor in determining radio purchases as the decade progressed. Also, as urban stations improved more rapidly in quality and power after 1928, the discrepancy between urban and rural service widened.

Not only quality of reception influenced radio ownership; so did the standard and character of the programming. Here the case of rural Quebec, so markedly low in set ownership by 1931, is most illustrative. At first glance, it might seem that the low proportion of radio owners in rural Quebec related to poverty. But comparative statistics in the 1931 census indicate that, while Quebec farms were not the wealthiest in the country in terms of the value of annual production, they were by no means the poorest either.[65] Cash poverty alone is not enough to explain the abnormally low rate of ownership among Quebec farmers in 1931. Quebec radio historian Elzéar Lavoie has pointed out as well that, although Quebec farmers ranked very poorly in comparison with those of other provinces in terms of ownership of radios, automobiles, and telephones, they ranked relatively high in such amenities as electricity and running water.[66] Lavoie concludes that, forced to make an economic choice among a number of "luxury" items, Quebec farm households opted against radio, and he speculates that the reasons were as much related to ethnicity, that is, language, as to socio-economic status. The key factor, Lavoie argues, was rural Quebec's lack of access to French-language programming.[67]

Anecdotal and other evidence supports this suggestion. By 1932 there were only eight radio stations in Quebec. Most powerful by far were CFCF and CKAC in Montreal, which broadcast in English and in both languages respectively.[68] Sharing the equipment of these stations a few hours a week were CHYC, owned by Northern Electric, and CNRM, the CNR station (both broadcasting mainly in English with the occasional French-language item). In other words, even in the largest market in the province, there was no station broadcasting in the French language only.[69] The only all-French stations in 1932 were CKCV, CHRC, and CKCI in Quebec City, with a combined power of only one hundred watts.[70] CNRQ, the CNR's Quebec City station, shared the meagre facilities of CKCV and seems to have broadcast little but CNR network programs (mostly in English). The Radio Branch of the Department of Marine and Fisheries was not particularly sensitive toward the need to encourage French-language stations either. Only in 1927, for example, did the branch begin to correspond with French listeners and broadcasters in their language and to issue some of its licences and official publications in French.

The implications of the lack of French-language broadcasting stations touched the whole province of Quebec. Those living in rural areas within the range of the Montreal stations could receive bilingual broadcasts; those within about fifty miles of Quebec City could hear the relatively unsophisticated programming of the tiny stations there. Otherwise, in large areas of Quebec, the only stations regularly available were American, especially KDKA Pittsburgh and WBZ Springfield, Massachusetts. J.E.R. Tremblay of the Chicoutimi Chambre de Commerce told the members of the Aird commission in 1929: "Ici à Chicoutimi nous devons limiters [sic] aux postes américains. Nous prenons Montréal et Toronto avec difficulté."[71] Receiving only American stations might be acceptable to many in rural English-speaking Canada, but it was not so appealing to unilingual francophones. One may surmise that low radio-ownership rates were a direct consequence.

The data about 1931 set ownership in other provinces confirms the argument that access to good broadcasting was a central factor in radio ownership. Consistently the most remote areas of the country, those farthest from all broadcast signals, had the fewest radios. In northern parts of the prairies, in northern Ontario, in the francophone counties in eastern Ontario, and in the three Maritime provinces where geographical configurations made all outside reception difficult, ownership rates were uniformly and disproportionately low.[72]

Thus radio, which had been particularly touted by its early enthusiasts as a boon to the isolated and remote, in fact served those Canadians poorly, if their many individual decisions not to own a receiving set are any indication. Cape Breton farmer William Burrows summed it up with a colourful simile in a letter submitted to the Aird commission in 1929: "A radio in a Cape Breton Home, before Station C.J.C.B., began too Broadcast, was like a Farmer, with a cream seperator, and a barn full of dry Cow's. The seperator, was no good, untill the cows became milker's. And the Radio in Cape Breton was no good until station C.J.C.B. began to operrate."[73] In Canada by 1931, radio sets were very unequally distributed, and the principal reason seems to have been unequal access to broadcasting services. To understand why that was so, we must look at the development and spread of broadcasting stations in the 1920s.

AS ALREADY INDICATED IN THE FIRST CHAPTER, the initial rush of enthusiasm over radio inspired a number of individuals and businesses to set up broadcasting stations. In April 1922, foreseeing in at least a rough way the shape of the future, the Radio Branch of the Department of the Naval Service introduced three new categories of radio licences: for private commercial, public commercial, and amateur stations set up "for the purpose of broadcasting entertainment or information." Private-commercial broadcasting licences were so deemed because they were intended for stations broadcasting commercial messages only from the firm owning them. Public-commercial broadcasting licences were for stations that planned to broadcast paid messages from the public (that is, other businesses); this approximately paralleled what in the United States was termed "toll broadcasting" because it resembled toll-charge telephone or telegraph service. In fact no licences for public-commercial broadcasting were ever issued in Canada; third-party advertisements were allowed on private commercial stations almost from the beginning. Amateur broadcasting licences, which seem to have been unique to this country, were granted only to organizations of amateurs (radio clubs) and were restricted to very low power to serve small local areas, usually those lacking commercial stations.[74] By

1932 there were seven surviving amateur broadcasting stations in Canada, mainly in small towns in Ontario and Saskatchewan, broadcasting an average of one to two hours per day.[75] Some of these stations, for example 10BP in Wingham, Ontario, and 10AB in Moose Jaw, Saskatchewan, later evolved into commercial stations (CKNX and CHAB respectively). Only British subjects or companies incorporated in Canada could possess broadcasting licences but there were no restrictions on the nationality of those who actually controlled the broadcasting companies.

By August 1922, four months after the introduction of broadcasting licences, fifty-five had been issued, representing all provinces but Prince Edward Island.[76] Only thirty-six (at most) of these stations were actually functioning by that date, however, and many of the others never did begin operating. Three main types of organizations leapt into broadcasting in Canada at the earliest stage: large firms previously involved in the electrical-communications field, newspapers, and retailers (mainly small electrical shops and department stores but also including some garages because of the tie-in with battery sales). Of the three, the involvement of newspapers was the most significant in the very early 1920s.

The major newspapers in most Canadian cities entered broadcasting for two reasons: because they saw it as a fad providing entertaining stories and publicity and therefore sales, and because they viewed radio as a natural extension of and supplement to their role as media of communication. The Vancouver *Sun* emphasized the first. As its spokesman attested in his letter of application for a licence in March 1922, "It is purely a service innovation of ours, and the advantage we derive is publicity only."[77] Main Johnson, who was in at the beginning of CFCA, the Toronto *Star*'s station, agreed. Recording in his diary how he was asked in October 1923 to add radio to his other promotional responsibilities for the paper, he remarked that this was "a logical step, since radio, of course, was promotion."[78] On the other hand, John R. Bone, managing editor of the *Star*, tended to glorify the second motive. As he explained in making the paper's licence application: "We are prompted by a desire to render the best newspaper service to the public that science, through radio, permits. Our object is two-fold – first, to give the public a knowledge of this wonderful scientific development and secondly, to supply to the public by means of wireless, news of the day and high class entertainment."[79]

For the first few years of the 1920s, the newspaper-owned stations in the major Canadian centres were the most active and best-financed. The Radio Branch's first official list of broadcasting stations in Canada, as of 1 August 1922, included fourteen newspapers holding licences, all but three of them in operation. Among them were all three major Toronto papers, both the *Free Press* and the *Tribune* in Winnipeg, the *Sun* and the *Province* in Vancouver, the Calgary *Albertan*, the Edmonton *Journal*, the Regina *Leader*, the London *Advertiser* and *Free Press,* the Kitchener *News Record,* and Montreal's *La Presse.*

In the latter years of the decade, however, newspapers began to lose interest in broadcasting. By 1932 only eight papers still owned stations,[80] and of those only two, the London *Free Press* and *La Presse* in Montreal, had enough continuing commitment that they had upgraded to powerful transmitters. Many scholars have attributed this drop-out to the advent of advertising-financed broadcasting and the dawning realization on the part of publishers that radio stations competed for revenue with their newspapers.[81] While this was undoubtedly a factor, it should not be over-emphasized, for most newspapers had abandoned broadcasting before the competition for advertising revenue had reached proportions of any significance. As Main Johnson confided to his diary, there were a number of other reasons for the waning enthusiasm of the *Star,* at any rate, including the diminished publicity value as the novelty of radio wore off, the growing competition from other stations, sharply rising costs, and negative listener response when CFCA interfered with reception of American stations.[82] By the end of the 1920s good broadcasting was becoming expensive; reluctance to divert enough resources to make the continuing substantial investment necessary was likely at least as important as revenue competition in the decision of most publishers to get out of radio.

Electrical retailers commenced broadcasting for the most part out of the practical need to give their salesmen programs to demonstrate to potential purchasers of radio equipment.[83] Consequently many stations owned by retailers broadcast only during the daytime and often only very locally. The list of such broadcasters is long and varied; among the sixteen or so on the August 1922 list that can be clearly identified as retailers were such firms as the T. Eaton Company (CJCD Toronto), Dupuis Frères (CJBC Montreal), Wentworth Radio Supply (CKOC Hamilton), the Jones Electric Radio Company (CKCR Saint John), and the Motor Products Corporation of Walkerville, Ontario (CFCI). By and large, however, these were the weakest and most marginal of the early stations. As the number of other broadcasters grew, many retailers dropped out of the field. The process was well described in the reminiscences of Howard Hume, son of Fred Hume, who founded CFXC New Westminster in 1924:

My father had a store in New Westminster. He was an electrician, and in the store they sold electrical appliances, lighting fixtures and so on. He was persuaded to sell radios, and he found that he couldn't sell radios in New Westminster because there was no local station. So he got a licence and started a radio station called CFXC.

The studio was in the top floor of the Westminster Trust Building. The deal made with the Trust Company was that if the radio station mentioned the name of the building, they got their rent free ...

After a couple of years of operation, my father decided that radio broadcasting wasn't for him. It was thought he could stimulate the sales of radio sets with the broadcasting station, and it apparently didn't work out. [In 1926] he sold the radio station ... [for either $350 or $600] to the Chandler brothers in Vancouver. They bought what equipment there was, and they named it CJOR.[84]

By 1932, firms such as Hume's no longer needed their own stations because in the large cities enough other broadcasters were operating. It was only in such smaller and more isolated centres as Port Arthur (CKPR), Saskatoon (CFQC), and Fredericton (CFNB) that electrical retailers continued to be important broadcasters as well.

The third major group of broadcasters in Canada in the early 1920s, the giant telecommunications firms, were motivated to enter the field primarily in order to sell the radio apparatus they manufactured, or, in the case of the telephone companies, to protect other investments. The August 1922 list of Canadian broadcasters showed that Canadian Westinghouse had licences for six stations in Hamilton, Toronto, Montreal, Winnipeg, Edmonton, and Vancouver; Bell Telephone had two licences, in Toronto and Montreal; Northern Electric one in the latter city; and Eastern Telephone and Telegraph one in Halifax. In addition, Canadian Independent Telephone Company had a broadcasting licence in Toronto, and Canadian Marconi had four, in Toronto, Vancouver, Montreal, and Halifax.

This list gives a misleading picture of the involvement of the big manufacturers in Canadian broadcasting, however. Only the last five stations mentioned, CKCE and CHCB in Toronto, CFCB Vancouver, CFCF Montreal, and CFCE Halifax were actually operating in August 1922. Neither of the Bell Telephone stations ever opened, nor most of those projected by Canadian Westinghouse; Westinghouse's CHIC in Toronto only operated for a short time, and the same was true of the Canadian Independent Telephone station in Toronto and of Canadian Marconi's Toronto, Halifax, and Vancouver stations.[85] Northern Electric's station in Montreal existed only until about the end of 1929, after which it used time on CKAC on Sundays. Of all the manufacturers' stations listed in 1922, only Marconi's pioneer station, CFCF, was still in existence in 1932. (In addition, as already mentioned, Canadian radio manufacturer Rogers-Majestic had set up an important station, CFRB Toronto, in 1927.)

This situation was in marked contrast to that in the United States, where American Telephone and Telegraph, Westinghouse, General Electric, and their subsidiary RCA all poured huge amounts of money into both their flagship and secondary stations. Within a year or two of the beginning of broadcasting, in fact, the manufacturers' stations such as

Westinghouse's KDKA Pittsburgh, GE's WGY Schenectady, and AT&T's WEAF New York dominated North American broadcasting and set its standards. Although AT&T dropped out of broadcasting in 1926, the other corporations remained active leaders, particularly after the subsequent formation of the NBC network, which they jointly owned.

That the Canadian subsidiaries of these American corporations did not involve themselves in broadcasting in Canada (except to a limited extent as advertisers) is not surprising but very significant. Of all the major manufacturers in Canada, only Marconi had an incentive to spend any money on broadcasting in this country.[86] Quite simply, the subsidiaries of the American electrical corporations did not need to do so, because most Canadian listeners could easily tune into the parent firms' US–based stations. These companies manufactured radio apparatus for the Canadian market in Canada because of tariff barriers. But there was not and presumably could not be a barrier to radio signals flowing across the border, so there was no need to build stations or produce programs here.[87] Indeed, by the end of the decade American radio executives not only assumed but boasted that their American stations gave complete service to Canadian listeners, apparently insensitive to the fact that at least some Canadians might not find that quite so satisfactory a situation as they did.[88]

The lack of involvement of the major manufacturers in the Canadian broadcasting industry was crucial, however, because it meant that no organizations with large amounts of money had a compelling motive to set up strong stations here. More fundamentally, the problem was that the Canadian electrical industry had been largely a branch-plant industry since the late nineteenth century. It would have been equally undesirable to many to allow these US-based firms an important role in Canadian broadcasting.[89] While British-owned Canadian Marconi and domestically owned Rogers-Majestic tried to build good broadcasting organizations, their resources could never equal those of the US communications giants. Thus Canadian broadcasters remained a generally weak and poor lot throughout the first decade, and certainly so in comparison with their main American competitors.

A general picture of the spread of broadcasting stations across Canada in radio's first decade is given in Table 8, which shows the number of stations licensed on 31 March each year from 1923 to 1932.[90] The column showing "active" stations is the best indicator of total growth, which it may be seen took a considerable jump in 1926–27 but then ceased when the government imposed a virtual ban on new stations pending the Aird commission report and fundamental decisions on the future of Canadian broadcasting. The number of early stations that either never commenced operations or soon dropped out is revealed by the figures for the year ending 31 March

Table 8
Broadcasting stations in Canada, 1923–32

Year (as at 31 March)	Private Comm'l Broadcasting	Amateur Broadcasting	Total Broadcasting	Active	including Phantom[1]	Inactive
1923	62	8	70	–	–	–
1924	46	22	68	–	–	–
1925	63	17	80	56	12	24
1926	55	16	71	53	10	18
1927	73	23	96	90	16	6
1928	84	15	99	93	19	6
1929	79	12	91	85	14	4[2]
1930	81	10	91	88	19	3
1931	80	8	88	82	18	6
1932	77	7	84	79	14	5

[1] Used facilities of another station

[2] Discrepancy in original

1925, which show twenty-four of the eighty stations inactive. Shortly thereafter the Radio Branch became more reluctant to renew licences for inoperative stations, as indicated by the decline in inactive listings for the rest of the period.

As of 10 March 1932, when the House of Commons Special Committee on Broadcasting gathered the information it needed, there were seventy-seven private-commercial broadcasting stations in Canada, of which all but two were active. Thus the total number of active stations had more than doubled since 1922, a good but not astonishing growth rate. Of these stations, eighteen were "phantom" stations, that is, although they had their own owners, licences, and call letters, they used the transmitting facilities of another station. Jarvis St Baptist Church in Toronto, for example, broadcast its services under its own call letters, CJBC, on the facilities of CKGW, and *Le Soleil* (CKCI) did the same on CHRC in Quebec City.

In 1932, as a decade earlier, there were more stations in Ontario than in any other province, by far. Ontario had fifteen active stations in 1922; in all the other provinces combined there were twenty-one. By 1932, there were twenty-five stations active in Ontario, and forty-nine in the other eight provinces. Ontario's stations were more powerful too. In 1922 the power of each station was measured according to watts of input. On that basis, Ontario had about 9800 watts in operation in that year, the other provinces about 13,000 watts altogether. By 1932 a different power measurement was used, normally termed antenna power, which was from three to five times less than the input rating.[91] In 1932 Ontario's active stations together broadcast at an antenna power of over 19,000 watts in the daytime; the other provinces combined had just over 35,000 watts.[92] In both years, then, about 43 per cent of the total broadcasting power in Canada came from Ontario stations. (Ontario had about 33 per cent of Canada's total population.)

In 1922 the vast majority of Canadian stations were located in larger cities, such as Toronto, Montreal, London, Winnipeg, Calgary, Edmonton, Vancouver, Halifax, and Saint John. By 1932 there had been some broadening out but the clustering in or near centres of substantial population remained evident. While there were now small stations in such communities as Lethbridge (CJOC), Sydney (CJCB), North Bay (CFCH), Charlottetown (CFCY and CHCK), and Chilliwack (CHWK), they had very low power, as little as 50 watts in some cases. The most powerful stations were still in the major metropolitan centres. It is not possible to draw an accurate map of broadcasting coverage areas in the 1920s because radio-reception patterns are always irregular owing to the interference caused by natural geographical and man-made features. As a rule of thumb, however, Canadian engineers in 1932 estimated that a 5000-watt station could be heard acceptably within 125 miles in the daytime and a 500-watt station within twenty miles.[93] Twenty-one of Canada's stations broadcast at 500 watts in 1932; only eight at more than that. Four of those eight stations were in southern Ontario. In the Maritimes and British Columbia, there were no stations more powerful than 500 watts, and in Quebec only one (CKAC Montreal). Clearly, some parts of Canada had much better access to radio broadcasts than others.

In 1932, the six leading stations in the country in terms of antenna power were two newspaper stations, the London *Free Press*'s CJGC and *La Presse*'s CKAC in Montreal; CFRB Toronto, owned by Rogers-Majestic; CKGW, also in Toronto, owned by Gooderham and Worts distillers; CKY Winnipeg, owned by the Manitoba Telephone System; and CFCN Calgary, owned by two broadcasting entrepreneurs, W.W. Grant and H.G. Love. While many of the original 1922 stations had fallen by the wayside, there were some significant new categories of licensees. These included three churches (Jarvis St Baptist, CJBC Toronto, a phantom; the United Church of Canada, CKFC Vancouver; the Christian and Missionary Alliance, CHMA Edmonton), three universities (Queen's, CFRC Kingston; Acadia, CKIC Wolfville; University of Alberta, CKUA Edmonton), and four grain companies (Saskatchewan Co-op Wheat Producers, CJBR Regina, a phantom; Winnipeg Grain Exchange, CJGX Yorkton; Alberta Pacific Grain Company, CKLC Red Deer; James Richardson and Sons, CJRM Moose Jaw and CJRW Fleming, Saskatchewan). Most important, the government-owned railway, Canadian National Railways, held thirteen licences by 1932 and the privately owned Canadian Pacific Railway had one (a phantom licence used to coordinate the CPR network programs.) Before concluding this discussion of station ownership in the first decade of broadcasting, it is worth pausing briefly to examine separately the Canadian stations owned and operated by public corporations: those of the CNR and the Manitoba Telephone System's CKY Winnipeg.

The work of Canadian National Railways was the most interesting experiment in broadcasting-station development in Canada in the 1920s. The CNR stations will be treated only briefly here because they have received more attention from previous historians than other stations, but the role of the national railway, especially in chain or network broadcasting, is so important that it does need special note.[94] Moreover, the CNR case, like that of CKY, illustrates the point that the drive for publicity and markets was a central motivation for virtually all the organizations that became involved in broadcasting in its early years.

The CNR was formed as a government corporation in 1919 as a means of amalgamating the remains of a number of near-bankrupt private railways. The corporation's first president, Sir Henry Thornton, faced the formidable task of welding together a large and disparate number of employees and a scattered physical plant into a single nation-wide organization that could balance its accounts. In late 1923 the railway announced that parlour cars on certain of its trains would be equipped with receiving equipment for the entertainment of passengers during the periods when the train was within areas of radio reception. Shortly thereafter the company decided that it would itself set up broadcasting facilities in key cities to provide programming for passengers on nearby trains and also for local listeners. The first such station, CKCH Ottawa (later CNRO), began operations in February 1924. By 1932, the CNR held thirteen licences, ten of them for phantom stations renting the facilities of other broadcasters. Three stations, CNRA Moncton, CNRO Ottawa, and CNRV Vancouver, were wholly owned and operated by the railway.

In 1929, the CNR's brief to the Royal Commission on Radio Broadcasting stated that the company had gone into broadcasting with five aims: to advertise the railway, to publicize Canada's attractions to tourists, to entertain passengers, to communicate with company employees in order to "create a proper spirit of harmony among them and a broader appreciation of the Management," and to assist colonization by providing radio service for remote settlers.[95] While it remains a moot point which of these motives predominated, others at the time, including government officials, viewed the CNR's stations as existing primarily to provide publicity for the railway.[96] In the opinion of most contemporary observers, the company's purpose was parallel to that of the newspapers which had set up stations: broadcasting was a not-unnatural extension of the role of a firm already involved in the communications business and a particularly appropriate means of self-advertisement for such a company. Nevertheless, Thornton and other CNR managers also seem to have perceived a somewhat larger "national" role for their stations than did other owners in the 1920s. Some of this was rhetorical flourish, but their actions also demonstrated this special sense of national purpose befitting a national corporation. From the beginning, the CNR's radio department planned a "complete" service from coast to coast; the choice of station locations demonstrates this intention, as do the early attempts at tying the stations together into networks – a subject that will be discussed more fully in the next chapter.[97]

In 1923, the CNR spent $10,146 on its radio operation, all of it for providing receiver service on trains. In 1925, including both broadcasting and train service, the radio department spent $240,686; annual costs reached a maximum of $441,082 in 1929 before being cut back by general Depression-induced retrenchment.[98] Of that total annual cost, however, a fair amount went for the equipment, wages, and accommodations needed for the train operations. In 1929, for example, about $161,000 was spent on the train operation, around $53,000 on general expenses, and approximately $222,000 on broadcasting out of the total amount allotted to the radio department.[99] Over ten years, the CNR spent approximately two and a quarter million dollars on its radio operation, nearly 60 per cent of it on broadcasting. Its capital expenditure on stations and studios amounted to over $130,000.[100] On the other side of the ledger, there can be little doubt that the radio operation attracted additional passenger revenues and helped finance the upgrading of CN telegraph lines in the late 1920s. CN Radio Director Austin Weir, admittedly not an unbiased observer, insisted that as a whole the income the railway received from increased business "very substantially exceeded the installation, operation, and broadcasting costs."[101] The CNR Radio Department also partially covered costs after 1929 by accepting advertisements. In November 1931, under heavy pressure from the Railway Committee of the House of Commons, and much to the disappointment of Weir and Thornton, the train service was ended, and a year later the CNR's Board of Directors decided to dispose of the radio stations and studios too. In early 1933 they were sold for $50,000 to the newly formed CRBC; many staff transferred as well. Indirectly, some CNR stations and staff ultimately became part of the CBC.

The CNR was not the only public corporation to own broadcasting stations in Canada in the 1920s. Indeed, the case of CKY Winnipeg, owned and operated by the Manitoba Telephone System (MTS), is in some ways more interesting and certainly less widely known. The significance of the story of CKY lies in the fact that the station was owned by a *provincial* government organization and that it possessed a monopoly on broadcasting in Manitoba for most of the first decade.[102]

The origins of CKY lie in the early concern of the government of

Manitoba that the use of radio for communication by private businesses might endanger the revenues of the provincially owned telephone system.[103] In early 1923, when John E. Lowry, Manitoba's commissioner of telephones, conceived the idea of taking the MTS into broadcasting, there were already two stations functioning in the province, both in Winnipeg, operated by the *Free Press* and *Tribune* newspapers.[104] The two papers apparently agreed quite readily to drop out of broadcasting in favour of the MTS, and negotiations with the federal government soon produced an agreement ratified by an exchange of letters and a May 1923 amendment to the Radiotelegraph Act covering the unique status of a provincially owned station.[105] While the federal government would retain regulatory authority over such crucial matters as licensing and wavelength assignment in Manitoba, unprecedented rights were granted to the province in the form of the return of 50 per cent of the licence fees collected there to help finance CKY and, even more important, a veto over all broadcasting station licensing in Manitoba. Between 1923 and January 1932 a total of $84,035 was paid to Manitoba under the first provision.[106] As to the second, the minister of telephones (on Lowry's advice) exercised it vigorously against all other attempts to establish stations in the province. With the exception of the phantom CNR station set up in 1924, which used CKY's equipment, the MTS had a monopoly on commercial broadcasting in Manitoba from 1923 on.[107]

CKY was operated from the first to earn a profit. Neither the MTS nor the financially strapped provincial government was interested in subsidizing its service. Thus the station's first manager, Darby Coats, who had left Marconi and Montreal in 1922, spent much of his time seeking inexpensive programs and willing advertisers. His hard work, coupled with the money garnered from the share of licence fees and the income from the CNR phantom, meant that CKY balanced its books most years.[108] The taxpayers of Manitoba were never asked to pay for CKY. The station was founded to protect the MTS's revenues, not to be a public service, although after the fact Lowry tried to justify it in those terms in order to obtain special privileges. CKY was a commercial enterprise owned by a public corporation primarily to protect its other communications interests.[109]

In that context, CKY's monopoly position was controversial and difficult to defend. In 1928, after failing in several attempts to establish a station in Manitoba, James Richardson and Sons, one of Canada's largest grain merchants, was granted a licence for a transmitter at Fleming, Saskatchewan, three miles from the Manitoba border, connected by CPR telegraph wires to a broadcasting studio in the Royal Alexandra Hotel in Winnipeg. Although Lowry protested furiously, federal-government officials, who had clearly begun to doubt the validity of the MTS monopoly, insisted that the Richardson station, CJRW, was licensed in Saskatchewan; therefore it did not violate the veto arrangement.[110] In early 1932, with a judicial decision granting full authority over broadcasting to Ottawa in hand, the federal government rescinded the Radiotelegraph Act amendment giving Manitoba 50 per cent of receiving licence fees on the grounds that "it discriminated in favour of Manitoba as against the other Provinces."[111] In 1933, shortly after the CRBC took over jurisdiction of broadcast licensing, it cancelled the veto agreement as well. Richardsons immediately closed down CJRW Fleming and reopened it as CJRC Winnipeg. Thus within the space of eighteen months, at a time of flux for all Canadian broadcasting, CKY lost its special status; Canada's only experiment with government monopoly broadcasting was over. The station continued to exist under MTS ownership, however, and became the *de facto* centre of the CRBC western network. The station was finally purchased by the CBC in 1948 and renamed CBW.

The participation of government organizations in broadcasting in Canada in the 1920s should not be viewed as precursory to public broadcasting. As with other enterprises engaged in the radio industry in the first decade, the need to expand or protect markets was the primary motivation for the entry of both the CNR and the MTS into the new field. The problem for the two governmental bodies, as for all the other Canadian firms involved in broadcasting, was that the domestic market was limited. While the number of listeners expanded considerably over the decade, they remained a minority of the population and scattered over a vast territory. Receiving-set manufacturing rested largely in the hands of American subsidiaries. Most Canadian broadcasting was therefore conducted by small or at best mid-sized entrepreneurs and businesses. Few if any of the stations in existence in either 1922 or 1932 were owned by firms with large amounts of capital or with much invested in the success of broadcasting as an industry. Their marginal position became increasingly obvious as the decade passed and the costs of constructing and operating a broadcasting station soared.

3 "Who is to Pay for Broadcasting?"

As radio broadcasting became more sophisticated in technology, programming, and audience, it also became increasingly costly. Rising expenses led the original broadcasters to seek more and more urgently for means to increase their revenues. Ultimately the solution to these twin problems was found in the interrelated phenomena of advertising-sponsored broadcasting and national networks, but the outcome was by no means a foregone conclusion from the perspective of the pioneers.

In the very early 1920s, one could open a station with little more than a licence ($50 per annum), some used parts, an ingenious engineer cum announcer (often seconded from other duties), and a stack of records. But that soon changed. In 1923 the minister of marine and fisheries estimated that it cost anywhere from seven to twenty thousand dollars to set up a good broadcasting station and between two and six thousand a year to maintain it.[1] A 1924 US survey showed that almost half of all stations had been installed for $3000 or less and cost less than $1000 per year to operate but that, at the other end of the scale, three American stations cost over $100,000 to build and more than $100,000 annually to operate.[2] Although the stations were not identified, clearly they were the flagship stations of the major manufacturers, those setting the standards by which all other broadcasters, American or Canadian, were judged.[3] By the end of the decade, one well-informed observer estimated, a "total investment" of $54,100 was needed to construct a 500-watt station and $168,400 for one with 5000 watts of power. Another calculated that it cost an average of $14.95 per watt to operate a broadcasting station in the United States, not including depreciation or programming; that is, on top of the expense of the original plant, a 500-watt station would have an annual operating outlay of about $7500 and a 5000-watt station ten times that.[4] Canadian costs were comparable. C.P. Edwards, director of the Radio Branch, estimated in 1928 that high-power 20,000-watt stations cost $300,000 each to build and $75,000 annually to operate.[5] Gooderham and Worts, according to quite reliable figures, spent $111,203 on transmitting and studio equipment for CKGW (5000 watts) in 1928, with operating costs (including salaries and telephone but excluding talent) estimated at almost $58,000 yearly.[6] Four years later Edwards told the Special Committee investigating broadcasting that it would cost $120,000 to construct a 5000-watt station with a daylight range of 125 miles.[7] The five Canadian stations then at that power or more had replacement costs, according to the Radio Branch, ranging from $114,000 (CJGC London) to $150,000 (CFCN Calgary).[8] Because the amount of electrical interference was steadily growing and the tolerance of the public for static and fading diminishing, that much power had become a virtual necessity by that time. Clearly, establishing and operating a broadcasting station required a substantial investment by 1932; particularly in the context of the Depression, the ability of Canadian business interests to come up with that kind of financing was increasingly in doubt.[9]

Programming costs rose dramatically as the decade progressed as well. While records and amateur talent sufficed in the first two or three years of radio, listeners became more sophisticated and demanding as time went on. Government regulations required that most programs had to be live[10] and audiences began to insist that they be "high quality." In the United States, one authority estimated that talent of high calibre could cost up to $1500 an hour by 1930.[11] Again, it was programming such as this that set the example for all of North America. Figures for two special series broadcast by CN stations in 1930 and 1931 give some idea of how expensive the best programming was. The orchestra, guest artists, and other miscellaneous costs for the twenty-six Toronto Symphony programs totalled over $27,000, while station rental (this was a network offering) came to almost $10,000 more. The much-celebrated Romance of Canada historical drama series that same winter cost $12,500 for eighteen programs, not including station rental.[12] Of course most programming was much less expensive, but broadcasts of this quality had to be offered if radio were to fulfil its potential.

The most complete and reliable statistics about the actual costs of operating Canadian broadcasting stations in the 1920s come from CKY Winnipeg and the CNR stations. Austin Weir, who was director of radio for the CNR beginning in May 1929, saved documents that give a breakdown of the disbursements of the Radio Department to the railway. Table 9 shows the operating expenses for the six largest CNR stations for the year 1929. Most indicative are the figures for the three stations owned by the railway,

Table 9
CNR Radio Department, total actual cost of operation for 1929, selected stations ($)

Station	Rent of Station	Rent of Premises	Light and Power	Talent	Wages	Mainte-nance	Telephone & Telegraph	Other	Total[1]
CNRA Moncton – owned	–	757	105	9,287	6,137	1,324	3,071	1,972	21,754
CNRM Montreal – phantom	11,500	333	–	17,034	2,614	277	545	243	32,546
CNRO Ottawa – owned	–	1,763	194	27,911	8,705	1,319	230	757	40,885[2]
CNRT Toronto – phantom	3,900	2,151	–	25,356	3,663	84	135	1,184	36,443
CNRW Winnipeg – phantom	14,410	403	–	14,866	708	525	3,886	1,064	35,862
CNRV Vancouver – owned	–	775	473	17,701	8,907	789	1,056	717	30,417

[1] Slight discrepancies due to rounding
[2] Slight discrepancy in original

those in Moncton, Ottawa, and Vancouver, which cost respectively $21,753.68, $40,884.86, and $30,416.67 to operate that year. For the sake of comparison, the expenses of CNRV Vancouver had been $17,422.02 in 1926, and in 1927 and 1928 in the range of $21,000 to $22,000.[13] While the wholly owned and operated stations were the most expensive to run, of course, even the phantom CNR stations had considerable outlays in 1929: talent (that is, programming) for the Toronto phantom station cost more than $25,000, and rental charges for the facilities of other broadcasters were also quite substantial, especially in the cases of the Winnipeg and Montreal stations. In turn, of course, for the stations providing the equipment, CKY and CKAC respectively, the revenue received from these rentals was welcome income. As another example, CKY Winnipeg cost the MTS $18,000 to build in 1923. The station's outlay for operation in its first year was $6000; by 1926 that figure had grown to over $15,000. In 1932 it cost almost $93,000 to run the station, including $43,259 for artists' fees, and CKY recorded a net loss of $15,470 that year.[14]

Although they were in the public domain, CKY and the CNR stations were probably fairly typical in their expenditures compared with the better privately owned stations. In the spring of 1932 the House of Commons Special Committee sent a questionnaire about current value, revenues, and expenditures to all Canadian stations. While the results were not checked for accuracy and great variations from station to station appeared, Table 10 gives some indication of the financial affairs of Canadian stations in 1931.[15]

This data indicates that the least profitable stations generally were those of 500 watts, while the more powerful stations up to 5000 watts had the greatest profits. Although these larger stations spent much more on programs and operations, their enhanced advertising revenues more than compensated. Considerable differences between stations is disguised in these averages, however. For example, CKGW had revenues of over $208,000 but the equally powerful CKGC London brought in only about $53,000. While this gave CKGW a profit of just over $25,000 for the year, CKGC made only $6920. Meanwhile, CKAC Montreal, with revenues of almost $188,000 and expenses of less than $137,000, made the most of any Canadian station in 1931, over $51,000.[16] CFRB (which has not been included in the totals because of inadequate information) apparently only made about $5000 profit, and that of CKY was little better, namely $5600.

Similar variations are evident among the less powerful stations. Of the sixteen 500-watt stations reporting, revenues ranged from around $4000 (CKX Brandon and CNRA Moncton, both largely rebroadcasting stations) to almost $142,000 (CKNC Toronto), with many clustering between $25,000 and $35,000. With the exception of CNRV Vancouver and CKNC, none spent more than $20,000 a year on programs and most spent less than $5500.

Table 10
Average revenues and expenditures by power class, 1931[1]

Power Class	Number	Av Revenue	Programs	Av Expenditure Other[2]	Total	Av Profit
50 watt stations	5	$ 8,256	$ 1,440	$ 6,400	$ 7,840	$ 416
100 watt stations	10	10,624	1,169	7,754	8,923	1,701
250 watt stations	3	1,667	150	2,667	2,817	−1,150
500 watt stations	16	28,085	9,754	23,584	33,338	−5,253
1–5 kilowatt stations	6	98,317	26,307	57,843	84,150	14,166
All stations	40	$29,794	$ 8,331	$21,049	$29,380	$ 415

[1] Based on replies from 40 of 57 commercial stations in operation in 1931

[2] Operation, interest and depreciation

Profits were rare, as the average loss of $5253 indicates. The three stations in this class that did best all had monopolies or near-monopolies in their small-city markets: CFBO Saint John, CFQC Saskatoon, and CHNS Halifax. The three CNR stations and James Richardson and Sons' CJRW Fleming, Saskatchewan, each lost more than $14,000 in 1931; all were subsidized by their controlling organizations.

For the eighteen stations of 50, 100, and 250 watts, those with the highest revenues in 1931 were CKWX Vancouver ($33,000), CFCH North Bay ($18,870), and CHML Hamilton ($17,430). CFCH, owned by Roy Thomson, made the most profit among these smaller stations – $5400 for the year. CHML lost about $500 in 1931. One reason for the difference was that CFCH spent only $1465 on programs, while CHML spent $3800. Of this group of stations, CKWX Vancouver, at $7000, paid by far the most for programming. As was also the case with the larger stations, those in the lowest power classes normally spent several times more on operations than on programming. Only one station in all of Canada, CKNC Toronto, allocated more to programs than to operations ($88,300 versus $54,100). This was probably because it was a relatively weak station (500 watts) in a big market where programming was well supported by advertisers; it also originated chain programs. CKNC's revenues of $141,800 were third highest in the country; nevertheless, it lost $610 on the year.

As Canadian broadcasting developed over its first ten years, the cost of producing good programs on powerful stations grew considerably. Most stations claimed, most of the time, that they lost money; despite the profitability of the largest stations, the average profit for all the stations analyzed in 1931 was a measly $415.[17] Station-owners, whether individuals or corporations, of necessity became more and more preoccupied with the central question of early radio: "Who is to pay for broadcasting?"[18]

Throughout the first decade of broadcasting, the issue of its financing received considerable attention in many countries, from those both within and outside the industry. Aside from certain schemes contemplated but never much tried, such as seeking patrons or voluntary listener contributions,[19] four main alternatives were considered and attempted in various parts of the world. The first was the method that dominated in North America in the early 1920s, namely that stations were set up and carried as "loss leaders" by those who stood to profit directly or indirectly from the growth of the radio industry in general.[20] The stations established by radio manufacturers, retailers, and, less directly, newspapers fell into this category. In many cases, these firms wrote the cost of the broadcasting station off as an advertising expense. Ultimately, of course, the real cost of the broadcasting done by these stations was borne by those who purchased the products of the owner. As H.S. Moore, manager of CFRB in Toronto, owned by the manufacturers of Rogers batteryless radios, told the Aird commission in 1929: "We take a loss on the station. We never expect to make any profit on it; we did not build it to pay. The loss that we suffer is charged over to advertising which naturally in the long run gets into the cost of your product ..."[21] But even the largest manufacturers soon found the expense of operating a good station too great to be written off completely against other profits. Another source of financing was needed, if only as a supplement.

The second option was that adopted in Britain and a large majority of European countries, namely requiring the listeners to pay a substantial licence fee to the government, part of which was forwarded to the broadcaster(s) to help cover expenses. This method was also advocated in the early 1920s by some prominent American industry spokesmen, but it was a difficult measure to introduce in the United States once listeners had become accustomed to the "free" service provided by the pioneer stations.[22] Another method with a somewhat similar effect also used in Britain in the early twenties was the imposition of a special tax or royalty on each radio set produced, that cost of course being passed on to the radio consumer as well.[23] The licence-fee alternative was considered in Canada in the 1920s. As we have seen, from the beginning annual licence fees were collected by the Radio Branch of the Department of Marine and Fisheries from receiver owners, and in 1923 an amendment was made to the Radiotelegraph Act enabling the branch to share this revenue with broadcasting stations in order to ensure continuing programming. As branch officials explained:

There is the possibility that at some future date existing Canadian broadcasting stations will begin to drop out. This would not be a good thing for Canada, having regard to the many powerful stations to the south, and it is desirable that the Canadian stations should receive support. The only way, so far evolved, to achieve this end is the collection of a license fee by a central body such as the Federal

Government, and to remit a portion of this fee to the different stations to assist in their upkeep. In this way the broadcast listeners in any area will be directly contributing to the support of the local stations which serve them.[24]

Despite the 1923 amendment, however, with the single exception of the money given to the Manitoba Telephone System's CKY Winnipeg, licence-fee receipts were never distributed to Canadian stations for use in financing broadcasting. Rather, the revenue collected went into the federal government's consolidated revenue fund and some of it was then allocated to the Radio Branch to be used primarily to investigate and solve technical problems such as electrical interference.[25] As in the American case, the early establishment of broadcasting stations on a private-ownership basis militated against later adoption of the option of licence-fee financing. Canadian radio listeners were certain to object to the higher fees such a scheme would necessitate. More important, Canadian officials were extremely sensitive to the potential for complex and embarrassing political repercussions from a system that involved handing government-collected licence fees over to privately owned stations. It was one thing to distribute such moneys to a consortium of manufacturers, as in the case of the early British Broadcasting Company, or to a publicly owned entity such as the BBC or the Manitoba Telephone System,[26] but private entrepreneurs were another matter. As Deputy Minister of Marine and Fisheries Alexander Johnston cautioned Jacques Cartier, general manager of CKAC Montreal, who wrote promptly after the passage of the 1923 amendment to inquire how his station might share in the largesse it augured: "There is no question that the service given by CKAC reflects the greatest credit on its management, the bilingual feature being especially commendable. The station is, however, being primarily operated for the purpose of advertising 'La Presse,' and the question at issue is whether the Government could, with propriety, subsidize a station operated for such purpose. This, of course, applies not only to 'La Presse,' but to all stations of a similar character."[27] On the whole, then, Radio Branch officials were inclined to leave well enough alone "so long as commercial companies and private individuals [were] prepared to operate first class broadcasting stations at their own expense ..."[28] This combination of concerns meant that, except in Manitoba, licence-fee receipts were not used to finance Canadian broadcasting stations before 1932.

A third option was direct government financing from general tax revenues, the practice in a few European nations. As in the previous case, however, it was extremely awkward for a government to subsidize any station other than one it owned, and the Canadian broadcasting system had initially been formed without government-owned stations. The stations set up and run by public corporations in the 1920s, the CNR stations and CKY, as we have already seen, were operated to generate profits or at least to break even. If they did not always do so, any subsidies were granted reluctantly and were as small as possible. Moreover, it was politically difficult to request funds from general tax revenues for a service to which less than one household in three had access. The Aird commission in 1929 explicitly rejected the idea of financing the publicly owned system it advocated out of general revenues on these grounds, for example. Thus no private broadcasters were given direct government subsidies in Canada in the 1920s; indeed the option was never seriously considered.

The final alternative for financing broadcasting was, of course, advertising. In effect, as various scholars have pointed out, broadcasting paid for by advertising approximates a telephone model; that is, the broadcasting station may be likened to a giant pay-telephone booth with an extensive party line that can be rented for periods of time by anyone wishing to convey a message to the public.[29] The party originating the message pays for the use of the communications equipment; the listener pays nothing for the message. In truth, of course, as in all the options being discussed here, the consumer pays in the end – not necessarily the broadcast listeners only in this case, but all consumers of the product being advertised. To put it another way, the real transaction occurring in advertising-sponsored radio broadcasting is that the broadcaster sells the audience (the commodity) to the advertiser (who is really the consumer). The programming is merely a delivery vehicle; for efficiency it must appeal to the largest possible number.[30]

The gradual move toward advertising-financed broadcasting in North America in the 1920s was also a move toward the concept of radio broadcasting as a separate, self-sustaining, commercial enterprise. Indirectly, advertising was the basis of all private-enterprise broadcasting in Canada and the United States from the beginning. Most of the newspapers, retailers, and manufacturers opening stations in the earliest days did so at least in part for publicity, that is for the advertising value of the frequent repetition of the company name. Soon various other kinds of indirect advertising commenced. As already mentioned in Chapter 1, even before it received its first broadcasting licence, the operators of Marconi's experimental station XWA/CFCF announced the name of the store from which they borrowed the records they played and the brand name of those records. Later in the decade it became common for a firm to advertise that it had paid for a program not only by regular reiteration of that information but also by its title (for example, "The Eveready Hour") or by the nomenclature of the performers ("The Ipana Troubadours," for example, or "The Lucky Strike Orchestra," or, the epitome of this genre, "Paul Oliver and Olive Palmer," the singing celebrants of Palmolive Soap).[31] In both the United States and

Canada throughout the twenties, these forms of indirect advertising were generally accepted by both broadcasters and listeners on all stations at any time of day.

Direct advertising, that is the use of explicit messages promoting specific products in the context of a sponsored show, and especially the mention of prices, however, was much more controversial in the 1920s and much slower to gain acceptance than one might assume from today's perspective. So were "spot" advertisements, those conveying a brief 100- or 150-word message but not implying sponsorship of the full program. Unusual in the very early period, spot ads were becoming increasingly common by 1932 and are of course the main type of advertisement on commercial radio or television today. The fiercely defended monopoly of the giant American Telephone and Telegraph Company over "toll broadcasting" in the United States initially discouraged other stations from soliciting direct advertising.[32] Even after AT&T began issuing licences for this right in 1924, and then bowed out of broadcasting altogether in 1926, considerable reluctance to utilize direct ads remained. For at least the first half of the decade, virtually all leading spokesmen condemned direct advertising on radio as an unacceptable intrusion of the world of business into the privacy and sanctity of the home, or, as one American magazine colourfully put it, "as a snake of commercialism in an Eden of entertainment."[33] While such practices might be barely tolerated during business hours, they were quite unacceptable during the evening, which should be reserved for leisure activities. Even those involved in the advertising industry opposed overly-direct and commercial advertising on radio, probably because they sensed a threat to the traditional advertising forums from which they still derived the bulk of their incomes and because they feared that negative listener reaction might hurt the credibility of the whole ad industry. The Montreal Publicity Association in 1924, for example, went on record as supporting the complete prohibition of direct advertising on the grounds that "an evening's amusement – listening in – to delightful concerts is a sincere pleasure, but to have this pleasure marred by direct advertising is a pity." To indirect advertising, on the other hand, the organization felt there could be "no possible objection."[34]

Similarly, in 1929 R.W. Ashcroft, one of Canada's leading advocates of commercial broadcasting, told the Aird commission that he thought all direct advertising should be banned, and as late as 1932 he claimed to find spot advertisements so objectionable that the station he managed, CKGW Toronto, deliberately charged a prohibitively high rate for them. Ashcroft admitted that he did, reluctantly, accept a few spot ads, from such reputable firms as Eaton's, Simpson's, and the Toronto *Star* – but never would he advertise such a product as a corn plaster.[35] This "moral" objection to direct advertising on radio, which was even shared at least rhetorically by such ardent devotees of private enterprise as US Secretary of Commerce Herbert Hoover, resulted in informal self-regulation by the better American stations that restrained its use until the latter 1920s; not until 1932 did the major networks allow prices to be mentioned in their advertisements. In Canada, more formal rules were in effect. Here, direct ads were restricted to daylight hours from 1923 until 1926 and then banned altogether until 1928, after which time stations were required to obtain individual dispensation to air them.[36] Whether deliberately or not, these rules and attitudes tended to keep the potential of radio advertising in the hands of those who could afford to own a station or subsidize a full-length program.

Partly because of the early restrictions on ad use, but also because of lack of data about radio audiences and because they felt more comfortable with traditional media such as newspapers, magazines, and billboards, advertisers and advertising agencies alike were slow at first to turn to broadcasting.[37] Even in the United States it was not until 1928 that all the factors came together that made it practicable to conceive of the sale of advertising time as the principal means of permanent financial support for broadcasting.[38] Among those factors, increasingly sophisticated broadcasting technology and regularized, precisely timed program formats were crucial. Even more important, however, was the creation of national networks, both a cause and an effect of expanded use of radio by national advertisers. Indeed, advertising and networking were symbiotically linked; it was, for example, precisely the ability of AT&T to create networks by the use of its wirelines that made it attractive to major advertisers in the earliest days, while advertiser revenue was in turn necessary to pay the wireline expenses of networking.[39]

Growing levels of audience acceptance were also important to the increased use of advertising by broadcasters by the end of the 1920s. More and more, listeners seemed to accept that they must trade off intrusive ads for the free entertainment they were beginning to crave. By 1932 *Fortune* magazine in the United States reported that listeners seemed "actually to like" advertising, and that sponsors were "likely to lose more listeners by adding a symphony than adding a sales talk."[40] Additionally, by making the importance of informed consumption more evident, the onset of the Depression helped destroy lingering prejudices against direct ads within both the business and regulatory communities. The firms first venturing into radio advertising tended to be those in flux: trying to expand their territories, introducing new brand-name products, facing harsher competition, and so on. They also were more likely to manufacture products either directly related to radio (for instance, batteries, tubes, receivers) or of the type that involved frequent small discretionary purchases (cigarettes, candy, toiletries, and the like).[41] In 1932, nevertheless, radio advertising still constituted only 5 per cent of total ad revenues in the

United States. In that year, an American study showed that 36 per cent of air time had commercial sponsorship.[42]

Although little hard information exists about the amount spent on advertising on Canadian stations in the first decade, it is highly unlikely that many of them were able to sell enough advertising time to break even, much less show a profit.[43] Little CFBO in Saint John, New Brunswick, for example, which was on the air for 572 hours between January and June 1929, had commercial sponsorship for only eighty-eight of those hours. CKY Winnipeg earned the quite considerable sum of $10,696.35 from advertising as early as 1926; without additional revenue from its share of receiver-licence fees and from the rental paid by CNRW, however, it would have been almost $10,000 in the red for the year.[44] In the two months between 1 December 1931 and 31 January 1932, out of a total of six hours programming each day, CJCJ Calgary had sponsors for only ten minutes; for its more than seven hours of daily programming in the same period, CKCK Regina had sponsorship for only an average one hour and three minutes. On the other hand, CJOR Vancouver had six hours and ten minutes sponsored out of a total of fifteen, and CKAC Montreal more than five and a half hours sponsored out of a total broadcasting day of thirteen hours and forty-four minutes. On the average across Canada, 28 per cent of air time was sponsored during those two months; in Alberta, however, that figure was only 18 per cent, and in Prince Edward Island only 16 per cent, whereas in Quebec 38 per cent of broadcasts were sponsored, and in Manitoba 41 per cent (demonstrating again CKY's commercial orientation).[45]

More than just the amount of sponsored air time is involved in determining the importance of advertising, however. A station's ultimate profitability depended as well on the rates it could charge for those ads. According to the testimony of Ernest Bushnell before the 1932 Special Committee of the House of Commons, CKNC in Toronto was able to cover its whole $177,000 operating expense in 1931 from ad revenues.[46] Similarly, by 1931 CKGW Toronto apparently had sufficient advertising revenue that it made a profit of almost $60,000; yet, as with the CKNC figure just quoted, depreciation was not taken into account.[47] Even the CNR station in Ottawa, despite various claims both then and since that CN stations were totally non-commercial, had enough ad revenue in 1930 to come close to breaking even; the station's expenses were $28,853.95 that year, its revenues $26,442.11.[48]

Advertising rates varied a great deal from year to year, hour to hour, and station to station. Indeed the lack of consistency in broadcasting ad rates illustrated the tentative nature of the venture. In 1932 Commander Edwards of the Radio Branch estimated that they ran from $25 to $225 per hour on Canadian stations, a very wide range depending upon the power of the station, estimated number of listeners, time of day, length of the advertising contract, and so on.[49] CKY Winnipeg, a mid-size urban station, for example, charged $100 per hour at night for one broadcast, reduced to $90 for a commitment to 13 broadcasts. The charge was only $70 per hour in the daytime. Short announcements were billed at $3 for less than 25 words, $6 for 26 to 50 words, and so on up to $15 for the maximum of over 150 words.[50] In Toronto in 1930, a spot announcement could be purchased on a small station for as little as $3 per minute, but an hour on CKGW in the evening cost $150.[51] Radio advertising rates were determined by the market.

Beginning as early as 1926, and increasingly common by 1932, broadcasting bureaus came into existence to act as brokers between radio stations and advertisers. The first such service was probably the one provided by Ernest Bushnell and Charles Shearer who in early 1927 began soliciting ads for CJYC Toronto.[52] As was to be the case later when more established advertising agencies began to take on broadcasting business, part of Bushnell and Shearer's job was to arrange the programs for the sponsors. They thus became booking agents and announcers as well. While Bushnell and his friend did not make much of a success of this particular job (although both went on to important radio careers), others followed them in the field, including such organizations as National Radio Advertising (Toronto), the British Columbia Broadcasting Bureau (Vancouver), and the Canadian Broadcast Bureau (Montreal). Rupert Caplan of the last organization (which in 1932 changed its name to the Canadian Broadcast Company) explained that his work consisted of "building and presenting programs, supplying talent, writing continuity and generally preparing Radio presentations for commercial or non commercial use."[53] Most of these companies worked primarily in the local field, although some did arrange cross-Canada chain broadcasts as well. As of 1930, still only about 15 per cent of Canadian programs were handled by agencies. Normally, the agencies received 15 per cent commission, paid for by the radio station (paralleling the standard practice in the newspaper business).[54]

Before 1932 the viability of such bureaus was as marginal as that of many stations. The contrast between the situation of a station such as CFBO or CJCJ and that of CKNC and CKGW in Toronto is important. The most powerful stations in the largest markets inevitably attracted the most advertising dollars. R.W. Ashcroft put it succinctly when he advised a group of advertisers: use the "most powerful and most popular stations you can secure," he suggested, because otherwise you will be broadcasting "mainly to the sun, and the moon and the stars." "Just as lineage in a newspaper or magazine with 100,000 circulation is worth ten times that of a publication with 10,000 circulation," he went on, "so is an hour on a popular 5,000 watt station worth ten times the price of an hour on a 500-watter ..."[55] The first comprehensive study of radio advertising in Canada, prepared for the Cockfield-Brown agency in Toronto in 1930, reached the same conclusion. While cautioning that radio coverage of the scattered prairie population was too expensive for most advertisers to contemplate, the author of the report pointed out that the Ontario and Quebec markets, within which resided 63 per cent of national purchasing power, could be "cheaply and thoroughly covered by radio," and he recommended that the firm encourage its clients to consider this option.[56] Thus the reliance on advertisers to finance broadcasting encouraged a situation in which the most powerful stations and those located in the largest market areas had the largest revenues.

It was not, however, the sole reason for regional inequalities. Broadcasting in Canada from the beginning had operated on a commercial basis, which had encouraged concentration in areas of higher density and higher income. Access to skilled technicians and performers also gave urban centres an advantage. As the decade progressed and advertising became more important to station financing, the gap between the service provided by small stations and that provided by the big-city stations widened considerably – which in turn bolstered the advertising revenue of the latter even more. Dependence on third-party advertising revenue reinforced a tendency innate in the business from the start.

The 1932 House of Commons Special Committee on Broadcasting heard quite a bit about advertising as a means of paying for radio programming, both pro and con, from various parties with various interests. In the early 1920s everyone in the industry had wondered who would pay for broadcasting. By 1932 it was clear to all that if private broadcasting continued in Canada it would be primarily financed by commercial sponsorship. Even the Aird commission of 1929 had recommended that the fully publicly owned system it advocated should be partly funded by indirect advertising. In the context of a system in which stations had developed under private ownership, with listeners accustomed to "free" radio shows and to the American model, no other alternative seemed feasible by the time the first decade of broadcasting ended, whatever the consequences for quality of programming or equity in distribution.

IN ADDITION TO ATTEMPTING TO ATTRACT third-party revenue, the other obvious way for broadcasters of the 1920s to attain profitability was to keep costs to a minimum. Because technical expenses were relatively fixed and rising steadily in the context of public and other pressures for more power and better tone, programming costs became the focus of attention. For those responsible for financing a broadcasting station, whether manufacturers, governments, or groups of advertisers, decreasing the programming cost per listener without lowering quality was a sensible goal. Three main methods of achieving the "economy of centralized pro-gramming"[57] were attempted by early broadcasters. While all these exper-iments involved the creation of larger and ultimately national audiences, however, their proponents were not motivated solely by commercialism. From the days of DX-ing and silent nights, the notion of radio as a unique medium by which listeners could experience distant events had survived. Equally, the utility of radio for "national" purposes such as coverage of major political events was much touted from the beginning and the cre-ation of a nation-wide audience became a matter of prestige as well as prof-its.[58] Nevertheless, the economic motive of decreasing per-unit cost in an era of rising demands predominated in the search for the best tech-nology for audience-enlargement.

One of the alternatives developed, one that became quite common in the late 1920s and for many years after, was the use of electrical transcriptions, ready-to-air recordings of programs complete with commercials, shipped from central studios to stations across the country. Although convenient, these transcriptions were initially unacceptable to many listeners because the reproduction quality was often substandard and because they destroyed what was considered the single most attractive feature of radio program-ming – its immediacy. Radio Branch regulators viewed transcriptions as infe-rior to live programming and strictly limited their use in the prime evening hours.[59] There is also some evidence that in the more heavily settled parts of the country electrical transcriptions were more expensive than other alternatives.[60] For these reasons, although electrical transcriptions offered many advantages, they did not become a central feature of programming prior to 1932.[61]

A second option, much touted in the United States, was the erection of "super-power" stations transmitting at 25,000 or even 50,000 watts, thereby covering vast distances, attracting huge audiences, earning high revenues, and airing the best programs money could buy. The movement for super-power stations was led by RCA.[62] Amidst considerable controversy, the US Department of Commerce, the regulatory body for American broadcasting, authorized experimentation with super power in late 1924. By November 1925, two US stations were broadcasting at 25,000 watts (25 kilowatts).[63] In 1926 both WGY Schenectady, owned by GE, and WJZ in Bound Brook, New Jersey, an RCA station, were authorized to experiment with 50 kilowatts. By the end of the decade five stations were operating at that power and experimenting with up to 200 and 400 kw. But there were a number of dif-ficulties with super-power stations. First, these stations had to be assigned their own frequencies (clear channels in the American terminology), which were scarce, and they often generated complaints that they "blan-keted" the receivers of listeners who lived near their transmitters, preventing them from picking up other stations. Stations of this power were also enormously expensive to build and to maintain. Smaller broadcasters and others feared that the licensing of super-power stations simply strengthened the already-massive domination by the large manufacturers over the American radio industry. It also became clear as experiments continued throughout the decade that no matter how strong the signal, random interference could mar evening reception beyond 150 miles; the radius of reliable coverage could not be expanded indefinitely.[64] Even super-power stations, then, while they could increase audience size and improve rural reception, would never provide the national coverage that listeners, broadcasters, and advertisers craved.

In Canada there was no serious attempt before 1932 to build super-power stations for the purpose of creating a national audience, although their existence in the United States certainly had repercussions on the Canadian broadcasting situation. Rather, the Canadian coast-to-coast service essential to the creation of a national audience was eventually accomplished by the method that in the end dominated in the United States as well – by the formation of chains or networks of local stations, linked by wire, broadcasting the same program simultaneously with only the added cost of line rental.[65]

In the United States, early network development was carried out almost entirely by AT&T because that company controlled the long-distance telephone wires necessary for the practice.[66] The first network program was broadcast on 4 January 1923 simultaneously over AT&T's WEAF New York and privately owned WNAC Boston. By the summer of that year WEAF was involved in frequent networking with WCAP in Washington; in the fall of 1924 the telephone company put together a twenty-three station chain for a speech by President Calvin Coolidge; by the end of 1925 there were twenty-five stations extending to Kansas City linked in a regular AT&T network offering such shows as "The Eveready Hour," "The A and P Gypsies," and "The Gold Dust Twins" in regular time slots.[67] Not all the early networks were created by the telephone company; by 1925 the so-called Radio Group (RCA, General Electric, and Westinghouse) also had a fourteen-station chain using WJZ as the key station and Western Union telegraph lines (acoustically inferior to telephone lines) for linkage. In these networking arrangements, as was to remain the case later, the stations involved were for the most part independently owned and the network programs provided were only a part, although an increasingly important part, of a total schedule that also included much locally produced material.

In 1926, after considerable conflict and negotiation among the major corporations involved in American radio, AT&T withdrew from the broadcasting business and left the development of networks to the National Broadcasting Company (NBC), at first created as a subsidiary of the Radio Group and after 1930 fully controlled by RCA. From nineteen stations regularly connected in late 1926, the NBC networks ("Red," "Blue," and for a time "Pacific Coast" or "Orange") grew to fifty-six outlets stretching across the continent by the end of 1928 and eighty-eight by 1933. A few of the stations were owned and operated by NBC, the others were permanent affiliates subscribing to network programming for a part of each day. Other stations also were able to tie in for just the occasional program. NBC built production studios in New York ("Radio City"), sold the advertising for its programs, and supplied "sustaining" programs to fill in the hours when no sponsored programs were scheduled. The connecting lines were leased from AT&T, which, incidentally, derived a substantial profit therefrom.[68] NBC's major source of income was the sale of advertising; from about the end of 1928 on, the network made a profit. Meanwhile, the Columbia Broadcasting System was also organized in the latter years of the twenties, and purchased by William S. Paley in 1928. By 1932 NBC and CBS were major factors in the increasingly mature North American broadcasting industry.

Despite the disadvantage of time-zone incompatibility, network broadcasting was a great success, not only from the point of view of NBC and CBS, but in the eyes of local station owners. The affiliated stations gained access to relatively inexpensive high-quality programs which allowed them to attract listeners and higher advertising rates for their other programming. The advertisers appreciated the convenience of having to deal with only one organization. By 1932, 28 per cent of all American stations were on one of the networks, including the vast majority of the most powerful stations on clear channels. As early as 1927, in fact, NBC-affiliated stations possessed 61 per cent of the total power of all US stations; by 1931 stations affiliated to NBC and CBS between them had 76 per cent of the power in the United States.[69] Equally significantly, and of course not coincidentally, 63 per cent of all radio advertising expenditure went to the networks by 1932.[70] While not precisely monopolistic, because based on small independently owned stations that continued to present local programming, the networks nevertheless dominated American broadcasting almost completely by the mid-1930s. Private-enterprise broadcasting in the United States thus did not result in a multiplicity of stations of relatively equal strength owned by individual entrepreneurs but rather in control by two large organizations, one of which was also linked to the corporations that dominated the radio manufacturing industry. The progression from 1927 on toward this conclusion had important repercussions in Canada.

Canadian chain broadcasting was initiated by the CNR. Indeed the very first CN broadcast, on 31 December 1923, involved a hook-up that allowed several speakers, including Sir Henry Thornton, to be heard simultaneously on both CHYC Montreal and OA Ottawa, the station of the Ottawa Radio Association, the connecting link being provided by Bell Telephone lines.[71] Information about other early networking attempts is scattered and often inconsistent. It seems, however, that in the summer of 1924 the occasional program from CKCH, then the CNR's Ottawa station, was simultaneously heard on a second station; CKAC, CHYC, and CFCF in Montreal were all apparently involved in these demonstrations.[72] Over the next couple of years intermittent experiments involving Montreal, Ottawa, and Toronto continued.

The biggest step toward national Canadian networking was taken in 1926 when CN decided to replace its telegraph lines with the more sophisticated carrier-current type whose greater capacity freed the wires for other uses after 6 p.m. and whose higher transmission quality made them more appropriate for broadcasting use. From then on the company looked increasingly to the possibilities of chain broadcasting, both through its own stations and by renting its lines to other networking organizations. By early 1927 network shows between the Montreal, Ottawa, and Quebec City CN radio stations had become a regular feature of the schedule. Sometimes these programs were the more expensive and original type, such as radio dramas and operas, which would have been too costly for each station to produce separately. For example, CNR program schedules show that on 23 November 1927, CNRO Ottawa, CNRM Montreal, and CNRQ Quebec City linked together for "Maritana," a three-act opera performed by the CNRO Operatic Singers. A few months later the troupe performed an abbreviated version of Gounod's "Faust" for the same chain.[73] By the winter of 1929 hockey games were aired on the chain. Often, however, the chain broadcasts were relatively routine musical concerts and dance programs.

On 1 July 1927, for the celebration of the Diamond Jubilee of Confederation, the first-ever coast-to-coast hookup was arranged. CNR personnel and stations were closely involved in this effort, as well as many private stations; both CN and CP telegraph wires were used, along with telephone lines, to link briefly twenty-three stations all told.[74] In December 1927 the first hook-up tying Winnipeg into the Toronto-Ottawa-Montreal circuit along CN telegraph lines on a regular schedule commenced. A year later, on 27 December 1928, a special holiday program originating at CNRM Montreal, in French and English, was broadcast on a fifteen-station nationwide network, including ten CN and five private stations.[75] Finally, in the fall of 1929, regular coast-to-coast network broadcasting on CN stations and lines began; programs were heard Sunday afternoons from 5 to 6 p.m. and Tuesday and Thursday evenings. There was also a four-station French chain which connected on Tuesday evenings. That same year the first programs were broadcast from Winnipeg to the east.[76] The network broadcasts, which continued through 1930 and 1931, featured many of the high points of CN programming, including the Toronto Symphony Orchestra and the Romance of Canada series of historical dramas.[77]

The CNR network did not develop from quite the same roots as NBC and CBS in the United States. For one thing, regular CN network programming appeared only on its own stations. In addition, networking and national advertising were tightly intertwined in the American case, while for the CN commercial advertising revenue, while not irrelevant, was a secondary consideration. The railway's motivation for networking seems to have been fourfold. First, it was an efficient way to provide better programs more cheaply. Secondly, broadcasting programs utilized the company's telegraph lines in what would otherwise have been idle time, presumably thereby expanding the railway's total revenues. Thirdly, CN management's desire to keep in touch with the company's scattered employees had from the first been part of the reason for entering the radio field and only a coast-to-coast network really satisfied that goal. Nation-wide radio seemed a logical accompaniment to nation-wide train service. Finally, the CNR as a public corporation was run by a group of men representative of Canada's nationalist élite; as such they were interested in promoting Canadian national feeling and saw the airing of public events of national interest as part of their mandate. Much of the rhetoric and mythology associated with the CNR's contribution to the history of Canadian broadcasting refers to this final motive; too often, however, the other more practical reasons for the CN Radio Department's deep involvement in network programming have been forgotten.

Although the pioneer of Canadian networking and the best remembered of the early chain broadcasters, the CNR was not alone in this work in the 1920s. Many of the private broadcasters experimented with network arrangements on occasion.[78] Usually these *ad hoc* chains were put together by advertisers or advertising bureaus for special programs or series. For example, Canadian General Electric's "Vagabonds" was heard nationally in the 1931–32 season on a specially created chain of about twenty stations. In addition there were at least two Canadian companies that existed for the sole purpose of arranging network programming with stations and advertisers. The first and most important of these was the Trans-Canada Broadcasting Company, formed in June 1928 to sponsor inter-city links of private stations. Harry C. Hatch, president of Gooderham and Worts, was the financial backer, and R.W. Ashcroft of CKGW the manager of the chain.[79] Ashcroft outlined how the company operated to the Aird commission members as follows: "It functions in a similar way to the National Broadcasting Company and the Columbia Broadcasting System in the United States, viz: It negotiates the sale of 'chain' broadcasting programs to various sponsors, prepares and supervises the programs, and purchases 'time' from various radio stations, and also the necessary local and inter-city wire facilities."[80] Like its counterparts in the United States, this company was not under government regulatory authority because it did not have a broadcasting licence; it simply used CKGW Toronto as its key station to originate programs to be picked up by any other station so inclined.[81] Among the important public events broadcast on this network were the opening of

Parliament in 1930 and the king's Christmas Day message in 1931. Its more routine fare included such sponsored programs as the "Canadian Wrigley Review," "The Maple Leaf Milling Company Program," and "Jack Frost and his Anti-Freezers."[82] As in the case of the CN network, Trans-Canada concentrated its program development at a major station in a major urban centre. So, while networks improved the distribution of good programs, they encouraged the centralization of program production in Montreal and Toronto.[83] Further, as was true in the United States, the networks normally chose to utilize the more powerful of the local outlets available in each distribution location. Again, this reinforced and widened the gap between the more successful and the poorer stations, and especially between urban and rural ones.

By 1930 a second network company called the Canadian Broadcasting System was also in existence, using CKNC Toronto as its flagship station. CKNC's brief to the Special Committee in 1932 claimed that such national advertisers as William Neilson, Wm. Wrigley Jr., Tuckett Tobacco, Imperial Tobacco, and Bell Telephone had all used CKNC studios to develop programs for chain broadcast.[84] Other more *ad hoc* networks existed too: a prairie chain, a maritime chain, and, in 1931–32, a cooperative one organized by Vic George of CFCF Montreal.[85] In February 1930 (once its carrier-current lines were in place) the Canadian Pacific Railway began chain broadcasting, providing programs (mainly orchestral and other music, both sponsored and sustaining) via its own telegraph lines to a network that eventually comprised twenty-one stations. The CPR's programming was arranged by Ashcroft of Trans-Canada Broadcasting and CKGW; the company set up studios in the Royal York Hotel and received a phantom licence for CPRY but it utilized the transmitting facilities of CKGW.[86] According to CPR President Edward Beatty's testimony to the 1932 parliamentary committee, his railway's network was on the air over 1400 hours between February 1930 and the end of 1931.[87] In all of these cases, hook-ups were tailor-made; each was negotiated separately and individual stations could opt in or out of any program at will. Despite the fluidity of the situation and the relatively high costs of transmission lines, the total number of hours of Canadian network broadcasting grew steadily, from 264 hours in 1929 to 646.5 hours in 1930 and 844.5 hours in 1931. The number of national advertisers grew from sixteen to twenty-one in the same period, many of them subsidiaries of firms already using radio in the United States.[88]

In the meantime, however, a very important new element had entered the Canadian broadcasting picture: private-station links with the two American networks. While many Canadians had listened to American programs directly from American stations since the birth of broadcasting and Canadian stations had for many years picked up the occasional

American program for rebroadcast, the direct wiring in of Canadian stations to NBC and CBS represented a portentous development in continental broadcasting.

The American networks first used Canadian outlets on a station-by-station and program-by-program basis. In the spring of 1929, CFRB Toronto had its first hook-up with CBS and that summer CKAC Montreal joined this network as well; CKGW Toronto became affiliated with NBC in November 1929 and CFCF Montreal in 1930. From the occasional *ad hoc* arrangement, the links quickly became much more frequent and regular; sometimes Canadian-generated programs were also fed to the whole network.[89] By 1932 both CKGW and CFCF were permanent affiliates of NBC; CKAC and CFRB remained in the position of picking up only selected programs from CBS, although CFRB in particular took a great number.[90] Rumours were also circulating in the spring of 1932 that CFCN Calgary and a new station in Windsor, Ontario, were about to become affiliates of American networks as well. Essential to these arrangements was the long-term lease of the Bell telephone lines linking New York with Toronto and Montreal.

R.W. Ashcroft of CKGW and Trans-Canada Broadcasting was the most vocal in justifying the tying-in of Canadian stations to the American networks. He was quoted in the Toronto *Globe* in 1929:

It is far from our intention to Americanize Canadian radio, but it is our job to give the Canadian radio public what it wants, and it has told us, in over-whelming fashion, that it wants good music and first-class entertainment, regardless of its source, and we are giving it.

The sponsored NBC programs we are accepting are as much Canadian as they are American. Their sponsors are domiciled in Canada; they have heavy investments here; they employ thousands of Canadians, and each plays its part in promoting and fostering the prosperity of our country. Why should they be asked to spend an additional amount of from $2,500 to $15,000 a week to stage up here a duplicate of their performance in New York or Chicago, when, by mechanical means, it can be brought to a Canadian station and reach us with perfect clarity? If we tried to duplicate their efforts, we would have to import most of the talent in order to do so.[91]

Similarly, in early 1930, just as CFCF's affiliation with NBC was finalized, Merlin Aylesworth, president of the US network, wrote to reassure Prime Minister Bennett that of course his organization would cooperate with the Canadian government in whatever decisions it made regarding broadcasting. He also emphasized that NBC's move into Canada came as a result of frequent and importunate requests:

More than a year ago the Mayors of many cities and towns in Ontario addressed communications to me requesting that we send the programs of the National

Broadcasting Company by wire to Station CKGW, in Toronto. I gathered from these letters that the many people in Ontario who were listening to our programs on distant stations were having difficulty in receiving them clearly and that they thought by this direct connection with CKGW the programs could be more clearly heard in Ontario. Upon investigation I found this to be a fact and our many friends in Toronto urged us to comply with these requests ...

For more than three years, officials of the Canadian Marconi Company have contacted with us [*sic*] requesting a number of National Broadcasting Company programs through their broadcasting station CFCF, in Montreal ... During this period we have had letters from the heads of organizations in Montreal requesting the National Broadcasting Company service.[92]

Ashcroft elaborated further to the 1932 Special Committee in terms that were paradoxical if not sophistical: "We pick and choose what we want," he assured the committee members, so "we have weaned the Canadian radio public ... away from their habit of continuously tuning in American stations." "In other words, we have been policing the Canadian-United States border and only allowing into the country such programs as we consider suitable."[93] While this statement was somewhat more sensitive to Canadian nationalist concerns than his remarks of three years earlier, nevertheless the message was the same. Ashcroft was pointing to a phenomenon that could not be ignored: Canadians were going to listen to American stations regardless; what the network affiliation provided was interference-free access to a limited number of the most popular American programs, with some of the financial benefits accruing to Canadian businesses.

The whole subject of the desire of Canadian listeners for American programs was and is so controversial that hard facts are difficult to verify. Nevertheless, anecdotal and other evidence suggests that throughout the 1920s many Canadians listened to American stations not only when there was nothing else available, but by preference. Frequently, for example, when the Radio Branch reassigned the wavelength of a Canadian station or boosted its power, it received letters of complaint from listeners who found their ability to tune into American channels blocked. A letter from S.H. Henry after the Toronto wavelengths were altered in 1928 was typical:

Last September there appeared in the radio columns of "The Globe", some comment on the possibility of the 475 m. wave being assigned to Toronto stations. At that time (Sept. 2) I wrote you, and also to "The Globe", protesting that those of us whose receiving sets were not very finely selective would have difficulty in tuning out the local stations when attempting to get the key stations WEAF and WJZ of the National Broadcasting Co.

Now the blow has fallen, and the Department of Marine and Fisheries has licensed the Toronto suburban stations to use the higher wave. Last night I tried to get Louise Homer and her daughters from WEAF, and also the Utica Jubilee Singers from WJZ. In both cases it was quite impossible ... I have inquired the opinion of a large number of friends who have receiving sets, and have yet to find one who has not the same opinion as I viz: ... that it is an unthinkable crime against Toronto lovers of good programmes, to allow the offerings of WEAF and WJZ to be interfered with.[94]

The attraction of American programs to Canadian listeners was well known at the Radio Branch and to some extent even viewed sympathetically. In reply to John E. Skelton of Fesserton, Ontario, who wrote in 1925 complaining that Canada did not have strong enough stations to counteract the blasts of American "boosting" coming in across the border, Deputy Minister Alexander Johnston replied:

Do our Canadian listeners turn their dials to the Canadian stations? I am afraid they do not! In the first place there is the glamour of receiving concerts from a long distance, which, for some reason, the listeners think sound better than those from near at hand, and, secondly, I am afraid we must admit that the average programme turned out by the best stations in the United States is superior to the average programme of the best Canadian stations, by reason of the fact that the former have so much more talent to draw from. These are facts which it is not desirable to voice publically [sic], but which have, nevertheless, got to be faced.[95]

Some very unscientific polls taken in the later 1920s also confirmed that Canadians listened to – and enjoyed – American stations regularly. A questionnaire in the Toronto *Telegram* in the fall of 1925 asking readers to name their favourite non-local station ranked American stations in the first seventeen places (the top five were KDKA Pittsburgh, WGR Buffalo, WGY Schenectady, WEAF New York, and WBZ Springfield – all owned by major manufacturers).[96] In 1930 a survey in southern Saskatchewan found that over 45 per cent of listeners preferred KOA Denver and 11 per cent KSL Salt Lake City, compared with only 26 per cent for the local station, CKCK Regina.[97]

Whether simply because of accessibility, or owing to an infatuation with the more polished products of American popular culture, there was already by 1930 an audience of fans for American programming in Canada that responded enthusiastically to the availability of American network shows on static-free local stations. In reply to a heavily loaded question in a CFRB survey cited to the 1932 Special Committee, 98 per cent of the 2500 answering favoured US network tie-ins. More convincingly, a more neutral question asking about favourite programs revealed that six out of ten of the respondents' favourite programs were CBS-originated, including the top three.[98] Similar examples could be added, none of them alone convincing enough to prove the point, but all taken together strongly suggesting that many Canadian listeners in Toronto and Montreal were quite satisfied with a broadcasting system that provided them with substantial amounts of American fare on static-free local stations and that listeners in other centres envied that service.

Whatever the truth about the listeners' point of view, at least there is no doubt that by 1932 private Canadian broadcasters thought US network affiliation was marvellous (and so, presumably, did the US networks, which were always interested in moving into profitable markets).[99] As Ashcroft explained to the Special Committee, CKGW as an affiliate got access not only to NBC's popular sponsored shows but also to sustaining programs that cost "$10 million a year to produce." While the figure was no doubt an exaggeration, a private Canadian broadcaster certainly would have been hard pressed to offer programs competitive with the New York Philharmonic, the Chicago Civic Opera, or even "Sunday at Seth Parker's."[100] Tied into a US network, the Canadian broadcaster had the best of both worlds. For instance, in exchange for handing over to NBC some of its prime evening hours (two to two and a half hours per day by 1932), CKGW guaranteed to air another three or four hours a day of network sustaining programs. If the Toronto station did not want all of the latter, NBC paid it the difference. While NBC collected the advertising revenue for its sponsored shows, the Toronto station could sell spot advertising just before and after they were scheduled; according to Ashcroft, advertisers clamoured for a spot just before "Amos 'n' Andy," for example.[101] Moreover, listeners were then more likely to stay tuned to the station for local programming, improving ad sales on them too.[102] The result was clear. Instead of all the advertising revenues attracted by the most popular radio shows accruing to the American stations Canadians tuned into, now at least some money also wound up in the hands of Canadian broadcasting stations. How could CKGW lose, unless its listeners revolted? But why would listeners mind; were they not getting clear local signals of highly touted shows put on by what were reputedly the most talented artists in North America? A 1931 Toronto questionnaire revealed that the first-ranked station in that city was CKGW, followed by WGR, CFRB, "other U.S." and NBC.[103] It was no coincidence that CKGW and CFRB, the only local stations to place in the top five, were those with US network affiliation.

By early 1932 CKAC Montreal was offering an average of 54 minutes per day of US chain programs, CFCF Montreal 4 hours and 22 minutes, CKGW 5 hours and 36 minutes, and CFRB Toronto a huge 7 hours and 15 minutes. Much of that time was in the prime evening hours. In the week ending 25 January 1931, American programs constituted 33.5 per cent of the total broadcasts on the four stations with US affiliation. Fully 49.4 per cent of all programming on CFRB Toronto originated with CBS that week.[104] W. Arthur Steel nicely summed up how things stood in a memo prepared for Prime Minister Bennett: "The Aird Report stated that in 1929 the majority of programmes heard in Canada came from outside sources. That was because Canadians were largely listening to broadcasts from American stations. The situation is much worse to-day, but for a different reason. Over 50 per cent of the programme material broadcast from our best stations is in the form of chain broadcast material brought in from the United States by the National and Columbia Broadcasting Companies."[105]

By 1932, when the Special Committee of the House of Commons finally made the concrete recommendations that led to the Radio Broadcasting Act of 1932, the CNR, in severe financial difficulty because of the Depression, was in the process of pulling out of radio. The only Canadian-originated network broadcasting was being undertaken by Trans-Canada, and that only twice a week, owing to lack of advertiser interest as economic circumstances worsened.[106] National network broadcasting in Canada had always suffered from the disadvantage of relatively high wireline costs because of the expense of bridging the large unpopulated gaps dictated by geography. Austin Weir of the CNR Radio Department calculated in mid-1931 that an advertiser could get access to almost 70 per cent of Canadian listeners in the major urban centres of Ontario and Quebec for a wire cost of $86 per hour. But to extend that coverage west to Edmonton and encompass another 15 per cent of listeners would cost $700 per hour; to reach to British Columbia and Halifax and cover all Canadians would cost at least $1000 per hour.[107]

Additionally, of course, the expense of creating the program and hiring the talent had to be considered. Graham Spry estimated that in total it would cost an advertiser from $50,000 to $100,000 to run a 26-week series of one-hour programs.[108] The inexperience of advertisers and agencies with creating high-quality programs also was a discouraging factor. In the prevailing depressed economic circumstances, it is not surprising that trans-Canadian costs seemed insurmountable to many national advertisers. The consequence was that by early 1932 "national network broadcasting had ground almost to a halt."[109] Increasingly, Canadian sponsors concentrated their expenditures on stations in the larger urban centres of central Canada – the same stations and centres also being favoured with direct links to NBC and CBS. The conclusion seemed obvious: with their inherent financial weaknesses exacerbated by the Depression, neither independent stations nor Canadian networks seemed capable of providing high-quality service from their own resources. Even in the largest Canadian centres, access to US network programming was apparently becoming necessary to attract listeners, advertisers, and revenues.

The economic reality by the end of the first decade of broadcasting was that in the context of steadily accelerating costs, private stations could be made financially viable only by reducing the programming cost per listener, and the networking concept had evolved as the preferred method of achieving that end. But the inexorable logic of profit-making did not respect national boundaries: if small Canadian networks achieved some cost efficiencies, larger American networks achieved even more. Given that advertising markets and popular cultural tastes had already become largely continental even before broadcasting began, an ever-increasing penetration of Canadian broadcasting by the American networks seemed inevitable. The same economic and geographic realities by the end of the 1920s also seemed to lead to the concentration of good Canadian service in the larger urban areas. Appreciation of the implications of these trends helped convince some key Canadian political and cultural spokesmen by the early 1930s that alternative means of financing Canadian broadcasting must be considered. Before turning to the debate about that idea, however, we should lay more of the groundwork by examining Canadian radio programming in the 1920s and the role played by the federal Department of Marine and Fisheries as the regulator of broadcasting.

4 Listening In

Broadcasting evolved during the 1920s from a diverting novelty to a fully rounded entertainment medium. Programming developed out of the interplay between broadcaster and audience within a particular economic and cultural context. Both the private-enterprise nature of most Canadian broadcasting, which led to its use as an advertising medium, and cultural habits, including traditional expectations of entertainment forms and the longstanding exposure of Canadians to American popular culture, moulded the format and content of radio programs in the early period. By 1932 the shape of future radio programming on private Canadian stations was clearly identifiable, although only the major city stations as yet provided the types of shows characteristic of the golden age of the 1930s and 1940s.

To appreciate what Canadians listened to on their radio sets in the 1920s and how programming evolved up to 1932, it is necessary first to determine how broadcast schedules were structured, that is, *when* the programs could be heard. At the very beginning, during the period broadcasting was still in the experimental stage, there were no set schedules. Early radio engineers or amateurs simply sent broadcasts at their own convenience and hoped someone somewhere was tuned in. But this initial stage passed quickly. Soon word-of-mouth spread news of broadcasting times and radio went public. To become truly accessible broadcasting stations had to operate on reliable, advertised schedules so that listeners would know when and where on the dial they might find a program. Indeed, the practice of regular scheduling is one of the central components of the definition of broadcasting as distinct from other forms of electronic transmission of messages.[1] As already explained in Chapter 1, many newspapers soon found it in their interest to cooperate in publicizing radio-program hours.

Throughout much of the period under consideration, Canadian stations broadcast for only limited periods each day, often at widely scattered times; their scheduling was discontinuous. For an example, one may take the programming hours on Canada's first station, CFCF, the Canadian Marconi station in Montreal, which remained a fairly typical city station during the decade. In February 1922, at a point when it had been broadcasting with some regularity for over a year, CFCF was in operation a total of only two hours a week, on Monday and Thursday evenings from 8 to 9 p.m., with a grab-bag of "music, news, stories, etc."[2] Eight months later, however, the schedule was considerably expanded; CFCF was on the air every weekday from 1 to 1:30 p.m. and from 9 to 9:30 p.m. with music and entertainment, news, and market reports.[3] By June 1923 the station was broadcasting daily except Sundays from 1 to 1:40 p.m. with weather reports and forecasts, financial and livestock market reports, and news, and from 7:30 to 9:30 p.m. on Monday, Wednesday, and Friday with bedtime stories, music, and telegraph instruction.[4] This represented a total of about ten hours a week of service, give or take a bit at times when the amateur vocalist failed to arrive, the stack of records was too small, or the equipment malfunctioned. CFCF was no longer broadcasting nightly in 1923 because it now shared its wavelength with CKAC, the *La Presse* station, which had the time between 4:30 and 5:30 weekday afternoons, Tuesday, Thursday, and Saturday evenings, and Sunday afternoons, for a total of about twelve hours a week.[5] Altogether, then, by 1923 Montrealers had approximately twenty-two hours of local service each week, at scattered times. "Prime" time, it was already clear, was in the evening hours.

By 1927, the Montreal wavelength was also shared with CHYC, owned by Northern Electric, and CNRM, the CNR phantom station (which used CKAC's facilities and part of its time slot). In that year CKAC broadcast slightly over twenty hours a week, CFCF seventeen, CNRM about seven, and CHYC four.[6] The two larger commercial stations each had some broadcasting time every day except Sunday, which was reserved exclusively for church services on CHYC; CNRM was heard only a couple of times a week. In other words, by 1927 the residents of Canada's largest city, after six years of broadcasting development, had access to local radio programming, via four different stations, for a total of about fifty hours each week.

Toronto had two wavelengths by 1927. The six stations (including phantoms) assigned to the city channel broadcast a total of about fifty-six hours a week; the three on the district channel about fourteen. In Winnipeg, where CKY had a monopoly, the local station could be heard about three and a half scattered hours each weekday, and anywhere from two to four hours on Monday, Wednesday, Thursday, Saturday, and Sunday evenings, for a total of about forty hours per week. The station was silent on Tuesday and Friday nights.[7] In Vancouver and Victoria, the five stations were on the air a total of eighty-eight hours each week by 1927, but only later than 11:30 p.m. on Saturday nights, when CFDC broadcast until 1 a.m.[8] In Halifax, CHNS broadcast only three nights a week, from 7 to 10 p.m. on Sundays, 9 to 11:30 p.m. on Mondays, and 7:30 to 10 p.m. on Wednesdays – for a grand total of eight hours a week of local broadcasting.[9] In smaller centres, of course, broadcasting times were even more truncated and random. Little CFJC Kamloops was only heard on Wednesday nights in 1927, although by mid-1928 it provided programs for three and a half hours a week, on Monday, Wednesday, and Friday evenings. CFCY, Charlottetown's only local station, was broadcasting daily by mid-1927, but at very sporadic times and totalling only twenty-two hours a week.[10]

In contrast, the strongest American stations, those most accessible to Canadian listeners, were able to broadcast on much more extended schedules from the beginning. Whether CFCF may claim primacy over KDKA as the first North American broadcasting station or not, by February 1922 the Westinghouse station completely outclassed its Canadian counterpart in hours of service. Although scattered throughout the day, and never for longer than one hour at a time, KDKA music and news programs were on the air for almost three hours each day (fifteen hours a week) by early 1922. Two years later, in April 1924, KDKA was broadcasting nightly from 6 to 11:30 p.m., with late concerts after that on Tuesday and Thursday.[11] By 1927, when CFCF was, it may be recalled, available to local listeners for seventeen hours each week and *all* Montreal stations for fifty, KDKA was broadcasting continuously from 8 a.m. until 10:30 p.m. daily, and often later – a grand total of over one hundred hours weekly. Other leading American stations operated on similar schedules by the mid-twenties – WEAF New York from 6:45 a.m. to midnight without a break, the Chicago *Tribune*'s WGN from eight to twelve hours daily, and so on.[12] By February 1927 the airtime of all the local stations in New York City totalled over 700 hours per week.[13] *No* Canadian station was broadcasting continuously in 1927; indeed, no Canadian city had continuous broadcasting even when the hours of all the local stations were added together.

The two main reasons for the lag in broadcasting service in Canada are discussed in detail elsewhere. Briefly, Canadian station owners lacked the financial resources to purchase programming talent to fill continuous daily schedules, especially given that records were partially banned and advertising revenue was scarce. Additionally, the combination of the shortage of wavelengths available to Canadian stations and the apparently adverse reaction of Canadian listeners to dual or simultaneous broadcasting led the officials of the Radio Branch in Ottawa to require time-sharing, thereby restricting each station's total hours of service and producing discontinuous, patchwork-like schedules in each city.

More important in terms of "listening in" were the results of short, choppy schedules on the habits of the Canadian radio audience. Regardless of whether American radio programs were especially appealing in style or content to Canadians in the 1920s or not, they were simply more *available* in the formative period up to 1927. While American daytime programs were usually out of range because ground waves did not carry as far, in the evenings, long after the Canadian stations had finished their two or three hours of concerts, American programs came in loud and clear. Canadians became habituated to American programs and performers and therefore not surprisingly responded eagerly when the US networks began to wire in Canadian stations after 1928. Accessibility was a central factor in the popularity of American stations in Canada in the 1920s.[14]

American broadcasters realized very early that continuity was one of the keys to radio listening.[15] Listeners were lost when stations switched on and off. Hence the practice of presenting "sustaining" programs in the hours when commercial sponsorship was unavailable. Up until the very end of the decade, Canadian broadcasters either by choice or necessity followed the opposite practice (also the custom in Britain) of scheduling breaks between programs. Sometimes the silences lasted hours, from one popular time slot to the next. But even in the periods when a station was continuously on the air, there were gaps of several minutes between programs – long enough for listeners to weary of waiting and begin searching for an alternative. The logbook of CHYC Montreal in late 1925 graphically illustrates this point. On Sunday, 4 October, the log reads, the station aired the "Emmanuel Congregational Church programme" from 7 to 8:58 p.m. At 9:08, after a period of dead air extending ten minutes, the "Traymore Quartette" commenced, continuing until sign-off at 11:18 p.m. Consider also the CHYC log records for the next three broadcast nights:

7 October: French Political Meeting, 7:58 to 10:26 p.m.
              Ritz Carlton Hotel, 10:44 p.m. to 1 a.m.
11 October: American Presbyterian Church, 6:58 to 8:40 p.m.
              Studio Programme (French), 9:02 to 10:45 p.m.
14 October: Political Speech (Lachine), 8:08 to 9:20 p.m.
              Windsor Hotel (Radio Show), 9:38 to 10:55 p.m.[16]

That this type of hiatus was deliberate is indicated by a notation some months later on an occasion when it was inadvertent: "Delay of 12 minutes in starting programme at Studio due to late arrival of artists."[17] The British apparently espoused the concept of breaks between shows because it forced fans to take an active part in program choice.[18] But the BBC had a monopoly; its listeners could either leave the wireless tuned to the BBC, try to locate a distant European station, or turn it off. In North America, most of the time another station could fairly readily be brought in when the local station went silent; the effect of discontinuity on listener loyalty was thus much more damaging. It is possible that many small Canadian stations were forced into this practice by the need to recharge the batteries on their transmitters.[19] Nevertheless, by the end of the 1920s Canadian stations that frequently went off the air, for whatever reason, sounded primitive and amateurish compared to the professional, smooth-flowing programming of the trend-setting US stations.

Between 1928 and 1932 the scheduling gaps on the major Canadian stations began to fill in. A number of factors contributed: the Radio Branch's gradual acceptance of simultaneous broadcasting in the major centres, growing listener demand for good-quality local programming, rising advertising revenues, competition with other stations, and access to both Canadian and American network shows. The change occurred rapidly. Again, we may use CFCF as an example. In May 1928, the station was on the air for twenty hours each week, only nine of those in the evening. Less than a year later the station's schedule comprised fifty-four hours of weekly programming, including continuous broadcasts from 3:00 p.m. to midnight or later three days a week. By January 1932, the station was broadcasting a minimum of fifteen and a half hours on weekdays, slightly less on the weekends, for a total of 105 hours per week. Of that, about thirty-four hours was network programming, mostly from NBC.[20] Finally, eleven years after it began regular broadcasting, CFCF was a full-time station.

By 1932 Canadians living in or near the largest cities had access to broadcasting on a continuous basis from one or more local stations. Yet, in many parts of the country, that was still not the case. Some stations broadcast as little as one hour each day, and the average number of hours broadcast per station remained low, as Table 11 illustrates.[21] All-day continuous service from a local station still remained a goal in most Canadian centres in 1932. The habit of listening directly to other, often American, stations during the hours when the local station was silent remained common. Increasingly, however, because of the competition from American stations, Canadian broadcasters felt impelled to offer similarly long hours of service whenever possible, whether they could afford to fill them with good programs or not.

LISTENING IN WAS AN ACTIVE, RATHER than a passive, venture in the earliest days of radio. Bcls sat close to their sets, fiddling with the knobs to maintain best reception. The thrill of the new medium's capacity to bring the

Table 11
Average broadcasting hours per station by province, 1931

Province	No. of stations	Average hours/day/station
Alberta	8	4 hrs. 58 min.
British Columbia	10	6 hrs.
Manitoba	2	6 hrs.
New Brunswick	3	4 hrs. 40 min.
Nova Scotia	4	3 hrs. 30 min.
Ontario	18	6 hrs. 54 min.
PEI	2	7 hrs. 16 min.
Quebec	3	11 hrs. 11 min.
Saskatchewan	6	5 hrs. 54 min.
Total Canada	56	6 hrs. 15 min.

world into one's living-room encouraged the search for new and distant stations. Until about 1925 DX-ing remained a popular pursuit; listeners logged and mapped their achievements, then wrote to the stations they had heard, however faintly, requesting postcard confirmation of their feats. As an early columnist in a radio magazine put it: "It is usually a fairly difficult job to convince the average radio fan that the home-town station can be compared with that of some city 1000 or 1500 miles distant. More often than not, they would rather hear the elementary piano class of the Pumpkin Centre high school make a mess of Franz Liszt at distance of 1000 miles than to tune in on Ignace Jan Paderewski at home."[22] After 1926, partly as a result of poor atmospheric conditions in the winter of 1925–26 which turned DX-ing from a challenge to a frustration, city listeners turned increasingly to local stations. The transition was nicely described by a vendor of radio sets: "Today distance is not the first thing in radio. It still has its fascination, of course, but radio is no longer a fad. You know, in the early days of the automobile, everybody was crazy about speed. Today, whilst there are plenty of speeders, the thought in most buyers' minds is not how fast, but how smoothly will this car take me? So with radio, it is not so much a question as to how far a set will reach out, but how good will my set get what it does get?"[23] Only in rural areas, of necessity, did the search for distance continue into the 1930s.[24]

In 1925 *Radio News of Canada* ran a competition to celebrate Canadian Radio Week in which it encouraged readers to report their listening habits. First prize was won by a Saskatchewan farmer, Arthur Elson. A few excerpts from his weekly log give an excellent picture of what mid-1920s listeners heard, and both the exasperation and the wonder they often felt.

Monday: In the evening, tuned into CFAC [Calgary] in time to hear the solo, "Morning," and a couple of instrumental selections. Switched off to Regina to hear

Announcer Hooper apologize for the non-appearance of someone or other and consequently he was closing down ... Back along the dial to pick up CJCA [Edmonton] to hear Dean Howes give an address on Agricultural Work at the University of Alberta. One of the finest talks we have heard, and most interesting to farmers.

Tuesday: Tried CKY, Winnipeg. Picked them up in their last item, when they switched to Roseland Dance Gardens, but Grace Church at Calgary drowned them out. Tried to pick up some Eastern station, but did not have our usual luck. Back to CKY, cut through Bill Grant's [CFCN Calgary] and heard a very successful relay experiment – CKY rebroadcasting KYW [Chicago] and WOAW [Omaha].

Wednesday: In the evening, picked up CFCA [Toronto]. Heard a tenor solo, "The Land Across the Sea," followed by "Far From the Land," so we got well out to sea anyway. KFOA, Seattle, were on the same wavelength, so moved back to Regina to hear what CKCK were doing. Found the Kiwanis Club in charge, and just giving a little skit on "How to Get a Motor License." This was followed by a chorus, "Round Her Neck She Wore a Yellow Ribbon." ... Listened in to CFCK [Edmonton], CNRC [Calgary], and finished up at CKCD, Vancouver, to get the news items of the day.

Friday: Noon market reports as usual. Wheat prices now worse than sick, getting real bad. Picked up the weekly organ recital from Knox Church, through CFAC, in the evening ... Tried CKY, but KFOA was again interfering. Looked in at CKCK to get initiated into the How Do You Do Club. We heard a bunch of initiations, then a solo, "Queen of the Earth," followed by "Oh, How She Lied to Me." ... We cleared up the interference at CKY and heard an able address on "The Aims and Objects of the Manitoba Radio Association." Peeked in at Edmonton to find a splendid program at CNRE; a Hawaiian Orchestra, with many popular song hits and novelty music numbers.

Saturday: Evening – Tuned into CKCK Regina, for the hockey game, Regina vs. Vancouver ... The cheers of the crowd and comments of nearby spectators were distinctly heard all through the game.

Sunday: Tuned in to [amateur broadcasting station] 10NT at Unity, Sask., and heard a couple of good items before that station signed off. In the evening, we picked up CJCA broadcasting the service from the First Baptist Church at Edmonton ... a fitting climax to a week of splendid radio....[25]

These diary excerpts have been quoted at length because they convey so well the flavour of Canadian radio listening at mid-decade. They are unusual in two respects. Mr Elson chose deliberately not to listen to any American stations during the week in question. He also did more dial-spinning than would have been the norm in late 1925, partly for the sake of the contest, but also because distance reception was better on the prairies than in many other parts of Canada. Otherwise, the programming and the problems Mr Elson described were typical and reveal the extent to which a radio had become, for some, a complete home-entertainment centre by 1925.

The vast majority of programming in the 1920s was music.[26] For this, there were technical, financial, and cultural reasons. Music, especially vocal and orchestral music, was transmitted fairly successfully even on primitive early equipment. It was inexpensive too. In the periods when records were allowed, a phonograph and a stack of borrowed disks could provide many hours of programs. (Restrictions on the use of records will be discussed in more detail in Chapter 6.) The rest of the time aspiring local singers and instrumentalists were happy – up to a point – to perform for nothing. "Amateur hours" were extremely popular, especially with the broadcasters.[27] One pioneer recalled: "In the initial stages, I could get anyone to come down to the studios and broadcast for me because I sent a taxi for them, and that was wonderful payment ... In the early days, to be invited to be on radio was a heaven-sent gift ... The glamor, the glamor ..."[28] Musical programming was also attractive to early cost-conscious programmers because the same songs could be played over and over again; indeed, unlike plays or comic skits, familiar, oft-repeated material was frequently the most popular.[29]

Culturally, early radio did not depart from traditional popular-entertainment forms but simply transferred them to the new medium.[30] The single most common type of studio program in the early 1920s was the "concert," a mixture of instrumental and vocal solos and duets with favourite poems and dramatic recitations, identical to the performances given in countless church basements and school auditoriums for several generations. Indeed, the word "concert" was used interchangeably with "program" for several years. Programs of this kind were not repeated on a regular weekly basis; they happened only once. The music offered was familiar, respectable, and middle class, uplifting and conformist. When it first began, "broadcasting ... was a system looking for content" rather than vice versa, and this type of programming helped make the new medium culturally acceptable to the classes that could afford to buy the receiving equipment.[31]

Music does seem to have been what the listeners wanted. An informal poll in *Radio* in early 1924 reported that most listeners (who were described as being primarily young and male) in Canada and the United States wanted popular, classical, and jazz music, while few expressed any interest in speeches or addresses.[32] Another survey conducted at about the same time by three Chicago stations which elicited 122,000 responses (4000 of them from Canada) showed that 29 per cent preferred popular music, 24.7 per cent classical, and 18.4 per cent jazz, while all other types of programming together attracted less than 28 per cent.[33] Later, one of the few Canadian surveys, conducted in southern Saskatchewan in 1930 for an advertising agency, asked the question "What type of radio program do you prefer?" Twenty per cent of the 116 respondents preferred classical music, 40 per cent popular, and the other 40 per cent "50–50 or variety."[34] Similarly, a questionnaire submitted by 769 Toronto residents to the Cockfield-Brown advertising agency in 1930 indicated that dance music was the most popular program, with 27 per cent of the vote, classical music next with 21 per cent, followed by comedy (20 per cent), playlets (14 per cent), educational (10 per cent), and religious (7 per cent).[35] Again, in 1932, a partial telephone-survey undertaken in North Bay, Ontario, revealed that 31 per cent of respondents preferred popular orchestral-dance music, 29 per cent classical and operatic music, 29 per cent old-time music, 9 per cent popular ballads and songs, and a meagre 2 per cent lectures and educational talks.[36] Finally, a survey of the preferences of CFRB listeners also conducted in 1932 showed on a point system (the method of calculation is unclear) that "musical programs of a lighter type" received 307 points, "other light entertainment" 159 points, and sports 87. Meanwhile, educational shows received 33 points, news 32, and religion 17.[37]

Music is certainly what the listeners got. One analysis shows that the four Montreal stations among them broadcast an average of 38.6 hours of music a week between 1924 and 1927 – which constituted no less than 93 per cent of their total programming.[38] Likewise, in a sample week in 1927, 55 per cent of programming on CKY Winnipeg was music, and 60 per cent of that on CFCA Toronto.[39]

The music broadcast was primarily of three types: dance music, classical and semi-classical recital fare, and old and Tin Pan Alley favourites.[40] By 1921 equipment was devised to make it possible to broadcast from locations outside the studio by use of telephone lines. The presentation of sporting events and church services by this method received much publicity and has tended to stick in the historical memory, but by far the most common "remotes" were from hotel ballrooms or other locations providing dinner and dance music. CKAC Montreal, for example, in 1924 filled well over half its programming hours with "Rex Battle and his Mount Royal Hotel Concert Orchestra" (in the early evenings) and "Jos. C. Smith and his Mount Royal Hotel Dance Orchestra" (after 10:30 p.m.).[41] In Toronto, the *Star*'s CFCA started out ambitiously in 1922 with concert programs six nights a week using a six-piece orchestra and soloists costing $3000 a month in wages. In late 1923, however, owner Joseph Atkinson ordered the station's manager, Main Johnson, to reduce expenses. Johnson promptly fired the music director and orchestra and under the direction of Foster Hewitt "extended much more vigorously" CFCA's remote control system to all available venues. As Johnson explained in his diary, "With the exception of the Massey Hall line, which only cost us $7.10 a month, we made everyone in remote-control concerts pay not only the telephone lines but the expense of the transportation of our radio equipment." Actually, Johnson was quite delighted with the order, for he had felt the concert programs were monotonous and predictable and the musical director, Reginald Stewart, "a typical Toronto pedant who regarded jazz as a cesspool." Although Johnson admitted that under the new regime "the classical standard may not have been so high," the programs now provided the "essential characteristic novelty" he considered necessary for a newspaper station and, even better, they cost almost nothing.[42] By 1925 CFCA was broadcasting from its studio only one night a week.

With respect to orchestral remotes, the CNR stations had a distinct advantage, for they could broadcast CNR hotel orchestras *ad infinitum.* But other stations did not have much difficulty interesting orchestra leaders and hotel and restaurant managements in broadcasting, for all recognized the publicity value of radio concerts.[43] The dance music broadcast was light, popular, with pleasant tunes and good rhythms. At the dinner hour it was sprightly yet soothingly traditional; pieces such as "Valencia" and "In a Little Spanish Town" were popular. Late at night it was a bit more daring and included a smattering of real jazz, usually a "hot" solo slipped in between dance-band numbers.[44]

Jazz, of course, was the focus of much controversy in the twenties and its popularity became intertwined in the minds of many with the arrival of radio, although in fact, because of the conservatism of station owners, little jazz was aired until near the end of the decade.[45] To some extent, a generation gap existed between the pro- and anti-jazz forces. While elders solemnly lectured on the dangers of jazz to the nation's identity, morals, mentality, and musical taste,[46] many radio listeners, on the whole younger, demanded that their favourite stations provide it. Darby Coats reported, in his account of how he selected programs for CKY Winnipeg, that he fed his listeners "large doses of jazz" because whenever he scheduled lectures and other serious programs, an outcry of "What do you think you're doing?" and "Tell that guy to get lost" erupted.[47]

On many stations, classical music constituted a high proportion of music programming at first, although this declined as the decade wore on, probably because of the growing commercial imperative to attract large audiences.[48] Despite less-than-perfect reproductive qualities, radio was much superior to four-minutes-per-side 78 rpm phonograph records in the presentation of lengthy classical selections.[49] For the most part, the classics heard were from the light-concert repertoire: Elgar's "Pomp and Circumstance," the "Overture" from William Tell, Ketelbey's "In a Monastery Garden," Dvorak's "New World Symphony" – these titles appear again and again in program listings. Operetta was very popular too, especially from such composers as Victor Herbert, Sigmund Romberg, and of course Gilbert and Sullivan. On the Ottawa, Toronto, and Montreal CNR stations, complete operettas were performed live in the studios from time to time.[50] Very occasionally a complete symphony, cantata, or opera was scheduled. CKCK Regina, for example, broadcast a full opera every Sunday evening during the winter of 1930–31, of which four were live performances and the rest records.[51] It was all somewhat educational and uplifting and a treat for those outside major centres who rarely had the opportunity to attend a live concert. Like the dance music heard on radio stations, however, this classical music tended to be light and melodious, selected less to challenge than to entertain.

The third major category of music most frequently heard was the vast popular repertoire, from traditional sentimental songs like "Home Sweet Home" and "Mighty Lak a Rose" to Tin Pan Alley ballads like "Mother Machree" to current hits like "Ain't She Sweet," "My Blue Heaven," and any number of other more forgettable titles.

Exactly what type of music one might actually hear on a given station varied with the time of day and the inclinations of the owner (or technician, or manager, or, possibly by the end of the decade, the program director). Usually the program planning was completely unimaginative, ranging from the extremes of one classical vocal solo after another to a hodgepodge of every possible type of music crammed indiscriminately into a forty-five minute slot.[52] Indeed this juxtaposition of musical genres that had previously been performed for differentiated audiences was one of radio's cultural innovations.[53] As the decade progressed, however, programmers became more skilled, more dependent on advertisers, and more responsive to audience tastes. This led simultaneously to more sophisticated, more structured, and less spontaneous program offerings. In general, however, "le divertissement" remained the principal object of all the musical programming – that is, of the vast majority of all programming – throughout the twenties.[54]

For those who had held lofty ideals about the utility of radio in uplifting and acculturating the farm, immigrant, and working-class populations, the demand for jazz and other light music – and the commercially driven willingness of broadcasters to cater to that demand – were matters of both disillusionment and concern, and a not unimportant factor in the calls made by the end of the decade in both Canada and the United States for structural changes in the broadcasting business as a step toward program reform.

IT WAS WITH RESPECT TO MUSIC, especially popular music, that broadcasting copyright became an issue in the 1920s, and a brief pause to consider this subject is appropriate before turning to other types of programming. In 1921 Canada passed the Copyright Act, effective 1 January 1924, which made clear, among other things, that copyright belonged to the author of a musical work (or to whomever the author assigned it) and that the author or assignee controlled the right to perform the work publicly and could demand royalty payment for such performances. No specific mention was made of broadcast performances, although "acoustic representation ... by means of a mechanical instrument" was included.[55] The act was so unsatisfactory to a number of interests that lobbying began immediately for amendments. In February 1925, a bill of amendments (Bill 2) was introduced in the House of Commons and a special committee set up to gather information. Among the amendments proposed was one which called for broadcast performances to be specifically mentioned in the act but which also recommended that an exception be made if the broadcast were made "for no gain or interest direct or indirect."[56] According to E.R.E. Chevrier, an MP from Ottawa and the sponsor of the amendment, this was simply a "clarification." To him there was no question that broadcasting was already covered by the act; he simply wished to specify that point and to exempt non-profit stations.[57]

Two positions on the issue were presented to the Special Committee and in other forums. On one side were the authors and composers, just in the process of banding together into a royalty-collecting organization (the Canadian Performing Rights Society or CPRS) and the music publishers (the Canadian Music Publishers and Dealers Association). They argued, as one might expect, that all broadcasters should pay for the music they used just as they paid for their rent, their equipment, and their staff.[58] "Radio, in essence, is simply a new means of publishing or bringing ideas to the people," insisted Gordon V. Thompson of the music publishing firm Leo Feist. "Why should radio be treated any different under the copyright law than other institutions such as the press, the stage and the auditorium?"[59] Most of the representatives of this group who appeared before the committee asserted that the question was not really one of money but of control. An author or composer of a song, they argued, must possess the power to limit or encourage its distribution as he or she saw fit; otherwise, for example, its popularity might be ruined by over-exposure.[60] On the whole, these producers and publishers expressed themselves satisfied with the existing (1921) legislation, for they were convinced that under British legal precedent the "public performance" clause covered all broadcasting.[61] They also agreed that the best method of collecting payment would be for the government to forward them a percentage (perhaps 10 per cent) of each receiver-licence fee it collected.[62]

On the other side were the broadcasters, who were galvanized by the copyright issue to form the Canadian Association of Broadcasters (CAB),[63] and representatives of the radio manufacturers and retailers (the Canadian Radio Trades Association), both also claiming to represent the views of the radio-listening public. These interests argued that radio broadcasting was offered as a public service, that authors and composers received free publicity from the airing of their works, and that payment of copyright fees would destroy the fledgling Canadian broadcasting industry, leaving Canada even more open to American radio.[64] In an open letter rallying radio manufacturers and dealers to the battle, the secretary of the Canadian Radio Trades Association asserted: "The radio industry in Canada must use every endeavor to arouse the public and Parliament of Canada to the truth of the situation, which is that broadcasting is *not* a public performance for private gain. Broadcasting to-day is a public utility, giving entertainment, amusement and instruction free of charge to the people of the Dominion, and as such should not be taxed by the owners of the copyright."[65] In other words, all broadcast performances should be clearly exempted from the Copyright Act. Supporters of this viewpoint, among them Joseph Atkinson of the Toronto *Star*, were convinced that the villains of the piece were the music publishers, vested interests trying to reap profits from the vulnerable new broadcasting industry.[66]

One of the chief instigators in the formation of the CAB was A.R. McEwan, acting director of radio for the CNR.[67] At the Special Committee hearings, however, the interests of the CN and the other broadcasters diverged. Norman Guthrie, counsel for the railway, argued passionately that the CN's radio stations above all others were operated "as a public enterprise" without profit in mind. He also remarked, however, without recognizing any contradiction, that the CNR was involved in radio "as a means of advertising the railways, pure and simple."[68] Others were quick to pick up on the point and to suggest that the CN's stations deserved exemption no more than those operated by newspapers which similarly made no direct profit but which, by stimulating sales, benefitted their owners considerably. No distinction should be made among broadcasters, they insisted; either all should be liable for copyright payments, or none.[69] Those in favour of royalties, of course, agreed: whether or not a radio station was operated for profit, it "exploited" authors and composers when it did not obtain their permission to use their works or compensate them appropriately for that use.[70]

In the end, the controversial amendment was not passed by the committee and the radio trades congratulated themselves on a victory.[71] Nevertheless, there remained the question of what exactly was covered by the 1921 legislation. In late 1926 the Performing Rights Society got injunctions against a number of Canadian theatres and radio stations preventing them from using music controlled by its members.[72] For two years a test case, *Canadian Performing Rights Society* v. *Famous Players Canadian Corporation*, wound its way through the courts. The case rested on the question of whether all works had to be registered with the Copyright Office in Ottawa in order to be protected; in 1929 the Judicial Committee of the Privy Council (JCPC) ruled that they did.[73] Again, the broadcasters rejoiced, for very few of the works in question were in fact registered.

Immediately, however, the CPRS and its allies began lobbying for revisions to the Copyright Act. Eventually they were successful and in 1931 amendments were passed which not only stated specifically that the act covered broadcasting (on *all* kinds of stations) but eased the registration system. As a result, the CPRS henceforth controlled the rights not only to the works of most British and Canadian musical authors and composers but also to those of artists in a number of European countries, and, by an arrangement with ASCAP (the American Society of Composers, Authors and Publishers), in the United States as well. In other words, CPRS controlled the rights to about 95 per cent of modern music.[74] Broadcasters, theatres, bands, and others who wished to perform any of these works had to obtain a licence for all of them from CPRS, the cost of the licence depending, in the case of broadcasting, upon the power of the station and the proportion of its time devoted to music.[75] Continuing controversy over the rates and the power of the CPRS "super-monopoly" finally induced the federal government to appoint a one-man royal commission on the question of performing rights and licensing fees in 1935. On the recommendation of the commissioner, Judge James Parker, more amendments to the act in 1936 set up a copyright appeals board and laid out in detail the responsibilities of the various parties involved. Thus the issue was resolved for the moment, but it was a precursor to a problem still challenging Canadian legislators today: how best to adapt copyright legislation to new technologies.

TO RETURN TO THE DISCUSSION of radio programming in the 1920s, while music dominated the airwaves, of course there were non-musical programs as well and a few words should be devoted to them. One of the most obvious uses of radio was to provide information. Broadcasters successfully introduced such information services as time signals, weather forecasts, stock- and farm-market reports, and sports scores. The announcers on these programs – as throughout radio in the first decade – were almost invariably men, a product of a combination of historical development (technicians, then as now mostly male, doubled as the first announcers), technical factors (women's voices did not project well on the earliest equipment), and cultural bias (reluctance to give women an authoritative voice and their own culturally conditioned hesitation to venture into a non-traditional field).[76]

The broadcasting of news reports was the most problematic in the 1920s. What news there was consisted almost entirely of reading short items from the local daily newspapers. Newspaper-owned stations most commonly presented news reports but some papers that did not own their own stations also made arrangements for short news broadcasts on independently owned stations. In both cases, however, the intent was to keep the items brief and tantalizing in order to stimulate, not diminish, newspaper sales.[77] Some stations, such as those owned by the CNR, had no news broadcasts at all.[78]

Not only did radio stations in the 1920s lack news staffs, they had no independent access to such services as Canadian Press (CP). In fact, the majority of newspapers affiliated with CP perceived broadcasting as a threatening competitor and actively fought extension of news services to radio stations.[79] A directive issued by J.F.B. Livesay, general manager of CP, regarding the 1926 federal election campaign, for example, warned not only that members "must not permit Canadian Press Election Service to reach any commercial broadcasting plant in any shape or form unless that plant is for that night designated by their own newspaper name," but laid down the general principle that all reports broadcast "should be designed to whet the public appetite rather than satiate it." "The radio service should give a good general idea of the result of the election," the memorandum continued, "but the newspaper reader would have to fill in the story from the published print."[80] It may be noted that this memo predated substantial advertising on Canadian radio; simply the threat of competition for ad revenue combined with the desire to retain control of news distribution in the country was sufficient to invoke considerable hostility within CP towards radio news. In 1930, after a similar battle in the United States led to the capitulation of Associated Press, CP began to allow its members to broadcast news "of wire bulletin value." Rather than receding, however, CP's fears increased as time passed, and although there was at least one semi-successful attempt to set up a rival broadcaster-owned news collective, broadcasting stations in general remained news-starved until the late 1930s.[81]

As already mentioned, much radio programming in the 1920s came via telephone lines from out-of-studio locations. Generally, sports broadcasts were among the first and most popular remotes, replacing simple game scores and summaries with play-by-play descriptions of hockey and football games, boxing matches, and horse races, among other events.[82] Church services were also common remotes. By the end of the twenties, in most cities Sunday morning services were available each week, usually from different churches of the major denominations in rotation, and often evening services were broadcast as well. Both church and sporting organizations had reservations that broadcasting might cut into attendance but the majority had concluded by the end of the decade that the benefits outweighed the risks.[83]

Political speeches were also broadcast from meeting halls during federal, provincial, and local election campaigns in the latter part of the decade. For the most part this sort of political broadcasting, rather than developing new forms of political communication, simply made radio "an extension of the platform."[84] Nevertheless, it brought the voices of politicians to the hearthside in an unprecedented manner so that those, especially women, who would not normally attend a political meeting now had occasional access to the hurly-burly of politics. Imagine the reaction in the homes of Montreal bcls tuned in to CHYC in September 1926, for example, when, as the station's logbook laconically recounts, a Conservative Party rally held in a hall at the corner of Plessis and Ontario streets began to get "rough," "so the mikes were shut off while the police endevoured [*sic*] to restore quiet" and eventually, by decision of the studio director, "the station was closed down without making any final announcement."[85] (Interestingly, it seems that the riot was *caused* by the fact that the meeting was broadcast. According to the Montreal *Gazette* the next day, Liberal rowdies deliberately broke up the Conservative speeches because for three days in a row the Conservatives had held "control of radio in Montreal"; the "barrages of malodorous eggs" and "smashing of furniture" were intended deliberately to end the broadcast as vengeance for this "dirty trick."[86])

One of the very few early broadcasters to confront the question of fairness in political broadcasting was Darby Coats of CKY Winnipeg, who was of course especially sensitive because of the public ownership of his station. CKY was also one of the few stations in the period before 1932 to broadcast in-studio political speeches. As he recounted in his manuscript autobiography, Coats made a policy decision shortly after taking charge of the station that "use of CKY's microphone must be available to all political parties on the basis of equal time and equal payment therefor." He accordingly announced that "on the day prior to an election, free and equal time (fifteen minutes) would be allowed for each of the local candidates to state his or her platform in a period to be arranged. The order of introduction at the microphone would be that in which the candidates arrived at the studio ..."[87] J.A. Dupont had a similar arrangement at CKAC, although he always gave the party in power the final say.[88]

Notes made by E.A. Weir regarding the 1930 federal election indicate that the CNR radio management was also aware of the danger of a charge of partisanship. Weir apparently ordered that whenever one party requested airtime, the other party be offered the equivalent. Weir's memorandum indicates that more Liberal than Conservative speeches were aired on CNRA, CNRO, and CNRV in 1930 but explains that this was because R.W. Ashcroft of CKGW, who handled the Conservative radio bookings, avoided using a CN station if he possibly could.[89] The CNR, incidentally, made almost $6000 from political rentals during the campaign.[90] Generally, during the 1920s politicians were feeling their way with respect to the use of radio; by and large political broadcasting was not extensive, innovative, or controversial in that decade.

The remainder of the schedule of the typical Canadian station in the 1920s was filled with a variety of other informative programs. These included morning exercises, health and gardening hints, cooking lessons, and other programming directed at women in the home during the day-time. Lectures by experts in various fields were heard irregularly. More were broadcast on university-owned stations such as CKUA Edmonton, on the CNR stations, and on CKY; these even included on occasion such features as remotes from the university classroom, complete language courses, or regular winter-long series.[91] CKUA, run by the extension department of the University of Alberta, for example, in the 1928–29 season broadcast weekly religious lectures by faculty of the United Church and Roman Catholic affil-iated colleges, a farmers' program of lectures by members of the faculty of agriculture, and a general lecture series on such subjects as "A Day in Old Rome" and "The French Language in Alberta."[92] Some of the commercial stations also broadcast lectures from time to time. CFQC Saskatoon aired regular talks by agricultural experts for its farm listeners and the department of extension of the University of Western Ontario presented a series on CJGC London in 1929 comprising weekly fifteen-minutes talks on topics ranging from "Oliver Goldsmith" to "The Why and Wherefore of Anti-Freeze" and "Mars and Its Inhabitants."[93] CHNS Halifax ran a number of lec-ture series between 1927 and 1931, including League of Nations Society talks, French lessons, and Dalhousie extension department lectures. In 1929–30, CKAC Montreal in cooperation with the Université de Montréal ran a "university of the air" series for the general public along the same lines, and during the winter of 1931–32 a coast-to-coast lecture series was run by Trans-Canada Broadcasting in cooperation with the National Council of Education. Because for the most part the lecturers involved were not paid, series of this type were attractively cheap "fillers" for expanding broadcasting schedules, although by 1932 the willingness of radio educa-tors to perform for nothing was beginning to evaporate.[94]

Nova Scotia was apparently the first province to begin using radio reg-ularly (if informally) for educational programs for children; by 1932 these programs were aired every Friday afternoon for two hours.[95] CKY was also cooperating with the Manitoba Department of Education to produce programs for children throughout the province by 1928. In Saskatchewan, six private stations carried correspondence courses for children in rural areas.[96] There were also, of course, entertainment programs directed exclusively at children, especially bedtime stories and interactive "clubs" such as Uncle Dick's "Cosy Corner" on CNRO Ottawa and CJCA Edmonton's "Igloo Hut Eskimos" run by "Big Chief Polar Bear."

Last but not least in significance were the dramatic productions broad-cast on the radio in the 1920s. Media theorists and historians have argued in recent years that radio's essence is dramatic, that it has made best use of all its material when it has given it a dramatic form.[97] But drama *per se* was slow to arrive on radio. The main reasons were probably financial and organizational. Although serious drama was cheaper to produce than such alternatives as symphony orchestras or operas, it also required more adaptation; light and popular dramas, conversely, were more expensive and complicated to arrange than popular music.[98] Aside from short sketches serving mainly as fillers, as far as can be determined the first plays were performed on Canadian radio stations in late 1924, when the "Drama Players" presented a one-act play on CNRO Ottawa.[99] Soon after, in March 1925, La Société des Concerts de Longueuil presented Molière's "Le médecin malgré lui" on CKAC Montreal; however, this was followed by only four more theatrical presentations on that station in the next three years.[100] In May 1925 "The Rosary" was presented on CNRA Moncton; more plays were broadcast on that station before 1932, although it is not clear how many. All of them were popular stage plays transposed to radio.[101] The first Canadian play written exclusively for radio was apparently Madge Macbeth's "Superwoman," aired on CNRO Ottawa in May 1926.[102] CKUA, the University of Alberta station, began regular live drama broadcasts in 1928.[103] Most significantly, CNRV Vancouver had the only continuing weekly drama program in the 1920s, using the professional CNRV Players under the direction of Jack Gilmore. Between 1927 and 1931, they produced ninety-five radio plays, most of them adaptations from classical plays and fiction but some of them original and some written by local authors.[104] The achievements of the CNRV Players have often been emphasized by Canadian broadcasters and historians, but it should also be remembered that while they may have been precursors of the "Golden Age" of Canadian radio drama, in the twenties they were unique – even among the CNR stations.

BY THE EARLY THIRTIES, WITH THE introduction of network shows and serials, the program format on the major Canadian broadcasting stations was beginning to change significantly, although it remained more traditional on smaller poorer stations. Planning and production had also become more sophisticated, as had measures (introduced primarily by advertisers) to monitor audience responses.[105] Musical programs continued to fill the largest number of hours. One study has calculated that music constituted 52 per cent of the programming on CKAC Montreal for the week of 1 to 7 January 1931, and 70 per cent of that on CKGW Toronto.[106] An analysis from CFRB Toronto presented to the 1932 Special Committee on Broadcasting indicated that in the week ending 25 January 1931, of a total program time of almost 97 hours, about 69 per cent was music, including both records and live performers. Fifty-six per cent of the music was described as popular, 23 per cent as dance, and 21 per cent as classical or religious.[107]

The big change, however, was that most of the best of these musical programs were neither produced in the local studio nor brought in on remotes but came via wire lines from other stations or network studios, and often, for listeners in Toronto and Montreal, from the United States. These included such prestigious features and series as "The Imperial Oil Hour of Fine Music" (Trans-Canada Broadcasting Company, 1929–31, weekly), "The General Electric Vagabonds" (eighteen-station national chain, 1931–32, weekly), the New York Philharmonic (CBS), "The Eveready Hour" (NBC), "The Atwater Kent Hour" (NBC), "The A and P Gypsies" (NBC) and many others. Such musical shows were the most popular programs on radio. In the early 1932 CFRB survey, for example, CBS's "Street Singer" was listed as the single most popular program; other musical programs ranking among the favourites of CFRB listeners were the Neilson Hour (Canadian chain), the Blue Coal Radio Revue (CBS), the Army and Navy Bands (CBS), and the New York Philharmonic (CBS).[108]

By 1932 comedy, mystery, and dramatic serials from the American networks were beginning to appear on the major stations in Toronto and Montreal, as well, of course, as being accessible directly from American stations. These programs were a product of a relatively new phenomenon in North American broadcasting, the creation of programs by advertising agencies, which by 1931 produced virtually all network commercial programming in the United States. From this arrangement the sponsor gained control of the content and thus a greater ability to ensure that the show would appeal to the largest possible audience; the broadcaster got a ready-made high-quality popular program.[109] "Amos 'n' Andy" had been the first popular serial of this type, becoming available to Canadians on local stations affiliated to NBC in the two largest cities in late 1929.[110] Among other favourites listed by CFRB listeners in early 1932 were "The Eno Crime Club" and "The Funnyboners." These programs still formed quite a small part of the total day's programming, however. Only later in the thirties and forties were they to dominate the airwaves to such an extent that they have become virtually synonymous in the minds of many with early radio.

Almost no Canadian programming of this type was produced in this period, a deficit that is still evident in the 1990s in the television popular-drama and "sitcom" genres. As for serious indigenous drama, the CNR's "Romance of Canada" series was the most significant production of the early 1930s. That series of historical dramatizations, written by Merrill Denison and directed mostly by Tyrone Guthrie, has received due attention from other historians primarily interested in it for its nationalist import and as a harbinger of later CBC radio drama.[111] Again, however, it must be remembered that, while programs like the "Romance of Canada" series may have set high standards, they were most certainly the exception in North America in the pre–1932 period. Light musical entertainment dominated both program schedules and audience tastes in the first decade of broadcasting.

Primitive wire tape recorders were not available until about 1933 and magnetic tape recorders not until the end of the Second World War. Broadcasters of the 1920s who wished to preserve programs for posterity could do so only by pressing a record. Consequently, only a few special and atypical presentations such as Mackenzie King's speech on the Diamond Jubilee of Confederation have been saved from the early days of Canadian broadcasting. An extended content analysis of what Canadians heard on their radios in the 1920s is therefore impossible. The historian attempting to piece together and analyze the programming of the 1920s must rely on anecdotal accounts, published program listings, and the very occasional station log. As British broadcasting historians Paddy Scannell and David Cardiff put it, "Reconstructing the character of output [is] more akin to archaeology in which shattered fragments allow a conjectural piecing together of what the whole must have been like."[112] It seems clear from the sources that do exist that most of the material aired consisted of the replication of traditional cultural forms on the new medium. There were indeed novel developments at the level of format and effect, both in the sense that a musical selection heard on the radio affects the listener differently than one heard in another milieu, and in terms of access, in that small-town and rural dwellers now could enjoy performances previously available only to the residents of the largest cities. Yet the actual content of the programs did not move on to such innovations as the radio serial until almost the end of the period being examined here.

Several concluding remarks may nevertheless be made about radio programming in the first decade of Canadian broadcasting. There is a tendency when thinking about early radio to confuse the 1920s with the 1930s. Many recall "Amos 'n' Andy" as a typical show of the first days of broadcasting, when in fact it was not widely heard until late 1929. Similarly, people often forget that national network radio, American or Canadian, did not arrive until near the end of the twenties. Prior to that all programming was determined by local stations and it was quite different from what the networks provided in later decades. In Canada, radio historians have tended to emphasize the programming of the CNR stations and to ignore the reality that they were only a few of the many stations in operation in the 1920s. Memories about the CN stations have been selective too. The dramas and lectures they aired have been justly celebrated; the fact that the bulk of their programming consisted of popular musical selections has been forgotten – as has the fact that in many cities the CNR phantom stations broadcast only two or three hours a week.[113] In most markets in Canada, the programming practices of the private commercial stations dominated the market throughout the 1920s, as they do today.

Despite the fact that we cannot now play back a typical day or even hour of radio from the twenties, certain conclusions may be drawn from what we do know of content and schedules. To begin with, it is clear that most of the conventions of broadcasting were formed in the medium's very early days – in the days before networks, before commercial sponsors, and before most broadcasting stations became separate business enterprises.[114]

The first such convention, accepted pretty well everywhere in the world by 1930, was that radio must provide variety.[115] Stations broadcast a little of everything to suit diverse listener tastes, partly out of the conviction that wavelengths were too scarce to allow for specialization but also for commercial reasons. Satisfying the "greater good of the greater number" was the common goal; broadcasters were acutely aware that their audiences comprised individuals of all classes, experiences, and tastes and that programming must take that unprecedented fact into account. As early as 1923 the CKY magazine *Broadcasting* proclaimed under the heading "Something to Please Everybody": "An impossible task? Well, perhaps it is. Our programmes cannot be expected to please all our listeners all the time. We can keep trying, however, to please most people most of the time, by so proportioning classical and jazz music with educational lectures, news items, market reports, etc. as to make each listener feel that his particular fancies are not being overlooked."[116]

In a very important sense, considering the schedules as a whole, early radio stations served an undifferentiated audience, both middle and working class, low and high brow. Well-performed classical music, to cite just the most obvious example, became more accessible to those who lived outside the major urban centres and those who could not afford the price of a concert-hall seat than it had ever been before, particularly after sponsorship and networks made the presentation of large orchestras and star performers feasible.[117] While it has been convincingly argued that in the latter part of the nineteenth century (in the United States at least) a previously rather homogeneous cultural audience was "streamed" into high and low (popular) segments, the arrival of radio for a few years halted or even reversed this process – or at least masked it.[118] By 1932 in Canada, however, some of the differentiation of types of programs and of audiences was beginning to reappear openly again, implicit in the debate about public (educational) versus private (commercial) broadcasting.

Secondly, from the beginning radio was primarily a medium of entertainment, mainly musical entertainment, not of information or commentary, and this entertainment function became even more dominant as the audience widened and sponsored programs proliferated.[119] This was not necessarily inevitable. For example, the best-seller lists of the 1920s demonstrate that self-improvement was very much in vogue among the middle classes, those who were most likely to be able to afford radios. Yet one sees only limited reflection of that fact in programming.[120] There are a number of reasons why. Radio began, it must be remembered, as a faddish toy for teenage boys and young men. Only gradually did it achieve recognition as a serious and respectable medium. It seems from what evidence is available that even as late as 1932 radio listeners were disproportionately young. While their parents sought to better themselves by reading heavy tomes such as *The Outline of History*, the younger members of the family danced to radio music. For them, radio was not serious but rather a supplement to the cinema and the phonograph in providing diversion and enjoyment. One "Radio Fan" made the point succinctly in a letter to the Victoria *Daily Times* in 1927: "What, I ask, is the motive that prompts anyone to purchase a more or less expensive radio set? Is it so that he or she can listen for an indefinite time to talks on 'the ills that the flesh is heir to,' or other dry subjects too numerous to mention? No, Sir! What the receiving set owner wants is music, entertainment, the best that can be secured."[121] For those whose priority was information, newspapers still provided it relatively quickly; magazines and books remained a familiar and widely available source of commentary. Meanwhile, radio had developed its own identifiable group of fans who demanded entertainment above all – and broadcasters were quick to give them what they wanted. Even in Britain, where the BBC tried to shape broadcasting to be an agency of public service and cultural uplift, one authority argues that by 1927 "the evidence suggests that for most people most of the time, irrespective of class or education, radio was treated as no more than a domestic utility for relaxation and entertainment – a convenience, a commodity, a cheerful noise in the background ..."[122] This was undoubtedly even more true in North America, where few broadcasters had sought to present anything else.

Thirdly, programming followed the clock and the calendar. While this particular convention was somewhat slower to dominate in Canada, by the end of the 1920s the major stations, particularly at the urging of advertisers who wanted to be sure they got their money's worth, presented all their programs in carefully timed segments, usually repeated daily or weekly.[123] Performers learned to time their presentations to the minute and listeners adjusted their daily schedules to accommodate their favourite programs.[124] Variety was provided through the balance of programs in the total weekly format of offerings.[125] As in the United States, by the end of the decade it was only a slight exaggeration to say that "weekly regularity, ease of identification, and split-second timing became characteristic of programs, and programs became characteristic of radio."[126] By then it had also become accepted that programming must be continuous, although as we have seen this was more a goal than an achievement on many Canadian stations by 1932.

Finally, as suggested above, by the end of the 1920s an audience or more correctly a set of audiences ("taste publics") had been created for radio – groups of people for whom radio was a (or the) preferred means of entertainment.[127] The Crawford-Harris survey conducted in southern Saskatchewan in 1930 discovered that in the average radio-owning home, town or country, the set was on for 7 hours and 22 minutes per day.[128] These faithful listeners were those to whom the stations catered. In the absence of formal opinion surveys, their telephone calls, postcards, and responses to advertising promotions provided station managers with the feedback that helped determine their programming choices.[129] Moreover, by tuning in for so many hours each day, these listeners indicated that for them radio had become a habit; no longer was conscious choice and careful selection involved in listening in as it had been in the early days of broadcasting or as it was in attending a film or a concert. Because it was so simple and continuous, available right in the home, radio listening had become for a certain segment of the population a routine and almost decisionless activity, "an agreeable background for passing and wasting time," by the early 1930s.[130] That this type of listener was most apt to be solicited by the advertisers and broadcasters reinforced the tendency toward the use of radio primarily for light entertainment.

What exactly did fans get out of radio in the 1920s? Communications theorists, sociologists, and others have debated the "effects" of mass media on individuals for many years, but have come to no generally accepted conclusions. The most popular recent theories have stressed the "uses" to which listeners put what they hear, the extent to which they are not passive subjects upon whom effects happen but rather active participants in the *process* of communication. How an individual responds to what he or she hears on the radio is subject to many other influences from family, peer groups, other media, and so on.[131] While the programs offered by broadcasters in the 1920s were selected (as much as possible given the primitive audience research of the day) primarily according to commercial priorities, local and family cultural practices mediated radio's effects on each individual.[132]

At this point, of course, we cannot question 1920s listeners directly about their responses to radio. Certain facets of the radio experience in that decade can be deduced, however, from both contemporary comments and later research.[133] The greatest element of appeal in radio seems to have been its "presentism," its ability to simulate in an unprecedented manner the direct emotional experience of actually being in the concert hall, the church sanctuary, the dance pavilion, or the hockey arena.[134] Listeners of the twenties remarked with wonder and excitement at the fact that radio was instantaneous, it was *now*.[135] Competing media such as phonograph records and cinema could effectively reproduce sound and pictures and allow the consumer more power of selection but in both cases there was a lengthy delay before presentation. Through the "miracle of the ether," on the other hand, events many miles away could be brought instantly right into the home. In addition, and on a more practical level, once the equipment was purchased, radio had a much lower per-use cost than the other two media. This factor became particularly important when the Depression began.

Early radio listeners were also thrilled with the sense that they were part of a vast unseen audience, all sharing a single experience simultaneously. While listening in was in this sense communal, it was at the same time intimate; the intimacy was in turn reinforced by the transiency of the experience.[136] Each listener could feel that he or she was being addressed directly and personally by the announcer. Both these aspects of radio, one may speculate, found a ready response in an age commonly characterized as increasingly impersonal and alienating. Ironically, the new mass medium perhaps most appealed because it helped the anonymous individual feel more like a person and the mass more like a community. As Lesley Johnson has written of the Australian experience:

Although radio stressed the sanctity of the individual's private life and promoted the family as an inward-looking institution, it also ensured that its audience was drawn back into the whole. The notion of privacy employed was a contradictory one: it trod a fine line between separating individuals from each other, and yet at the same time needing to ensure that they did not sever their relationship with the society ... In the face of an increasing fragmentation of society associated with ... changes in the workplace, radio created a sense of belongingness – to a community of other listeners, to the nation and its public events, and to the Empire.[137]

Thus, although chronologically broadcasting developed in an environment in which consumers had already been exposed to such other mass media as newspapers, magazines, records, and movies, and although a certain amount of competition among them existed initially, eventually radio found its niche because it provided certain experiences the other media did not.[138]

Radio also began to affect leisure-time habits in the 1920s. Initially, as we have seen, radio listening was a solitary occupation involving headphones and much tinkering with dials. Jokes abounded about the radio widows and radio divorces caused by the fanaticism of some early devotees. By the mid-twenties, with the development of loudspeakers, listening in was becoming increasingly a communal family activity, or at least so it was portrayed by advertisements showing families sitting around the living-room staring at the receiver with a mixture of concentration and delight. Exactly how common this was needs further investigation, however, because the powerful loudspeaker sets remained quite expensive until at least 1930. Indeed only a third of Canadian homes possessed a radio set of any kind at the end of the first decade. Thus, while by 1932 radio was beginning to alter the leisure habits of some Canadians and its cultural effects were already evident, the more widespread effects on lifestyle were a phenomenon of the later thirties.

Nevertheless, by the time the Radio Broadcasting Act was passed in 1932 the basic conventions of radio programming and format were in place. These conventions were mainly the product of technical and commercial decisions of broadcasters. While listeners' likes and dislikes were solicited and heeded, so that on the surface program development seemed reciprocal and interactive, listeners could not respond to what was not offered. The programs presented took on an existence of their own and created a set of expectations among the audience. By the end of the 1920s, listeners assumed that they would receive variety, quality, regularity, and continuity from their broadcasting stations. Above all, they anticipated that they would be entertained. Any decisions about the future of Canadian broadcasting would have to take that context of expectations into account.

PART TWO

5 Government Regulation: Licensing

From July 1922 until early 1933 the administration of radio in Canada under the Radiotelegraph Act was the responsibility of the Radiotelegraph Branch of the Department of Marine and Fisheries. Among the duties of the branch was the operation and supervision of navigational and direction-finding stations and beacons on both coastlines and along the Great Lakes and of a variety of commercial, ship, and long-distance stations. The branch also handled the telegraph-traffic accounts for all commercial, government, and international stations, as well as the examination and certification of all radio operators.[1] These aspects of the branch's work accounted for most of its expenditures during the twenties and, at least in the early days, for most of the time of its employees. They will not be further elaborated on here, except insofar as they sometimes overlapped with our main concern: the branch's role as the supervisor of radio broadcasting.

The personnel of the Radio Branch exhibited remarkable continuity throughout the first decade of broadcasting. From the time the branch was transferred to Marine and Fisheries in mid-1922 until the Radio Broadcasting Act came into force in early 1933, the same six men in effect ran Canadian radio; indeed most of them had careers in government radio administration which extended either before 1922 or after 1933 or both.

Alexander Johnston, mentioned earlier as the Nova Scotian Liberal MP and newspaperman who helped bring the Canadian government together with Marconi at the turn of the century, was the deputy minister of Marine and Fisheries from 1910 until his retirement on 31 December 1931.[2] (The department was administratively split under two deputy ministers in

1927 and divided into two separate departments in 1930. Johnston and the Radio Branch stayed with Marine through these changes.) Although Johnston was responsible for many other aspects of the department's work besides radio, he was actively involved in supervising the policies of the Radio Branch during the 1920s. H.E.A. Hawken, a career civil servant with special expertise in shipping, was assistant deputy minister for the whole ten years being covered here and acting deputy minister on those occasions when Johnston was absent or ill and after his retirement.

Charles P. Edwards, the director of the Radio Branch from 1909 until 1936, was the most important federal official by far throughout the ten-year period of the early development of Canadian broadcasting policy. A big, burly man with a brush cut, Edwards was born in England in 1885. He studied electrical engineering there, came to Canada as a Marconi employee (in charge of erecting the stations at Camperdown and Sable Island, Nova Scotia), and joined the federal civil service in 1909. He held the rank of lieutenant-commander in the Royal Canadian Navy during the First World War, and then returned to direct the Radio Branch until 1936, when he became chief of air services in the Department of Transport. He served as deputy minister of Transport from 1941 until his retirement in 1951.[3]

Commander Edwards's most important assistants in the Ottawa headquarters also were all there throughout the period 1922 to 1932. They were W.A. Rush, another British-born Marconi man, who was superintendent of the Radio Service from 1919 on; Donald Manson, a Scot, also a Marconi employee in the early days, who during the twenties was senior and later chief radio inspector as well as secretary to the Aird Royal Commission and who eventually became general manager of the CBC; and G.C.W. Browne, born in Ireland in 1889, a wireless ship operator during the war and wireless instructor at headquarters afterwards, appointed radio inspector in 1922 and senior radio inspector in 1926. Browne also went on to a later career as a senior bureaucrat in the Department of Transport.[4] In addition to these six men, there were a couple of electrical engineers on headquarters staff, as well of course as support personnel. On the "outside service" the two most important officials were E.J. Haughton, superintendent of the Pacific Division throughout this period, and Alex Sutherland, superintendent of the Atlantic Division after 1926.

All these officials served under a number of ministers during the decade: Ernest Lapointe was minister of Marine and Fisheries in the Liberal government from late 1921 until August 1922; Jacques Bureau and J.H. King were successively acting ministers until P.J.A. Cardin took over the portfolio in January 1924. Cardin held the post until 1930, with a brief interruption in the summer of 1926 when Conservatives W.A. Black and E.L. Patenaude succeeded one another as acting minister. Subsequent to the Conservative victory of 1930, Alfred Duranleau was minister of Marine during the period of debate and passage of the Radio Broadcasting Act.

It may be noted that all four of the senior civil servants in the Radio Branch during the 1920s were immigrants from the British Isles. In 1931, in response to a complaint from a New Brunswick wireless operator that Canadians experienced discrimination in job opportunities with the branch, Prime Minister Bennett initiated an investigation into the birth-place, date of appointment, and residence status on appointment of all its employees. The lists provided to Bennett by Deputy Minister Johnston showed that not only on the headquarters staff but throughout the coun-try a considerable proportion of wireless employees (22/79 at headquarters, 131/303 on the outside service) had been born outside Canada. Johnston argued, however, that for many years trained Canadian radio operators had been impossible to find and that the situation was now righting itself.[5]

The complaint was undoubtedly an instance of a resentment among some white-collar and skilled Canadian workers against perceived British domination of civil-service jobs at all levels – an attitude that manifested itself, for example, in the strength of the voluntary organization called the Native Sons of Canada in the 1920s and 1930s.[6] In this case, it was probably an inappropriate criticism of those holding the senior jobs, at least, for these men had all been hired between 1907 and 1916 when their special skills were indeed rare in Canada and they had all been resident in Canada for some time before appointment. Throughout the period examined here there is no evidence that their origins resulted in a pro-British bias in their policies; indeed they supervised a broadcasting system much more like the American than the British without any noticeable anguish and even with some pride. A much more important determinant in their decision-making was the fact that these key bureaucrats were all originally trained as wireless-telegraph engineers in the early days of the technology. They were technical experts, with little experience in dealing with the political, social, and cultural ramifications of radio which became increasingly important once broadcasting commenced.

The 1913 Radiotelegraph Act, although passed almost a decade before broadcasting began, gave the federal government one decisive supervisory power, namely the authority to set the terms for the licensing of all wireless equipment.[7] In practice, the Radio Branch's activities in regulating broad-casting fell under four or five main headings: licensing, inspection, sup-pression of interference, and wavelength and power assignment, which will be dealt with in turn in this and the next three chapters. The branch involved itself in the regulation of the content of broadcast messages only in three respects: in ensuring that obscene or inappropriate material was not aired, in monitoring the wording of advertisements, and in controlling the use of pre-recorded material. This content regulation (which will be covered in detail in Chapter 6), was minimal, however, compared with the activities of the branch in more technical areas. "The function of this Department is to administer the technical requirements of radio ...," Director C.P. Edwards bluntly told J.E. Lowry of CKY in 1926.[8]

Before turning to the details of broadcasting regulation, a few general comments about the branch's records and activities are in order. The surviving files of the Radio Branch held by the Government Archives Division of the National Archives of Canada are of two main types. Primarily they consist of the complete record of the correspondence between branch officials in Ottawa and each licensee; there also exists a much smaller group of files on particular topics such as the use of mechanical reproductions.[9] These files are fairly complete from 1 July 1922 on; unfortunately, in most instances the files from the very earliest period of broadcasting, when the Radio Branch was still within the Department of the Naval Service, have apparently not survived. Only in rare cases is there any record of the actual policy-making process within the branch and few signs remain of consultations at the ministerial level. Other evidence, such as the virtual absence of discussion about broadcasting in the House of Commons in the early twenties, suggests that there was little or no ministerial or Cabinet involvement in decision- and policy-making on the subject of radio broadcasting before 1928 when the non-renewal of the broadcasting licences of the International Bible Students Association (IBSA) suddenly made radio licensing a hot issue. In other words, one may infer that policy was developed primarily within the Radio Branch, subject to the approval of Deputy Minister Johnston.

Similarly, there is little record of formal or informal contacts between the Ottawa bureaucrats and individual broadcasters or listeners on any but specific issues. This is in direct contrast to the situation in the United States, where because of the weakness of his legal authority to regulate broadcasting, Secretary of Commerce Herbert Hoover made a point of calling together broadcasters, manufacturers, and other interested parties to try to establish a common base for action. Four national radio conferences were held in Washington between 1922 and 1925 (Canadian government representatives attended the last three); no similar gatherings were ever held in Canada.[10] Rather, it seems, Edwards and his officials relied upon informal meetings and telephone contacts to keep them in touch with the opinions of those most interested in the directions broadcasting regulation was taking. Because of these circumstances, then, the only way to assess either the intent or the success of broadcasting regulation in Canada in the 1920s is by a careful examination of day-to-day policy as it was applied to each station.

As already mentioned in Chapter 1, in 1922 a change in classification of radio licences was instituted in response to the many advances in the field of wireless telephony in the previous three years. Before 1922 broadcasting had been conducted mainly by holders of experimental licences; individuals who wished to transmit and/or receive were required to hold amateur licences. Now two new classes of licences more appropriate for the coming era were introduced: for private-commercial broadcasting, and for receiving only.

The receiving licence was the more controversial. When amateur licences for receiving only had first been issued (as early as 1911) they were subject to most of the same requirements as those for amateur transmitting, except the need to demonstrate one's ability to send code at a given speed.[11] In 1922, with the introduction of the new receiving-licence classification, some additional restrictions, such as that the holder be a British subject and that he (or in a tiny minority of cases, she) sign a declaration of secrecy, were dropped.[12] However, the rule that all Canadians with receiving sets must purchase a $1 licence annually was retained; more precisely, under the new regulations the sets were licensed, not the individuals, and if one person owned two sets he must purchase two licences.

The initial motivation for the licensing of receivers seems to have been a desire to keep track of radio owners. Radio Branch Director C.P. Edwards claimed that he wanted licensing in order to be able to compel receiving-set owners to modify their apparatus if necessary, for example if it interfered with others'.[13] Receiver licensing was also the practice in Britain, where it was justified on the basis that wireless telephony, like wireless telegraphy, involved a transmission *system*, both ends of which should be supervised. Whatever the initial motivation, in Canada by the middle of the twenties the desire for revenue had superseded it. The Radio Branch offered a number of services to receiving-set owners; it was felt that those who benefitted from those services, rather than the general public, should pay for them.[14] As demands upon the branch's resources multiplied, the reluctance to give up this source of income (which amounted by 1931–32 to over $500,000 per annum or 90 per cent of the branch's revenue[15]) prevailed over any inconvenience and all objections and complaints from Canadian radio fans. In fact, as may be seen from Table 12,[16] the branch's revenues from licence fees far exceeded its expenditures on services to broadcast listeners in every year of the 1920s for which accurate records exist. Graham Spry claimed in 1932 that the Canadian government "owed" radio listeners a cumulative total of $1.3 million in this respect.[17]

Not surprisingly, the biggest problem the government had with requiring receiving-set licences was enforcement. The licences had to be renewed annually on 1 April; although every attempt was made to make renewal as

Table 12
Radio branch revenue, expenditure and inspectorate, 1922–32

Year	Revenue from Licence Fees[1]	Expenditures[2]	Permanent Inspectors	Part-time Inspectors
1922–23	$ 16,223.20	–	5	11
1923–24	37,659.35	$ 27,500.00	7	27
1924–25	103,108.10	–	9	29
1925–26	124,011.25	58,657.49	–	–
1926–27	200,789.50	111,782.05	10	33
1927–28	243,979.50	154,543.19	15	30
1928–29	266,307.05	166,775.89	15	32
1929–30	403,043.70	225,264.70	18	33
1930–31	459,192.32	221,655.90	18	39
1931–32	518,807.40	216,906.12	18	40

[1] For the first three fiscal years, the figure includes the revenue from broadcasting-station licences as well as receiving licences and does not deduct the Manitoba subsidy (50 cents per licence issued in that province); for the rest of the decade the figure gives net revenue after deducting commissions to radio dealers and the Post Office and the subsidy paid to Manitoba.

[2] The figure for 1923–24 gives only the expenditure for inspection; the figure for 1925–26 includes all expenditure on broadcasting, including inspectors, headquarters clerical staff, printing, and so on. The figure given for the fiscal years 1926–27 on is for all expenditures on "the general improvement of reception conditions," including engineers, electricians, cars, and office staff but not including inspectors' salaries.

easy as possible, many set owners evaded the regulation. Before 1922 all owners of radio equipment of any kind had to send to Ottawa for their licences. Obviously, such a system was impractical for the growing numbers of broadcast listeners, so arrangements were made to have receiving-set licences available from radio inspectors where they existed and also throughout Canada at staff post offices and eventually from a large number of radio retailers and agents as well. The Post Office received a 5 per cent commission for handling licences, the dealers 10 per cent. Permission to sell receiving licences became a means of widespread small patronage under the Conservatives.[18] Although annual renewal reminders were not sent out individually, notices were broadcast on Canadian stations and placed in major newspapers and radio publications.[19] By the fiscal year 1931–32, almost three-quarters of the licences were sold through private dealers and retailers, about 20 per cent at post offices, and the remainder by the Manitoba Telephone System, the RCMP (in remote areas), or directly from Ottawa.[20]

Nevertheless, as the figures cited in Table 6 in Chapter 2 indicated, there was widespread disregard of the set-licensing requirement. In early 1922 one observer estimated from his own experience that half the owners ignored the rule. A year later a Saskatoon region radio inspector similarly thought that only about half the receivers in his district were licensed. A few months later Divisional Superintendent E.J. Haughton of Victoria confided to Edwards that he suspected as many as 25,000 sets were in operation in British Columbia, of which only 2,769 had been licenced in 1923–24. And so on.[21] Haughton did not just bemoan the situation, however; he had a concrete proposal to make. He had been in touch with the RCMP, he reported, who had recommended that the only way to enforce the sale of licences was to take people to court.[22] The officials in Ottawa took heed of the message.

In June 1924, after seeking legal advice from the Department of Justice on various technicalities, the Radio Branch began an enforcement campaign by selecting a number of cities for a search-and-seizure program. Edwards issued a set of instructions to radio inspectors on how to seize radio apparatus for non-possession of a licence under Section 8 of the Radiotelegraph Act, the most important point of which was the ninth: "You will endeavour to get all the publicity possible in the local press regarding any seizure you make." As the covering letter explained: "It is anticipated that one or two examples will be sufficient to obtain compliance with the Law ..."[23] The result does seem to have been a flurry of confiscations, prosecutions, and hasty licence purchases by transgressors. Response varied from locality to locality, depending among other things upon the enthusiasm of local inspectors, as witness Edwards's letter to Alex Sutherland, the Halifax inspector, complaining that Halifax was the only centre with a permanent inspection staff that had recorded no seizures. "We cannot believe that the city is 100% licensed," Edwards grumbled. In Ottawa on the previous Friday alone, he pointed out, the inspector had visited eighteen houses with radios and found four of them unlicensed. "A decided stimulus to the sale of licenses has been the result," he informed Sutherland happily.[24]

Despite sporadic attempts to enforce the regulation through the rest of the decade, non-compliance remained common. One difficulty was that with improving technology, exterior aerials became unnecessary, so radio inspectors could not tell which homes had sets without conducting complicated direction-finding tests that necessitated two men and two radio-equipped trucks.[25] To put it bluntly, the law was increasingly unenforceable. Even worse, the fee was so unpopular that its evasion troubled the consciences of few radio fans. Many different criticisms were voiced. Some said the sum was so small that individuals forgot or could not be bothered to pay it. It was simply, they claimed, a "nuisance tax," a "joke" aimed solely at discovering how many "suckers" there were around.[26] Others felt they were not getting good service for their money; even Sir John Aird, chairman of the 1928 Royal Commission on Radio Broadcasting, admitted publicly that "I hesitate myself sometimes to pay my dollar for some of the stuff you get over the air now."[27] (Aird's misperception that the fee was somehow connected to radio programming was a common one.) Some complained that it was unfair to charge the same fee regardless of the value of the set or the time of year it was purchased.[28] Above all, the receiving-licence fee was denounced because American radio listeners did not have to pay it. A Mr J. Smith of Montreal put it well in a letter to Prime Minister Bennett in 1931: "I am not an American and I have no axe to grind but if you wish to please the people Mr. Bennett and win their approval make radio free for everybody like in the States ..."[29] (Interestingly, however, one of the principal reasons for the reluctance of American legislators to impose a receiving-licence fee there, namely the belief that licensing requirements in general endanger freedom of the press, was not used as an argument against the law in Canada. In the United States as well, large manufacturers were a much more powerful lobby against measures such as this that might reduce sales.[30]) In the context of widespread dislike and disregard of the set-licensing requirement in Canada, then, it is little wonder that when the idea of financing public broadcasting with a markedly increased licence fee was mooted, it received a widely negative reaction – almost, in some cases, to the point of panic.[31]

At various times Radio Branch officials considered making it compulsory for all manufacturers to attach a warning sticker to new sets about the need for a licence or alternatively forcing retailers to sell a licence with every set, but they decided against both measures in the end.[32] The branch did, however, make a point of denying services to those who had not paid their receiving-licence fees. When petitions began to pour in on the subject of cancelling the broadcasting licences of the International Bible Students Association stations in 1928, for example, Radio Branch staff went to an enormous amount of work checking to see which signatories had paid for licences; the opinions of all others were apparently invalid.

In total, 1076 persons were convicted of operating radios without a licence between 1924 and 1929. In a concerted push in early 1930, another 1050 were convicted.[33] Later that year, however, after the province of Quebec challenged the regulatory authority of the federal government, prosecutions against evaders ceased. The pause was motivated not only by the constitutional question but by growing concern among branch officials that the irregular enforcement of the law caused by staff shortages was perceived to be discriminatory by the few caught and was very damaging to the good will built up over years of service to radio listeners. It was also doubtful whether it was cost effective to pursue individuals who owed the government one dollar.[34] Nevertheless, once the regulatory case was decided in the federal government's favour, on 1 April 1932 the receiving-licence fee was raised to $2 and prosecutions began again. Despite continuing resentment against the receiving licence and its cost, the revenue generated continued to be important enough to the government that receiver licensing was not discontinued until 1953, when the government of Louis St Laurent decided that it was "a greater nuisance in political and administrative terms than it was an asset." In the end, Canadian authorities had to succumb to the reality that the system of licensing receivers did not work in an environment "dominated by the American idea that radio services were a free good." [35]

The Radio Branch was also responsible for licensing the private-commercial broadcasting stations in Canada. A broadcasting licence cost the relatively nominal sum of $50 per year regardless of the size or power of the station; with it came a regularly lengthening list of terms and conditions imposed on the licensee.[36] The branch performed the essential task of deciding who should have the privilege of using the scarce resources of the electromagnetic spectrum. The Radio Branch's authority to determine who would be licensed and under what conditions was the essential factor giving it control of the development of Canadian broadcasting.

During the first rush of enthusiasm over broadcasting, the branch seems to have issued licences to all who complied with a few relatively simple requirements – the payment of the $50 fee, a description of the apparatus being constructed or used, and the hiring of a qualified operator being the most important. The branch's willingness to license all comers in 1921 and early 1922 was critical to the ultimate structure of the Canadian broadcasting industry, so it is particularly unfortunate that no record remains of the debate that determined this policy. It seems, however, that the decision was rooted in a number of particular circumstances and assumptions.

One factor, more or less common in Britain, Canada, and the United States, was that wartime bans and controls on amateur stations and experimental work had resulted in a pent-up demand for access to the airwaves, exacerbated by the technical improvements of the war period and the widening circle of skilled operators. In both Great Britain and the United States, military authorities were interested in extending their wartime control over radio into peacetime and were consequently chary about allowing others access to wavelengths. In the United States, the Navy failed in this endeavour but ensured that the largest corporate interests would control the future development of the radio industry as a whole. The desire of manufacturers such as General Electric and Westinghouse to sell receiving equipment led them, as we have seen, to establish and fund powerful stations that became the prototypes for the "best" in broadcasting. Because the 1912 Radio Act did not allow the Department of Commerce to deny broadcasting licence applicants, however, large numbers of smaller broadcasters also immediately sprang up, equally anxious to develop the commercial potential of the new technology.[37] In Britain, military influence delayed the establishment of experimental broadcasting after the war; while a Marconi station was allowed to broadcast in mid-1920, its transmissions were banned that fall and only amateur broadcasting at less than 10 watts was allowed until a new Marconi station was authorized in January 1922.[38]

The exact details of what happened in Canada remain unclear, but the military influence seems to have been much less significant here. With the amalgamation of the Department of the Naval Service into the Department of National Defence shortly after the war, the transferral of authority over radio back to a civilian department was accomplished, it seems, with little friction or resistance. Even before the transfer, however, the Naval Service had granted experimental broadcasting licences generously. It began allowing engineers at Marconi and other electrical firms to experiment with voice transmission almost as soon as the war ended and the ban on amateur licences was lifted in May 1919. When other organizations, especially newspapers, began requesting the right to broadcast in the winter and spring of 1921 and 1922, they were also accommodated without apparent opposition and that practice was then continued under the Department of Marine and Fisheries.

Two assumptions seem to have lain behind this open-handed policy. One was a standard free-enterprise belief that the development of this new science (and art) would be stimulated by allowing competitive service. The precedents of private ownership in telephone, telegraph, and wireless telegraphy were significant as well, although in those cases more oligopolistic arrangements had eventually resulted. The second assumption was that Canada, because of its vast size, not only could but should have a large number of broadcasting stations to provide service for all.

Both of these assumptions also prevailed in the United States, but the situation in Britain was very different. With a small territory, close to European countries also beginning to demand broadcasting frequencies, and with the military complaining about the danger of interference with its activities, British authorities (that is, the Post Office) were much more reluctant to begin granting licences to all applicants. Hence they delayed long enough to see that in the United States (they do not seem to have paid much attention to the Canadian example) the open policy had created confusion and chaos.[39] That confirmed Post Office officials in their decision to limit severely the number of broadcasting licences granted and to insist that the manufacturers interested in broadcasting set up a government-sponsored consortium (the British Broadcasting Company).[40] Thus, although public ownership did not begin in Britain until the BBC was founded in 1927, British broadcasting was monopolistic from the start, whereas in both Canada and the United States it was competitive.

Despite their early generosity in granting broadcasting licences, as early as 1 May 1922 Canadian Radio Branch officials felt it necessary to institute a brief pause in licence-issuing except in small and isolated localities until they could assess whether the forty stations so far authorized were running into problems such as interference.[41] Insofar as concern was shown about the open-handed policy, then, it was for technical, not economic or cultural reasons. The branch's subsequent policy on the granting of private-commercial broadcasting licences was best summed up in a 1927 letter from Deputy Minister Johnston to J.E. Lowry of the Manitoba Telephone System: "Provided the Department is satisfied that the stations are going to be established for some useful purpose and are going to give real service to the broadcast listeners and can be fitted in without being a source of interference with other stations, we are prepared to consider the issue of licenses."[42] In other words, while the branch was inclined to be generous in granting licences, it also had a great deal of discretionary power which it could exercise if it chose.

To what extent this power was used to deny worthy applicants is not clear but such instances were probably uncommon in the early years. Many applicants did have to be put on waiting lists as frequencies became crowded after the middle of the decade but what information has survived (only the successful files were kept) suggests that most serious applicants did eventually get a wavelength by assignment or transfer and did commence broadcasting.[43] Beginning in mid-1928, however, when the Aird Royal Commission was set up to investigate the future direction of Canadian broadcasting, virtually all new licensing was frozen. By 1932, when the Radio Broadcasting Act was finally passed, there was a backlog of at least one hundred presumed legitimate applicants.[44]

The branch's officials learned early on that they must require a new licensee to begin operations within six months and to maintain his equipment in operating condition. Otherwise various kinds of abuses were apt to ensue.[45] Yet the rules were not always enforced consistently. For example, in June 1925 the branch issued a licence to an organization called the Canadian Broadcasting Corporation (not to be confused with the CBC) to build a station (CKCW) near Toronto, promising it one-third time on the 329.5 metre wavelength and allowing it until 31 March 1926 to begin broadcasting.[46] Despite the fact that no work at all had commenced by that date, the licence was renewed until 30 September 1926, with a warning that no further extension would be granted. In mid-August the station's spokesman, Toronto lawyer Charles Millar, wrote asking for more time so he could reincorporate with better financing. Commander Edwards was hostile to the request, explaining in a memo to Deputy Minister Johnston that "we have been holding the wavelength for this station for one and a half years, and, so far, they have done absolutely nothing ..."[47] Edwards went on to advise Johnston, however, that he had been told that "the project was backed by Sir Henry Drayton and Senator Murphy." (Drayton at that point was government house leader in the short-lived Meighen administration; Charles Murphy was an influential Liberal of long standing.[48]) The memo bears a marginal note from "A.J." which says simply: "You better extend for 6 months." Edwards did so.

Ten days before the expiration of the extended deadline, on 21 March 1927, the Radio Branch was asked to approve the transfer of the licence (for a consideration of $1) from the Canadian Broadcasting Corporation to the large distillery firm, Gooderham and Worts. The transfer was expeditiously approved. Gooderham and Worts asked for a change of the call letters to CKGW and eventually began operations in the late autumn of 1927; CKGW ("Canada's Cheerio station") soon became one of the most powerful and influential stations in the country. The abortive history of CKCW had meant, however, that one of the scarce and much-sought-after frequencies in the Toronto area had been held unused for more than two years, despite explicit branch policy designed to prevent such an occurrence. Moreover, the breach of the normal rules was clearly in response to political pressure.

Most of the station-licensing decisions taken by branch officials were fairly routine, although cumulatively they resulted in informal and sometimes formal policy-making. These policies often were openly expressed only when a particularly complicated or even bizarre situation arose. Such was the case of CJCJ Calgary. In early 1926, T.A. Crowe, owner of the Radio Service and Repair Shop in that city, applied for a broadcasting licence.[49] Commander Edwards immediately contacted the part-time Calgary radio inspector, A.V. Evans, as well as the two existing licensees in the city, the Calgary *Herald* (CFAC) and W.W. Grant (CFCN), asking whether there would be "any objection" to licensing a third Calgary station, which would have to share a wavelength with the other two. Evans recommended granting the licence but both W.J. Watson of the *Herald* and Grant objected, arguing that local listeners wanted some silent hours free of local broadcasting to hear distant stations, that two stations sharing the rest of the time was sufficient, and that the Radio and Repair Shop was not likely to use high-quality equipment.[50] On 22 March, Edwards informed Crowe that his application had not been granted, on the grounds that "the radio needs of Calgary are being adequately provided for by the existing stations." Crowe, most unhappy, complained that he had already spent $1700 on equipment in anticipation of receiving a licence and voiced the suspicion that the *Herald* lay behind the refusal. "What their particular objections are, we are not in a position to say," Crowe wrote Deputy Minister Johnston, "but we cannot see just why a private enterprise should be permitted to exercise its influence in the granting of a public privilege to another concern. In other words, we cannot see why a private firm should be permitted to maintain a monopoly under government protection."[51]   Simultaneously, Crowe handed the matter over to his lawyers; his legal firm was the one with which prominent Conservative R.B. Bennett had long been associated.

During May and June, Crowe peppered the Radio Branch with a series of letters of complaint against the *Herald* station, alleging among other things that it was not using the hours allotted to it. Upon checking, branch officials discovered that this was indeed true but that perhaps the station was simply operating on a summer schedule. They also learned that the newspaper remained firm in its opposition to a third licensee in Calgary, although Grant had dropped his objections. The irate letters from Crowe did not cease and so, on 30 July, Deputy Minister Johnston wired R.B. Bennett in Calgary (by this time Bennett was acting minister of Finance in the Meighen government), quickly outlining the facts and concluding, "Would appreciate your advice." Bennett, however, just lobbed the ball back into Johnston's court with a query about the implications for listeners of the licensing of a third station. The Independent Labour Party member for Calgary East, H.B. Adshead, did support Crowe by writing on his behalf to the minister on 23 October. What happened next behind the scenes is not clear, but Commander Edwards ultimately came down on Crowe's side on the grounds that the *Herald* was not in fact using all its available hours. After a hiatus of a few months, Crowe was issued a licence on 14 December 1926, for station CJTC, the call letters soon altered at his request to CJCJ. Although there were some initial difficulties in getting the three stations' time allotments synchronized, everything was straightened out and apparently operating satisfactorily by mid-1927.

That fall, however, in need of more financing, Crowe converted his business to a limited company in which he could sell shares, which involved the transfer of the licence from the Radio Service and Repair Shop to a limited company of the same name (who provided the financial backing is not clear). The following year, in September 1928, the *Albertan* Publishing Company, which had been using CJCJ facilities for its phantom station, CHCA, purchased ownership and control of the Radio Service and Repair Shop. Another transfer of CJCJ's licence, to the *Albertan*, was then approved by the branch. Unfortunately, Crowe had not realized when he sold shares in CJCJ in 1927 that he had thereby risked losing control of the station, which he in fact had continued to operate, so he was rather distressed to find that the *Albertan* had bought it out from under him without his knowledge. The new Calgary inspector, R. Ainslie, reported to Commander Edwards: "Apparently after receiving this letter he [Crowe] refused to put the Albertan programme on the air and when Mr. G.M. Bell, President of Albertan Publishing Co. together with his Manager, Mr. Gemeroy, visited the station on Saturday evening to straighten matters out a fight took place and police were called."[52] Crowe was promptly fired but legal proceedings threatened by both sides apparently never materialized. Crowe dropped out of sight of the Radio Branch, to resurface only briefly when he helped the International Bible Students Association set up their radio station, CHCY, in Edmonton; the *Albertan* continued to own and operate CJCJ for many years thereafter.[53]

The story of CJCJ Calgary has been recounted in some detail because, although it contrasts considerably with the vast majority of much more routine cases, it reveals several aspects of the branch's licensing policies and its manner of dealing with broadcasters in the 1920s. First, it shows that licence applications could be turned down because of adverse advice from interests already established in the market involved. By this kind of consultation branch officials did indeed put themselves in the position of protecting or seeming to protect the privilege of some private entrepreneurs against competition from others, as Crowe suggested in his letter to Johnston. Making choices about who should have the privilege of using the portion of the electromagnetic spectrum allotted to broadcasting is, of course, the essence of regulation. In these early days, the regulators at the branch were still feeling their way and only gradually developing guidelines and principles on which to base these important decisions. Not surprisingly, some individuals felt aggrieved when they were passed over for ill-explained and seemingly unfair reasons.

In fact, the branch did evolve certain standards. Most evidently, it almost always granted the so-called "pioneer" broadcasters, the first in any given market, those who had chronological priority, the greatest privileges – closest consultation, first choice among wavelengths, the best time slots, and so on. Although not explicitly stated, another of the principles of priority that evolved informally within the branch was also illustrated in the Calgary case, at least initially, namely that newspaper-owned stations were in general favoured over others.[54]

Secondly, the example of CJCJ reveals the branch's gradually emerging policy on the crucial question of the sale and transfer of broadcasting licences (as distinct from the trade in transmitting equipment, which was never controlled). There were three possible variations when a broadcaster decided to give up his business. If he wished, he could simply decline to renew and thereby abandon his licence. This was non-controversial. Alternatively, he could try to sell his licence to someone else. If this were allowed, it would mean that a spectrum assignment, a scarce and many would argue public resource, could become a means of private profit-making. The third possibility was that the licence could be relinquished but on the understanding that it would be reissued to another party already identified (in practice, usually the purchaser of the station equipment).

According to Section 21 of the broadcasting licence, "Except with the consent in writing of the Minister, the licensee shall not assign or sublet this license." But under what circumstances should the minister give his consent? The branch's policy on this delicate subject was laid out in a memorandum written by Donald Manson and approved by Edwards in July 1926:

It is recommended that the following ruling be made as a guiding principle in dealing with applications for the transfer of Private Commercial Broadcasting Licenses, viz: –

In order to obviate the trading or selling of wavelengths or other privileges conveyed by a Private Commercial Broadcasting License, for money or other consideration, the Department shall not in general authorize the transfer of such licenses from one party to another.

Nevertheless at its discretion and upon satisfactory evidence being furnished that no money or other consideration has been charged for the priveleges [sic] above named or agreements made for the subsequent conduct of the station, the Department may then cancel the license for an existing station and authorize the issue of a new license for the same station to another party.[55]

Simply put, then, as the CJCJ case illustrated, the branch did in fact on a discretionary basis allow licence transfers in the sense that it was willing routinely to authorize cancellation and reissue to a party selected by the seller. The reasoning was straightforward. The equipment of a broadcasting station was of no use in the absence of a licence to use it; without the inducement of a near-guarantee of a licence, it could not be sold and service would end. "After all," the Pacific Division superintendent wrote, "the license is the chief incentive in connection with the purchase of the equipment."[56] In the interest of stability, continuity, and expanded broadcasting service in the early days, virtually automatic reissue was preferable to loss of service, and became in fact the practice. A year after Manson's memo, branch official W.A. Rush admitted to the Calgary inspector: "For your personal information, I may say that while the Department does not give any encouragement to transfers of ownership of stations and licenses, this has been done in a few cases and there is nothing very objectionable about the procedure as long as it does not involve the licensing of an additional physical station."[57] It was by means of such a transfer in a period (1930) when virtually no new licences were being issued, for example, that young Roy H. Thomson, owner of a company that distributed automotive and radio equipment, acquired the licence of Abitibi Power and Paper's Iroquois Falls station, CFCH, and moved it to North Bay, there to begin building one of the largest media enterprises in the world. As in the case of the far less successful T.A. Crowe of Calgary, the persistent and skilful lobbying of local and national politicians played an important role in Thomson's effectiveness in persuading branch officials to authorize the CFCH transaction.[58]

As noted, Donald Manson specified in his memo that the branch must determine that no money changed hands in licence transfers. This provision was virtually impossible to enforce. One large loophole was that the price of the equipment could be inflated to include the value of the spectrum assignment. More important, there is almost no evidence in the many files of stations that were transferred from one owner to another that the branch ever checked up on what "considerations" had passed between buyer and seller. They had neither the staff nor the desire to investigate in this manner. In the CKCW/CKGW case, the $1 purchase price was volunteered by the parties involved, but in many other instances where no details about the arrangement were provided except the identity and address of the new applicant, approval was just as prompt. Indeed, sometimes the branch even lost track of who owned a given station – and moreover showed little concern. For example, at one point in late 1927 some confusion apparently existed in Ottawa as to who owned CFCY Charlottetown. In the margin of a letter in which Atlantic Division Superintendent Sutherland admitted that he had been unable to sort out whether the station belonged to K.S. Rogers or W.E. Burke, Edwards jotted, "We don't care who the actual owner is as long as the licensed apparatus is at the address given ..."[59]

Two recent students of Canadian broadcasting history have written disapprovingly of the branch's licence-transfer policy on the grounds that it denied businessmen the opportunity to make a legitimate profit when selling their stations.[60] The literature on regulation is full of the debate about whether the spectrum is a scarce and/or a public resource, and whether it is justifiable to allow its commercialization.[61] In the specific case of Canada in the 1920s, however, the point is not so much what Manson's policy document said but how it was used in practice. All the evidence, such as Rush's letter in the CJCJ case, suggests that both before and after 1926 such transactions were routinely authorized by the branch with little or no scrutiny as to who the new owners were or what payments might have been involved. The branch's officials bent over backwards to enable stations to survive by allowing virtually automatic licence transfer; their general failure to query the terms suggests that they were less concerned about the possibility of the commercialization of the spectrum than about providing continuity of broadcasting service.

Given the marginal nature of most early broadcasting stations, the emphasis on stability was justifiable; nevertheless, precedents were set that were difficult to overturn later. It remains the practice of the current regulatory body, the Canadian Radio-television and Telecommunications Commission (CRTC), for example, to consider only the licence applicant selected by the vendor when a broadcasting station is sold; no other interested parties are allowed to compete for the spectrum assignment except in the rare cases when the designated purchaser is denied the licence.[62]

The Radio Branch's informal policy on the multiple ownership of radio stations was also revealed by the CJCJ case. In late 1927, in the midst of the considerable confusion over who was going to own, operate, and finance the station, a rumour surfaced that Alberta Pacific Grain wished to purchase it. The problem was that the company already owned a station in Red Deer; should it be allowed to own another in the same province? The answer was yes; if the stations were not too close together, the branch had no difficulty with multiple ownership. It was "distinctly opposed," however, to two stations with the same owner in the same market.[63]

Fourthly, the CJCJ tale illustrates, as did the story of CKCW Toronto, that political consultation was not unusual in tricky licensing decisions. In this instance, it was the branch officials who initiated the approach to the most prominent local MP, Bennett, who apparently washed his hands of the affair. It also worked the other way around, as with the plea from Adshead. In addition to the usual pressures on politicians to represent the interests of supportive constituents, the heavy involvement of party-linked newspapers in the broadcasting business helped cause a carry-over of old partisan habits into the new medium. These types of contacts were mostly informal and off the record but enough scraps of evidence have survived to suggest that they were not at all uncommon. For instance, when the Victoria Radio Club wired Edwards about its dissatisfaction with the service provided by station CFCT, some branch official pencilled in the margin for the director's benefit, "Hon. Mr. Tolmie is interested in this case – please note."[64] When in 1930 the owner of CFCY Charlottetown (it had eventually been determined that it was Keith Rogers) had to give up certain broadcasting hours to a new station, CHCK (owned by "strong Liberals"), and then was denied a power increase to 500 watts, he got two MPs, Thomas Cantley and Chester McLure, to put in a good word with the Radio Branch, which they promptly did.[65] Someone in the branch jotted down "Endorsation by M.P. noted" and Rogers got his increase. Similarly, in 1927 David Rogers of CFRB Toronto (no relation to Keith) asked James Malcolm, minister of Trade and Commerce, also successfully, to speak to Edwards on his behalf regarding a change of wavelength for the Rogers's station.[66] Two years later, when the licence of little CJPC Preston, Ontario, was transferred from Wallace Russ to the Metal Shingle and Siding, a branch official assured the acting deputy minister that "the Honourable Mr. Euler has no objection ..."[67] And before Edwards would authorize the transfer of the Midland, Ontario, station's licence to a group in Fort William in late 1930, he warned his deputy minister that Dr Manion was "vitally interested" in the case and must approve the transfer in writing.[68] Of course, in many instances attempts to apply political pressure probably failed. But they succeeded often enough to cast doubt on the even-handedness of the branch's decision-making, particularly after 1930 when, in the context of pending revisions of the broadcasting system, Prime Minister Bennett personally took control of all major aspects of radio regulation.

Finally, the case of CJCJ Calgary reveals that small entrepreneurs could easily get in over their heads in the early days of broadcasting in Canada, and that the great flexibility the branch showed in dealing with Crowe *et al.* was probably necessary in the interests of broadcasters and listeners alike. But there is little doubt that such flexibility and discretionary authority also left room for abuse.

The power to licence broadcasters was the biggest weapon in the Radio Branch's regulatory arsenal in the 1920s. Despite the central importance of licensing, the branch's policies and procedures in this area throughout the decade seem to have been *ad hoc* and even arbitrary, with virtually no written guidelines. Although certain priorities gradually evolved, they were liable to change at a moment's notice and frequently were not publicly known. While even under the most ideal circumstances regulators are subject to pressure from interested parties including politicians, when clear, visible rules exist and are more or less followed, the regulators are less vulnerable to accusations of favouritism and/or incompetence than was the Radio Branch in the 1920s. The weaknesses in the licensing process were among the most important factors leading to the almost universal call for the creation of a non-partisan regulatory body by 1930. The problem was not a lack of legal authority, as it was in the United States before 1927, but rather a lack of public debate about what that authority entailed and how it should be exercised, compounded by the placement of the regulatory function in a government department vulnerable to partisan pressures.

6 Regulation of Interference and Content

Once a licence for a broadcasting station was granted, the branch prescribed a variety of rules and regulations for its operation, some of them printed on the four-page licence form, others communicated on irregularly issued mimeographed sheets. Among the rules in force by 1926 were specifications regarding the wavelength to be utilized, an injunction against interfering with other radio stations, and requirements that a wavemeter be used to keep track of the wavelength, that a proces verbal of all signals transmitted be kept, that all operators be British subjects, and that all apparatus be completely and accurately described on the licence application. Additionally, the licence contained a list of instructions regarding sharing of time allotments and the hours that could be utilized for recorded music, advertising, and testing.[1] This chapter will assess the major regulations and the strengths and weaknesses of the enforcement policies of the Radio Branch before 1932 by analyzing the branch's inspection service and its endeavours to eliminate interference and to oversee content. The next two chapters will continue the discussion with an examination of the branch's policies regarding wavelength and power assignments.

The enforcement of the rules and regulations of the Radio Branch with respect to all aspects of radio, including broadcasting, was in the hands of a team of radio inspectors. The inspection service dated from before the First World War, when staff members were placed in port cities to monitor ship and shore stations to ensure that they were licensed, did not interfere with one another's transmissions, and so on. The advent of broadcasting, bringing with it more transmitters, more receivers, and therefore more possibilities for interference and other abuses, necessitated the enlargement of the inspection staff and the appointment of these so-called "ether cops" to inland communities. Beginning in the 1922–23 fiscal year, the branch also appointed part-time inspectors in many localities, most of them holders of amateur licences who had received radio training during the war. The part-time inspectors were paid a nominal fee of between $15 and $30 a month; many of them were patronage appointments. By 1932 the inspectorate comprised at least seventeen full-time in major cities from coast to coast and thirty-three part-time in smaller centres, with a supervisory staff in Ottawa headquarters directed by Manson and Browne (see Table 12). While not all their time was spent on matters related to broadcasting, the inspectors in inland centres in particular devoted a large part of their efforts to making radio listening as pleasant as possible for its new fans.[2] According to contemporary accounts, the Canadian radio-inspection service was the largest and most effective in the world, with the possible exception of some Swiss cantons.[3]

The principal task of the "ether cops" was to listen in regularly (usually nightly) to the stations in their local area in order to identify any problems of interference or breach of regulations on the part of either amateur or commercial broadcasters or listeners. In effect, they were the branch's field men, with a good deal of discretionary authority to warn offenders of problems, to attempt to clear them up amicably, but if necessary to bring Ottawa officials in on the case. From 1924 on they inspected the facilities of each broadcasting station annually and sent detailed reports to headquarters. They also provided the branch with direct on-the-spot information about local conditions and opinions, an important feedback function during a period when all were experimenting together with a new medium.[4]

A large part of the inspectors' time was spent dealing with the complex problem of interference, which Commander Edwards called in 1926 "one of the greatest detriments to the future of Radio."[5] Interference – various kinds of static, hums, whistling, fading, and the like – could and often did make radio listening a misery rather than a pleasure in the earliest days. One radio columnist described it this way: "How many times have you looked forward to some broadcast program of particular interest, only to be greeted by a flood of jumbled harshness belching from the horn of the loud speaker. It interferes with the program, it grates upon the nerves of the listener, and tries the patience of those people who desire quality reception unaccompanied by this objectionable noise."[6] The branch's files were full of complaints about interference problems; one survey conducted in southern Saskatchewan in 1930 found that, of a total of 116 respondents, 66 complained of at least some interference when they tried to listen either to local or distant stations.[7] In periods or places where interference was particularly acute, the sale of radio receivers was noticeably affected. For example the slump in licence sales in 1927–28 was generally attributed to the particularly bad static conditions in the winter of 1926.[8]

Interference had both natural and man-made causes. About the former, the product of various kinds of atmospheric disturbances, little could be done except to realize, as radio experts gradually did, that it was an inevitable and insoluble problem for long-distance broadcasting but could be virtually eliminated within a reasonable range (say 150 miles) by increasing the power of transmissions.[9] Until high-power stations became the norm, however, atmospheric interference remained a problem varying in intensity from year to year. In most of Canada, the reception was excellent during the early radio rush of 1921–22, very poor during the first four months of 1926, and then much better in the winters of 1930–31 and 1931–32.[10] This type of interference was always a greater problem in summer than in winter, to the point that in the early 1920s radio listening tended to be mainly a wintertime activity.

Man-made interference had three main causes: faulty and inefficient power lines and other electrical equipment, radio transmitters usurping one another's channels, and inferior receiving equipment. In an attempt to deal with the first of these problems, the Radio Branch in 1924 made a grant of $3000 to the Research Council of Canada to investigate possible means of suppression of electrical interference. Enough by way of positive results was obtained that in February 1925 the branch set up a special inductive-interference section to handle suppression activities. Initially, the section comprised an engineer and three electricians, two of whom staffed a truck sent on a tour of one hundred Ontario and Quebec communities; 203 sources of electrical interference were investigated that first year, of which 124 were cleared up immediately and most of the others later.[11] Soon three more trucks were purchased and permanently stationed in Toronto, Ottawa, and Montreal. By the time of the 1931–32 *Annual Report* of the department, there were twenty-four such trucks covering most of the more heavily settled parts of the country. (In comparison, in the whole of the United States there were eight test trucks in 1931.[12]) In addition to these on-site investigations and an advice-by-mail service, the inductive-interference staff in collaboration with Research Council engineers produced a booklet dated 1 May 1925 entitled "Radio Inductive Interference," which in relatively non-technical language discussed both a number of the causes of and some of the solutions to the most common problems of interference experienced by broadcast listeners. The booklet was available to anyone for fifteen cents; three thousand copies were produced, in English only. A second more technical bulletin was issued in 1932 and a supplement in 1934.

As may be seen from Table 13,[13] in approximately 75 per cent of the cases investigated by the special staff the problem proved to be caused by electrical apparatus, most often power lines tapping against one another in the

Table 13
Interference investigation by the radio branch, 1926–32

| Type | Sources of interference investigated | | | | | |
	1926–27	1927–28	1928–29	1929–30	1930–31	1931–32
Electrical-distribution systems and power lines	n/a	4,383	4,271	6,405	7,719	7,688
Domestic and commercial electrical apparatus	n/a	901	1,650	2,123	3,763	3,385
Defective receivers and radio apparatus	n/a	152	356	723	1,346	1,605
Total	2,793	5,436	6,277	9,251	12,828	12,678
Action taken						
Sources definitely reported cured	2,432	4,880	5,273	8,301	10,709	11,082
Sources not yet reported cured	361	465	855	782	1,953	1,467
Sources having no economic cure	–	91	149	168	166	129
Total	2,793	5,436	6,277	9,251	12,828	12,678

wind, trolley tracks "sparking," and so on. The 1929–30 *Annual Report* cited a fairly typical instance of the work done by the interference engineers: "The interference from a single source frequently travels many miles along the power wires and affects thousands of broadcast listeners. An example of such a case was recently located by our investigators near Three Rivers. The 15,000 volt line was making intermittent contact with a guy-wire and ruining radio reception all the way from Ste. Anne de la Pérade to

Three Rivers, Quebec, a distance of about twenty-five miles."[14] Once the source of the problem was identified, the staff had to rely upon cooperation to correct it, for nothing in the Radiotelegraph Act gave the federal government the power to compel suppression of interference. As the table shows, most of the problems were readily cleared up, and the branch always claimed that it was delighted with the cooperation it received from all offenders, especially the public-utilities companies which were most often to blame. According to official Radio Branch spokesmen, the power companies were universally pleased to have faults in their systems pinpointed before they became serious enough to damage equipment or before a dangerous accident occurred. Public utilities also recognized the need to maintain public good will. As the decade passed, these companies became more meticulous about keeping their lines in perfect condition and gradually they replaced obsolete equipment with improved modern apparatus less likely to cause problems.

For some cases of electrical interference, however, an "economic" cure was not easily found; these included electro-medical apparatus such as dentists' drills and x-ray machines, high-voltage power lines, and electric-railway and trolley wires. Although official reports did not admit it, difficulties did occur with lack of cooperation from some offenders in these categories. Indeed, there were enough complaints voiced before the Aird commissioners in their tour of the country in the spring of 1929 that their report recommended "the earnest consideration" of legislation to compel users of interfering apparatus to correct faults.[15]

Shortly after that recommendation the subject of electrical interference came up at a meeting of Toronto-area radio inspectors, leading to a difference of opinion about how to deal with these situations. While S.J. Ellis, the chief Toronto inspector, repeated the headquarters' line that publicly identifying offenders should be avoided "due to the fact that such splendid co-operation is obtained," some others from smaller centres disagreed. All the inspectors felt that diplomacy was preferable to legislation, but they voted in the end almost unanimously in support of a law for use against persistent offenders, mentioning specifically problems with movie equipment and dentists' drills.[16] The 1932 Radio Broadcasting Act, however, did not contain the "big stick" they desired.

In fact, however much cooperation or legislation existed, it was not and could never be enough to cope with the constantly growing emissions of an increasingly electrified and urbanized society. Despite its best efforts, the interference inspectorate by 1932 found itself falling further and further behind because the greater sensitivity of more sophisticated receivers exacerbated the problems faster than improved suppression apparatus could alleviate them.[17] The ultimate solution, and the main reason we do not normally experience excessive static, hums, and whistles on our radio receivers today, lay, as in the case of atmospheric interference, in high-power transmitters and the receivers appropriate thereto, with 50,000 watts now the standard output of most urban stations, more than one hundred times the Canadian norm in 1932.[18]

The second serious source of man-made interference was radio stations, including ship and amateur stations as well as broadcasting ones, intruding on one another's assigned frequencies. Interference between amateur and broadcasting stations was a problem only in the very early 1920s. Once broadcasting began the amateurs were moved to wavelengths well away from those used by broadcasters and "ham" operators were at first encouraged and later required to switch to continuous-wave transmitters, because their old spark sets emitted such a broad wave that they interfered on much of the dial. The general policy of the branch was to encourage the hams to regulate themselves, and with the aid of the various amateur organizations, this goal was by and large reached without too much difficulty.[19] Sensitive to the fast-growing numbers and influence of the broadcast listeners, the amateurs voluntarily established a silent period between 7:30 and 10:00 every evening. Eventually, regulations were passed so that, if an amateur's transmissions caused problems for broadcast listeners in a particular area, he could be legally banned from 7 p.m. to midnight.[20] Although this caused some grumbling among the hams, who suspected that they were often shut down because of someone else's inferior equipment, the system based on mutual respect between branch officials and the heads of the amateur organizations meant that amateur interference was not a significant long-term problem for radio broadcasting in Canada.

A much more serious form of station-to-station interference in some parts of the country was that from ships and coastal direction-finding transmitters. The branch took early action with respect to the coastal stations it owned or leased, replacing spark with continuous-wave apparatus at considerable expense. Interference from ship sets was much more difficult to eliminate, for it required international agreement. Since the war, most countries had required wireless equipment on all ships over a certain tonnage. The 1906 International Wireless Conference at Berlin, however, had assigned wavelengths of 300 and 600 metres for ship-to-ship and ship-to-shore communications – the former right in the middle of what by 1922 had become the broadcast band. Worse, most of the equipment used for code transmission by merchant ships was of the broadly interfering spark type which shipowners were reluctant to pay to replace.[21] As a result, in the early 1920s Canadian radio fans who lived in coastal areas were often annoyed by having a concert program interrupted by a series of dots and dashes from some ship. The problem was alleviated considerably when, at Canada's initiative, a conference was held in New York in

January 1924 at which Newfoundland, Canada, and the United States agreed that ship and shore stations would move to either 2000 metres or more or to between 625 and 735 metres.[22] This arrangement was extended to include Great Britain by an exchange of notes in September 1925 and by March 1926 it embraced eleven countries in all.[23] Although this did not eliminate the problem of ships of non-signatory nations near Canada, especially the vexing problem of French trawlers on the Grand Banks and the French coastal station on St Pierre, it did substantially reduce the interference experienced by Canadian bcls in British Columbia and the Maritimes.[24] At the Washington International Radio Conference in 1927, it was resolved that no spark transmitters could be used at wavelengths above 300 metres, but thirteen years of grace for compliance by ship-owners were allowed. Spark transmitters took a long while to vanish; as late as 1935 40 per cent of British merchant carriers were still so equipped.[25]

The third main source of station-to-station interference was between broadcasting stations, and to this the inspectors and other branch officials devoted much time and attention. Frequently throughout this early period of broadcasting, stations moved off their assigned wavelengths by three or five or even ten or twenty metres. As wavelengths were assigned in 10-metre bands, this "straying," sometimes accidental, sometimes not, often caused interference with the transmission of another North American station.

The first step in correcting the problem was the development of equipment to measure precisely the wavelength being utilized. In early 1922 the Radio Branch asked the National Physical Laboratories in Great Britain to develop and build an accurate wavemeter for Canadian-government use. This device, which cost the branch over $1000, was received and installed in late 1923; subsequently all broadcasters were required to possess wavemeters calibrated to the Ottawa instrument. Operators were told to check their frequency prior to each transmission and at least hourly thereafter. Henceforth no station had an excuse for slipping off its assigned frequency, although of course it continued to happen. To cite just one example, the logbook of CHYC Montreal for a period of sixteen months in the mid-1920s reveals seventeen occasions when either an inspector called the station or vice versa with some sort of problem about its transmission frequency.[26] Experiments at the Bureau of Standards and in the Westinghouse laboratories in the United States eventually led to the development of extremely accurate piezo-electric crystals that held stations to their assigned frequencies; first introduced in 1925, these became standard equipment for the better Canadian stations by 1930 although many of the smaller ones continued to use the less satisfactory wavemeters.[27] In 1932 Commander Edwards conceded to the Special Committee of the House of Commons that, while the Radio Branch officially allowed a station to slip off its frequency by only 300 cycles (in the updated terminology), some Canadian stations with older equipment still strayed as much as 1000 cycles. He admitted that the branch normally let itself be guided by the volume of listener complaints in determining how rigorously it enforced precise adherence to frequency assignments.[28] Typical of the branch's flexible policies, this practice was no doubt based on the knowledge that with time outdated equipment would be replaced.

Another transmitter-created interference problem whose solution depended upon technological improvements was the so-called "heterodyne" or beat effect. This was caused by the harmonic radiation that is a characteristic of all wave motion; in radio, harmonics are multiples of the fundamental frequency of operation. So, for example, a station transmitting at 400 metres has a second harmonic at 200 metres that can cause interference for another station. Problems with second harmonics were worst in the years when atmospheric conditions were best, because the transmissions of each station carried further. The solution to second-harmonic interference lay in technical refinements in transmitting equipment gradually worked out by radio engineers during the decade.[29] For the most part, broadcast-station owners and managers gave branch officials their full cooperation in rectifying station-to-station interference; after all, it usually hurt them as much as the other fellow. Like problems with amateur stations and with electrical equipment, then, interference of this kind was usually fairly readily cleared up.

That was not the case with the last major source of interference in early radio, regenerative receivers. Here the problem lay with a larger and less skilled group, the listeners. The sensitive single-circuit regenerative receivers that became popular in 1923 and 1924 because of their good long-distance reception required very delicate tuning to get the maximum volume without causing oscillation. If the dial was over-adjusted just a fraction and oscillation began, the receiver in effect became a small transmitter and caused whistles and squeaks on neighbouring sets for several blocks around. In the period when these sets were popular, about 1924 to 1927, regenerative interference was by far the greatest single barrier to enjoyable radio listening in urban areas. One expert warned in late 1923: "This interference is a hundred times more extensive and dangerous to the future development of the art than most radio enthusiasts realize."[30] He was soon proved right. The Radio Branch was deluged with complaints about the "super squealadynes," especially in early 1926 when poor atmospheric conditions compounded the problem. One unhappy listener wrote to the Montreal *Star* in January of that year to denounce roundly the selfish "pests" who interfered with their neighbours' listening pleasure and to predict direly that the days of broadcasting were numbered if the problem persisted.[31] The author of this letter, along with many of the other complainants, including many radio clubs and organizations, called on the government to ban the manufacture of this type of receiving set.

This demand put the officials of the Radio Branch somewhat on the spot, for in late April 1925 they had received an opinion from the Department of Justice that the government had no authority to prohibit the "importation, manufacture and sale of a specified type of receiving apparatus" under the Radiotelegraph Act or any other.[32] Moreover, after some consideration branch officials decided that passing legislation to deal with the problem was impracticable. Similar legislation had been recommended in the United States in 1924 but never enacted; the British, in a more controlled market situation, had attempted to ban single regenerative receivers but with such mixed results that they abandoned the idea after a year.[33] Edwards explained the basic difficulty to one radio listener:

Under Canadian Law every man is innocent until he is proved guilty, and the trouble lies in producing evidence before a Court, which would be accepted as proof that a man [who] had listened in on a certain date and at a certain time caused his receiver to oscillate. Direction finders on properly equipped Radio cars will give a general bearing, and in the case of an isolated house might be accepted as proof, on the other hand, it is not the man in the isolated house who causes most of the trouble.[34]

Likewise, a ban on the manufacture of these sets would not solve the problem of already existing or home-made sets, or the impossibility of patrolling the border for imports.[35] Thus, branch officials reluctantly concluded, legislation was not the solution to this admittedly serious problem.

Instead the Radio Branch took a pragmatic and flexible voluntarist and educational approach to the crisis over regenerative-receiver interference. In the fall of 1925 a special circular was sent to every licence holder to instruct fans in the proper tuning of their sets.[36] Inspectors responded to as many individual complaints as they could and warned any offenders they were able to identify. Even broadcasting stations apparently got into the act. One newspaper reported that once a persistent offender was publicly identified by name, address, and telephone number, "he is usually kept so busy answering the phone that he cannot tune his set."[37] For the most part those in the radio trade, including both manufacturers and retailers, were happy to cooperate in gradually discouraging the production and sale of regenerative sets, for they fully realized the damage done to the whole industry by dissatisfied customers. By mid-1926 one or two manufacturers were boasting in their advertising that they no longer made these problem-plagued sets, and the rest soon followed.[38]

The regenerative-receiver problem was not solved in one fell swoop but gradually over several years by a combination of developments. By the mid-twenties bcls began to find more pleasure in the clear reception of good entertainment than in logging distant stations; the gradual increase in the number of strong local stations made more attractive the purchase of selective multi-tube superheterodyne receivers that did not cause this type of interference. By late 1928 the standard branch reply to complaints about regenerative receivers was the assurance that they were rapidly becoming obsolete, so the problem would soon rectify itself. At the 1929 meeting of Toronto-area inspectors already mentioned, it was agreed that complaints about regenerative interference now had the lowest priority for action. Technological improvements and their acceptance in the market-place had eliminated one of the most serious barriers to enjoyable radio listening in the 1920s.

One important lesson had been learned, however. As an article in an early radio magazine put it, the development of broadcasting paralleled that of the automobile in many ways. As increasing numbers became involved in the pursuit, more regulation became inevitable. But legislation was not enough. Educational campaigns to teach people to observe certain common courtesies were also essential in easing the widespread adoption of a new technology.[39]

FEDERAL-GOVERNMENT RADIO REGULATORS concerned themselves little with the content of what was broadcast. "The jurisdiction of this Department over broadcasting stations is limited to technical matters, hours of working, interference, etc., and ... we exercise no censorship over the actual programs," Radio Branch Director C.P. Edwards informed one correspondent.[40] Edwards's relief was evident. Neither he nor his officials believed the branch had the mandate or the expertise to dictate program content to privately owned broadcasting enterprises. Edwards's statement was nevertheless inaccurate. There were three areas in which the branch did regulate what was heard on the air: the use of obscene or offensive language, the playing of records, and the wording of advertisements.

Not a great deal was said or apparently done about obscene or offensive language on Canadian broadcasting stations in the 1920s, with the important exception of the 1928 crisis over the programming of the stations owned by the International Bible Students' Association which will be discussed in detail in Chapter 9. The branch's official policy was that expressed by Edwards in the quotation cited above: censorship of program content was neither the government's interest nor its concern. In reality, however, the officials had to accept the fact that the power to issue licences did implicate them in controlling unacceptable material to some extent. Edwards admitted as much to J.E. Lowry in 1926 when, in the context of a discussion of programming on an IBSA station, he wrote, "Unfortunately, as the

Department is charged with the issue of licenses, we cannot evade certain responsibilities."[41]

Yet the definition of what was unacceptable was drawn narrowly. With the exception of the IBSA case, usually branch officials took it upon themselves to rap a broadcaster on the knuckles only when listeners or local inspectors complained about hearing obscenities over the air. In early 1929, protests were received that a salacious conversation had been heard on CKMO Victoria, including the word "bloody" at least twice and "drunken bugger." The station's owner insisted that a private telephone conversation had been accidentally broadcast because of a crossed BC Telephone wire. The regional inspector did not agree; he was convinced, he wrote Edwards, that the listeners had overheard a quarrel between two operators in the CKMO studio. Nevertheless, the inspector's queries constituted the only warning the station received and its licence was routinely renewed a couple of months later.[42]

Around the same time, CJOC Lethbridge was attacked by a listener who objected to "dirty" songs that she feared might have a deleterious effect on suggestible young people and "foreigners." Such lyrics as "She let me stay all night/ Tho' she knew it wasn't right" and "Oh what a night for love/ You know what I'm thinking of" were cited. The branch paid no attention to this aspect of the listener's complaint, although it did investigate her allegation that the station operator had "maliciously" broadcast her name. The furore ended with the listener offering a written apology, the "impulsive" operator resigning, and the branch officials, probably thankfully, closing the file.[43] Incidents such as these cropped up rarely, however. For the most part broadcasters regulated themselves, by requiring for example that most announcements be pre-scripted.[44] It was not in their interest to offend the listeners.

One other quite exceptional case involved broadcasts deemed offensive coming from an unlicensed station. In early December 1930 Edmonton part-time inspector W.G. Allen reported hearing, on an unauthorized wavelength, a voice speaking in broken English declaring that he was "Comrade Trotsky" on the air from Leningrad and Moscow. The following week the man was heard again, this time claiming that there were fourteen communist radio stations such as his in Canada and predicting that the workers were prepared to seize all "pianos, automobiles, radio sets, and all luxuries." Despite the fact that Alberta inspector R. Ainslie (based in Calgary) dismissed the whole thing as a hoax (pointing out among other things that Trotsky had been banished from the Soviet Union), the Radio Branch went to great efforts to track this station down, including having RCMP officers listen in all day every Sunday for a month, notifying all western inspectors to keep checking for broadcasts from the other thirteen reputed stations, and sending out direction-finding trucks to tour likely districts. Inspector Allen did identify a promising suspect, an eighteen-year-old radio-store employee named Schultz whose father was a Russian immigrant. Although the young man had transmitting apparatus he lacked a power supply, so Allen on his own authority decided that successful prosecution was unlikely; indeed Ainslie routinely recommended the renewal of Schultz's amateur licence immediately thereafter. Edwards was furious when he heard what had been done. He decided without further evidence that Schultz was the guilty party, refused to renew his licence, and ordered his equipment dismantled immediately.[45] While ostensibly a matter of unlicensed broadcasting, quite clearly it was the content of the messages being aired that caused the overreaction in Ottawa.[46]

In 1932 R.W. Ashcroft of CKGW Toronto told the Special Committee of the House of Commons investigating broadcasting that in his view the government, through the Radio Branch's licensing authority, possessed "complete control over Canadian broadcasting."[47] If they ordered us to take "Amos 'n' Andy" off the air, he asserted, we would have to do it. On closer questioning, Ashcroft conceded that in fact the government had no power to make a station improve its programming by adding more educational material; it could force a station to eliminate the objectionable but not to add the excellent. Actually, Ashcroft was incorrect. The government had as much authority for the one as for the other under the Radiotelegraph Act.[48] It was not a legal but a policy choice that led branch officials throughout the 1920s to steer clear of anything smacking of interference in programming. Given the wide acceptance of the principle of free speech, the lack of legislative guidelines and the enormous risk of being accused of political bias, it was an understandable decision.

On the use of recorded material, the branch took a much more activist approach. This, the bureaucrats apparently felt, was not a sensitive matter of free speech versus censorship but rather an area where government regulation could be justified as being in the best interests of the whole radio industry. What was best, however, was not necessarily always clear in this formative period, as the officials soon discovered.

The earliest programs broadcast were mostly records, the easiest and cheapest means of filling up the occasional hour to which the amateur radio operators and the new category of bcls could listen in. Transmission was accomplished by placing the horn of a gramophone as close as possible to a primitive microphone; the quality varied from poor to awful. Pioneer broadcaster Gerry Quinney reminisced: "We did a lot of programming. It was all recordings, and it was all 78 rpm, and you had to change the [steel] needle for every side. So that you were stuck there ... Your records ran two and a half, three minutes ... If you wanted to go to the toilet, you had to put on a 78 rpm that ran for maybe four minutes. Then you made a fast, wild dash to the back."[49] In Sydney, Nova Scotia, Nathan Nathanson, the owner of a book and music store, installed a radio station on the second floor above his shop. One of his employees recalled: "Since we were a record store, we had a girl in the store who would pick out the records and bring them up, ... a stack of records so high, and we would play those at noon and just flip them over and play the reverse sides at night ... You'd get a good cross section of music all the time."[50] Such programming was simple to arrange, inexpensive, and apparently quite popular. The stores and record companies were pleased, for the most part, to receive the free publicity.[51]

Nevertheless, by 1925 the Radio Branch had introduced a regulation barring all broadcasting stations from using "mechanically operated musical instruments" between 7:30 p.m. and midnight without permission; records (and, of less significance, instruments such as player pianos) could be used only in the less popular daytime hours.[52] This restriction seems to have been motivated by the belief that excessive recorded music would harm the growth of broadcasting because listeners did not want their radios simply to duplicate their phonographs, because such programming was of lower quality, and because it constituted a deception of the public. Recorded music was viewed as artificial and (implicitly) as alien and external to the local listening community.[53] As in many policy matters in the 1920s, the branch deferred to what it believed were the wishes of Canadian listeners. "The Department is endeavoring to administer broadcasting to the satisfaction of the public," one of the Ottawa officials informed a broadcaster who wanted permission to use records extensively, "and has found from experience that the reaction of the majority of radio listeners, is unfavorable to this class of entertainment."[54]

In one sense the concern expressed was justifiable. Listeners who already owned good phonographs were not apt to purchase radios merely to listen to records; not only was the reproduction quality poor but the sense of immediacy, one of radio's main attractions, was missing. Moreover, the locally rooted live programming on the pioneer stations was one of their greatest attractions to many radio fans. On the other hand, the complete ban on records in the evening hours imposed hardships on many broadcasting stations – and their listeners. While most broadcasters accepted the premise that live programming was best, records were useful to provide continuity between items or in emergency situations when a line was faulty or a scheduled artist did not appear at the studio on time. Many stations were so poor that they could not afford to hire good artists; they filled up the evening hours instead with second-rate performers and "amateur hours." The resulting programming, while genuine and community-based, was nevertheless musically inferior to what could be produced from a good record collection, a factor that became increasingly important as sophisticated American stations began to set the standards for the whole continent. Darby Coats of CKY Winnipeg put the case to his local radio inspector:

During the summer months there are occasions when we have our choice of broadcasting inferior local talent or the very best music reproduced by a modern phonograph. It seems to us that on such occasions we are serving the public better by providing the good phonograph music rather than the inferior human talent.

Listeners in the country districts especially, tell us that they hear music in this way which they could not possibly hear otherwise on account of their inaccessibility to phonograph stores or for economic reasons. It should be said that we have not permitted many hundreds of requests of this kind to influence us to the extent of broadcasting phonograph music in excessive quantities. We use only the occasional record to fill in gaps and preserve continuity in the programs. Sometimes artistes [sic] arrive late or some other accident happens which can very well be taken care of by the running of a few records ... Therefore we would like to have permission from the Department to broadcast phonograph music in emergencies and on the distinct understanding that the privilege would not be abused.[55]

Although Ottawa officials claimed they were imposing this regulation, like many others, at the request of the listening public, they soon found that quite a few bcls agreed with Coats's position.[56] When CFCT Victoria began using its new Victrola to supplement local talent on evening studio programs in 1925, the local inspector was asked to determine the opinion of the local radio association. Immediately, the Victoria Radio Club declared that it was "in favour of Western Canadian broadcasting stations being permitted to use gramaphone records to the extent of 25% of their programme during broadcasting hours, providing that only the best of records are used, and these played only upon the latest type of gramaphones."[57] Similarly, 97 of the 117 Saskatchewan residents surveyed by the Crawford-Harris agency in late 1930 stated that they had no objection to recorded programs, while only twenty disliked them.[58]

Responsive to changing opinion, the branch backed away from its total ban and began in 1926 to authorize limited use of records in the evening hours on some smaller stations, among them CFCT.[59] The broadcasters were cautioned that permission would be rescinded if listeners objected and local radio associations were requested to report their views. This was the first time the branch instituted a policy recognizing that the capabilities of small stations differed from those of larger ones.

By the end of the decade two factors arose that stimulated broadcasters' desire to use more recorded material. Technical advances, particularly pick-ups linking the phonograph output directly with the transmitter, made it possible to broadcast recordings that sounded almost perfect. More significant, under the aegis of advertising agencies newly involved in program production, high-quality electrical transcriptions of full programs complete with advertisements were made available to stations. While these pre-recorded 16-inch disks (they provided 15 minutes of playtime at 33 1/3 rpm) had the disadvantage of loss of spontaneity, they were an easy source of relatively sophisticated programming for many stations, especially those that could not arrange network hookups, and requests immediately began to arrive at the branch to allow their use. Beginning in 1929, limited airing of electrical transcriptions was authorized. Again, the response of listeners seems to have been positive.[60]

In August 1930, as station managers began preparing their fall schedules, the branch suddenly found itself deluged with requests from a number of the larger stations for permission to use the packaged series of electrical transcriptions being offered by various advertising agencies.[61] All the transcriptions in question were made in the United States and carried the promotional messages of national American advertisers. A policy review was clearly called for. On 26 September 1930 all local radio inspectors were instructed that "no further broadcasting of records was to be permitted after 7:30 p.m., except in the case of the few stations which had already been given limited privileges in this reference in the past, these stations to be allowed to continue, for the moment, until the final policy of the Department has been determined."[62]

On 8 October, at the request of Sonora Corporation, one manufacturer of the transcriptions in question, a meeting was held in Ottawa to which some of the major broadcasters and advertisers were invited. Ralph Ashcroft of CKGW spoke for the latter, proposing that the ban on electrical transcriptions after 7:30 p.m. be cancelled entirely. Alfred Duranleau, the minister of Marine in the new Conservative government, who attended part of the meeting, cautioned that his government would oppose transcriptions if they advertised American goods or were manufactured outside of Canada. He also suggested that it was unpatriotic for Canadian stations to accept advertisements such as the recent Chevrolet series touting "America's War Heroes." Duranleau's intervention was significant, for it represented the changing attitudes of the post-Aird commission and Depression milieu in which broadcasting-policy decisions would have to take into account such factors as Canadian jobs and growing concern about radio as a Canadian cultural industry. The new government's general sensitivity to broadcasting issues was also evident; at the end of the meeting the deputy minister warned the broadcasters and advertisers present that they might have to wait some time for a decision on electrical transcriptions, for this was a matter that must be decided by the government as a whole.[63] A couple of years earlier such a policy decision would have been routinely handled by a Radio Branch bureaucrat.

Almost immediately another interested party surfaced: the unions representing Canadian musicians hard pressed by the early days of the Depression and by the takeover of the movie theatres by the "talkies" and determined not to lose their jobs in radio studios as well.[64] Once the Department of Marine received a hint of the musicians' viewpoint, Deputy Minister Johnston wrote to H.H. Ward, the deputy minister of Labour, who in turn contacted G.B. Henderson, president of the Canadian division of the American Federation of Musicians, to urge strongly that he come to Ottawa as soon as possible to present his case.

On 21 November the musicians' representatives were warmly received by Duranleau, who assured them that his greatest concern was the employment of Canadians and the preservation of "Canadian Institutions." The musicians' position was that no recorded material of any kind should be allowed on Canadian stations after 5 p.m. and that Canadian broadcasters should not be permitted to tie into US networks. They expressed themselves willing, however, to live with the current ban on records after 7:30 and with a rule that 50 per cent of the programs on Canadian stations should be Canadian in origin.[65]

Three months elapsed while Duranleau consulted with his Conservative colleagues on the question of electrical transcriptions. During this period the branch had to contend with a lot of unhappy broadcasters, some of whom had made commitments to advertisers which they now had to renege on. A number of station owners and managers thought that the moratorium on record permissions was unfair; those who for one reason or another had received the right to use records before September 1930 could now use that time for lucrative transcription contracts, while those who had faithfully stuck to live programming were out of luck.[66] All in all, a whole radio season passed by under the moratorium, and resentment grew among some broadcasters against a government department that arbitrarily restricted their ability to present popular programs and earn advertising revenue.

The new policy on records and electrical transcriptions was finally announced on 10 March 1931. It represented an ingenious compromise recognizing the different needs of stations in centres of different sizes and offering unprecedented protection to Canadian musicians.[67] The use of phonograph records was still prohibited between 7:30 p.m. and midnight but a proviso was added that upon application "low power stations located in the smaller cities and towns" might be granted an exemption. Records could also be used by any station for short periods in emergency situations at the discretion of the local inspectors. Electrical transcriptions were, like records, to be permitted freely between midnight and 7:30 p.m. but in the prime evening hours were restricted to one-half hour daily or, if the program required more than half an hour to air, a total of three and one-half hours in any one week. No electrical transcription could be broadcast more than once in any one area and the transcriptions had to be produced and manufactured in Canada. This last provision, of course, was to protect musicians' jobs. It constituted the first Canadian content requirement ever in Canadian broadcasting.[68] The effect was weakened, however, by a subsequent ruling that it applied only to the transcriptions aired in the evenings.[69] Finally, reflecting the longstanding assumption that recorded material somehow "wilfully deceived" the radio listener, it was decreed that "phonograph records and electrical transcriptions shall be so described and announced at the beginning of the programme, and at least once every 15 minutes thereafter."[70] (A similar injunction had been placed on American radio stations in 1928). This was to remain a requirement for Canadian broadcasters until 1959.[71]

As soon as the new regulations were proclaimed in the spring of 1931 a number of small stations wrote requesting the promised special permission to use records in the evening. Under this pressure, Donald Manson finally drafted a clear statement classifying stations into three groups according to the size of their community; he decreed that no additional time would be granted to stations in cities larger than 100,000, that one-half hour extra per day would be allowed for stations in cities between 25,000 and 100,000, and that one hour extra would be permitted those in communities of less than 25,000. A number of exceptions were also made, however, most of which had the effect of reducing the number of eligible stations in the second and third groups. In the end, only the little stations in ten small communities (such as Lethbridge, North Bay, Kamloops, Summerside, and Moncton) were allowed the full extra hour of use of records or transcriptions per day; those in twelve others were allowed something less. A very special exception was made for two university stations, CKIC Wolfville and CKUA Edmonton, which were given permission to use recorded educational material up to seven hours per week regardless of its origin.[72]

As of 1932, therefore, live programming remained the rule and the norm in the evening broadcasting hours when the greatest numbers were listening in. Records, however, filled a large portion of the rest of the day. Statistics presented by the Radio Branch to the 1932 Special Committee showed that the fifty-six stations studied during December 1931 and January 1932 presented an average of three hours per day of "original talent" and three hours and fifteen minutes per day of recorded programs (three hours and three minutes of phonograph records and twelve minutes of electrical transcriptions). Only on some of the major urban stations, especially those tied into the American networks, was there substantially more live than recorded programming.[73]

By 1932 the lack of original Canadian live material available on Canadian radio stations was becoming a matter of concern to those who believed that the new medium should be playing an active role in Canadian cultural life.[74] This was not the issue to which the regulators of the 1920s had responded. Their assumption had been that records were inferior for technical and market, not cultural reasons. Their mistake was in the initial regulatory requirement banning records in the evening hours on all stations. In the United States, where the Department of Commerce lacked the regulatory authority of the Radio Branch in Canada, small stations in the early years were free to program as they wished. Once the Federal Radio Commission (FRC) was established in 1927 it adopted a flexible policy enunciating that "the question of the use of these instrumentalities is one for the station to determine, and each station's record in connection therewith is judged by the commission on the basis of a number of factors, such as the time and extent of the use of records, the purposes for which they are used, the availability of local talent, etc."[75] While the excessive use of records was equally frowned upon in the United States, more responsibility was placed upon the broadcasters to regulate themselves. In fact, the largest American stations used records rarely and the networks not at all.[76] Only with the greatest reluctance did the Canadian Radio Branch officially recognize that this was a case where the needs of small stations might differ from those of large. The branch's general policy of treating all stations equally in fact hampered Canadian broadcasters in their attempts to attract Canadian listeners away from US stations.

The control of advertisements on the air was a bigger, more contentious, and more important regulatory issue because it was linked to the key question of how broadcasting was to be financed. Even before the first broadcasting stations were officially licensed, Radio Branch authorities received queries as to their policy on advertising. In a June 1922 telegram to Basil Lake, radio editor of the Toronto *Star*, one Ottawa official stated: "Broadcasting licenses so far issued do not specifically forbid advertising but Department discourages same and if Public opinion and the press demand that advertising be limited or cut out altogether Department is quite prepared consider Establishment of a regulation to this effect."[77] In fact the branch promptly did so. When the broadcasting-licence system was instituted in Canada the following month, the main class of private-commercial broadcasting stations was prohibited from levying or collecting tolls or charges for any services. Only the owner could announce his sponsorship of the programs. While, as previously mentioned, the branch expressed its intention to create a class of public-commercial stations on which toll-type broadcasting would be allowed, this class was never set up. Instead, when pressure began to mount (which it did very soon) to allow private broadcasters to garner some income by selling advertising time to others, an ingenious alternative was concocted.[78] Each advertiser was issued his own licence for a private phantom station on which he was entitled to advertise his own wares as much as he wanted. He in turn paid the owner of the physical station to rent the equipment over which the messages were broadcast. W.W. Grant of CFCN Calgary, to cite one example, apparently collected close to $200 a month in this period from rentals to phantom-licence holders.[79]

Phantom licences, however, were impracticable as a long-term solution to the growing need of those who held private-commercial broadcasting licences to make their businesses viable. Alarmed at the rate at which broadcasters were failing, in mid-May 1923 Commander Edwards advised his deputy minister: "With the dropping out of Canadian Broadcasting Stations, the question of ways and means is becoming serious, and representations have been made that owners of private broadcasting stations should be permitted to rent their stations for advertising and other purposes. As far as we have been able to sense public opinion, we are not at all sure that this will be a popular move. The only way to ascertain this would be to try it out ..."[80] Accordingly, Edwards recommended that Section 4 of the Private Commercial Broadcasting Licence be amended to allow advertisements. While there is no direct evidence, it would seem that the notion of creating a separate class of toll-collecting public-commercial stations was abandoned at this time for the same reason: to channel the potential revenues to the broadcasters already in business and already in need.[81]

Under the regulations that came into effect 15 May 1923, two classes of advertising were specified. Indirect advertising, which was allowed at all times, was described as follows: "A departmental store renting the station for a couple of hours and putting on a first class entertainment, with no advertising in it at all, the only connection between the store and the programme being the announcement of their name and the fact that they were contributing the concert, before and after every number."[82] Direct advertising, which the new regulation made clear was experimental, was permitted only with the written consent of the minister of Marine and Fisheries and not between 6:30 and 11:00 p.m. The branch's example of direct advertising was: "An automobile firm renting the station for, say, ten minutes, for the purpose of extolling the virtues and merits of their particular make of machine." The Radio Branch's regulations did not make any mention of possible advertising rates. Subsequently, inquirers were informed that rates were under the jurisdiction of the Board of Railway Commissioners (which regulated telephone and telegraph charges in Canada); however that board never did in fact become involved in setting radio advertising rates.[83] Instead, they were left to the market-place.

During the experimental period a number of stations, including most of the major ones, applied for and received permission to use advertisements. Such permission was granted lavishly. One broadcaster wrote in to Ottawa simply to inquire if Canadian stations were allowed to charge fees; within days the reply came: "Permission to charge such tolls is hereby granted."[84] Similarly, J.E. Lowry of CKY Winnipeg requested in March 1925 that the branch retroactively endorse the tolls he had been charging since his station's inauguration two years earlier; he had just noticed, he claimed, that apparently this was necessary. Authorization was immediately given without a murmur.[85]

In March 1926, after two years of experimental direct advertising in the daytime only, the Radio Branch canvassed various groups to ask their opinion about whether Canada should return to a ban on all direct advertising. Responses varied. A.R. McEwan, secretary-treasurer of the newly formed Canadian Association of Broadcasters, replied that the twelve principal stations submitting their views were all unanimously opposed to direct ads between 6:00 p.m. and midnight and some went so far as to object to them at any time.[86] This position was probably the result of the fact that a number of the members of the CAB were newspapers which owned radio stations and therefore were particularly sensitive to competition from radio advertising. J.E. Lowry of CKY expressed quite a different point of view in a letter to Edwards dated 9 June 1926. First, Lowry pointed out, CKY listeners had been surveyed the previous year as to their opinion of direct advertising and had made it clear that they had "no objection whatever ... so long as it is not overdone." Secondly, any ban on direct advertising was a kind of censorship being imposed by eastern interests on the listeners of Manitoba, who should be allowed to hear what they wanted to. Finally, such a ban was bound to run into difficulties of interpretation that would make it unenforceable. All in all, Lowry concluded, and on this he certainly had the agreement of the Ottawa officials, "the tastes of the public ... should generally govern."[87] The question remained, however, what the public really wanted; lacking any precise measurement of opinion, branch officials acted on their hunches.

Edwards's reply to Lowry was not encouraging:

As regards advertising, in this we are frankly following the lead of the United States, who, under their licenses forbid direct advertising. The point is that wavelengths are extremely scarce, and they are too valuable to allot to some store to come on at all hours of the day or night and advertise bargains. The underlying idea is also that the proper place for this type of advertising is in the columns of the newspapers.

This office has gained the opinion that the listeners, as a body, object most strongly to direct advertising ... [88]

Thus the Radio Branch director laid out the rationale for a new ban on direct advertising: negative listener reaction, scarcity of wavelengths,

American practice in banning direct ads and the mention of prices, and the objections of newspapers. The implication was that the financial situation of Canadian broadcasters was not now so precarious that it overrode these other considerations.

Accordingly, in March 1926 the regulations were revised once again, and all direct advertising prohibited with the minor exception that the minister could give special consent in individual cases such as advertising for a charitable organization.[89] According to official statements, this action was taken because, while many stations were utilizing indirect ads extensively, "practically all direct advertising would appear to have been abandoned, in other words, the broadcasting stations have apparently reached the conclusion that the reaction of the radio listener to direct advertising is unfavourable and that it is not a desirable function of radio."[90] That there was some listener resistance to direct advertising was no doubt true.[91] But neither privately nor publicly did Edwards mention the additional possibility that stations were not airing direct ads because they had failed in their efforts to interest advertisers to experiment with a new medium in the less favourable daytime hours.

While the regulation banning all direct advertising remained in effect until the end of the period under consideration, it began to be whittled away within a year of its proclamation. In April 1927 Darby Coats, newly appointed manager of the James Richardson and Sons Moose Jaw station, CJRM, wrote to Edwards indicating surprise and concern that some stations were broadcasting such "undesirable material" as the names and prices of specific articles of merchandise. Edwards's reply revealed his discomfort with the implications of the ban on advertising and his willingness, as usual, to apply the rules flexibly:

I have your favour of the 7th April, with regard to direct advertising ... The special rule covering this point is intended to give us control over what may become an abuse of radio. We make no pretense of censorship of the stations and the limitation in regard to direct advertising is merely an endeavour to voice the feelings of the listeners.

For some time direct advertising practically disappeared, but now, apparently, its head is cropping up again. The Department, however, has not been able to arrive at any definite conclusion as to whether or not this comeback is due to the fact that the listeners want it or the fact that the broadcasters can make money thereby.

We are accordingly disposed to treat each case on its merits, and if the Department is satisfied that the majority of listeners covered by any one station desire direct advertising, then my angle is that they certainly should be allowed to have it if the broadcasters want to give it to them. ...

The general regulation of the Department that there must be no direct advertising in the evenings, continues in effect. The listeners apparently continue to be unanimous in their views that the evening hours should be kept as clear of advertising as possible.[92]

The Radio Branch soon went further. In December 1927 it granted CFCY Charlottetown permission to air direct ads up to 6:00 p.m., convinced by the argument of the station's owner that local businesses were unwilling to sponsor programs indirectly, so it was either direct ads or the cessation of operations.[93] By the end of 1928 three more small stations, CHGS Summerside, Prince Edward Island, CKMO Victoria, and CJOR Sea Island, British Columbia, had received similar permission, although at least two stations, in Edmonton and Calgary, had been denied it.[94]

No sooner had these exceptions to the rule been authorized, however, than the branch began to back away. CFCY lost its privilege to carry direct advertising at the end of September 1928 after a complaint was lodged by the radio inspector, egged on by a commercial rival. The station's owner was understandably miffed, and again made the point that if small operators were denied the right to finance their stations with direct advertisements, either local broadcasting would vanish or else the federal government would have to subsidize it.[95] At the beginning of the 1930–31 fiscal year, all the other stations that had been granted special permission for daytime direct ads also found it rescinded, ostensibly because of multiplying complaints from listeners.[96] After the fact, Branch Director Edwards admitted that the real reason for the action was the difficulty in applying a policy that discriminated against the larger stations.[97]

A much more significant erosion of the ban on direct ads, however, occurred as the result of an expansion of the definition of indirect advertising. Increasingly after 1929 stations pressed the word "indirect" to its limits, and branch officials responded in a manner that revealed their ambivalence on the whole question. The following message aired on CJRM Moose Jaw, for example, was decreed "indirect" although it clearly went far beyond the description promulgated back in 1923:

The new Victor Super Heterodyne Radio is creating a great sensation among those who have had the pleasure of seeing them ...

The New Victor 8 tube Super Heterodyne is far different from anything you have ever known. New in design. New in construction and new in appearance. It offers you a totally new and greater measure of enjoyment, at a price never before dreamed of.

Heintzman and Co. are located at 121 Main St. Moose Jaw and maintain a representative stock in Cumming's Jewelry Store, Swift Current.[98]

In the end, after a whole series of individual decisions, the definition of indirect advertising was stretched to the point that lengthy dissertations about the qualities of the product in question, where it could be purchased and at what savings, were judged acceptable so long as there were no complaints from listeners. As Edwards put it to the Special Committee in 1932, it was all "a difficult problem" but it seemed that only one commandment remained: "Thou shalt not mention prices or money."[99] Even on that point, however, interpretation was slippery and the branch's decisions were generous. So, for instance, "Dollar Cleaners" was permitted, as was "One Cent Sale."[100] One unkind radio owner chastised the Radio Branch itself because its spot announcements reminding listeners that they must purchase receiving-set licences mentioned that they cost $2 per year. Edwards was as generous in applying the rules to his own department as he was to others: this was a fee, he asserted, not a price, and therefore permissible.[101]

Regulating advertising was one of the trickier tasks the Radio Branch took on in the 1920s and its waffling on the matter is not really surprising. While determined on the one hand to give the listeners what they wanted and convinced that they did not want ads, the Ottawa authorities came to realize that commercial broadcasting stations could not be denied such a lucrative source of income. The on-again off-again regulations were the direct consequence of the contradictions between the two positions; the steadily expanding definition of "indirect advertising" represented the branch's final acquiescence to the concept of advertising-funded commercial broadcasting. Nevertheless, that acceptance came only with considerable reluctance. In early 1932 Edwards wrote to New Brunswick MP R.B. Hanson summarizing his own feelings:

We appreciate that a station's sole source of revenue is advertising, and we allow every latitude. The one thing, however, not permitted, is mention of any prices; no station in the country is allowed to do this ...

Personally I think the advertising which is now going over the air is more than sufficient, and while I quite appreciate that a rule which would apply in Toronto need not of necessity apply in Fredericton, I do not want to see the bars let down on this "price" business, otherwise you will find the broadcasts from some of the stations resembling the full page "ads" of a departmental store, and I think you will agree with me that the function of a radio channel is primarily to carry entertainment, news, education, etc., and not the price list of a "corner drugstore," just because the latter would sooner pay $10.00 to advertise over radio than in a newspaper.[102]

In September 1932 both the CBS and NBC networks announced that because advertisers were boring listeners with long-winded circumlocutions, as well as increased public interest in the cost of goods owing to the poor economic conditions, henceforth prices could be directly mentioned under very strict conditions.[103] Immediately, of course, the Canadian stations affiliated with the networks (and others) appealed for similar privileges in Canada. Edwards believed that he had no choice in the matter. "I am not in favour of stations mentioning prices," he wrote to J.N. Thivierge, "but once the higher grade stations in the United States adopt such a policy, I do not think we should withhold the same from Canadian stations which are trying to make a living in these hard times."[104] Edwards accordingly recommended the adoption of CBS's rules (up to two direct price mentions in a fifteen-minute program and up to five in an hour) to his assistant deputy minister, who in turn passed the recommendation on to Hector Charlesworth, the chairman of the newly created Canadian Radio Broadcasting Commission, under whose aegis such matters now lay.[105] The CRBC did not in the end lift the ban on the mention of prices in advertisements, however, and it remained in effect, with modifications, well into the 1940s.

The approach taken by the Radio Branch to regulating advertising demonstrates the two general principles that governed the branch's policy-making: the rules were to be flexible and the wishes of the listening public were to be paramount. As Edwards summarized it as early as 1924: "Every station is established fundamentally for the purpose of advertising somebody or something, and the Department at this moment is giving the stations as much latitude as possible in regard to advertising with a view to ascertaining what the public wants in this regard."[106] But the Radio Branch did have a point of view. It established, for example, one of its informal guidelines to encourage stations to remain if possible advertisement-free. "In arranging hours of working for the different private broadcasting stations in any area, preference will be given to the requirements of broadcasting stations which do not undertake advertising service," the deputy minister informed the owners of CKAC Montreal in 1923.[107] Direct advertising was accepted only reluctantly by the branch as one of the few possible solutions to the problem of financing a Canadian broadcasting service.

THE OFFICIALS OF THE RADIO BRANCH pursued the various problems caused by interference aggressively. In this, they responded to a definite demand from the public and the industry. Clear reception was fundamental to the further growth of broadcast listening. Branch employees were obviously intrigued by and comfortable with the sorts of technical challenges involved in this aspect of their work as well. They were much less active or decisive concerning the more complex questions surrounding programming, questions that became increasingly pressing towards the end of the decade as concern mounted in certain circles that Canada was being inundated by American broadcasting. The real solution not only to the main interference problems prevalent in the 1920s but also to the cultural ones lay in developing powerful stations in as many Canadian centres as possible. While there were financial, demographic, geographic, and other factors that limited the ability of Canadian enterprises to build a strong private broadcasting industry, some of the branch's decisions exacerbated rather than alleviated those difficulties. Specifically, its policies on wavelength and power assignment, to which we will now turn, reveal some well-intentioned but faulty judgments that seriously undermined Canadian broadcasting in the 1920s.

7 Frequency Assignment: Negotiations with the United States

The most complicated and touchy duty of the Radio Branch was the assignment of wavelengths or frequencies to broadcasting stations. The issues were difficult because many different interests had to be satisfied, because incorrect frequency assignments could cause objectionable interference, because changing technology required constant adjustments, and because frequency allocation was not only a national but an international question, involving branch officials in a close but not always harmonious relationship with their counterparts in the United States. The threads are tangled; in this chapter and the next both the actions and what can be deduced about the intentions of the officials of the Radio Branch will be unravelled as much as possible. The issue of North American frequency allocation will be covered first because it was one of the major factors determining the margins of manoeuvre for domestic decision-makers. Before that, however, a few explanatory remarks about the limits imposed by the electromagnetic spectrum are necessary.

Essentially radio transmission involves the carriage of sound on an electromagnetic wave from a sending to a receiving instrument.[1] Electromagnetic waves, as the name suggests, are indeed wave-like in shape, undulating up and down at regular intervals. While all these waves travel at the speed of light, when measured from crest to crest they vary greatly in length; the electromagnetic spectrum encompasses the whole range of such waves, from very short to very long. In the early 1920s, a particular place on the spectrum was described by a wavelength measurement (the length of the wave from one crest to the next in metres). The first Canadian broadcasting stations were therefore assigned to 400 metres, 410 metres, and so on. After about 1924 or 1925, the terminology of measurement in common usage changed from wavelength to frequency.[2] The frequency of a transmission is the number of wavelengths that pass a given point in a second; originally stated in kilocycles per second (kc), this measurement is now termed kiloHertz (kHz). Thus the longer the wavelength, the lower the frequency.[3]

The alterations in terminology make it difficult to be consistent when writing about the 1920s. In this discussion, a relatively loose approach has been taken. For the most part, the vocabulary appropriate to the issue under consideration is utilized. On occasion, where necessary, both wavelength and frequency figures are given. In general comments, however, the terms wavelength and frequency are used virtually interchangeably, as was conventional in the 1920s.

The AM-radio broadcast band was established initially between 550 and 1500 kHz, not because this was technically the best for either local or long-distance broadcasting but because it fit nicely between previously allocated ship and military services.[4] In fact, for the first six or eight years, broadcasting was normally restricted to 550 to 1100 kHz because, as a result of ground absorption, less distance can be achieved at the higher frequencies; the low frequencies were accordingly preferred because less power was required to achieve equivalent coverage. On this band, stations were generally from the beginning assigned in ten-metre (later ten-kHz) jumps.

The electromagnetic spectrum has three dimensions: frequency, time, and space. Theoretically, a transmitter located at point x broadcasting at a specific frequency sends out radio waves in a concentric pattern, fading proportionally with the distance from x. Close to the transmitter, reception is strong and clear; the further the receiver is away from the transmitter, the weaker the signal, until it completely vanishes. Two transmitters located too close together, transmitting on the same frequency, will interfere with one another's signals in the areas where they overlap at relatively equal intensities. The extent and location of this area will depend upon the power of the transmitters. There are four ways to avoid this problem: by locating the transmitters further apart, by having them use adequately separated frequencies, by reducing their power, or by having them broadcast at different times.

As might be expected, in reality the situation is not quite so clear-cut, and it was even less so in the 1920s. Irregularities in transmission patterns occur because geographical configurations cause refraction, reflection, and absorption of the radio signals, because transmitters and receivers have varying capacities in terms of power and frequency-selection, and so on. An additional complication is that radio waves travel in two patterns: they follow the curvature of the earth (ground waves) and also (between sunset and sunrise only) are reflected back from the Heaviside layer in the lower atmosphere or ionosphere (sky waves). Generally, with natural fading, ground waves can be received clearly from ten to seventy-five miles. Sky waves fade with distance as well and suffer interference from atmospheric disturbances but, if conditions are right, a strong signal can travel up to fifteen hundred miles at night.

The 1920s comprised a long period of experimentation with station-power and frequency assignments, the result of which was a gradual accumulation of knowledge about how to define and achieve the best service in a technical sense. The location, power, frequency, and transmission times of broadcasting stations were juggled interminably in the process. Moreover, the regulators responsible for this technical task had also to be responsive to a variety of political and economic pressures and constraints, some of which have been discussed in previous chapters, such as the fact that most stations were located in major urban centres in southern Canada.

The electromagnetic spectrum was brought into the international public arena as early as 1903 because of an underlying assumption that it was a scarce and limited resource whose allocation raised critical foreign-policy questions. Domestically as well, economic and political issues about whether a spectrum assignment was public or private property came increasingly to the forefront in the early decades of radio. While the assumption of spectrum scarcity has been called into doubt by recent literature,[5] what matters here is that it was accepted unquestioningly in the 1920s. The regulators of that era endeavoured to understand and cope with assignment issues within what they assumed was an almost inflexibly defined broadcast band providing room for a finite number of channels (at the time, less than one hundred for North and Central America). Despite the many factors limiting their manoeuvreability, the officials of the Canadian Radio Branch nevertheless tackled the technical questions involved in frequency assignment with energy and enthusiasm derived from their radio-engineering backgrounds.

The scarcity assumption prevalent in the 1920s not only tied the hands of regulators technically but made the economic question of how the spectrum should best be allocated even more crucial. Thus (as we have seen) the regulators of the 1920s also had to wrestle with questions about the optimal use of licences, who could possess them, whether they should be sold, and so on. While broadcasting was for the most part not a very profitable endeavour in Canada in the 1920s, licences to use a spectrum frequency did have value in that they were a privilege accorded only to a few. Economic implications affecting licensing and allocation policies also followed from the fact that the spectrum requires expensive equipment to utilize it. Thus the officials of the Radio Branch found themselves involved in a complex juggling act through the 1920s as they attempted to sort out the principles on which to base critical decisions, the consequences of which echo down to the present.

As of April 1922 the Radio Branch (still with the Department of the Naval Service) began licensing commercial broadcasters in ten-metre increments in the band between 400 and 450 metres (750 to 666.6 kHz). Although fifty-two stations were licensed within one year, because they were in widely separated localities and broadcast only occasionally, the problem of their interfering with one another, even on technically primitive crystal sets unable to discriminate between frequencies, did not arise. Neither did interference from American stations pose a problem at this stage, because all US commercial broadcasters were operating at 360 metres (833.3 kHz) for entertainment and general programming and at 485 metres (618.6 kHz) for crop reports and weather forecasts. This happy situation soon came to an end, however. Because of the rapid multiplication of stations in the United States and consequent difficulties with time-sharing and interference, the US regulatory authority, the Radio Service of the Department of Commerce, reassigned a limited number of strong stations (called "Class B") to 400 metres in August 1922. Immediately problems of interference with Canadian stations around that frequency commenced, and these were multiplied many times when a further American rearrangement effective 15 May 1923 assigned the high-power stations to various frequencies between 300 and 545 metres, while leaving the weakest stations (usually educational or religious institutions) at 360 metres and giving broadcasters with medium-power (up to 500 watts) frequencies between 222 and 300 metres.[6] In other words, in response to its own pressing needs, the United States began licensing stations throughout most of the broadcast band "without any regard for Canada."[7] That Canadian authorities were not contacted is not really surprising, however, given that the Department of Commerce's authority to make this reassignment was legally questionable. While Secretary of Commerce Herbert Hoover was successful in obtaining the necessary cooperation from the various interested parties in the United States, his lack of clear authority gave him an excellent excuse for not approaching Canada even had he wished to do so.[8]

For over a year a very "unsatisfactory state of affairs" prevailed.[9] In April 1924 Deputy Minister of Marine and Fisheries Alexander Johnston wrote to D.B. Carson, the US commissioner of navigation, explaining how difficult the American action had made things for Canada. Since the United States had begun using the whole band, the Canadian government had received many protests from listeners about excessive interference, Johnston complained, adding: "To avoid the same we were compelled, in turn, to allot wavelengths out of the band 250 to 500 metres, endeavouring, however, at the same time, to select wavelengths likely to cause the least interference with United States stations."[10]

What made things particularly difficult for Canadian officials was the fact that the United States continued to hand out frequency assignments without regard for the Canadian presence even after the problems became evident. As an example of "lack of co-operation," Johnston cited for Carson the case of CHYC Montreal, the Northern Electric station. The Canadian Radio Branch had given CHYC the 341-metre wavelength and it had operated well there for some months until the US Department decided to give the same frequency to KFKX Hastings, Nebraska. As a result of numerous complaints that CHYC could no longer be heard reliably, the Canadian Radio Branch had to shift it up to 350 metres, a less desirable location. Johnston's letter closed with a tentative draft of Canadian station assignments, presented, he said, as "an endeavour, as before stated, to organize our stations so as to fit in with yours." The draft specified twelve frequencies for Canadian use, only one of which (435 m. or 690 kHz) was apparently intended for use in more than one Canadian city. The draft also posited two separate frequencies for two cities, Calgary and Montreal.

The response of A.J. Tyrer, acting commissioner of navigation in the United States, was partially satisfactory. Although Tyrer pointed out the unfortunate fact that "the Secretary of Commerce has not the authority under the existing law to limit the number of stations," he also promised that "this office will endeavor to protect from interference as far as possible the important stations in Canada which you have indicated." [11] Shortly thereafter, Canadian representatives were invited to the Third National Radio Conference, which began in Washington on 6 October 1924 because, as Carson admitted, "our previous conferences gave no consideration to the needs of the Canadians."[12] At the conference, the Canadian officials (Johnston and Radio Branch Director C.P. Edwards were both present) met and talked over their mutual problems with their American counterparts. At this time the US representatives specifically committed themselves to "regard six of the channels in the upper part of this broadcast band as belonging exclusively to the Dominion" and to "share" an additional five wavelengths.[13] This "Gentleman's Agreement" became the basis of North American frequency allocation.

The six frequencies subsequently viewed as "exclusively" Canadian were 690, 730, 840, 910, 960, and 1030 kHz (434.5, 410.7, 356.9, 329.5, 312.3, and 291.1 metres), although NAA, the US Navy station in Arlington, Virginia, also used 690. All of these "clear" wavelengths, as well as most of the shared ones (580, 600, 780, 880, and 1210 kHz), were in the range between about 550 and 1070 kHz, the spectrum band considered preferable for broadcasting at the time. In this band there were fifty-three or fifty-four possible frequencies, using the norm of ten-kHz intervals between them established in January 1925. The forty-three frequencies between 1080 and 1500 kHz (288.3 – 200 metres), which were assumed to be suitable only for small stations with limited range, were not discussed with the Americans at this time.[14]

For awhile, the arrangement proved fairly satisfactory from the Canadian point of view. Although demands for frequencies from Canadian broadcasters and potential broadcasters were growing and a fair amount of negotiating had to be carried on regarding wavelength sharing in Canada, nevertheless the Canadian officials were not noticeably unhappy with their situation or their relationship with the American radio officials. Throughout 1925 there were numerous letters back and forth between the two departments ironing out specific cases of interference, and a cooperative approach prevailed on both sides. As Edwards explained to a correspondent in July 1925: "There is, and has been, severe interference between United States stations, but comparatively little between United States and Canadian stations. Our inspectors keep careful watch on the aether and the minute one of our stations gets interfered with, we promptly telegraph a complaint, giving date, time, etc., and the Department of Commerce, with equal promptitude, sit on the station which is causing the trouble."[15]

But the situation was not quite as rosy as Edwards painted it, for developing technology and policy changes regarding transmitting power were already posing new problems. At the Third National Radio Conference, the American radio community had taken the decision that the erection of stations powerful enough to be received over wide areas should be seriously considered. Consequently, the Class B stations were given permission to experiment with higher power. In November 1924 six American stations increased their output power to 1500 watts on an experimental basis; by late 1925 almost twenty stations were broadcasting at 5000 watts (5 kw) and two on experimental licences at even more.[16] The consequence, of course, of increased power and therefore greater distance was interference with stations previously problem-free. By February 1925 Edwards was pressing US officials for a couple of wavelengths on the east coast clear of the high-power stations at Springfield and Schenectady and in July he complained once more, this time about Springfield again and about KDKA Pittsburgh, whose strong signals made use of adjoining wavelengths for Canadian stations next to impossible. He reported: "There is just one continual stream of complaints from the Stations and from the listeners in regard to interference from high power stations."[17] The complaints were not always one way, however. As Edwards confided to Carson, "I think about 90% of the Canadian listeners on the East Coast, at least, regard Springfield and Schenectady as their own stations, and a week ago this office was swamped with complaints ... that the high power [trans-Atlantic radiotelegraph] stations at Glace Bay had developed a harmonic on Springfield, and one would think the world was about to come to a sudden end."[18]

Edwards's jocular remark revealed an additional and very severe complication for Canadian radio officials – the demand by Canadian listeners for good reception not only of Canadian but of American stations. So, for example, when the Americans moved powerful KGO Oakland from 299.8 to 361.2 metres, where it began to interfere with Calgary stations at 356.9, Commander Edwards immediately shifted the Calgary frequency assignment because, as he assured his American colleague, "I need hardly say that we will certainly arrange our service so that Calgary does not spoil KGO's concerts, which are just as popular in Canada as they are in the United States."[19] Canadian radio listeners wanted to hear American programs and Canadian radio officials believed that the wishes of listeners came first. Thus they endeavoured, despite the considerable difficulties involved, to provide their listeners with interference-free listening to both Canadian and American stations.

In November 1925, before setting off for the Fourth National Radio Conference in Washington, Edwards drafted a letter to Carson, offering the Canadian position on the North American wavelength situation. "The broadcast situation in Canada is far from happy," he began, "and I would like to set out our point of view for your consideration."[20]

At the present time, as you are aware, this Dominion enjoys six exclusive channels out of the 53 channels available in the "Class B" broadcast band (280 to 545 metres), the remaining 47 channels being regarded as belonging to the United States.

We have 35 stations to provide for in the "Class B" band, and as two of our channels cannot be used on the east coast on account of high power stations on your side of the line using adjoining channels, we are suffering from serious congestion. This situation has been greatly assisted by the co-operation we have received from the Department of Commerce in permitting us to duplicate on five of the channels allotted to southern United States stations, but in spite of this, we are only carrying on by compelling all our stations to share time, and, at the moment, not a single Canadian station enjoys an exclusive wave, and, in some cases, as many as five physical stations in one area are sharing the time on the same wavelength.

I appreciate to the fullest extent the difficulties the Department of Commerce must encounter in trying to meet the requirements of your own broadcasting stations; nevertheless, having regard to the large area of this Dominion and the peculiar value of radio to a sparsely populated country such as ours, I think I am justified in respectfully requesting that Canada be allotted a few more channels out of the 53 above mentioned, and I would therefore submit for the consideration of the Honourable the Secretary of Commerce that, for the time being, the band be divided in the proportion of 43 to the United States and 10 to the Dominion of Canada.

The letter went on to point out that Canada had established prior use of the frequencies between 400 and 450 metres before May 1923, and then concluded: "I am anxious that I should not be understood as submitting the foregoing observations in the nature of a protest, or of even a complaint. I very deeply appreciate the difficulties in the way of securing a mutually satisfactory arrangement. My purpose is to place before you certain facts in an endeavour to establish that there is sound basis and precedent for our request for four additional channels."

By late 1925, then, even before the United States Department of Commerce began to have the jurisdictional problems that threw the whole situation into great confusion, Canadian officials were feeling the need for more frequencies and were preparing their case. That case already rested on two grounds: prior use of the wavelengths in the 400- to 450-metre band, and the extent of geographical area Canadian broadcasters had to serve. The first point was later dropped, possibly because Canadian officials recognized that it was unreasonable in a context where maximum flexibility was desirable for and beneficial to both countries.[21] The second argument, however, that of territory, subsequently became the cornerstone of Canada's case for a larger share of the wavelengths in the broadcast band.

While he was in Washington for the Fourth Radio Conference, Edwards held consultations with American radio officials about the increasingly difficult situation. On Saturday, 14 November, he met with Secretary of Commerce Hoover. When the meeting ended, Edwards cabled back to Ottawa the news that Hoover was "developing [the] idea" that North American frequency allotment would eventually have to be covered by "something [in the] nature [of a] treaty" but that this would "require legislation first meantime."[22] Edwards perceived this to be merely a delaying tactic, and proposed an interim measure that was rather complex but in effect would make fourteen wavelengths truly available for Canada (six exclusive, eight shared), which he felt would "see us through for some time to come." This proposal, he reported, had been accepted by the American radio officials and by judge Stephen B. Davis, solicitor to the Department of Commerce, and, at the time the telegram was sent, awaited only Hoover's approval. The new deal was confirmed on 18 November: Canada could now share three additional channels (890, 930, and 1010 kHz), and the American officials promised not to authorize power increases for stations on frequencies close to Canadian ones without consultation. Johnston deemed the arrangement "very satisfactory."[23] In mid-1926 three more shared frequencies also became available to Canada (630, 1120, and 1200 kHz).[24]

Unfortunately, this state of affairs lasted less than two months, for in early January 1926 the whole frequency-allocation question was thrown open by a direct challenge to Hoover's power to regulate. The story has been told in detail elsewhere.[25] Briefly, the secretary of commerce's legal authority over broadcasting under the US Radio Act of 1912 had been suspect from the beginning and all of Hoover's radio regulation up to 1926 had in fact consisted of a "painstakingly fashioned" "extralegal structure" based on cooperation among the many interests involved.[26] Numerous attempts in the early 1920s to get legislation through the House and Senate all failed for one reason or another; the only legal decision in the period, the Intercity Radio case, which ruled that the Department of Commerce had no authority to deny a licence to any applicant but that it could use its discretion in assigning wavelengths, remained moot because it did not go to the Supreme Court. In December 1925 Eugene McDonald of the Zenith Radio Corporation in Chicago decided to force a court challenge which he hoped would rid American radio of what he termed Hoover's "one-man rule" and convince legislators finally to agree on a better regulatory system. Consequently, he had Zenith's radio station, WJAZ Chicago, which had been authorized to transmit at 930 kHz on Thursday evenings only, broadcast at 910 kHz or 329.5 metres on the nights of 2, 6, and 7 January 1926. The case was doubly embarrassing for Washington radio officials; not only did it challenge the Department of Commerce's authority over domestic radio but 910 kHz was one of the frequencies reserved for Canada by the Gentleman's Agreement. As Solicitor Davis told the attorney-general of the United States in requesting the prosecution of Zenith, this sort of violation "would result in an international conflict on wavelengths with consequent utter confusion and on our part would be a breach of good faith with our Canadian neighbors."[27]

Formal litigation began in the US District Court of Northern Illinois on 18 January 1926. The decision was announced in mid-April: the secretary of commerce had no authority to assign frequencies to broadcasting stations under the 1912 Radio Act. The department then requested the attorney-general's opinion on the situation. On 8 July 1926, that opinion was made public: the Illinois judge was correct. Secretary of Commerce Hoover immediately announced:

The Department will, therefore, in accordance with the opinion, not assign wavelengths, but will merely recite on the face of the license the wavelength selected by the applicant as the normal wavelength of the station. Under the Attorney-General's opinion, no authority exists in the Department, or elsewhere, to compel adherence to this wavelength, and the Department must issue licenses to each applicant.

The general effect of this opinion is that regulation has broken down and stations are under no effective restriction as to wavelength or power used. The 1912 Act under these various constructions has failed to confer authority for the prevention of interference which was its obvious intent.

Persons desiring to construct stations must determine for themselves whether there will be wavelengths available for their use without interference from other stations. They must proceed entirely at their own risk.[28]

The effect of the attorney-general's ruling on American broadcasting has been a matter of some dispute. While some radio historians describe the resulting interference as "chaos," others suggest that self-regulation soon took effect and that "confusion" is a more appropriate term.[29] It is also claimed that Hoover deliberately fostered the "bedlam" in order to get better radio legislation passed.[30] What certainly did occur was a period of "staking of claims" in anticipation of new legislation.[31]

Whatever the case on the American side of the border, Canadian radio officials found the situation "intolerable."[32] Despite Hoover's appeals to American broadcasters to avoid "trespassing upon the Canadian assignments," two Canadian wavelengths were being usurped by the end of July and others were threatened. Canadian officials therefore decided to take Hoover up on the hint he had made six months earlier and to attempt to get a United States-Canada treaty that would protect certain frequencies as exclusively Canadian. American broadcasters could be compelled to comply with such a treaty regardless of the state of internal US regulatory legislation.[33] Accordingly, in early August 1926 the Department of Marine and Fisheries approached the Department of External Affairs with a request that it commence negotiations for a treaty allocating ten exclusive channels to Canada, plus another ten shared, out of the full ninety-five available on the 200–545 metre (550–1500 kHz) band, and External Affairs passed these representations on to the British ambassador in Washington, who contacted the State Department on 19 August 1926.

The United States accepted the proposal to negotiate and the first meeting was tentatively set for January 1927. However, in late November the Americans requested that the date be held open, pending the passage – finally – of a new US Radio Act. The legislation passed the House of Representatives on 29 January. On 17 February, the day before the act went through the Senate, the Canadian officials received a telegram asking them to hurry to Washington to negotiate a treaty in time to submit it before the Senate adjourned 4 March. The Canadians hastened to comply. Before they got there, however, on 23 February, President Calvin Coolidge signed the long-awaited Radio Act of 1927, which placed regulatory and licensing authority for radio in the hands of a Federal Radio Commission. All broadcasting licences in the United States were terminated as of the date the act became law and a sixty-day period was allotted to working out a whole new system of station wavelength assignments. This was in fact the real motivation behind the new-found urgency to deal with Canada: American officials desired to straighten out the international situation before beginning new domestic assignments.

The meetings were held on 25, 26, and 28 February 1927. The Canadian representatives were Alexander Johnston, deputy minister of Marine and Fisheries, C.P. Edwards, director of the Radio Branch, Jean Désy of the Department of External Affairs, and Laurent Beaudry, first secretary of the newly established Canadian legation at Washington. On the US side, although the FRC had been created, it had no members yet (and indeed political wrangling and other factors delayed the appointment of a full complement of five commissioners for a considerable period), so the chief American negotiators were men still formally related to the Department of Commerce: judge Stephen B. Davis, the department's Solicitor, and W.D. Terrell, chief radio supervisor, accompanied by W.R. Vallance of the State Department.

The opening positions of the two sides were a long way apart. The US submitted a draft treaty that proposed granting Canada five exclusive and nine shared frequencies, while the Canadians asked for fifteen exclusive and sixteen shared, which they almost at once reduced to twelve exclusive and sixteen shared.[34] Immediately judge Davis, the chairman, suggested that the solution might lie in granting Canada a larger number of shared frequencies, but the Canadian delegation found this unacceptable because shared wavelengths could be used for only medium-power (500 watt) stations, and "Canada's plans for the future of radio ... contemplated a number of high power stations which can only function on exclusive waves."[35] This demonstrated a concern that was fairly new for the Canadians and one related more to future than to current needs. Although no Canadian station at that time was operating at more than 5000 watts, it was becoming increasingly evident that high-power stations were the key to the future development of radio. The Canadians calculated that no more than two high-power stations, one in the east, one in the west, could share each exclusive wavelength. They therefore stuck to their demand for twelve clear channels for Canada.

What happened next may be quoted directly from the memorandum Johnston prepared for his minister after returning to Ottawa:

The United States delegation in the morning session of the 26th. February, appeared to acquiesce in the proposal that a division of the broadcast band in the ratio of 12 channels to Canada and 83 to the United States, with a certain number of shared channels, was not unreasonable, and there appeared to be some hope that the proposal would meet with their approval. At the afternoon session, however, Judge Davis informed the Canadian delegation that owing to the pending establishment of the United States Radio Commission, and the transfer of the control of radio from the Department of Commerce to that Commission, they did not feel they could proceed further with the matter until the Commission had been appointed, when a member of the same would be placed on the United States delegation, and that unless Canada was prepared to accept the Treaty as originally submitted by them, they would request an adjournment of the negotiations.[36]

This was clearly a stalling move; after all, it had been the Americans themselves who had initiated the negotiations in this transitional period. On behalf of the Canadian delegation Johnston rejected the American draft treaty out of hand, pointing out that far from increasing it actually reduced the number of exclusive wavelengths allotted to Canada. There was obviously no point in continuing the talks but, at Johnston's suggestion, a meeting was arranged between Hoover and Vincent Massey, the new Canadian minister at Washington, for 28 February.[37]

According to Massey's memorandum of this brief conversation, Hoover opened with an expression of regret that Canadian wavelengths had been pirated during the previous few months and promised that this "unfortunate situation" would end as soon as the new FRC was instituted. Massey then "as forcefully as possible" presented the Canadian position that twelve exclusive wavelengths was a minimum demand because "anything below this number would leave us sooner or later in a serious predicament" and "our people would not fail to consider it utterly inadequate." The memo continues: "Mr. Hoover's reply meant that he was rather inclined to look at the problem from the standpoint of existing conditions, which rendered it extremely difficult to disturb the large interests involved on his side of the border, and of some practical arrangement to be made by the technical experts to accommodate the two countries with as little trouble as possible for the vested interests." The meeting concluded when it became clear to Massey that absolutely nothing could be accomplished until the FRC was in place.[38]

Three weeks later, on 21 March, the Canadians were again hastily summoned to Washington to renew negotiations "with a view to having the matter settled before the Radio Commission commenced to allot waves." Judge Davis was replaced as chairman of the negotiations by Orestes Caldwell, acting chairman of the new commission. At the first of this second round of meetings, the Canadians again submitted their proposal for twelve exclusive wavelengths for Canada, sixty-seven for the United States, and sixteen shared. Caldwell countered with the suggestion that the ratio of the populations was a more logical basis of division and that, according to the latest census, this would give eight exclusive waves to Canada and eighty-seven to the United States. Johnston, on the other hand, argued that the coverage of the total area involved should be the determining factor and that, to "give a service of similar intensity" as that in the United States, Canada should have twenty-five channels.

That evening, an informal meeting was held among Edwards, Terrell, and Caldwell. After a detailed discussion they "formulated a suggestion" of eight exclusive wavelengths for Canada, seventy-one for the United States, with sixteen shared, which proposal Caldwell put to the full group the next morning. However, after discussing the proposal with Massey, the Canadian delegation decided to reject it, on the grounds that Canada "could not provide radio adequate facilities with less than eleven exclusive waves." At this point the Americans asked for an adjournment to consider the modified

Canadian proposal. During the break the Canadian delegates held their own consultation and reached the conclusion that, if the United States did not agree to the eleven wavelengths requested, they would have to return to Canada to discuss the situation with the Canadian government. As far as one can tell from the minutes, these about-faces indicate that some members of the Canadian delegation must have wanted to hold out for eleven exclusive frequencies, while others thought that eight were at least better than the prevailing six. One may deduce that Edwards was one of those agreeable to compromising at eight, as he had been a party to the drafting of that proposal the previous evening. Edwards probably also felt that the Americans would have to accept eight frequencies for Canada, for Caldwell himself had cited the population figures supporting that number.

But it was too late. When the conference reassembled on the afternoon of 22 March, the United States formally withdrew the draft proposal, stating that "on examination of their situation" they had discovered "difficulties ... with regard to the possibility of execution" which meant that they could not grant eight exclusive wavelengths to Canada, although they would make "every effort" to protect the six frequencies the Canadians had been using since 1924. That was that. The Canadian delegation withdrew and the negotiations ended. Thus Canada was left with what it had had before, six exclusive and eleven shared frequencies, but at least with the assurance that the FRC under the new legislation could enforce that allocation.

A few conclusions may be drawn about the negotiations of February and March 1927. The majority of the Canadian delegation knew full well that they risked the break-off of the talks if they refused the offer of eight exclusive wavelengths but they felt they had to do so anyway because, as Massey put it in a report he sent to Prime Minister Mackenzie King, "we feared that the lure of a gain at best very slight and probably illusory would only result in our retreating from our original position and committing ourselves to unsatisfactory arrangements which would jeopardize the solution of the future problem as to radio control in Canada."[39] Massey, for one, hoped that once more high-power Canadian stations were built, Canada would have a stronger case. He also maintained that "after all, no very serious offer [was] ever made by the other side." Massey believed that the American intent from the beginning had been simply to make the informal arrangements of the Gentleman's Agreement "binding upon us for a definite length of time and likely to become permanent in consequence of the conditions thus created." Massey's report concluded, then, that he felt the Canadian delegation had taken the correct action in refusing to be locked into a less-than-adequate arrangement. He ended by urging that there be "careful consideration ... at an early date" of "the question of radio broadcasting in Canada in its national aspects" – probably the first such call from an influential Canadian official.

Nevertheless, the hard-line position advocated by Massey did apparently cost Canada its opportunity to gain eight exclusive frequencies. Perhaps Massey wanted to look tough in one of his first actions in his new post; he was likely urged on by Hume Wrong, the legation's chargé d'affaires, as well. Edwards, on the other hand, who had worked closely with American radio officials for years, was more cognizant of the real difficulties – practical as well as political – that the FRC would have faced in granting Canada twelve clear channels in 1928.

As for the Americans, it seems fairly clear that there existed some differences of opinion as to how generous to be with Canada and that those who counselled obduracy won out. Massey's analysis had suggested that the Department of Commerce's representatives held to the harder line because of Hoover's desire to protect "large interests" in the United States. To put it a bit more charitably, there was at the time enormous pressure on the wavelengths the United States had available; it is not surprising that Hoover and his officials wished to spare themselves the grief of having to double up more stations, as would have been necessary if even two more wavelengths had been given Canada, much less the five or six the Canadians demanded. While the phrase "vested interests" connotes wealthy and powerful stations, most likely it would *not* have been the big US stations that would have been squeezed out of good frequencies but rather more of the medium- and low-power non-commercial stations.

Department of State officials involved in the negotiations seem to have been rather more sympathetic to the Canadian case, presumably because they were more concerned about the general goal of maintaining smooth relations with Canada. Hume Wrong in 1928 offered the analysis that "Mr. Hoover is known to be personally opposed to the Canadian demands and to be convinced that Canada has all, or even more than, her proper share of wavelengths under the existing arrangement. Mr. Kellogg [Secretary of State Frank B.], on the other hand, is inclined to favour the Canadian view and has, on several occasions, brought pressure to bear without avail on the Radio Commission in attempting to secure a modification of its attitude."[40] In fact, this sort of difference of opinion between the two departments was frequent in this period. The State Department often perceived Commerce to be too narrowly business-oriented and lacking in tact in dealing with other nations and Hoover's "apparent indifference" specifically to Canadian feelings created a bit of controversy.[41] Nevertheless, as one American historian has concluded, on the whole in these interdepartmental conflicts Hoover "gained the upper hand" – as he certainly did in this case.[42]

Canada's *bête noire* seems to have been Orestes Caldwell, who chaired the second round of talks although his official appointment to the FRC was delayed for another year because he was perceived by many in the US Senate to be too much "Hoover's man."[43] Only days after the talks ended he delivered a speech in New York in which he argued that Canada was doing very well with six exclusive and twelve [*sic*] shared wavelengths, for that meant that Canada had one-fifth of the wavelengths (eighteen out of ninety-five) with only one-twelfth of the population. "Hence," he concluded, "the present division of channels would seem really to favor rather than to discriminate against our Northern neighbors."[44] It may be recalled, however, that during the treaty negotiations he had made the calculation somewhat differently and had concluded that according to population ratios Canada did deserve eight exclusive channels. Clearly, much rested on how valuable one considered the shared frequencies. Caldwell's (second) calculation indicates that he considered them just as good as clear channels, at least for Canada, but other American officials, including Admiral W.H.G. Bullard, the first permanent FRC Chairman, admitted that only low-power stations could be used on shared channels, which reduced their utility greatly.[45] This view corresponded more closely with the Canadian position and with the technical reality of the time.

It is also worth noting that, although under the Radio Act and the subsequent Davis Amendment of 1928 the American regulators themselves divided licences, wavelengths, and power equally among five zones equal in population but very different in area, this system had to be abandoned in 1936 because of its impracticability. Elmer Smead, author of *Freedom of Speech by Radio and Television*, confirmed the validity of the Canadian stance in his analysis of the 1936 American reallocation: "A large zone, like the Far West, needed more stations and power than a smaller zone having a more concentrated population. If the facilities of these two zones were equal, listeners in a smaller one would be getting better service than those in a large one."[46] The territory to be covered did matter in frequency and power assignments, then, not just the population. Later, when the North American allocation of short waves (1500 to 6000 kHz) was undertaken in 1929, Canada stuck to its guns more successfully and managed to get over 30 per cent of the total 293 channels.[47]

It is possible to look at the American stance from a larger perspective as well. Radio was regulated within one section of the US Department of Commerce, which in the 1920s under Hoover's leadership was undertaking an energetic economic expansion into Canada, among other foreign countries. As one student of the period has put it, in the Hoover era Commerce's "tacit and occasionally explicit" policy toward Canada was "not merely to integrate the North American economy, but to do so in ways which would be of profit to the economy of the United States."[48] What this meant in practical terms was that Hoover encouraged trade rather than investment expansion; he believed that the best interests of the United States lay in creating a demand abroad that would then be satisfied by American-manufactured goods.[49] Radio policy was only a small part of this mission but it was nevertheless significant for a number of reasons. First, the more wavelengths under American control, the more opportunities for its own broadcasters and manufacturers to prosper. Secondly, the more high-power American stations on exclusive wavelengths near the Canadian border and the fewer good Canadian frequencies or stations, the more Canadians would listen to American stations. Thirdly, and most importantly, the more Canadians tuned into American stations, the more they were exposed to advertising of American products and lifestyles.[50] Whether these factors were explicitly stated or not, they were part of the relationship between a particular view of the work of the Radio Section and of the external trade drive of other sections of the Department of Commerce, a relationship facilitated by their placement in the same administrative unit. The unbending position of the Americans in the wavelength negotiations with Canada was an excellent example of the principles of Hoover's Department of Commerce in action.

When the Federal Radio Commission took over responsibility for American radio on 15 March 1927, forty-one US stations were transmitting on Canada's six wavelengths.[51] On 24 March orders were issued that these channels were to be cleared by 24 April; henceforward, 690, 730, 840, 910, 960, and 1030 kHz were reserved by the FRC as exclusively Canadian wavelengths.[52] Eight months later, in December 1927, Deputy Minister Johnston asked the Department of External Affairs to request an additional exclusive wavelength between 550 and 700 kHz in order to accommodate an increase of power for the publicly owned station CKY Winnipeg, adding that this request was "intended to cover the present application only" and in no way implied that Canada had abandoned its claim to a total of twelve exclusive frequencies.[53] After some delay, the American officials offered CKY 1500 kHz, which Canadian officials found unacceptable because it was completely out of the broadcast band Canada had been using for years and was unsuitable for high-power transmission.

At this point the Americans also tentatively offered a new deal: nine exclusive wavelengths and nine shared, evenly distributed along the broadcast band. This offer the Canadians also repudiated, because it entailed a sacrifice of one or two exclusive and four shared channels at the "good" end of the band; Johnston reiterated at this time that he "would hesitate to reopen negotiations unless there was reasonable ground to believe that what has been given as the minimum requirements of Canada would receive favourable consideration."[54] To this suggestion, the reply from the FRC via the State Department, although couched in the usual polite diplomatic language, was a firm No. Again, the Americans argued they were really the aggrieved party in the case, for while Canada had only 8 per cent of the population of the United States, it had 20 per cent of the wavelengths. They also pointed out that American frequencies were much more heavily utilized, with an average 8000 watts of power in use on each, while Canada had only about 2200 watts on each of its wavelengths. (To these claims the Canadians replied, first, that they had nowhere near 20 per cent of the important exclusive wavelengths and, second, that the lack of crowding on Canadian frequencies was because of more stringent licensing policies deliberately designed from the beginning to avoid channel over-crowding.[55]) The American note then concluded that "the benefits of this highly perfected American broadcasting are ... shared in to a high degree by our Canadian neighbours."[56] This was possibly the first but by no means the last time highly placed American spokesmen were to use this argument, which explicitly stated the conception of an integrated North American broadcasting market that the Department of Commerce's policies had always implied, and that, along with the spread of American networks northward, was beginning to alarm a growing number of Canadians.[57]

In the face of this further rejection, Canadian officials had two choices: to back down or to demonstrate their unhappiness by defying the American allocation of 1927, to which they had never agreed. Strong representations to opt for the latter course came from Hume Wrong in Washington, who wanted the Radio Branch simply to assign a choice wavelength to CKY and present the Americans with a *fait accompli*. Wrong argued that the situation was urgent, for the possibility that Herbert Hoover might soon be president would undoubtedly stiffen rather than soften the American stance.[58] Vincent Massey agreed. He wrote to O.D. Skelton in late October 1928:

I very much hope that before the Winnipeg station commences operations, we shall have been able to secure proper accommodation for it, but I cannot help feeling that the actual operation of this station, with its increased power and wider range, is the sort of thing which is needed to show the United States Radio Commission that we in Canada are serious in our contention as to the wave lengths we require. To maintain on paper that we have certain requirements is one thing and to demonstrate it in practice is another.[59]

The advice apparently had some effect, for CKY was soon authorized by Radio Branch officials to increase its power to 5000 watts on a shared wave-length, contrary to the normal practice of allowing only 500 watts on such channels. Despite American protests, this assignment remained fixed.[60]

For the first time, the Radio Branch had altered its earlier policy of always adhering impeccably to the Gentleman's Agreement in order to hold to firm moral ground in all negotiations.[61] In fact, the branch had been pushed to the point of declaring that it did not consider either the agreement of 1924 or the FRC allocation of 1927 binding.[62] To one correspondent Johnston declared that "until an agreement satisfactory to Canada has been reached, the division of channels in this [broadcast] band remains an open question and Canada is at complete liberty at any time to utilize any channel ..."[63]

In practice, over the next three years Canadian officials pursued several different options to break the impasse. Intervention by international radio authorities was, to their regret, not particularly likely, in part because the United States now was the dominant radio power in the world. In October 1927 the fourth International Radiotelegraph Conference, the first such meeting since 1912, had discussed wavelength allocation issues at its Washington meeting. It had quickly become clear that the delegates would be unable to resolve allocation disputes such as the one between Canada and the United States. Instead, they simply agreed on how to divide the spectrum from 10 to 60,000 kHz for different services, "leaving each nation untrammeled to license individual stations as it saw fit within the service divisions agreed upon" as long as it "consider[ed] the allocations made by others with a view to avoiding interference."[64] Late in 1928, however, when the Radio Branch was asked to submit Canada's frequencies for the official list being compiled by the International Telegraph Bureau at Berne, it formally registered its dissatisfaction. After some delay, the Department of Marine and Fisheries sent the information, but with a disclaimer that it considered the wavelengths Canada was currently using "temporary and inadequate."[65] The Canadian hesitation was well justified. In the years to follow, the United States chose to consider that such lists established "priority rights," to the considerable disadvantage of less developed countries which had been slow to establish services.[66]

The issue remained alive for the Canadians into the early 1930s, especially as a period of excellent transmission conditions in 1931–32 and the erection of high-power stations in Mexico and Cuba on Canadian frequencies exacerbated interference problems again. Edwards told one American correspondent: "Things are in bad shape up here ... Every channel we are using has foreign interference on it."[67] Between 1929 and 1932 Canada (like Mexico, whose needs had never been considered) began placing stations on what were called "split" channels, that is, halfway between two American frequencies, ignoring the rule of thumb that a 10-kHz separation between channels was mandatory. By 1932 ten small Canadian stations were placed on these so-called "holes in the ether" at such frequencies as 645, 665, 685, and 815 kHz.[68] The only factor apparently holding the Canadians back from further usurpment – and it was a major one – was that the virtually certain fate of a Canadian station placed on or too near an American frequency was to suffer from intolerable interference itself. Indeed, some of the split channels had to be abandoned for this reason.[69]

Another option considered in this period was the placing of stations outside the conventional broadcast band at 520, 530, and 540 kHz.[70] Although this was supposed to be a "guard band" for the international distress-signal frequency, it was agreed that it could be allocated to broadcasting if the stations were at least 1000 miles from any coastline. That plan, however, fell by the wayside when Canadian manufacturers pointed out that they could not easily alter the receivers they made because of their great dependence on parts and research from the United States, where 550 kHz remained the standard frequency limit. As J.W. Bain put it in a memo to Edwards: "The technical design of a receiver to tune from 1500–520 K.C. is no problem at all if the designer has any freedom and that is the crux of the whole question ... Many Canadian so called radio manufacturers are not manufacturers at all but merely assemblers of United States made parts"[71] To extend the reception capabilities of radios used in Canada would cost, a Canadian Manufacturers' Association (CMA) spokesman stated, about $7.50 for each set. The burden on the manufacturers would be onerous, for they would be forced to do their own research and engineering "with considerably higher costs, which have hitherto been controlled by contractual participation in the laboratories of the United States where the huge production warranted the expense." Not surprisingly, the Radio Manufacturers' Association and the CMA vetoed the idea.[72] Canada did, however, begin using 540 kHz for CKX Brandon in 1927 and in 1930 it registered it with the International Telegraph Bureau in Berne.[73] In June 1932 this wavelength was also assigned to a new station licensed in Windsor, Ontario (CKOK). Canadian representatives also continued to press for an extension of the broadcast band at international conferences in alliance with other nations that felt similarly disadvantaged.

Yet another alternative considered quite hopefully by the Canadians was the European *Plan de Genève*, adopted in 1926. This plan, which made wavelength allocations to European countries on the basis of a formula taking into account their area, population, and frequency of telephone and telegraph messages, seemed to bolster the Canadian argument. If it was applied to North America, Canadian officials argued, Canada would be allotted about twenty exclusive channels.[74]

But after the fall of 1929 there was no more time to persuade the Americans of the justice of this claim. The impending reorganization of Canadian radio occasioned by the Aird commission's report demanded that the situation be regularized. The concreteness of the plan actually to build and use seven high-power stations also gave the Canadians some leverage, as Massey had predicted. In mid-1931 the government arranged an informal meeting between Lieutenant-Colonel W.A. Steel, a radio-engineering expert with the National Research Council, and Dr C.B. Jolliffe, chief engineer of the Federal Radio Commission, to explore the possibilities for a break in the logjam.[75] While Dr Jolliffe admitted that modifications of the 1927 arrangement were necessary, he reminded Steel of the many constraints on the FRC, including US court decisions which suggested that the vested property rights of station owners were intimately linked to the frequency assigned.[76] Nevertheless, as Steel's memo about this meeting reveals, the American position was moderating, for both political and technical reasons. By this time the FRC was under intense pressure to negotiate an allocation agreement or treaty with Mexico, whose high-power stations (some of them owned by Americans who had been denied licences in the United States) were causing severe interference problems in the southern states and whose government seemed impervious to all appeals. The FRC apparently calculated that, if it could reach an effective but non-treaty agreement with Canada, this would improve its position in dealing with Mexico. Technically speaking as well, its members felt that they had more room to manoeuvre, a view premised on the utilization of some of the frequencies between 500 and 550 kHz and on the recent development of directional antennas making more sharing of wavelengths possible.

Consequently, on 5 May 1932, Canada and the United States exchanged notes confirming a new allocation arrangement. While the calculations are complex (and some of the provisions controversially unclear), Canada essentially ended up with nine clear channels (including 540 kHz) and twenty-seven shared (although on twenty of these power was restricted to 100 watts). Thus Canada gained three clear channels but lost access to four shared slots on which it could place middle-power stations.[77] Nevertheless, it was left with an allocation more suitable for the chain of high-power stations now being planned; the United States meanwhile lost little because it had no interest in utilizing frequencies such as 540 kHz for broadcasting anyway.[78] Subsequently, after two rounds of meetings among the major North and Central American countries, the Havana Treaty of 1937 creating the North American Regional Broadcasting Agreement (NARBA) was signed and, by 1941, ratified by all involved. It finally gave Canada a total of eleven channels for Class I-A and I-B stations, the type needed for high-power coverage and access to more than forty other channels for weaker stations on a shared basis.[79]

But this richness of spectrum resources lay far in the future for the radio regulators of the 1920s. Until 1932, the allocation of six exclusive channels to Canada by the Gentleman's Agreement in 1924, viewed by the Canadians at least by 1927 as only a *modus vivendi*, seemed engraved on stone; it created the narrow limits within which domestic wavelength assignment had to occur. There were many reasons for the failure to increase Canada's allotment in the 1920s. The crucial period was 1926–27, when the American situation was in transition. But the very fact that US radio regulation was in flux gave the Americans the tactical opportunity to delay serious renegotiation of the 1924 arrangement. Laurent Beaudry of the Washington legation expressed the frustration felt by the Canadian negotiators in 1928:

The United States Federal Radio Commission, which was created in 1927, has full power and refuses to make any concessions. Before the creation of that Commission, the answer of the United States authorities was that the radio situation in their country was rather chaotic and that they hoped that when the Federal Radio Commission was established there would be a possibility to deal with the difficulties existing between the two countries. With the establishment of the Federal Radio Commission, the situation has become worst [*sic*] since that body ... has proceeded with the task of licensing the available channels and paid practically no attention to the representations made by Canada last year. The danger is that the present situation may become crystallized and that we may not be able ever to get more than the present six exclusive wave lengths unless we start what has been called a radio war with the United States.[80]

Canada failed before 1932 to convince the United States to relinquish more exclusive channels for three main reasons. First, Hoover and later the FRC officials were determined not to grant Canada's demands, because of the pressure of domestic vested interests which not only occupied all the US channels as early as 1924 but were constantly pressing for more, and because they deemed it in the public and national interest of the United States to control most North American broadcasting frequencies.[81] A second reason for Canada's failure was, quite simply, its lack of clout. Canada had no power to force the United States to take it seriously. Nor could it turn to an international body with its case; the International Radiotelegraph Conferences were reluctant to meddle in regional allocations, and besides, by 1927 the United States dominated world radio regulators. Within the North American region neither Canada nor Mexico, not to mention the smaller countries, could do more than try to persuade the United States to change its policy.

Persuasion, however, did not get far once the United States had usurped the vast majority of available channels. The very early and widespread expansion of American stations onto ninety of the ninety-six frequencies in the broadcast band presented other North and Central American nations with a *fait accompli* not easily reversed. In the face of American intransigence, only two tactics really remained for the Canadians and they were both too risky to use fully. One was to begin placing stations at frequencies outside the traditional broadcast band. That was tried to a limited extent but fell afoul of international spectrum-allocation regulations and of the dependence of Canadian radio manufacturers, most of them branch plants, on US research and parts. The second possibility would have been for the

Canadians simply to move in and begin utilizing frequencies at will. But that was also contrary to the 1927 Washington agreement and was for the most part impracticable; the interference thereby created would harm Canadian as much as American stations, infuriating both Canadian and American broadcasters and listeners.

Canada's radio officials and politicians were thus, by 1927, caught in a trap from which the only escape was either to do violence to international agreements or to destroy the listening pleasure of North American radio owners. Neither was considered feasible. Domestic assignment decisions during the 1920s, therefore, had to be taken within the limits imposed by the fact, as Hume Wrong put it at the time, that Washington had taken "the lion's share of broadcasting channels and refuse[d] to disgorge."[82]

The third and most important reason for Canada's failure in 1927, however, was the weakness of its case. As Commander Edwards admitted to the House of Commons Special Committee in 1932: "At that date the situation was not really serious. That is to say, we had sufficient channels to take care of all the stations of the power we had and some to spare."[83] Only future needs were at stake, and they were much harder to demonstrate and fight for. In 1931 one of Prime Minister Bennett's advisers admitted that "our case against the United States is weakened so long as the number of radio sets in use remains relatively limited, the number of our stations small, and their broadcasting power still more limited."[84] As was already demonstrated in Chapter 3, some of the reasons for that situation were economic; others, however, were rooted in the policy decisions that will be examined more closely in the next chapter. Essentially the problem was circular: without high-power stations Canada's claim to more frequencies was weak; without more frequencies, Radio Branch regulators were reluctant to authorize high-power stations. Only in 1932, with the federal government apparently committed to supporting a national system of high-power stations, was the dilemma resolved.

8 Domestic Frequency and Power Assignment

Policies regarding domestic frequency and power assignment were constrained not only by the need to avoid the detrimental effects of interference and the practices of American radio authorities. Two other related factors also circumscribed the branch's actions: the technical capabilities of broadcasting and receiving sets and listener preferences. These "limits" were the key elements in determining the Radio Branch's assignment decisions, but within them its officials had some room to manoeuvre and made some choices that reveal the principles and assumptions underlying their approach to radio development in the early years.

The essential technical factor upon which optimum wavelength assignment depended was the gradual accumulation of knowledge about the spectrum and about the causes of and cures for station-to-station interference. Initially, as was mentioned earlier, wavelengths were granted on an experimental basis to Canadian broadcasting stations in ten-metre steps in the band between 400 and 450 metres (750 to 666.6 kHz). By June 1922 about thirty-six stations existed in Canada. If several broadcasters were operating in a single city, they were given wavelengths ten metres apart; thus in Montreal, the four earliest stations were assigned to wavelengths of 410, 420, 430, and 440 metres, the five in Vancouver used 400 to 440 metres, and the eight in Toronto used 400 to 450 metres, with three of them sharing 410. As more new stations were licensed throughout the rest of 1922 and early 1923, they were assigned these same frequencies.

Because the tuning devices of the time were very unsophisticated, however, even skilled operators with good receiving sets could not prevent interference if stations in the same city were broadcasting simultaneously on wavelengths closer than 30 or 40 metres.[1] Although Canadian officials were, of course, aware of this fact and were watching for interference problems, the branch's records do not indicate any serious difficulties in the initial period. Undoubtedly this was because a number of the stations licensed never actually began broadcasting and because those that did operated only a few hours a week. Nevertheless, Radio Branch officials were keenly aware that in order to encourage broadcasting development they must be flexible about frequency assignments. Their routine letter to the earliest licensees warned of possible frequency adjustments because "we must anticipate passing through an experimental stage before we can finally ascertain what can and cannot be done with the average receiving equipments [sic] in inexperienced hands ..."[2] The twin emphases on flexibility and on catering to the needs of the "average" listener were to remain constant through the rest of the decade.

During the latter part of 1923 and 1924 Canadian officials were forced continually to alter wavelength assignments because of interference caused by the American move, effective 15 May 1923, to place stations throughout the 222- to 545-metre band (1365 to 550 kHz). As already described in the previous chapter, avoiding interference with the rapidly expanding number of US stations forced considerable manipulation of Canadian frequency assignments and prompted the first Canadian use of wavelengths beyond the narrow 400–450 metre band. In early 1924 as well, adjustments were made to change the wavelength designations from metres to even kilocycles.[3]

The extent to which interference created problems for listeners in the 1920s depended to a large extent on the capabilities of their receiving sets. One great challenge for regulators was that the quality and capacity of receiving sets evolved rapidly during the decade. The officials at the Radio Branch not only had to keep up with the changes but, even more difficult, had to regulate for several different levels of sophistication simultaneously. In the early part of the decade, up to about 1925, crystal sets were in the majority. While precise figures do not exist, as many as three-quarters of sets in use as late as 1925 may still have been crystal sets.[4] Cheap and simple to construct and operate, the perfect "starter" sets, crystal sets could normally pick up only stations within twenty-five miles and could not separate stations closer together than 40 or 50 metres on the band. The next step up from crystal sets were non-selective one-tube receivers, the infamous regenerative receivers. Because they were capable of receiving more distant stations, these sets were the basis of the fad for DX-ing, or logging distant stations, which did not begin to fade until about 1926. DX-ing fans disliked local stations; they pressured to keep their power low and for the establishment of the local "silent" nights common until at least 1926. In the final years of the decade, more selective, powerful, and expensive multi-tube sets became increasingly widespread. Their owners were more interested in the quality of local broadcasting, both in terms of clear transmission and good programming, and tended to favour strong and competitive local stations.[5]

It was primarily with the needs of the owners of the relatively unsophisticated crystal and single-tube sets in mind that the major assignment decisions of the early 1920s were taken. As long as these sets dominated the Canadian market, the majority of fans made it clear to the Radio Branch that they preferred having only one local station broadcasting at a time. In 1924 the branch floated the idea of allowing "dual" or simultaneous broadcasting in Toronto but hastily cancelled the plan when "the local broadcast listeners ... evinced a very decided re-action [sic] against having two stations on the air at once."[6] A year later, another attempted experiment in the same city was torpedoed by an alliance of broadcasters, manufacturers, and radio dealers who feared "long and loud complaints" from listeners.[7] John R. Bone of the Toronto Star's CFCA wrote: "Dual broadcasting we believe to be at the present time out of the question. It would, we understand, involve the scrapping of ninety-five per cent. or more of the receiving equipment at present in use in the territory, and that would be a serious matter for the public."[8] In 1925, then, many broadcasters still perceived dual broadcasting to be to their disadvantage, primarily because they felt it would alienate listeners. Government officials were keenly aware of these sentiments.

After the Gentleman's Agreement of 1924 and with pressure increasing on the available frequencies, a major reallocation of Canadian frequencies was undertaken effective 20 February 1925. According to this plan, wavelengths were assigned by city. The exclusive Canadian frequencies were given to two cities at opposite ends of the country, while frequencies shared with the United States were used in isolated centres or for low-power stations. Thus, the exclusive wavelength of 410.7 metres (730 kHz) was assigned to the stations in Montreal and to those in Vancouver, 434.5 metres (690 kHz) to Calgary and Ottawa stations, 329.5 metres (910 kHz) to London, Saskatoon, and Victoria, and 356.9 metres (840 kHz) to Toronto.[9] Yet there was already so much demand for time in the three major cities that on an experimental basis they were each assigned a "district" wavelength as well; the transmitters for stations on this wavelength had to be located at least ten miles outside the city centre. With the exception of Montreal, Toronto, and Vancouver, however, which effectively had two (widely separated) frequencies each, all the stations in each Canadian city had to operate on the same wavelength.

In its effects, therefore, this 1925 assignment perpetuated the ban on simultaneous broadcasting in most of Canada. There is no record of the discussions that lay behind this decision but there is no doubt that it deliberately catered to those with the more primitive sets. In contrast, it may be noted, American frequency-assignment plans as early as 1923 had divided stations by classes and posited the existence of as many as three stations, one of each class, in any one locality, provided their broadcast frequencies were 50 kilocycles apart.[10]

The assignment of only one frequency per city did not imply only one station in each. On the contrary, the Radio Branch quite explicitly encouraged a number of stations to exist and compete in each locality by sharing time on the single wavelength assigned (or, in the three largest centres, on both city and district waves). A 1923 report explained it this way:

Practically no restrictions have been placed in the way of issue of licenses, and while it might at first sight seem uneconomical to allow more than one station in any one area, since only one or, at most, two can work at the same time, nevertheless this policy has the advantage that the friendly competition between stations in regard to quality of transmission and quality of programmes, has done much to develop the art, and had unquestionably functioned to the benefit of the broadcast listener.[11]

It is particularly noteworthy that this justification was presented in a report to a committee studying the British broadcasting situation, for it indicated either genuine belief in or at least rationalization of the competitive North American as opposed to the more tightly controlled British and European approach to station licensing and development – and on the grounds of satisfying the listeners.

In summary, throughout the early 1920s, the Radio Branch's policy was consistent. Most applicants were granted licences, but only on condition that they share time on the single frequency assigned per city. In each locality, the broadcasters themselves were responsible for reaching their own arrangement on time-sharing, but if they could not agree or if abuses occurred the authorities had the right to step in and determine schedules.

One typical example of a time-sharing controversy requiring branch intervention occurred in London, Ontario, in early 1924. On 25 April of that year, C.H. Langford, the London radio inspector, wrote to inform Commander Edwards that the two local stations, CJGC, owned by the London *Free Press*, and little 10-watt CFLC, owned by a C.G. Hunter, were quarrelling about their time allotments.[12] Langford assigned total blame to the uncooperative attitude of the *Free Press* station manager. As the problem looked serious, Edwards sent in S.J. Ellis, his full-time Toronto inspector, to see if he could bring the parties to agreement. Ellis reported back to Edwards on 12 May that he had found the *Free Press* station "terrible" and its manager "most uncivil," while Hunter seemed to be spending a lot of money to put on good programs. In fact, Ellis had not even managed to speak to Mr Thomas, the manager at the newspaper's station, and suspected the man was deliberately evading him. Ellis recommended that "the *Free Press* station be suspended until such times [*sic*] as they can agree to live up to the regulations and get their set in proper working order."

Edwards, on behalf of Deputy Minister Johnston, promptly wrote to the *Free Press*, commencing with a reproach for not meeting with Ellis but then going on to point out rather mildly that all the Radio Branch really wanted was to "ascertain your wishes" regarding schedules of transmission, a process made necessary by the licensing of the second London station. Thomas's reply was equally amicable: the contretemps with Ellis (whom he thought was named Lucas), he explained, had merely been a misunderstanding. He then told the branch precisely which broadcasting hours he would prefer for his station, they were subsequently granted, and Hunter was informed that he must fit his times in around those chosen by the *Free Press*. Hunter agreed and all was settled peacefully. Eventually, indeed, Hunter became the *Free Press* station operator.

This tale illustrates fairly standard handling of time-allocation problems by the Radio Branch. First the local inspector tried to deal with the situation, then a more senior inspector, and if neither of them had any luck, the muscle of the director of the Radio Branch was invoked. The latter step was only reluctantly taken, however; as Edwards put it to a correspondent on another case, "As a matter of general policy, this Branch is very averse to exercising its arbitrary power unless absolutely necessary."[13] Despite the hostility of both inspectors toward the *Free Press* station, based on both its technical capabilities and its management, the Ottawa officials bent over backwards to be conciliatory and granted it the choice of time allotments. This was consistent with the branch guidelines giving preference to newspaper stations and to those first established. Finally, it is worth noting that this whole fuss arose in the first place because neither station wanted to broadcast after 8:15 p.m.; neither wished to interfere with the ability of London listeners to tune in without interference to "the American concerts after that time."[14]

Radio Branch officials were not unaware that their policy of forcing all stations to share time had some disadvantages for Canadian broadcasters. In 1925 Edwards explained the dilemma he felt in trying to satisfy both listeners and broadcasters simultaneously to a correspondent who was concerned about the need for more and better Canadian broadcasting to counter the cultural threat from the United States:

There is, of course, a limit to the number of stations which can be operated in any one area. We have obtained the impression that Canadian listeners do not favour several stations on the air at the same time, the arrangement which exists in New York, Chicago, and other large U.S. cities. Our listeners' desires would appear to be only one local station on the air at a time.

You will appreciate that the problem is not a very easy one. Licensees built broadcasting stations and they naturally want to transmit all the time. If there are two or three in one area, this means the B.C.L. with the selective set can receive very little from outside stations, while the owner of the unselective set cannot get anything at all.

If we cut the stations down to one on the air at a time, it means that the licensee who builds a $15,000 station is only able to use it one or two nights a week. If we do not have Canadian stations, then all our listeners will be loaded with U.S. matter. So the best we can do is to effect a compromise in an endeavour to reconcile these conflicting interests.[15]

Despite Edwards's characterization of his policy as one of compromise, that was not really the case. The branch policy until the late twenties to assign only one or at most two frequencies per city and thereby to force time-sharing was heavily biased toward the interests of listeners with unsophisticated sets; the only concession to the broadcasters was the rule that no more than three stations could be assigned to one wavelength.

The effect was to deny continuity to even the best broadcasters and to limit their ability to hire good staff, which could not be financed on two and one-third days broadcasting per week. O.L. Spencer, business manager for CFAC Calgary (owned by the Calgary *Herald*), summed up the broadcasters' problem neatly in a 1930 letter to the deputy minister, in which he requested an exclusive wavelength for his station:

Our present wave length is 690 kilo cycles and we operate on this wave length, dividing the time by mutual consent with two other stations located in Calgary. We have, therefore, out of each twenty-four hours, only about five and one-half hours of actual broadcasting time available; and it is impossible with this small period of time each day for us to make the necessary progress in new equipment which should be made to keep up with modern broadcasting methods.

The cost of operating a station such as C.F.A.C. is between 12 and 15 thousand dollars per year, and with the limited time available it is impossible for us to secure enough revenue to break even.[16]

As advertising revenues became increasingly important to station financing the instability and impermanence of this type of arrangement caused more problems. Not only was income reduced by short hours but long-term advertising contracts were difficult to obtain when a station could not guarantee that its time allotment would remain undisturbed.[17] Similarly, in the latter part of the decade, shared time meant that stations were often unable to hook up to desirable chain programs when they wished without the considerable effort of making special arrangements with the other local stations. This undoubtedly made it more difficult for Canadian broadcasters to build networks. As Ernie Bushnell of CKNC Toronto explained in a letter pleading for a full-time wavelength for his station in 1931: "For our chain broadcasting it is almost impossible to synchronize our schedule with that of other stations operating every night, and for this reason we have had to forego programs from affiliated stations on our chain, originating in Montreal or London."[18]

Quite simply, then, the branch's policy of forcing time-sharing reduced the ability of Canadian broadcasters to develop and build their stations. Alex MacKenzie of CKNC Toronto told the Aird commissioners in 1929 that "if we can be assured of a clear wave length and seven days operation per week, we are prepared to give consideration to building and operating a high-powered transmitting station and to guarantee that only the best of programs be put on the air, and to make available without charge two hours per day for educational purposes, all without government subsidy."[19] It was not a promise, but MacKenzie's statement does suggest that considerable upgrading might have occurred had the better Canadian broadcasters felt financially more secure through the guarantee of full-time operation. Unfortunately, their sense of uncertainty was exacerbated by the long period of political indecisiveness that followed the submission of the Aird report and particularly by the warning routinely given to broadcasters from the end of 1928 on that the government would not necessarily provide compensation for money spent on station improvement in the event of nationalization.[20]

The introduction of "district" wavelengths for the major cities was the branch's mid-1920s solution to overheated demand for licences in these localities. Broadcasters assigned to the district wavelength could maintain their studios in the city but to reduce interference had to build their transmitters at least ten miles outside. So, from 1925 on, each of the major cities was theoretically capable of supporting six stations, three each on the city and district frequencies. Actually, time on the district wavelength, despite certain disadvantages because of extra wireline and staffing costs, was soon much in demand because other regulations (which will be discussed in more detail shortly) compelled high-power transmitters to be some distance from centres of population as well.

Nevertheless, branch officials authorized utilization of district wavelengths only with considerable trepidation. Toronto was first to be allowed dual broadcasting; in 1926 CJYC, the station of the International Bible Students Association, was placed on the district wavelength. Despite the large volume of complaints, the following year CFRB was also given a share of the Toronto district wave. Beginning in early 1928 when CKGW went into operation, a redistribution was initiated which opened up a third wavelength and by 1932 there were five different operative frequencies in the Toronto area, with separations of about 100 kHz.

The Toronto case (discussed more fully in the next chapter) was very much the exception, however. Not until the very end of 1928 was dual broadcasting allowed on a regular basis in Montreal, initially for stations CFCF and CKAC, and then only in the daytime and for two hours on Wednesday nights to test the reactions of listeners. The branch's caution about offending bcls was more than evident. Edwards wrote to Montreal inspector J.M. Colton, "We are not looking for any adverse criticism from the Montreal listeners, in fact rather the reverse, as the transfer of the Marconi station to the shorter wave will enable the local listeners with selective sets to hear WJZ [Bound Brook, New Jersey] and WEAF [New York], which they must have a hard time accomplishing at the present time ..."[21] In fact, there *were* complaints; for instance, one of the rare letters to the branch from a francophone claimed that "some of the best stations in the U.S.A." such as KDKA, WBZ, WBAL, and WTAM, "les endroits d'où venait la meilleure musique" (the places the best music comes from), were now difficult to hear in Montreal.[22] But negative reaction was judged slight enough that at the request of CFCF the dual broadcasting hours were extended the following spring to include seven more evening hours, and by March 1929 the two main Montreal stations were operating simultaneously all day and for two or three hours certain evenings.[23] In Vancouver, limited simultaneous broadcasting (6 to 8 p.m., Monday to Saturday evenings) was allowed by early 1927. By 1932 stations in Hamilton, Edmonton, and Calgary were also assigned to two different wavelengths and allowed to operate simultaneously. Nevertheless, in all of these cities – including Toronto and Montreal – there were still some frequencies on which time had to be shared among both physical and phantom stations and this practice was of course still necessary in the many other localities with only one channel as well.

The fundamental reason for the branch's continued reluctance to expand simultaneous broadcasting lay in its conviction that the wishes of the listeners were paramount – despite clear evidence that this policy catered to the technologically backward end of the market and to listeners whose primary objection to simultaneous broadcasting from local stations was that it interfered with reception of American stations.

With respect to the first point, contemporary opinion differed about how to deal with the difficult problem of a technologically diverse market. In the United States, the prevailing attitude was that "necessity is the mother of invention," and that while simultaneous broadcasting might temporarily inconvenience those with primitive sets, in the long run the purchase of better sets would be encouraged, enabling the assignment of more stations to more wavelengths, thus expanding the whole market and industry.[24] This view, propounded especially by the manufacturers, who had enormous influence with the Department of Commerce, was not held unanimously, however. One of the best-informed surveyors of the American radio scene, L.D. Batson, argued in 1930 that "the basing of broadcast policies on a prevalence of modern or highly sensitive receivers has not been found an effective practice. Instead of stimulating the market for new sets it has tended to annihilate interest on the part of those whose still serviceable sets have been rendered obsolete."[25]

There is no doubt that in Canada the Radio Branch was under regular pressure to remember the needs of those with more primitive sets.[26] The significance lies in its responsiveness to that pressure. The listeners came first at the Radio Branch, and as long as the majority of listeners had unselective sets, branch policies indulged their wishes. Radio manufacturers, who might have exerted a counter-thrust, were less influential here than they were in the United States; as we have seen, most receivers were imported until 1927 and even after that the factories were largely branch plants. What advice the Radio Branch did receive opposing its policy was ignored. In late 1924 R.H. Combs of Canadian National Carbon (owners of CKNC Toronto) wrote to Commander Edwards to make the case that the prolongation of the ban on dual broadcasting was inducing "unsuspecting" Canadians to continue to purchase cheap regenerative sets "which would not be worth a cent in any of the large American cities" and whose "squealing and yelping and wailing" were ruining reception and thereby "menacing the entire radio business."[27] While Combs's comment was noted and passed on to the inspectors, in fact policy did not change for some time – time during which much energy was spent looking for other solutions to the troublesome regenerative-receiver problem.

As to the second point, that branch policies deliberately pandered to Canadian listeners who wished to receive American stations, one more example will suffice. In reply to a Calgary fan who complained in 1924 that the local stations were broadcasting so much that he could never hear distant American stations, Edwards wrote with some sympathy:

I agree with you ... that it is exasperating to some of us who at times are wont to believe that the 'bird in the bush is worth two in the hand' and want to get some outside programmes ...

We do not wish to see any community get more than it bargains for and if at any time the Department should conclude that the broadcast listener is overburdened with local transmission in any city, suitable steps will be considered to remedy the situation.[28]

A 1925 letter to the Radio Branch from W.M. Turnley, manager of Dominion Battery, which wanted a Toronto broadcasting licence, reveals that some at least recognized the implications of the branch's actions. After being denied a licence on the grounds that no more stations could be allowed in Toronto because of the objections of local listeners, Turnley wrote to Deputy Minister Johnston in January of 1925:

We do not think that the protest from the local listeners is due to the interference of stations in the city between each other, but due to the fact that some of them cannot cut through on the lower wave lengths and reach the American stations, but it seems to us rather a strange situation that the Dominion Government would feel inclined to suppress Canadian Broadcasting Stations, so Canadians can listen to the American Stations, which naturally are sending out propaganda favourable to the United States, and the writer personally feels that we have enough propaganda coming from the United States through newspapers and magazines, without encouraging it on the air.[29]

Dominion Battery did in fact get its licence (CKCL) shortly thereafter, but on a strict time-sharing arrangement on the Toronto district wavelength.

Thus throughout the 1920s even the major Canadian cities offered many fewer local choices to listeners than did similar American communities; as early as 1925, for example, Chicago had ten stations on five wavelengths and New York eight on six wavelengths.[30] Legitimate Canadian applicants were still being denied licences as well. In 1926 E.S. Rogers's Standard Radio was held up for some months before being granted a Toronto licence because such previously approved applicants as the Loyal Order of Moose were being given every opportunity to get their stations into operation.[31] While Rogers had every reason – as well as the contacts and money – to persist, other applicants simply lost the opportunity to get into broadcasting because of the shortage of wavelengths. The problem, of course, was not that some applicants had to be denied licences. That was imperative given the marked scarcity (with contemporary technology) of the key resource, the spectrum band. Rather, it was that the branch officials artificially restricted the number of frequencies available by eschewing simultaneous broadcasting until long after it was technically feasible.

They also – as the Rogers case as well as those of the London *Free Press* and the Crowe case in Calgary illustrate – bent over backwards to be even-handed. Not always, but frequently enough, small 10- or 50-watt stations were treated as though they were the equals of 500-watt stations in which much more had been invested. W.W. Grant of Calgary complained in a 1924 telegram: "Unless some fair method protection no encouragement maintaining the leading Canadian station CFCN if any one can secure license for 5 or 10 watt set and secure same proportion broadcasting time in competition with station such as ours." While the branch replied to Grant that "quality of programme and class of equipment installed will be given due weight when hours of working are being arranged," as usual a great deal was left to its discretionary authority, with attendant uncertainty for broadcasters.[32]

In fact, the branch generally did follow a policy of treating all those to whom it granted licences as equally as possible. In theory admirable, this practice nevertheless created many difficulties. In earlier chapters instances were cited of blanket policies concerning use of records and permission to air direct advertising that hampered small stations. Concerning time-sharing, the same argument may be made in reverse. The refusal to allow full time to the higher-power stations discouraged their development. Little attempt was made to foster or promote the interests of the more stable and secure licensees, in direct contrast to the American policy enunciated at the Fourth National Radio Conference that "having a few stations broadcasting high quality programs was more desirable than having many stations offering mediocre programs."[33] Probably the lack of influence of the major manufacturers in Canadian broadcasting partly accounted for the differing approach here. Another factor was Ottawa's desire to have as many Canadian wavelengths occupied as possible, both to provide service to the far-flung population and to improve its tactical position in North American wavelength allocation negotiations. While on the surface appearing fair, this policy of equity in fact weakened Canadian broadcasting as a whole.

A final problem with the branch's time-sharing policy, and one of the most telling, refuted the claim that this arrangement improved broadcasting by enhancing competition. As W.W. Grant put it in a memo to his friend R.B. Bennett in 1931, the fact that the three Calgary stations shared a single wavelength had had precisely the opposite effect: "There is no competition because the three of us know that it is only a question of who has the time that governs who will do the broadcast. The result is that improvements in equipment and high standard of entertainment has not been maintained ..."[34] There was in fact little competition under the shared-frequency scheme; each local station had a monopoly in its time slot.

The Radio Branch's policy with respect to time-sharing, it must be stressed again, was in direct contrast to that of its American counterpart in the 1920s. There, from 1923 on, the stronger and more financially able broadcasters (including the major manufacturers) were deliberately favoured and encouraged to develop and innovate by the granting of exclusive wavelengths on which they could broadcast full-time.[35] This policy was, of course, much attacked and its effects on the non-preferred broadcasters (who tended, with time, to include most educational institutions, for example) were dire. On the other hand, the Canadian Radio Branch's more even-handed approach, its coddling of listeners with unselective sets, its apparent desire not to show favoritism among broadcasters, its unwillingness to allot anyone more than one-third of the week, weakened the ability of the Canadian private broadcasting system as a whole to compete with the one to the south. Canadian radio authorities do not seem to have recognized their greatest limit of all: Canada does not exist in isolation. Canadian broadcasters were forced, as a result of the easy access of Canadian listeners to American stations, to hold their own against arguably the strongest, most inventive, and best-financed broadcasting in the world. Any policy that weakened their ability to do so unintentionally undermined private broadcasting in Canada.

INEXTRICABLY LINKED TO THE QUESTION of frequency assignment was the issue of the power output of broadcasting stations, for the more powerful a station, the less flexibility the Ottawa officials had in determining its wavelength. Again, slowly accumulating technical knowledge, US practices, diverse receiver capabilities, and the demands of listeners all played a role in the decisions taken by the Radio Branch during the 1920s.

American broadcasters pioneered with both the advantages and the problems of increasing the power of broadcasting stations. The earliest US stations operated for the most part at low power, under 500 watts, until the reallocation of May 1923. At that time, as mentioned previously, a special classification of more powerful "Class B" stations was created, intended to serve listeners beyond the local area, with a minimum of 500 watts and maximum of 1000 watts (1 kilowatt). Despite complaints from listeners close to these stronger stations that they could not tune them out to hear anything else[36] and from those who feared the tendency to monopoly inherent in high power, Hoover's Department of Commerce officials, at the urging of the radio industry, encouraged experimentation with more and more powerful stations. By 1926 there were almost twenty American stations with power of 5000 watts; the following year three had moved up to the new maximum of 30,000 watts. By 1928 there were over fifty at 5000 watts or more and three at 50,000; by 1932 there were at least sixty-six American stations broadcasting at 5,000 watts or more and thirteen at 50,000.[37] The vast majority of these stations were assigned exclusive wavelengths; they were also, of course, the stations best received by Canadians.

Meanwhile, in Canada, there was a very marked lag in the development of high-power stations. Part of the reason for this was no doubt economic. As was explained in Chapter 3, high-power stations were very much more expensive to build and to maintain and the scarcity of large investors in Canadian broadcasting undoubtedly slowed the erection of such facilities. But the delay was also owing to the actions of the Radio Branch officials. As we have just seen, forced time-sharing decreased profit opportunities and therefore incentives for major investment. Moreover, unlike its American counterpart, the Radio Branch never actively encouraged stations to increase their power. On the contrary, throughout the 1920s Ottawa officials made little attempt to provide for regional coverage of Canada and often denied permission to broadcasters who wished to boost their output. By 1932 there were only six stations in Canada broadcasting at 4000 watts or more, the strongest being at 10 kw. Canada's first 50-kw station was not to be opened until 1937. The two main considerations lying behind this policy have both already been discussed with respect to the branch's assignment decisions. The first was excessive solicitude for the concerns of listeners with primitive receivers. The second was the practice of treating all broadcasters equally.

As with so many other technical issues relating to broadcasting, Radio Branch officials in the 1920s were still feeling their way on the question of how a station's transmitting power affected radio reception. In the early years they depended a great deal on trial-and-error and listeners' and inspectors' reports. By the end of the decade, however, much knowledge had been accumulated about the measurement of field strength or field intensity, that is, the value of the electrical field at any given reception point. It had been determined by then that field strength not only falls off with increasing distance from the power source and with decreasing length of the transmitted wave but that the patterns are irregular because of variations in the earth's surface, both natural and man-made, and interference. Canadian technical advisor W.A. Steel wrote in 1931:

Today *interference* is commonly defined as *any spurious or extraneous sounds accompanying radio reception which are present over 10% of the time. Good service area is similarly defined as that area in which satisfactory reception free from interference is obtained at least 90% of the time ...*

Broadcasting is used today just as much in daylight as at night, and, while phenomenal ranges are frequently covered by stations at night, it is only possible by using the reflected ray. Since this ray is subject to violent fading and distortion at all times, it follows that the *Good* service area of a station is the area served by the ground wave and this area is approximately the same by day as by night.[38] [emphasis in original]

By 1932 standards had also been arrived at: a field strength of 100 millivolts per metre gave excellent urban radio service, of 10 mv/m very good, and of 1 mv/m fair (a millivolt is one thousandth of a volt).[39] Considerably lower intensities were adequate in suburban and rural areas where there was less extraneous interference.

These standards, however, were based on relatively sophisticated five-tube superheterodyne receivers; on simpler, less selective sets, reception of this intensity from one station would likely blanket all others. Consequently, in deference to listeners who owned the more primitive sets, throughout the 1920s Canadian stations were kept to outputs considerably less than those recommended in 1932. The main regulation serving that purpose was the rule introduced in about 1924 limiting the output of transmitters located in heavily populated areas and requiring that more powerful transmitters (by which was meant at the time over 500 watts) be constructed in suburban or rural areas where their blanketing effect would bedevil fewer fans.[40]

A 1927 exchange of correspondence between Branch Director Edwards and Dr A.N. Goldsmith, chief broadcast engineer at RCA in New York, is enlightening in this respect. An RCA engineer had recently visited Toronto to install equipment at a Bowmanville location for the new Gooderham and Worts station, CKGW. Goldsmith wrote to Edwards to point out that his man felt that the 3.5 millivolt/metre strength the station gave in central Toronto was inadequate. Edwards, in reply, told Goldsmith that his mistake was in looking at the question from the "angle of the service you get in New York and the other big American cities." "Up here," he continued, "one millivolt per meter is regarded as a wonderful signal, as 90% of our stuff is taken from the States and we rarely get even [that]. With 3.5 you are doing very well, and my trouble is going to be to explain to the Toronto fans why the signal is so strong."[41] With Canadian radio listeners and authorities sharing that viewpoint, it is no wonder station power was kept so low.

Three years later Radio Branch engineer J.W. Bain prepared a memo for his superiors on field intensity that stated outright that Canadian output standards were considerably below those adhered to in both the US and Great Britain. This was nevertheless justifiable, he argued, because of the smaller number of congested urban centres and the superior interference-suppression service provided in Canada.[42] Bain suggested that the rural daytime minimum for "adequate service" should be .1 millivolts per metre, although he did admit that urban areas needed at least five times that intensity for comparable service, and that the three or four major Canadian cities might need as much as five or even ten millivolts. (At this standard, a 50-kw station could be heard about one hundred and seventy miles; a 5-kw station for one hundred and twenty-five.) He cautioned, however, against allowing any greater field intensity, because the resulting interference with reception of American stations would surely arouse objections from urban listeners.[43]

Until 1927, then, even the best Canadian stations remained much weaker than the continental standard. In 1927 and 1928, both CKGW and CFRB in Toronto were allowed to increase their power (CKGW to 5000 watts and CFRB to 4000), but only with the greatest caution and on condition that the augmentation could be cancelled on twenty-four hours' notice if listeners objected too strongly.[44] The increase, Radio Branch officials calculated, brought the stations' field strengths to somewhere between three and five millivolts per metre in the centre of the city (far below what would four years later be termed "very good" service).[45]

In fact there were no complaints at all from Toronto listeners when CFRB and CKGW increased their power and so the branch's extra-cautious policy began to be relaxed a bit. In early 1931 W.W. Grant's Calgary station, CFCN, with its transmitter located in Strathmore and in a less densely populated part of the country, was not only allowed to increase to 10,000 watts but was granted an exclusive channel because, as Edwards put it, "a high power station cannot be made to pay on a 'part time' basis."[46] In another interesting shift of emphasis, Edwards now championed Grant's station over that of the Calgary *Herald* (which had seniority in the market) because the broadcasting station was Grant's "sole business," while the *Herald* merely ran its station as an advertising adjunct to its main business, the newspaper.

By 1931 the branch was allowing a maximum of 10 mv/m field intensity in urban areas.[47] In December of that year CFRB Toronto was also permitted to increase its power to 10,000 watts, despite the fact that this doubled its field strength to 12 mv/m in central Toronto and to 15 in the northern suburbs (its transmitter was located in Aurora). To give it an equal chance to compete for commercial sponsors (because "the commercial advertiser always favours the high powered stations"), CKGW was also granted permission to go to 10,000 watts, although it did not in the end do so.[48] It might be noted that both the Calgary and Toronto power increases were sent for personal approval not only to Alfred Duranleau, the minister of Marine, but to Prime Minister Bennett.[49] Thus, as the reorganization necessitated by the new Broadcasting Act commenced in 1932, only three stations in Canada had been authorized to use 10,000 watts of power. By this time, it will be recalled, thirty-one American stations were routinely operating at this output or much more.

There were several reasons for the branch's move, gradual as it was, to permit higher power to Canadian stations. Rising levels of inductive and other interference were making more power necessary for optimum reception. The gradual acquisition of selective receivers was making broadcast listeners more tolerant and indeed more desirous of strong local stations.[50] The most important motivations, however, were related to the general North American situation. As early as 1927 Edwards had admitted to Ted Rogers that "in view of the large number of high power stations now in operation across the border, an increase in power at some of our own stations would be an advantage," although he had still added "provided that no undue inconvenience is caused thereby to Canadian listeners."[51] There were actually two aspects to the problem. One was discussed in the previous chapter: the need to prove Canada needed more exclusive channels in order to reinforce its North American allocation claims. Increasingly after

1927 Canadian officials showed a dawning realization that the only way to win the battle over wavelengths was by staking large claims for the northern half of the continent. The second was the difficulties caused by interference from high-power stations south of the border, particularly when they were on a channel adjoining a Canadian one. This was one of the main arguments used by CFRB (690 kHz) to get its increase: it claimed that it had lost a potential market in western Ontario because of the proximity of 50-kilowatt WLW Cincinnati on 700 kHz. As the decade ended, more and more listeners with more sophisticated sets and tastes were beginning to complain vociferously when programs on their favourite local stations were ruined, especially now that some of these stations also carried the most popular US network programs. "Canada's great need at this moment is more high powered broadcasting stations in order to offset interference from United States and Mexican stations," Alfred Duranleau wrote to the prime minister in December 1931.[52] Thus by late 1931, the Radio Branch had finally concluded that Canadian stations must be allowed to increase their power in order to compete in their local markets; otherwise the Canadian broadcasting industry would be severely damaged.

Until that time, however, the emphasis had been in the opposite direction. While it is unclear precisely how many requests for increased power were refused, such applications were routinely denied throughout the 1920s.[53] When increases were granted, it was at the initiative – frequently the oft-repeated initiative – of the broadcasters, never that of the branch. Even after 1931, when the need for more high-power stations was acknowledged by Ottawa, broadcasters granted an increase were still required to waive any claims to compensation for their expensive equipment in the event of nationalization. Thus in the crucial growth period, when the essential structures of the Canadian broadcasting industry were being formed, regulatory decisions helped contribute to the financial instability of Canadian stations and the inadequate local service they provided. While the Radio Branch was circumscribed in many ways in assigning frequencies and power to Canadian broadcasting stations, it also had considerable room for manoeuvre and sufficient discretionary authority to mould the development of Canadian broadcasting in many fundamental matters. Not only structural constraints but faulty regulatory decisions contributed to the weaknesses in the Canadian broadcasting industry everyone perceived by 1929.[54]

THE LAST FOUR CHAPTERS HAVE DISCUSSED how the officials of the Radio Branch used their authority to license, inspect, and assign wavelengths and power outputs to shape the growth of broadcasting in Canada. In 1986 the report of the Task Force on Broadcasting Policy (the Caplan-Sauvageau report) outlined four major processes that are involved in policy-making: defining the ends, choosing the means, carrying out the decisions, and evaluating the results.[55] The first of these tasks concerns the general, long-lasting objectives that overarch the other three; in the modern day these goals are defined by Parliament in the Broadcasting Act. Neither Parliament nor Cabinet nor even the minister of Marine and Fisheries, however, was involved in this sort of goal-setting vis-à-vis Canadian broadcasting prior to 1928. The only interest they showed in radio in the early 1920s was the occasional attempt to protect the business interests of their constituents or to bestow patronage; otherwise they left an area they considered primarily technical to the experts. The Radio Branch was thus a regulatory agency without a clearly defined mandate.

Nevertheless, in the course of exercising their authority Radio Branch officials had many decisions to make, decisions that inevitably involved value judgments. Lacking guidance from above, branch officials evolved their own priorities and policies. Two main principles underlay the actions of the Ottawa officials throughout: maintaining maximum flexibility and serving the listeners. Edwards summed it up to one correspondent: "We are here to endeavour to see that the public gets what it wants, and so far we have been chary about making regulations ... The fewer regulations we can get along with, the better for radio. On the other hand, once the Department is satisfied that a regulation on a certain point is essential in the public interest and demanded by the public, we will be only too pleased to put the same in effect, and, what is more to the point, strictly enforce it."[56] This approach, in both its aspects, was adopted with the best of intentions. Flexibility, virtually everyone believed, was essential in a context of fast-changing technologies, markets, and habits, especially on a continent dominated by the rapidly emerging world leader in broadcasting. No doubts were ever expressed about the Radio Branch's goal, oft-repeated from 1922 through to 1932, "to introduce as few restrictions as possible in regard to broadcasting, in order that the development of the art may not be hampered by unwise regulations."[57] The position seems on the surface both sensible and admirable. Indeed, the one clear case where it was not followed, the overly rigid decision to ban records, was the classic exception that proved the rule.

But radio, even in its earliest days, *had* to be regulated. Because of the limitations of the spectrum and the dangers of interference, both national and international regulation were instituted from the beginning. Canada was no exception. As a compromise between the desire for flexibility and the need to regulate, and in the absence of policy directives from Parliament, the Radio Branch's actions essentially came down to the practice of keeping the written rules to a minimum while making *ad hoc* decisions whenever necessary.

Some analysts of administrative policy-making have argued that this method of "muddling through," or less pejoratively, of "building out from the current situation, step-by-step and by small degrees," is the most desirable in a pluralist society and indeed the only realistic way to make public policy.[58] According to this argument, it is not only impossible but inappropriate for public administrators to attempt to clarify objectives rationally and comprehensively in advance – they simply cannot know enough. Rather, they endeavour continually to make small adjustments based on specific comparisons and choices. The Radio Branch's adoption of this approach certainly seems appropriate given the state of radio in the 1920s; it would indeed have been risky to lay down the law for all future development of Canadian broadcasting in 1922. Most other jurisdictions avoided this sort of prior commitment too.

There are, however, certain disadvantages to *ad hoc* policy-making that are also evident in the case of Canadian radio in the 1920s. One is that avoiding the clarification of values, objectives, and alternatives tends to lead to inertia, to an avoidance of change. This is particularly unfortunate in instances such as this one when new technology offering the possibility of new directions is ignored.[59] A second possibly disadvantageous result of the emphasis on flexibility also applies to early radio. How can one take an incremental approach to changing policies when there are no past decisions to build upon? Broadcasting in the 1920s was new; its problems had never been encountered before. Significantly, the only field in which the Radio Branch officials had commendable success – namely the suppression of electrical interference – was the one in which it *was* possible to build upon previous knowledge, and precisely the type of knowledge Radio Branch employees were most apt to possess. In other areas, in which technical knowledge was lacking or insufficient, or where value-laden economic, political, or cultural factors came into play, the branch's officials floundered, fudged, and often made decisions ultimately contrary to the optimum development of Canadian broadcasting.

Yet another flaw in the flexible, pragmatic, incremental approach to policy-making is that external pressures are a greater factor in the choices ultimately made than would be the case if general principles were laid down in advance.[60] Thus the marked vulnerability of the Radio Branch to listener desires and political influence. That it was part of a government department headed by a minister of course meant that the branch was necessarily political in the way a separate regulatory commission might not have been. But the lack of clearly enunciated principles exacerbated this vulnerability to a point that by 1928 had become intolerable to many.

The greatest weakness of the *ad hoc* approach, however, was that it hid the fact that rules were in fact constantly being instituted, enforced, examined, and revised during the 1920s. By the end of the decade a number of principles and priorities had been established that set the mould for all future broadcasting in Canada. But because they were formed by the process of the accretion of individual judgments, they lacked clarity, visibility, and coherence. Flexibility in a formative period is admirable, yet the accumulation of individual decisions implants a structure that is difficult and often impossible to alter. Choices once made make other alternatives difficult to recapture. The cumulative effect of many small policies was in fact a Policy for Canadian broadcasting, and one with many flaws. Incremental policy-making did have long-term consequences, intended or not.[61]

The desire to be flexible was primarily motivated by the branch's desire, at all costs, to please the listeners. Throughout most of the 1920s the branch's policies seem to have focused almost entirely on the goal of giving the listeners what they wanted – even when that meant catering to inferior equipment or to the yen for American popular culture. While listeners' opinions were not systematically sampled, their views were recorded and regarded. Local inspectors and radio listener clubs, especially, were solicited for their views on local broadcasting issues, and so were individuals.[62] "Always remember," Edwards wrote to an acquaintance in Victoria, "that we public servants are paid to attend to your requirements, but that not being mind readers, we have to be told about them before being able to attend to same."[63]

There were good reasons for this sensitivity to the listeners. As an early commentator remarked: "The future of broadcasting depends to some extent upon the success with which it can be brought to the listener who can afford only a low price receiving set." Edwards, in his *Annual Report* in 1924–25, spelled it out succinctly: "Without the broadcast listener, there would be no broadcasting and therefore in the administration of broadcasting, the wishes and the interests of the broadcast listener must be paramount."[64] But catering too much to listeners' preferences also wreaked great damage on early Canadian broadcasting, specifically by hampering the broadcasters in their quest for financial stability. Finding the balance between listener preferences and the general good of the industry was not necessarily easy; the problem was that up to 1929 if not later the Radio Branch threw all its weight on the side of the former at the expense of the latter. P.J.A. Cardin, as minister of Marine and Fisheries, justified the non-renewal of the broadcasting licences of the International Bible Students' Association stations in 1928 in precisely these terms: "After all the public at large, the listeners-in, are to be considered first; the welfare, the benefit and the enjoyment of the mass of the population which is composed of the listeners-in should be considered *before anything else.*"[65] [emphasis added]

The wishes of listeners were always diverse and, as radio developed during the decade, they changed. Again, the flexible approach adopted by the branch seems eminently sensible. But problems resulted here as well. Many listeners wished to be able to receive American stations clearly, so they wanted local stations to be few, weak, and limited in broadcasting hours. Lacking broader policy goals for the development of Canadian radio either as business or culture, the branch simply acquiesced to the listener lobby and adopted regulations whose consequences were harmful to Canadian private broadcasters. The difficulty was not so much that the listeners' views were solicited and respected; that surely is a good thing. Rather, it was the very narrow and short-term view of listener preferences, or to put it another way, the lack of any sense of a more broadly defined "public interest."

Many Canadian radio fans in the 1920s, like magazine readers before them and television viewers since, were attracted to American popular culture. Canadian regulators in the 1920s acknowledged and accepted that fact. But if they also believed in building a Canadian broadcasting industry alongside the American, they had to find ways to reconcile the two desires. Policy-making by "muddling through" prevented a creative or innovative or even self-interested stance on the question. The branch's deliberate avoidance of this or any other cultural issue left it vulnerable to criticism from all those individuals and groups in both English and French Canada who were beginning by the end of the 1920s to perceive that radio was a cultural medium of central significance to Canadian society.

The officials of the Radio Branch strove to create a broadcasting system that respected such fundamental Canadian principles as equity, efficiency, and individual liberty insofar as was compatible with the uncertainties of the technological and economic environment in which they had to operate.[66] However, they evinced little interest in two other traditional Canadian concerns: national identity and regional loyalty. Their unwillingness to deal with questions of regional and national identity – that is, to confront the cultural dimensions of radio – left them open to charges of failure by contemporary commentators and future historians alike. After 1928, when radio's cultural and national role came under increasing public scrutiny, the calls for a new regulatory agency capable of recognizing and administering these new priorities also grew in volume.

In sum, although a variety of beliefs, assumptions, and principles lay behind the decisions of Radio Branch officials in the 1920s, they never tried to lead Canadian broadcasters or listeners to a vision of a long-term goal for Canadian radio. But that, of course, was not their responsibility. The larger sense of purpose and leadership should have come from the minister, the Cabinet, and the government as a whole. Balancing the technical, political, economic, and cultural aspects of radio regulation in the formative period was by no means an easy task. The lack of political oversight and the bias of the Radio Branch toward maximum flexibility meant that guidelines replaced both rules and principles and that even these loose strictures were developed gradually and without external consultation or debate. Dissatisfaction with two outstanding failures of that policy approach led to the establishment of the Aird Royal Commission on Radio Broadcasting and eventually to the new regulatory system enshrined in the Radio Broadcasting Act of 1932.

PART THREE

9 The Aird Commission

When 1928 began, broadcasting had received very little public discussion in Canada. While the numbers of those who listened in was steadily growing, few concerned themselves with questioning the directions in which Canadian radio was developing, how it was regulated and controlled, or what its cultural implications might be. Neither had the subject reached the political agenda; aside from the occasional broadcast speech or attempt to aid a supporter who might want a broadcasting licence, politicians paid little attention to radio. Within a few months, however, the curtain was to be raised on a full-fledged debate which raged on and off for four years before finally resulting in the creation of the Canadian Radio Broadcasting Commission, a combined national broadcasting company and regulatory agency.

Two specific issues impelled the creation of the Royal Commission on Radio Broadcasting, commonly known as the Aird commission after its chairman, Sir John Aird. The first was the non-renewal in March 1928 of five broadcasting licences held by the International Bible Students Association and its affiliate, Universal Radio of Canada; the second was a partisan battle over the assignment of wavelengths in the Toronto area.

To understand the IBSA case, it is necessary to set it in the context of general Radio Branch policy regarding the licensing of religious organizations. As has already been mentioned, as early as 1923 commercial broadcasters began placing "remote" equipment in churches to broadcast Sunday services. Radio Branch officials had no problem with this practice and indeed granted preference in Sunday time allotments to stations airing church broadcasts.[1] They did urge the commercial broadcasters, however, to be broad and flexible in choosing which churches to serve in this way.[2]

Apparently pleased with the response from the isolated, elderly, and shut-in, during 1924 and 1925 several Canadian churches and religious organizations applied for and were granted licences for either phantom or actual broadcasting stations, including the Victoria City Temple (CFCT) and Toronto's Jarvis Street Baptist Church (CJBC). (The former soon passed out of the church's hands; the latter actually began broadcasting through CKGW only in 1930.) In Vancouver, First Congregational Church (after 1925 First United) set up CKFC, which broadcast its own services and those of a Presbyterian Church on Sundays and music on Thursday nights.[3]

It is not clear how carefully the Ottawa officials thought through the implications of their decision to grant broadcasting licences to religious bodies. Several difficulties were involved. Once one or two groups were granted licences, how could others be refused without risking a charge of religious discrimination? But broadcasting wavelengths were a scarce resource; how many could be tied up with religious stations? By the end of 1927 the Radio Branch had had to confront these issues but had essentially avoided resolving them by simply granting all requests. In at least one case, the 1927 licensing of the Christian and Missionary Alliance station CHMA in Edmonton, this meant forcing four stations to share a single wavelength, a breach of the standard three-station-per-frequency rule. Deputy Minister Johnston summed up the branch's policy on church stations in an admonitory letter to CHMA:

The policy of the Department, based on the wishes of the listeners, is to permit only one station on the air at a time in any city. On the other hand, the Department cannot favour one denomination at the expense of another ... We would very much prefer that churches should make use of available commercial stations, but if they insist on having their own apparatus, we are not disposed to refuse their applications, provided they thoroughly understand the severe limitations which must be attached to their license in order to preserve equality between the many denominations which desire to broadcast.[4]

In addition to those just mentioned, there were five other religious stations licensed in Canada by the end of 1927. One was CKSM, the phantom of St Michael's Cathedral in Toronto, which used CFRB's facilities. The other four, CHUC Saskatoon, CHCY Edmonton, CFYC Vancouver, and CKCX Toronto, were operated by the International Bible Students Association, a religious sect that had originated in the United States under the leadership of Pastor Charles Taze Russell in the early twentieth century and that in 1931 would take the name Jehovah's Witnesses.[5]

The IBSA apparently first applied for a licence in Toronto in 1922, but were turned down because "it would not be in the best interests of the .

public."[6] In 1924 another IBSA group made an application for a licence in Saskatoon. Commander Edwards wrote the local inspector, J. Macklem, to solicit his opinion, admitting that head office was "not at all enthusiastic about granting such licenses," partly because of complaints about the two or three IBSA stations already in operation in the United States.[7] Macklem, however, responded in favour of permitting a low-power, limited-hour station, on the grounds that the Bible Students were very popular in Saskatoon and that there were few other stations for lonely Saskatchewan settlers to listen to. On that advice, the station was licensed as CHUC late in 1924.[8] Similar stations were licensed in Edmonton and Vancouver on 1 April 1926.[9] In the meantime, in Toronto, some members of the IBSA along with "other prominent men of the City of Toronto" conceived the idea of forming a company called Universal Radio of Canada to erect a commercial station, CJYC.[10] Walter F. Salter, the Canadian general manager of the IBSA, became the president of Universal Radio, which was granted a licence in January 1926. That August, the IBSA was also granted a Toronto licence for the phantom station CKCX, which would use the facilities of CJYC.

The Radio Branch began to receive a significant number of complaints about the IBSA stations beginning in late 1926, of sufficient import that Deputy Minister of Marine and Fisheries Johnston made a special note in the file of CHUC that "the operations should be carefully observed and considered when time for renewal of license arrives."[11] Nevertheless, the licences of all five stations were routinely renewed on 1 April 1927. Over the next year listener dissatisfaction with the stations, particularly the one in Toronto, continued to mount. There is no doubt that the Radio Branch received far more criticism of these stations than of any others it administered in the 1920s. By March 1928 a total of about one hundred letters, many of them heated, had reached Ottawa, as well as a petition signed by 199 members of a Toronto radio club. Among those who wrote were ordinary listeners, local dignitaries, radio inspectors, mainline church officials, and several Members of Parliament. The subject was also aired in the letters-to-the-editor columns of some of the Toronto newspapers.

On 8 March 1928 Deputy Minister Johnston wrote to Universal Radio, informing the company that the licence of CJYC Toronto would not be renewed for the next fiscal year, and a similar letter was sent to the IBSA regarding the other four stations on the 15th of the month.[12] No reason was given. The act was almost unprecedented. No other operative Canadian station desiring renewal had ever been refused it, although, as we have seen, some had regularly breached various regulations. Because of a lack of surviving sources, it may never be possible to be absolutely sure why the Radio Branch officials took this step against the IBSA stations. Nevertheless, a closer examination of the accusations made against the stations and the defence offered by the Bible Students may help clarify at least how justifiable the action was.

Copies of all the complaints against the IBSA stations received by the Radio Branch before April 1928 were later tabled in the House of Commons at the request of two members of the Independent Labour Party (ILP), J.S. Woodsworth and A.A. Heaps. The criticisms differed somewhat from city to city. Of the five letters on file from Edmonton, four (including two from MP K.A. Blatchford reporting the views of numerous constituents) grumbled that CHCY interfered with reception of other stations, while one from the medical officer of health denounced a particular program that had condemned vaccination, inoculation, canned foods, and the medical profession. From Saskatoon there was a 1927 resolution from the Board of Trade requesting that the station be limited to Sundays only and several anguished letters from Mr Macklem, the inspector who had supported the station's licensing in the first place, detailing his attempts to get the CHUC management to be reasonable in its demands for weekday broadcast time and admitting that he had received "a continual deluge of complaints" about the station.[13] There seems to have been little protest from ordinary listeners in Vancouver, but the Greater Vancouver Radio Association and the Retail Trades Association sent in a recommendation in early 1928 that the injurious overcrowding of the Vancouver airwaves could best be cured by the cancellation of the licences of two stations inferior in both technical and programming quality, one of them being CFYC, the IBSA station.[14]

By far the largest number of letters were about the Toronto station. About twenty of the correspondents objected to CKCX's power and wavelength assignment, which they claimed prevented reception of many better stations such as WJZ and WEAF. Another ten or so were particularly upset because on a number of occasions CKCX cut into the CFRB broadcast of the Reverend W.A. Cameron's popular Sunday evening sermon from Bloor Street Baptist Church. About thirty of the letter-writers, as well as the 199 signatories of the Toronto Radio Club's petition, were primarily incensed about the Bible Students' message, which was deemed unpatriotic and seditious in its attacks on the British empire and slanderous and blasphemous in its references to the major churches.[15] Ordinary citizens in Toronto were probably more aware of the Bible Students' doctrine than those of many other cities because a large convention in the summer of 1927 had received quite a bit of local publicity. That convention had adopted a resolution condemning the "unholy alliance" of politicians, big businessmen, and the clergy of Christendom; the convention speeches of judge Rutherford, the sect's leader, were broadcast – a "nightly nuisance," according to an editorial in *Saturday Night* at the time.[16]

A few excerpts from letters to the Radio Branch give the flavour of the outrage about the Toronto radio station:

I think I can truthfully say that station CKCX is the most unpopular of any Toronto station. They seem to be on the air more than any other station and they are always broadcasting religious propaganda of the premilleniul [*sic*] type in a way that is offensive to all the leading protestant denominations as well as the catholic. [J.H. Cranston, editor, *Toronto Star Weekly*]

If there is a nuisance on the street, police will remove it. CKCX is a nuisance on the air and should be removed. [W. Strudwick]

It would seem to me that the Department of Radio through the government should advise a little more discretion on their part, because I am afraid any more lack of christian charity on their part will result in the future in a nation-wide agitation to remove them entirely from the air. [Dr H.H. Armstrong]

The CKCX nuisance is becoming intolerable. Their patriotism is poor and their religion is worse. I have given away my radio set rather than endure such gratuitous nuisance. [Ex-Radio Fan]

While these letters undoubtedly gave the Ottawa officials pause, even more significant were several from the reliable Toronto radio inspector S.J. Ellis. Ellis wrote to head office:

With particular reference to CKCX owned and operated by the IBSA, I might say that the verbal complaints against the class of programme broadcasted by this station have been innumerable. The main objection is to the controversial nature of the programmes, which the Radio Public, generally speaking, terms propaganda. On several occasions I have listened to the so-called Bible Students and have heard some slanderous statements made against the Roman Catholic and Protestant Churches and Clergy. As you know, I am in very close touch with the situation, and have yet to meet the person who approves of the type of programmes being broadcasted by Station CKCX.

In view of the above I would strongly recommend that the Department refuse to renew the license for the coming fiscal year 1928–29.[17]

It was suggested at the time and has been suggested since that the most influential opponents of the IBSA stations were the clergy and officials of the major churches and that, more specifically, Minister of Marine and Fisheries P.J.A. Cardin and Deputy Minister Alexander Johnston, both devout Roman Catholics, closed the stations down as punishment for the Bible Students' attacks on their church and its priests.[18] In the surviving written record, however, there are only four or five letters from clergy or church officials, none of them Roman Catholic. The most irate was A.C. Crews, who was in charge of Sunday School publications for the United Church. Crews wrote several times both to the Toronto inspector and to the

Ottawa office calling for some sort of censorship of the Bible Students' Toronto station for its attacks on the major Christian denominations. In one of those letters, he made a point which no doubt struck a responsive chord at the Radio Branch: "If these people wish to declare their doctrines in their own meetings, or if they desire to publish them in their books, they are, of course, free to do so. The people who disagree with them do not need to attend their services or to read their literature, but to have their harangues broadcast upon the air and forced upon the people generally is scarcely less than an outrage. ... Surely this is a misuse of the privilege which has been granted to them."[19] Another kind of chord may have been struck by a comment in Crews's final letter to the Radio Branch. After inquiring rhetorically whether there was any supervision whatsoever of the programs broadcast on Canadian stations, he warned, "If there is not, then an agitation must be begun at once to secure legislation to cover such a situation."[20]

The Bible Students did not hesitate to defend themselves or to condemn the Radio Branch. Petitions and letters supporting the IBSA stations, many of them solicited, poured into the branch, to individual politicians, to the prime minister, and to Parliament, and a number of protest meetings were held.[21] On several points, the Bible Students' case was sound. For example, the fact that their Toronto station interfered with reception of several popular American stations was entirely the responsibility of the branch, which assigned their wavelength. Any local station using that frequency would have had the same effect (although it is true that CFRB, with which CJYC shared the wavelength, aroused much less hostility).[22] As to cutting off Cameron's sermons, the Bible Students were quite justified in pointing out that they had been assigned by mutual agreement the time from 8:15 to midnight on Sunday nights and that it was not their fault if Cameron could not keep within his time limit.[23]

The Bible Students and their supporters, including a number of MP's who spoke in the parliamentary debate on the subject, also specifically condemned the cancellation of the licence of CJYC Toronto. That station, they claimed, was not a religious station but a commercial one, owned by a company separate from the IBSA, established at a cost of upwards of $50,000 and broadcasting material other than the programs of the IBSA phantom CKCX.[24] This position had considerable validity. The complaints the branch received from Toronto listeners named CKCX; few attacked CJYC as such. Religion dominated CKCX broadcasting on Sundays but the rest of the week was filled with a variety of sponsored and sustaining musical programs such as those on any other station.

As to the nature of their message, the Bible Students, along with some important allies, insisted that their teachings were neither abusive nor unpatriotic but simply represented their own search for the truth.[25] They were critical of secular authorities and other churches, yes, but that was only because they were attempting to herald the good tidings of "God's righteous Kingdom" which would soon supplant all nations. Surely they had the right to voice their beliefs. As one IBSA document put it:

No one holds the exclusive right to teach the Bible, and though not every one will agree with the Bible Students, all fair-minded persons will agree that every man should have the right to fully and freely speak the truth as he understands it, and all have the right to accept or reject as they may choose. Why should the Bible Students be discriminated against? In the city of Toronto, a few Sundays ago, services were broadcast from the Roman Catholic Church, the Anglican Church, the Jewish Synagogue, the Baptist Church and the United Church. Would not justice to all demand that the Bible Students be granted a like privilege?[26]

Thus the issue became one of free speech, specifically the freedom to express one's religious beliefs and the freedom to criticize authority, and on that ground the IBSA rallied to its side a number of important spokesmen, including representatives of organized farm and labour groups and, in the House of Commons, some members of the ILP and the Progressive Party.[27]

It was with respect to this argument for freedom of speech that the point made by Mr Crews of the United Church was important. How could the right to express one's ideas freely be put into practice on the new medium of radio? As already described in Chapter 6, the officials of the Radio Branch and the Department of Marine and Fisheries had bent over backwards from the day they began regulating broadcasting to avoid seeming to censor programming. Nevertheless, they believed that the radio spectrum was not and could never be a completely free market-place for ideas because of its unique ability to carry messages right to the family hearthside and because of the shortage of wavelengths available for broadcasters. Cardin used this point in the House as one of his main arguments in defence of his department's actions:

Certain people have said: Well we have freedom of the press, we have freedom of writing, and so on. But the same principle cannot be applied to radio broadcasting. If you are not satisfied with a book you are not forced to read it; similarly, if you do not like the way in which a newspaper is conducted you are not forced to read it, and if you are not in sympathy with the objects of a meeting you are not obliged to attend and listen to the speeches. But in view of the fact that radio receiving-sets are not yet so perfected as to enable you to eliminate any station whose broadcasting you do not wish to listen to, you are forced to listen or not use your receiving-set at all.[28]

In a very important sense, however, the issue of the Bible Students' stations was *not* one of free speech versus censorship. No one denied the organization the right to broadcast its views if it could find a commercial station willing to give it time, and throughout this period and later Bible Students' programs were heard regularly on many Canadian stations, including CKY Winnipeg, CJGC London, and CKMO Vancouver.[29] Although many neglected to make the distinction, it was the privilege of owning broadcasting stations that the IBSA lost in 1928, not the right to broadcast.

The problem with the branch's action against the IBSA stations was that it was a particular rather than a general attempt to deal with the dilemma of censorship and free speech. If the granting of broadcasting licences to religious organizations gave them too much freedom to espouse their own doctrines at the expense of others, why were the licences of the other church-owned stations not also cancelled in 1928?[30] If it was the specific message of the Bible Students which was so offensive to a large number of listeners, why were their broadcasts from commercial stations not also banned?[31] And how did one draw the line between the acceptable and the not, especially when there was no taped or written record of what had actually gone out over the air? Finally, why were the Bible Students not given adequate warning of their sins, and a fair chance to remedy them?

On this point the Radio Branch officials may definitely be faulted, particularly when one compares the treatment of the IBSA stations with the flexibility and tolerance shown to virtually every other station in the country during this experimental period.[32] Cardin admitted to the House that the IBSA stations in fact received almost no prior warning that their licences were in jeopardy.[33] The closest the branch came to admonishing them was a meeting held in January 1928 between Deputy Minister Johnston and Salter, at which they mainly discussed complaints that had arisen about airtime given to J.J. Maloney of the Ku Klux Klan on CHUC. Salter not only apologized both verbally and in writing for this indiscretion but made sure that the contract with Maloney was cancelled.[34] As he pointed out on numerous occasions later, however (never denied by Johnston), he did not conclude at all from this interview that there were any other more substantial problems with the stations' programming.[35]

Whatever the reasons for the non-renewal of the IBSA stations' licences, and undoubtedly listener and official disgust with the content of the messages being broadcast was central to that action, the Ottawa authorities mishandled the case. Their errors were caused by the virtually complete absence of policy guidelines for managing problems relating to radio's role as a transmitter of ideas and culture. Cardin claimed in the House of Commons that the Bible Students' licences had to be cancelled because that was the Radio Branch's only remedy for non-compliance with its regulations. But what regulations, the Bible Students quite justifiably asked, had they broken? The answer was none, because no rules about program content had ever been enunciated. Until 1928 Radio Branch officials succeeded in concentrating on technical questions and avoiding political and cultural issues. The crisis over the IBSA stations made it clear to all that that era was over.

SHORTLY AFTER THE CANCELLATION OF the licence of CJYC Toronto, Universal Radio's lawyers wrote a formal letter of protest to Prime Minister Mackenzie King. They claimed that upon interviewing "a number of persons interested in the broadcasting business," they had discovered unanimous agreement that the real problem with broadcasting in Toronto lay not with CJYC but in "the activity of a certain Journal ... who [sic] are seeking special privileges which apparently are denied to all others."[36] The journal to which the lawyers referred was the Toronto *Star*. Not only broadcasters but many others, including ordinary listeners, the Toronto *Telegram*, and the parliamentary opposition, agreed that the Radio Branch's assignment of an exclusive wavelength to the *Star*'s station, CFCA, which occurred virtually simultaneously with the non-renewal of the Bible Students' licences, was equally reprehensible. In Toronto and in Ottawa, the two issues became inextricably entangled. At least one Member of Parliament openly accused the government of cancelling CJYC's licence not because of its IBSA connections but for the ulterior motive of freeing a frequency for CFCA.[37]

CFCA was the pioneer Toronto broadcasting station. From 1922 to 1924 it was the only station operating on a regular basis in the Toronto market. In 1924 and 1925 two more stations commenced broadcasting, CKNC (owned by Canadian National Carbon) and CKCL (Dominion Battery). With CFCA they shared the 840-kHz wavelength.[38] Joseph Atkinson considered closing CFCA down at this point; although he decided in the end to leave it open, the station was starved for resources in the latter 1920s. Toronto became the first city in Canada with dual broadcasting in 1926. When the Bible Students' station CJYC was licensed in January of that year, it was assigned to the 1030-kHz "district" wavelength (later changed to 580 kHz), with its transmitter in suburban Scarborough. In early 1927, when CFRB (owned by Canadian radio manufacturer Rogers Majestic) began operations, it was required to share time with CJYC on 580, despite an attempt by Minister of Trade and Commerce James Malcolm to persuade Edwards to give "our friend Ted Rogers" a better wavelength.[39]

The pressure on the Toronto wavelengths continued to grow. As previously mentioned, Gooderham and Worts distillers purchased a licence from a defunct company in the spring of 1927 and set out to build a powerful modern station. When the Radio Branch approved the transfer of ownership of the licence it warned Gooderham and Worts that it would have to share time with not more than two other stations, but when the new station, CKGW, came on the air in early 1928 branch officials apparently decided that further time division on the two existing wavelengths was not feasible, so a third wavelength was authorized for use in the Toronto area, 960 kHz, and CKGW was assigned to it.[40]

On 13 February 1928 Main Johnson, director of CFCA, wrote Deputy Minister Johnston to complain about the arrangement which gave the new station full time on its wavelength while CFCA, the pioneer Toronto broadcaster, was forced to share time with two others. Three days later he went to Ottawa to press his case in person.[41] Exactly what decisions were taken when, by whom, and why unfortunately remains unclear, for they were the nub of the whole controversy. Privately, *Telegram* personnel claimed that "the Radio Division of the Dept. of M. & F. ... passed out of the picture early in the performance" and that the key to the whole affair lay in a meeting between Joseph Atkinson and Mackenzie King, who subsequently "took a hand" to insure that the *Star* was granted a more favourable position.[42]

On 8 March 1928 CJYC was told that its licence would not be renewed and on 9 March a general reorganization of the Toronto wavelengths was begun. CKGW was informed that it would henceforth have to share 960 kHz with CFRB; CKCL and CKNC were transferred to 580 kHz, and CFCA, the *Star*'s station, was left (alone) on 840.[43] The net result was that CFRB remained able to broadcast half the hours in the week, CKGW went from full to half time, CKNC and CKLC both went from one-third to one-half time, and CFCA went from one-third to full time. That trouble erupted should not have been a surprise in Ottawa, especially as the *Star*, whose station had gained the most in the shuffle, was a Liberal paper while the rival Conservative journal in Toronto, the *Telegram*, broadcast through CKGW, the station that had lost the most.

The ensuing political vituperation does not need much comment. Much was said about the relative merits of the various stations and the various wavelengths.[44] Much more was said about the bias of the Department of Marine and Fisheries, its minister, and the prime minister. Whatever the truth of the accusation that CFCA had been favoured because of the *Star*'s Liberal loyalties, the important point is that the case revealed another profound weakness in the regulatory structure overseeing broadcasting since its inception: its vulnerability to the charge of political influence. Instances of the involvement of politicians in the decisions of the Radio Branch have been detailed in earlier chapters; if that occurred in Toronto in 1928, as it probably did, it was certainly not unique. Partly because it was linked to the equally controversial IBSA decision, however, the Toronto wavelength assignment blew up into a storm of unprecedented proportions. The defensive and embarrassed minister, P.J.A. Cardin, told the House on 1 June:

We have reached a point where it is impossible for a member of the government ...

to exercise the discretionary power which is given by the law and by the regulations as they stand today, for the very reason that the moment the minister in charge exercises his discretion, the matter becomes a political football and a political issue all over Canada ... We should change that situation and take radio broadcasting away from the influences of all sorts which are brought to bear by all shades of political parties. This will avoid much trouble for the government, and I think will result in greater satisfaction for the public at large.

He continued:

We are not prepared to evolve a scheme at present, because we have not in our possession all the information we will need. We are inclined to follow that plan which has been established and which is operating at present in England; our idea would be to establish a company, the shares of which would be the property of the Canadian government and to appoint special men, who are called governors in England, to look after the issuing of licenses and the regulation of everything else in regard to this important business.[45]

The next day he asked Parliament to allocate $25,000 for the expenses of an investigative commission "to enquire into the radio broadcasting situation throughout Canada, and to advise as to the future administration, management, control and finance thereof." "We want to inquire in England, the United States, and Canada as to the best means for Canada to adopt in dealing with radio broadcasting," he told the MP's, and then hinted rather broadly at the anticipated conclusion: "We want this information before coming to parliament with a bill nationalizing the system, or some such method." The expenditure was authorized without dissent.[46]

Before proceeding with the discussion of the Royal Commission on Radio Broadcasting, one point needs clarification. A prime difficulty in assessing the positions and intentions of the various participants in the radio debate between 1928 and 1932 is that of vocabulary. Often words such as "national broadcasting policy," "national system," "government control," and even "public broadcasting" were used imprecisely. None of these terms necessarily meant government ownership and operation of Canada's broadcasting stations, much less a government monopoly. To some, they suggested only a better regulatory system and possibly more emphasis on broadcasting as a public service (for example, through some government-sponsored programming). Even the use of the phrase "like the British system" is less than clear. Until 1 January 1927, British broadcasting was run as a private monopoly, owned by the major equipment manufacturers under close government control; only after that date did it become what we would today call a crown corporation (although in both variations it was funded wholly by licence and other fees and carried no advertising).

After 1929, the language used in Canada tended to be less ambiguous, for the debate became focused on the Aird report's recommendations (although they were unclear in some respects as well), but generally great caution must be taken throughout to represent positions accurately. The terminology used in the text (as distinct from the quotations) in the next three chapters will adhere as much as possible to what is commonly understood today. Specifically, the terms "public broadcasting" and "nationalization" will be used only to mean a crown-corporation type of arrangement with government ownership of broadcasting facilities, although not necessarily in a monopoly position.

Despite some vagueness, however, Cardin's use of the term "nationalizing" along with his reference to the system "which is operating at present in England" suggest that he *was* hinting at the institution of public ownership of broadcasting in Canada. Nevertheless, it is curious that the minister so quickly suggested that nationalizing broadcasting "along the lines adopted ... by the British government" (to quote the phraseology he used on 12 April, the first day he faced questioning about the IBSA case in the House) was a possible solution to the difficulties that had made radio a "political football" in the spring of 1928. Previously, there had been virtually no public, official, or private discussion of such a possibility for Canada. Neither was it the only alternative to the regulatory problems revealed by the IBSA and Toronto wavelength cases: simply taking radio regulation out of the hands of the minister and giving it to a body operating at arm's length from the government would have been perfectly feasible. Indeed, this was the system the Americans had implemented just a year earlier with the creation of the Federal Radio Commission. One can only conclude, then, that although they were not much discussed in the parliamentary debate in April and May of 1928, fundamental questions about Canadian broadcasting beyond the issue of control and regulation were concerning Cardin considerably.

Why this was so is not completely clear, in part because neither Cabinet records nor Cardin's own correspondence have survived. Cardin himself had shown little evidence of interest in or concern about radio prior to this time; radio was only one branch of a multifaceted department where many other issues dominated. Mackenzie King's diary certainly contains no hint that the push came from his direction. In fact, the prime minister made no mention of the radio issue during the spring of 1928; his only comment about parliamentary business on 2 June, the day the radio commission was announced, was that the House had concluded its debate on supply for Marine and Fisheries.[47]

On one level, clearly the commission was a device to delay a political problem and get it out of the House for awhile. Cardin plainly was exasperated both with the situation and the system which had engendered it.

He was probably aware as well that by 1928 a number of countries, after five or six years of experimental development, were undertaking this same process of rethinking their broadcasting arrangements.

As to why he hinted at nationalization, it may be that Cardin shared with some of his English-speaking colleagues a tendency to look to Britain as a model for Canadian institutional arrangements. Once the flaws in the prevailing system were revealed, turning to the British alternative may have been almost second-nature. In France as well, the state was beginning to think about recapturing its monopoly of broadcasting by ceasing to issue permits to private companies. Perhaps the railway nationalization model was also in his mind; the CNR/broadcasting connection would have encouraged that.

It is also possible that the government's action was in part stimulated by the increasingly loudly expressed concerns of the nationalist élite in both English- and French-speaking Canada in the 1920s about the vulnerability of Canadian culture and ultimately of Canada's national identity to the flood of American popular culture pouring over the border. There is little doubt that this concern, as organized and orchestrated by Graham Spry and Alan Plaunt of the Canadian Radio League, had a political impact after 1930. It may not be going too far to suggest that the Liberal government was responsive to this issue as early as 1928. Certainly it had been very much "in the air" since the war ended, and any MP who read Canadian magazines, attended Canadian Club luncheons, or occasionally visited the National Gallery could not have been unaware of it. The plight of Canadian magazines in particular in the face of American competition had been debated in Parliament and had been before the Tariff Advisory Board.[48] As early as 1924 an article in widely read *MacLean's* had made the radio connection: "Just as it is a tremendous pity that American magazines flood our book shops and news stands, that American news is given so much prominence in our newspapers and that American-made photo-dramas monopolize our moving-picture houses, so it is unfortunate that nine out of ten radio fans in Canada will pick up more American than Canadian stations almost every night in the week."[49]

A network of lobbyists for Canadian culture had grown up over the course of the twenties, and their ideas were circulating widely by 1928. One of their great successes was the Diamond Jubilee celebration of 1927, largely orchestrated by the Association of Canadian Clubs, of which Graham Spry was secretary, which highlighted the first nation-wide radio hookup. Mackenzie King was apparently quite impressed with the power of broadcasting revealed on that occasion.[50] Thus, although there had been very little explicit discussion of radio as a vehicle of Canadian culture prior to 1928, the sudden revelation of difficulties in the broadcasting system occurred in an environment of considerable interest in questions of national unity and cultural identity in English Canada particularly.

Here the role of Charles Bowman, editor of the Liberal Ottawa *Citizen*, was significant. Bowman had developed an early interest in radio regulation partly because he was a neighbour of C.P. Edwards in Rockcliffe Park and in 1926 had visited the British broadcasting headquarters in London while accompanying Mackenzie King to the Imperial Conference.[51] According to his own testimony, he was so impressed with what he saw that he became convinced that Canada needed a new, national broadcasting policy.[52] Occasionally during 1927 and more systematically during the spring of 1928 he published a series of editorials in the *Citizen* (picked up by a number of other papers as well) urging a new radio policy for Canada and specifically warning that if nothing were done Canadian radio would suffer the fate of the Canadian movie industry, namely monopoly control by "some parent corporation in the United States."[53] Bowman's stance was strong from the beginning: "The problem to be decided is whether private vested interests are to be allowed to become established in a new public service, which by its very nature can only be satisfactorily operated for the public benefit under public control." Significantly, the editorial containing this statement appeared on 21 March, a week *before* the issue of the IBSA stations had even been brought before the House. Between then and the day Cardin first mentioned the possibility of nationalization of the system (12 April), three more editorials made the same case, mentioning as the major problems of the current Canadian system the North American wavelength dispute, excessive advertising, and the inability of Canadian private broadcasters to produce programs popular enough to counteract the appeal of American rhetoric and ideas.[54] On 4 April, an obviously leaked front-page story appeared: "Canada May Have Govt. Radio Control: Whole Broadcasting Business May Be Taken Over By State; Would Be Like British System." Clearly Bowman was either a catalyst or an accomplice in the decision taken by the Liberal government in the spring of 1928.

Another possible explanation as to why Cardin believed a complete, fundamental investigation was necessary, and why he made explicit the possibility that it could result in a radical restructuring of Canadian broadcasting, derives from the negative results of the attempt to gain a larger share of North American wavelengths. As was detailed in Chapter 7, Canadian officials reacted to the defeat in the Washington negotiations with a brave front and insisted that the Americans had not heard the end of the matter. There was much to be said in favour of the course urged by Vincent Massey at that time; "careful consideration" of "the question of radio broadcasting in Canada *in its national aspects*" (emphasis added) was necessary before the government would have any chance of success at renewed frequency-allocation talks with the Americans.[55]

In the fall of 1928 Massey was to argue even more explicitly in a letter to

O.D. Skelton, undersecretary of state for external affairs, passed on to Prime Minister King, that only the creation of a strong, sound, publicly owned broadcasting system would put Canada in a position to make a compelling case in Washington:

I feel very strongly that the appointment of our Dominion Radio Commission which has been pending for some time, and their operation as a national body investigating broadcasting in the interests of the Dominion as a whole, will have a very striking effect in demonstrating that we "mean business." Moreover, I do not think it is going too far to say that, should the Commission report in favour of Government control of broadcasting in Canada, this will be an even more graphic demonstration of the fact that broadcasting in Canada is regarded as a serious matter and must be treated as such, both within and without our national boundaries. If we think of the radio in terms of national welfare to the extent of giving broadcasting stations some form of Government control, we shall be in a much better position to deal with the problem internationally than if we are content to leave broadcasting in its present chaotic condition, in which, for the most part, the only programmes which Canadian people are permitted to receive from Canadian sources, are a by-product of advertising schemes ... Should broadcasting in Canada become a national matter, with the greater prestige which would result, then it is clear that the [U.S. Federal Radio] Commission's attitude to our Canadian situation would materially change ...

It is not within my province to discuss the broadcasting problem in Canada save in its international aspect, but I cannot help feeling that the national and international problems are closely related ...[56]

On the other hand, it was also necessary for Canadian officials to prepare for the eventuality that the failure to gain a greater share of North American frequencies was a permanent one and that Canada would be limited to six exclusive wavelengths for a long time to come. In that case, it was equally essential that Canada put its own broadcasting house in order. An improved means of distributing scarce frequencies among contenders was imperative.

That this matter of North American frequency allocation may have been a key to the decision to conduct a full-scale investigation and to the bias toward nationalization inherent from the beginning has a certain logic. Virtually the only official contact members of the Liberal Cabinet had had with radio policy prior to 1928 was over the allocation question. It had aroused special interest in part because it was among the first matters dealt with by the staff of the brand new Canadian legation in Washington in early 1927. Cardin himself had of necessity hovered over that affair more than he usually did over radio matters because it demanded inter-departmental handling. King, too, had been involved as secretary of state for external affairs. By the spring of 1928, then, there was in the Cabinet and the prime minister's office at best only vague and general awareness of the policy implications of such issues as the growing influence of the American networks or the coverage and financing of Canadian broadcasting stations, but there *was* official knowledge about the wavelength matter – perhaps enough to ring the alarm bells. The American intransigence about wavelengths was likely a central factor in the Liberal government's decision to solve a particular political problem regarding radio regulation with a full-scale inquiry leading perhaps to nationalization.[57]

During the summer parliamentary recess Prime Minister King decided that a royal commission would be the best instrument for investigating radio. Its membership and mandate were hammered out during the fall. The three men appointed to the commission were banker Sir John Aird, Charles Bowman, and Dr Augustin Frigon, director of the École Polytechnique in Montreal and director-general of technical education for the province of Quebec.[58]

Aird was nearing the end of a distinguished business career as president of the Canadian Bank of Commerce. He had no publicly expressed views on radio before 1928 but was apparently not a fan of the new medium.[59] The prevailing assumption was that Aird's presence on the commission was designed to reassure private interests; he was certainly no advocate of public enterprise.[60] On the other hand, as a major Canadian banker, Aird was typical of the indigenous "merchant capitalist" élite whose interests in the 1920s still lay in reinforcing Canadian economic and therefore cultural nationalism against the growing north/south imperative.[61]

Charles Bowman represented a group with a special interest in broadcasting; as a newspaper man he was well aware that in Canada, unlike Britain, radio was becoming increasingly a competitor for advertising dollars, although the exact extent to which this motivated him in 1928 remains unclear.[62] He was also, by his profession, one of what is often called the "new bourgeoisie," that segment of the middle class whose job it is to deal in words and ideas and who are consequently often the most ardent supporters of cultural nationalism.[63] His employers as well, the Southam family, owners of six newspapers across Canada, were little inclined to favour advertiser-financed broadcasting and several Southams were later to become active in the campaign for public broadcasting.

It is particularly interesting that Vincent Massey apparently suggested the names of both Aird and Bowman to Prime Minister King. Massey had also accompanied King to London in 1926; from Washington in 1927, as we have seen, he was the first Canadian official to suggest that a national broadcasting policy should be a priority. On 14 April 1928 he and Bowman discussed the need for a radio commission over lunch. Massey followed the commission's activities closely and on at least one occasion during the drafting process was consulted by Aird.[64] Later he actively supported the Canadian Radio League in its fight to get the Aird recommendations adopted. As both the scion of a powerful Canadian industrial family and a cultural patron, Massey personified the alliance that lay behind the push for strong national broadcasting system in Canada.

The third and youngest member of the commission, Dr Augustin Frigon, was both the representative of francophone Canada and the technical expert, an educator, and an engineer. Frigon was helpful in explaining technical points to the other commissioners; additionally, and inevitably, his particular concern became the protection of the special cultural interests of French-speaking Canada (more specifically, of the province of Quebec) in the formulation of a national broadcasting policy. According to Bowman's later accounts, Frigon was initially very wary of public broadcasting because of its vulnerability to politicization; neither was there a strong public-ownership tradition in Quebec.[65]

The secretary to the commission was Donald Manson, chief inspector in the Radio Branch of the Department of Marine and Fisheries. Manson subsequently became an ardent advocate of public broadcasting in Canada but his private views on the matter prior to 1929 are not clear. It was claimed that he was "at the outset cautious and opposed," as were his superiors, Alex Johnston and C.P. Edwards.[66] Significantly, however, in the fall of 1928 Manson accompanied Deputy Minister Johnston on a tour of most of the prairie and British Columbia stations, and reached the conclusion that in western Canada, at least, broadcasting was in poor shape. This is how he ended the report he made to Edwards on his return:

Reviewing Broadcasting as a whole West of Winnipeg ... I feel satisfied that the programmes given listeners by Canadian Broadcasting Stations are of a poor order in that part of the country. The Stations generally are poorly equipped; the personnel inadequate and largely unqualified (not from the technical viewpoint) and untrained to carry programmes into the homes of listeners in the dignified and edifying manner to be hoped for; facilities and financial standing are not possessed so that the quality of the programmes thereby suffers ...

The Commission about to be appointed will doubtless find a solution of these difficulties but whatever that solution may be, it is patent that the broadcast listeners in Canada deserve something better than they are now getting from Canadian Broadcasting Stations.[67]

It may be noticed that Manson's comments mainly concerned not the technical but the program quality of the western stations – something of a new priority within the Radio Branch. As a long-time branch employee, Manson knew far more about the development and condition of Canadian broadcasting than did Aird, Bowman, or Frigon when the commission began its work. His expert opinion that the prevailing situation was so deficient may have helped predispose the commissioners from the beginning to assume that fundamental and drastic reforms were essential.[68]

The three commissioners were appointed by Order in Council on 6 December 1928.[69] The order also included a brief analysis of the state of Canadian broadcasting and a detailed mandate for the commission.[70] There are several interesting aspects to this document, which was prepared by the Department of Marine and Fisheries; although it is not clear who actually wrote the document, it would certainly have been cleared with Cardin. The Order in Council begins with seven points describing the current situation in relatively neutral terms, listing the number of stations and receiving sets, and so on. The eighth point, however, is more subjective: "That a substantial number of Canadian listeners at the moment appear to be more interested in programs from the United States than in those from Canadian stations." So is the ninth: "That in the opinion of the technical officers of the Department, the remedy for the above lies in the establishment of a number of high power stations throughout the country, and a greater expenditure on programs than the present licensees appear to be prepared to undertake." Both of these statements may well have been perfectly correct; they clearly derived from the dilemmas Radio Branch officials had faced over the previous few years. Nevertheless, they contained elements sufficiently controversial that their inclusion in the mandate of the commission could well be seen as inappropriate. One might have assumed that the commission's task was to discover what Canadians were listening to and to inquire how much the current broadcasters were willing to spend on program development, not to be told in advance.

The tenth point had the same effect. It offered three alternative means of achieving the "desired end" (from the context, clearly, high-power stations with better programs that would wean Canadians from American stations). They were:

a) the establishment of one or more groups of stations operated by private enterprise in receipt of a subsidy from the Government;
b) the establishment and operation of stations by a government-owned and financed company;
c) the establishment and operation of stations by provincial governments.

Most significantly, the *status quo* whereby almost all stations were individually and privately owned and financed was not mentioned; the conclusion had already been reached that that arrangement was inadequate.[71]

Finally, the Order in Council's definition of the mandate of the commission used six crucial and unprecedented words. Because of the limited number of broadcasting frequencies available, the twelfth point read, it was desirable "to consider the manner in which the available channels can be most effectively used in the interests of Canadian listeners and *in the national interests of Canada*" (emphasis added). For the first time in an official document, the notion was inserted that radio broadcasting should not just provide a service for individual Canadians as listeners but that it should also function in the national interest. Once that assumption was made, the conclusion that broadcasting would no longer remain the sole domain of commercial concerns was nearly inescapable.[72]

Thus the genesis, mandate, and personnel of the Aird commission predetermined its conclusions to an important extent. At a very minimum, radio broadcasting was now defined as "in the national interest" and more government involvement in the financing of Canadian radio was assumed. For the next three and a half years, the debate about the future of radio in Canada occurred within clearly defined limits: the issue was not whether the government should finance Canadian broadcasting but rather which level of government should do so, to what extent, in what manner, and with what amount of control. Even more drastic changes were in fact strongly hinted from the beginning: a complete revision of the regulatory system was assumed and possibly nationalization following the British model. The royal commission did not begin its deliberations with a *tabula rasa.*

IN LATE 1928 AND EARLY 1929 THE THREE Aird commissioners and Manson journeyed to New York, the first stop on their information-gathering tour, where they met with top management at NBC. According to Charles Bowman's later accounts, this visit had a significant impact on Sir John's views. The discovery that NBC personnel simply assumed that North America comprised a single radio market which the network was destined to serve made Aird "thoughtful," Bowman wrote. At the next stop in London, Aird's anti-public ownership bias, again according to Bowman, was considerably softened by the favourable impression he apparently gained of the work of the BBC.[73] The commissioners also admitted to being impressed by the mainly government-owned and -controlled systems they saw in the six other European countries they visited, particularly the German arrangement dividing the technical and programming responsibility between the federal and state levels.[74]

On returning to Canada, the commissioners began in mid-April 1929 a cross-country tour of hearings in twenty-five cities including the capitals of all nine provinces. Altogether, in addition to the nine provincial governments, 164 individuals and organizations made presentations to the commission and another 124 written statements were received before the hearings wound up in Ottawa on 3 July. Unfortunately the transcripts of the meetings held in April and May in Victoria, Vancouver, Edmonton, Calgary, Saskatoon, Prince Albert, Regina, Moose Jaw, Brandon, and Winnipeg have apparently been lost and newspaper accounts of these sessions are too brief to be very revealing. However, full transcripts of the hearings from Port Arthur/Fort William east have survived, as well as many written submissions.

Succinctly summarizing what the commission members heard is difficult, because a great deal of information was conveyed and many disparate opinions expressed. Other scholars, especially Frank Peers in *The Politics of National Broadcasting*, have provided fairly detailed accounts of the major presentations. Most of the problems brought out by those giving testimony, such as the inequity in continental wavelength allocation, low-quality programs, lack of reception in remote areas, interference, excessive advertising, the burden of receiving-licence fees, and so on, have been discussed in previous chapters. To those administering Canadian radio, none of it was news. The commission hearings, however, afforded the first opportunity most Canadians, including many actually involved in the industry, had to express their views about radio service in a public forum. For the first time the fundamental questions of how best to finance and regulate Canadian broadcasting within the North American context were openly confronted and debated.

That most of those who appeared at the hearings deplored the current situation there can be no doubt. Yet much disagreement surfaced about what reforms were needed. As one might expect, most private broadcasters and their supporters wanted both private ownership and advertising-based financing retained, although they made various suggestions about how their businesses could be strengthened and their incomes supplemented. Many of them, including Ralph Ashcroft of CKGW and J. Arthur Dupont of CKAC, favoured the elimination of the small weak stations in favour of a few strong large ones. The Canadian Manufacturers' Association and the representatives of the radio trades both suggested that government subsidization of wire lines would solve the major problem of lack of coverage by making Canadian networks of private stations viable. Alex MacKenzie of CKNC put it well:

In our opinion all that stands in the way of furnishing real Canadian programs to all of Canada is the excessive cost of transmitting those programs over land lines from the few centres where the talent is available to produce these programs. We suggest that some means be developed whereby under the supervision of the

Radio Commission transmission lines from Toronto and Montreal to the other stations of the Dominion east and west be made available without cost to the sponsor.[75]

The friends of private broadcasting also made the points that Canadian
advertisers needed access to the new medium in order to compete with
American firms, that competition was the most efficient means of producing
better programs, that government ownership would be very costly (the CMA
estimated licence fees of $14 per annum), and that a government system
ran the risk of being a tool of political propaganda.[76]

The most thoughtful of the representatives of private broadcast interests,
including the Canadian Association of Broadcasters, which represented
forty-one broadcasting stations coast to coast, were conscious of the dangers
of too much advertising, of the need to utilize radio's capacity as a medium
of education and instruction, and of the necessity for strict but fair government regulation and/or control (the terms were used interchangeably).[77] Various different regulatory arrangements were recommended, but
no one denied that regulation was a necessity and that the government
should have a hand in it. Long-time amateur A.H.K. Russell, however, the
head of the Canadian section of the American Radio Relay League, made
a prescient point: "We are opposed to the proposal of a complete
Government monopoly because the Government's proper sphere is supervision. They cannot properly interpret the Radio Act if they are going to be,
on the one side enforcing the law and on the other side the person
against whom it is enforced."[78]

On the other extreme, such organizations as the All-Canadian Congress
of Labour and the Canadian Legion advocated a completely government-
owned and -financed system, largely on cultural-nationalist grounds. They
were greatly worried about the withering of patriotism, especially among
young Canadians, which they believed resulted from excessive listening in
to American stations. The legion's statement, read by J.A. McIsaac, nicely
summarized many nationalist concerns:

The Canadian Legion believes that the Canadian public would be better served by
some form of Federal government ownership and operation rather than by ownership and operation by private enterprise. This opinion is arrived at largely in view
of the inadequacy of the present Canadian broadcasting effort, and the over-
whelming of the Canadian listener by the flood of programs from powerful stations
of the United States, which are frequently heavily charged with foreign propaganda.
It is felt that Canadian private enterprises could hardly compete with United
States stations without very strong organization and the expenditure of great
sums, which the advertisers might conceive to be unwarranted from their point of

view. Furthermore, it is to be anticipated that radio, under private enterprise in Canada, would develop along similar lines to that in the United States which the vast majority of our membership regard as undesirable.[79]

From several Maritime centres came particularly impassioned pleas for the retention of local stations, both because topographical conditions prevented the reception of even high-power Canadian stations and because communication of matters of local interest and concern was so essential.[80]

Manitoba opinion about the possibility of government-owned broadcasting for Canada was particularly interesting with respect to the third option – the establishment and operation of stations by provincial governments – because that province in 1929 had the only provincially owned and -operated broadcasting system in the country. At the Winnipeg hearings of the commission, the provincial radio station got what the Winnipeg *Free Press* called "the razz." Very few had anything good to say about CKY or about what it suggested as a model for government ownership. Veteran broadcaster Darby Coats, who had parted from CKY a couple of years earlier, made it clear that if Canada moved to a publicly owned system, he would be heading south. On the other hand, as the *Free Press* pointed out editorially, CKY was in truth as commercially oriented as any other station in Canada and was run by one employee of the Manitoba Telephone System rather than by a more neutral or representative body such as the BBC board. It was therefore unfair to cite it as an example of government or (pejoratively) "civil service" broadcasting.[81]

Seven provincial governments declared themselves ready and willing to enter negotiations with the federal government "with a view to the organization of radio broadcasting on the basis of public service"; two, New Brunswick and Quebec, expressed their willingness to cooperate but asserted their position that, constitutionally, radio broadcasting lay within provincial jurisdiction.[82] Donald Manson came closest to putting all the views in a nutshell in a memorandum he sent back to Deputy Minister Johnston in the midst of the tour: "Broadcasting station owners and manufacturers giving information generally favoured the continuance of private enterprise, while those representing the listener were more inclined towards government ownership or control, in some form or other. It may be said that all were agreed that something should be done to improve Canadian Broadcasting."[83]

It is especially unfortunate that the transcripts of the western hearings have been lost, for by the time they arrived at the Lakehead, the statements and questions of Aird, Bowman, and Frigon indicate that they had already come to the conclusion that Canada needed a national broadcasting system organized primarily for public service rather than private profit.[84] As the tour wore on, the three commissioners increasingly led witnesses and interjected their own points of view. Aird, for example, kept pointing out that high profit margins made radio more costly than it need be and that in the United States the result of a competitive private-enterprise system had been a virtual monopoly in the hands of RCA. The implication was that Canadian broadcasting might also fall under the control of American corporations. He declared with great certainty that Canadians did not want to hear advertising on their radios but rather educational material. When A.H.K. Russell told the Toronto hearing that in his experience "the average listener is not particularly interested in the origin of his programme as long as it is a good one," Aird firmly replied that this must be a Toronto view, because it was quite contrary to what he and his colleagues had heard in the west.[85] Bowman sharply questioned witnesses who claimed that the BBC was very unpopular among ordinary British listeners and argued vehemently with those who suggested that radio stations were just the same as newspapers and should be given the same freedom of ownership and content. Rather, he insisted, Canadian radio was a "natural" monopoly that must be kept out of American hands.[86] Even Frigon, although the most reluctant to remove private enterprise from the system entirely, seemed to feel that one strong chain was preferable to many small and weak stations and agreed that the quality of programs deteriorated when their sole aim was the advertiser-driven need to attract the largest possible audience.[87] By the time the commission got to Charlottetown on 20 June, the hapless owner of CFCY, who dared to advocate the *status quo* supplemented with government subsidies to the private stations, found himself being raked over the coals by all three commissioners.[88]

So it is not surprising that when they sat down to marshall their thoughts and begin writing their report, the commission members found they had little difficulty in reaching the unanimous conclusion that, because of the shortage of revenue and wide dispersal of the population, Canada could not be served adequately by private-enterprise radio. Indeed, the net result of the experiment with private radio had been that "the majority of programmes heard" came from outside the country, so that the minds of Canadian young people were being moulded with "ideals and opinions that are not Canadian." Because radio played such an important educational and national purpose, therefore, in the "interests of the listening public and of the nation," "some form of public ownership, operation and control" should be implemented.[89]

The report recommended, first, the creation of a national organization, the Canadian Radio Broadcasting Company, with status and duties corresponding to those of a public utility, which would own and operate all broadcasting stations in the country. The company would have a governing board of twelve members, three representing the federal government and one from each province. Secondly, it recommended that "full control" over the programs broadcast in each province be given to a "Provincial Radio Broadcasting Director." This person would be the province's representative on the company board; the mode of his or her appointment would be decided by agreement between provincial and federal authorities.[90] Thirdly, each province would set up an advisory council on radio broadcasting, responsible to the provincial government.

The report then went on to elaborate more fully on the erection of stations, how they would be financed, and how programs would be created. The objective was to provide good reception of Canadian stations over the entire settled region of the country. This could best be accomplished, the commissioners felt, by establishing seven high-power stations (say 50,000 watts), one in each province except in the Maritimes, where one would serve for all three provinces. These stations would be the "nucleus" of the system; if local areas were still ineffectively covered, "stations of smaller power could accordingly be established" to serve them. (It was estimated that perhaps four such stations would be needed, three at 5000 watts and one at 500 watts.[91]) While the three commissioners felt there was no legal obligation to compensate the owners of stations taken over by the new company or shut down, they nevertheless recommended that "reasonable compensation" be offered through a special parliamentary appropriation. They suggested that the erection of the high-power stations should commence as soon as possible, but also proposed that on an interim basis one existing station in each area be taken over and operated by the company until its own stations were functional, at which time the stations providing the provisional service would be closed down.

The commissioners estimated that the capital cost of installing the seven powerful stations posited would be $3 million, with another $225,000 for the four supplementary stations. Operating costs for the total organization were estimated at a minimum of $2.5 million annually, without taking into account depreciation of the capital. As to revenue, the commissioners rejected the idea that the full cost be borne by general tax revenues, on the grounds that this would be unacceptable while many taxpayers were not yet radio owners. They did, however, suggest that the government should provide a subsidy of $1 million per year for the first five years, because broadcasting was "of such importance in promoting the unity of the nation." An additional amount of at least $900,000 per year could be raised by increasing the receiving-licence fee to $3 per annum. Finally, while stating that they were "strongly against any form of broadcasting employing direct advertising," the commissioners recommended that a limited amount of indirect advertising should be allowed, which would bring in about $700,000 per year.[92]

With respect to programming, the report briefly encouraged the exploration of ways to give Canadian listeners access to good programs from other countries, allocation of time for educational programs for both children and adults, supervision of religious and political broadcasts to prevent controversy, and training programs to ensure that all announcers were "competent and cultured." There was only a very brief mention of the desirability of chain broadcasts and "the interchange of programmes among different parts of the country."

Finally, the report called for the continuation of efforts to get a more equitable wavelength allocation from the United States and for the passage of legislation to compel users of apparatus interfering with radio reception to correct faults. The report also recommended that the Department of Marine and Fisheries retain authority over such matters as wavelengths, station power, and the collection of licence fees and continue its interference-suppression services.

LOOKING AT THE REPORT OF THE AIRD commission in the light of the previous seven-year development of broadcasting in Canada, certain aspects of its recommendations deserve special comment. The commissioners called for a radical transformation of the system: from competitive private broadcasting to monopoly ownership by a government-appointed company; from over eighty stations, many of them small and weak, to seven powerful stations supplemented by perhaps four with less power. One contemporary observer remarked: "It is impossible, reading the report, to escape the feeling that the Aird Commission was appointed not so much to investigate as to justify an already determined course of action."[93] While there is no evidence quite that strong, to some extent the conclusion reached *was* foreshadowed from the day Minister of Marine and Fisheries P.J.A. Cardin first suggested the need for a commission of investigation.

By 1928–29, radio was viewed by some Canadian leaders not only as an entertainment medium but as an instrument for the creation of national unity and the fostering of national identity. To that end, as well as in the interests of simple equity, it was deemed essential that all citizens of the country must be able to receive Canadian broadcasting service; because private enterprise had shown itself to be unable to provide this coverage, the government must do so. Moreover, given the relative lack of resources in Canada, duplication of transmitting facilities was viewed as inefficient; some sort of monopoly was necessary. This meant a fundamental departure from the pattern in which North American broadcasting had developed from the beginning. It also flew in the face of the wishes of vested interests in the Canadian broadcasting industry. The system which they had built up over the previous seven years was to be totally dismantled.

A new view of the role of the government vis-à-vis culture and the media was thereby implied. Never before had the state been assigned such control over a cultural field. While in the radio area the government had previously exercised more authority than in other cultural sectors, the Radio Branch of the Department of Marine and Fisheries had concerned itself mainly with regulating wavelengths, power, and technical operations. Now, however, it was recommended that the government should also bear responsibility for appointing and partially financing the company which would own all Canadian broadcasting stations and distribute all programs.

On the other hand, certain explicit and implicit compromises which bowed to the existing reality are also evident in the commission's conclusions. Even a broadcasting system completely owned and operated by a national company would never be as "pure" in Canada as it was in Britain. For one thing, the commissioners assumed that the maximum Canadian listeners would be willing to pay in licence fees would be $3 per year. (Bowman claimed he had difficulty persuading the other two of the feasibility of even this figure for they knew that many Canadians disliked the fees intensely.) The difficulty for the commissioners was that the revenue from even a $3 fee was not sufficient to finance the system they envisioned. A second assumption, that taxpayers would not take kindly to substantial funding from general revenues, derived from the knowledge that only a minority of Canadians possessed radios in 1929 and that many of those who did were envious of the American model of "free" broadcasting. Thus the compromise: indirect advertising would be allowed on the new national broadcasting stations to provide about one-quarter of the revenue.

The commissioners' willingness to accept advertising had a second and more significant root as well. They were swayed by the case made by some representatives of Canadian manufacturing enterprises that indigenous businesses needed access to this powerful new medium to compete with American firms that advertised on the big US stations still beaming into Canada. The Aird commissioners stated explicitly that they were somewhat persuaded by this argument. More important, they claimed that their system would actually benefit Canadian advertisers by providing them with powerful transmitters built at the listeners' and taxpayers' expense. Bowman, for example, argued in a pamphlet issued in January 1930 in reply to some of the attacks levelled on the report:

The cost of the Canadian radio stations will be shared by the advertisers, the radio set owners and the nation ... Radio advertisers will be required to pay only for the amount of public service they receive. Under private ownership, the whole of the cost of Canadian stations, including the unnecessary duplication of competitive stations, would have to be paid for out of advertising revenue ...

It is misleading to argue that private enterprise would be eliminated by the Radio Commission's recommendations. Wasteful competition in the building of too many stations would be eliminated, but private broadcasters would actually be furnished with better station facilities, nationally owned, than private capital could afford to build.[94]

Bowman also insisted that the competitive principle would be preserved in program creation; those who planned programs (presumably including advertising agencies) would compete with one another in lobbying the national company for airtime. Rather than the blueprint for a complete transformation of the Canadian broadcasting system, then, the Aird report, according to even its most nationalist author, was in fact a much more modest exercise, "essentially different from the system of the British Broadcasting Corporation" in that it retained provision for sponsored programs and "the element of competition by private enterprise."[95] The report outlined a system in which privately engendered and advertiser-sponsored programming was transmitted via an infrastructure of high-power stations built and maintained with the listeners' money. It assumed the continued existence of the profit motive in Canadian broadcasting, both on the part of the advertisers and their clients and on the part of the revenue-seeking national broadcasting company. If they had understood it in this light, manufacturers and advertisers might not have objected quite so strongly to the report.[96]

The only advertising to be permitted under the new system, according to the report, was the "indirect" type, which the commissioners defined strictly as "an announcement before and after a programme that it was being given by a specified firm." At the time the report was written, the Radio Branch was still adhering to a fairly strict definition of indirect advertising. Hence the hubbub of criticism from private broadcasters, manufacturers, and advertisers that this provision was totally impracticable: indirect ads would not serve the purposes of Canadian business or bring sufficient revenues to the company.[97] Nevertheless, the decision to depend upon advertising for over a quarter of the company's total revenues was the thin edge of the wedge. That much dependence on sponsors would inevitably affect programming and other policies. That the commission members not only accepted but celebrated the continued use of advertising to finance Canadian broadcasting was very important. Bowman's support for this measure is especially interesting because it indicates that, despite his newspaper background, concern about competition for ad revenues was not his principal motive for advocating nationalization of broadcasting.

The Aird report said far less about the preparation, content, and distribution of programs than it did about the technical equipment by which radio signals were to be transmitted nation-wide. Recently a number of scholars have argued that Canada (especially English-speaking Canada) has been prone to a sort of "technological nationalism" which assumes that adoption of the latest technology to enhance east-west communication lines in and of itself will ensure the creation of a sense of Canadian nationhood. The result has been, however, according to these authorities, the triumph of process over substance.[98]

The Aird report is a case in point. The general lack of emphasis on programming and the assumption of the commissioners that private interests would continue to create many of the programs broadcast by the company suggests again that the transformation they recommended in 1929 was somewhat less profound than it seemed on the surface. The commissioners' primary goal was the erection of strong stations that could be heard by all Canadians. While Montreal, Toronto, and some other parts of southern Ontario were fairly well served by the existing system, the outlying regions of the country lacked reliable and appealing Canadian broadcasting. In the context of the western and Maritime regional discontent of the 1920s, the provision of equal service to those regions was a high priority. The three commissioners concluded that because the necessary infrastructure could not be privately financed the government must step in. Notably, however, they placed considerably less emphasis on the programs that would be carried on the high-power system. Their statements about the national, educational, and informational uses to which these stations would be put were few and vague and responsibility in this area was handed primarily to the provinces. The recommendation of a provincially based programming structure that would in fact make networking administratively difficult along with the brevity of their only comment about the desirability of network broadcasting, indicate the extent to which the commissioners were either hesitant to concern themselves with central questions of content and message or oblivious to them.[99] Because of this lack of specifics, it is difficult to know exactly what a national radio system meant to the commissioners. In particular it is not clear whether the Canadian Radio Broadcasting Company was intended to fulfil primarily nationalist or primarily public-service goals. Those who have viewed the Aird report as a seminal document in Canadian cultural policy have often failed to notice its irresolution in these respects.

Another compromise in the document which has been rather neglected by the historians of Canadian broadcasting was the assertion that the company would encourage the use of good programs from other countries. While Great Britain was specifically mentioned, this statement by no means precluded the possibility that American programs of high quality or great popularity would be picked up on the Canadian stations. With hindsight, we know that both the CRBC and its successor, the CBC, did serve (and continue to serve) as vehicles for the nation-wide distribution of popular (and advertisement-rich) American programming. Similarly, the commissioners were very sensitive to the fact that Canadians would wish to continue listening directly to American radio stations. With reference to the seven high-power stations posited, they stated specifically: "It is well, perhaps, to point out here the necessity of locating broadcasting stations at suitable distances from centres of population to obviate blanketing [blocking] of reception from outside points. The need for this has been amply demonstrated to us."[100] The outside points referred to could only have been in the United States.

"Canadian radio listeners want Canadian broadcasting," the Aird commissioners wrote in 1929, in the most-quoted line of their report. But in 1932 both Bowman and Frigon told the Special Parliamentary Committee on Radio Broadcasting that of course they had not meant that Canadians wanted *only* Canadian broadcasting. Rather, they asserted, their intention had always been simply to obtain a better balance between Canadian and American service – at least a "50-50 share" of the domestic audience for Canadian stations.[101] "We do not want to interfere with the reception of Amos and Andy or ... Jack Dempsey or anyone else," Bowman assured the MP's.

This was a pragmatic and realistic position to take given the context of North American broadcasting in 1929. Canadians did listen in large numbers to American stations and to American programs rebroadcast on Canadian stations. They had been doing so since the dawn of broadcasting. Many clearly enjoyed and appreciated this particular form of American popular culture. Even if the government had wished to deny it to them, they could not have done so. The Canadian broadcasting system, whatever it was to be, would inevitably have to accept that reality and to coexist with American radio in Canada.

But that was not going to be easy. As Ralph Ashcroft of CKGW told the 1932 Special Committee:

The principle [*sic*] weakness in the report of the Royal Commission is that it totally ignores the main factor bearing on the situation in Canada, namely, viz: the competition which we have to the south of us and the methods that are in vogue in the United States.

It is conservatively estimated that at least $50,000,000 a year is expended in the United States for radio programs. This is for talent alone, and does not include station time or transmission ... How could Canada with a $1,000,000 annual expenditure for programs compete with a $50,000,000 radio show or even with a $15,000,000 show or $5,000,000 show ... I recall one program that we [Trans-Canada Broadcasting] broadcast from Winnipeg about two years ago which cost over $1,000 a minute for talent. At this rate of expenditure ... $1,000,000 would be eaten up in less than a day's broadcasting.[102]

In one sense he was quite wrong. The commissioners' main goal was to counter the competition from the rich and powerful American stations and networks with a strong Canadian system constructed and maintained largely with listeners' fees and public money because they believed that Canadian private interests lacked the resources to do so. He was right, however, in implying that they were not sufficiently concerned about the great expenses involved in competing with high-quality American programming. The fundamental problem of economies of scale in what was *de facto* a continental market-place was not going to be solved simply by the creation of a national broadcasting company.

Aird, Bowman, and Frigon reassured Canadians that competitive principles, the needs of Canadian manufacturers and advertisers, and the desire of Canadian listeners for diverse and entertaining (and American) programs would be respected. They did so because both they and the Canadian public at large believed in competition, free enterprise, and consumer choice. Despite the recommendation of a monopoly system, these principles remained sacred. On close analysis, the Aird commission's report proves to be somewhat less revolutionary than it seemed then or since.

Nevertheless, if not completely root-and-branch, the changes the report outlined for the Canadian broadcasting system were certainly major. Most important, the Aird commission introduced a new conception of Canadian broadcasting to the public forum, an "idealist" vision that suggested that radio was more than simply a business enterprise – it was also a cultural medium to be used, as the Order in Council had put it, "in the national interests of Canada." It remained to be seen what would happen to that vision when it entered the political process.

10 The Debate about Broadcasting

The Aird commission's report was issued on 11 September 1929, simultaneously in English and French. Parliament was not in session so it was not debated in the House. Prime Minister Mackenzie King's initial reaction seems to have been positive, for he commented to his diary, "[The report] is, I think, a good one."[1] Donald Manson was asked to prepare a draft bill for a new radio act to be presented to Parliament at the next session.

The bill was ready by early February 1930. It followed the report in most respects.[2] The name Canadian Radio Broadcasting Company was confirmed; according to an explanatory memo penned by Manson, this was because it suggested an "independent national Company" not subject to political suasion.[3] Provision was made for a twelve-person board of directors, nine representing the provinces and three the federal government. The provincial directors would control programs broadcast by the station(s) within their provinces with the help of honorary advisory councils. Following Bowman rather than Frigon, these directors were all to be appointed by the Governor in Council (essentially the federal Cabinet) although Manson's memo suggested that the nine provincial directors be nominated by the provinces. In addition to a chairman of the board, the Governor in Council could select and appoint a chief executive (general manager), a position that had not been mentioned in the Aird report. The company would report to Parliament through the minister of Marine and Fisheries.

The financial suggestions of the Aird report were followed almost to the letter in the draft bill. For five years a $1 million annual subsidy was to be paid to the company; on a permanent basis it would receive the full revenues collected from licence fees minus costs of collection and the interference service. The fee would be raised to $3 annually. Additionally, the company was to have all the income accruing from the rental of station time to sponsors; Manson argued that this was necessary "to augment its revenue so that a high class broadcasting service may be provided." No limitation on the type or length of advertising messages was mentioned. Finally, the company was given a fairly free hand financially and was allowed to borrow up to $3.5 million for capital expenditures. One restriction was that no real property could be acquired by the company without prior approval of the Governor in Council; any expropriations were to be paid for by the company (although Manson foresaw the need for a special appropriation for this). Manson contemplated that immediately the legislation was passed, most owners of existing stations would be informed that their licences would not be renewed. However, certain private stations "would be selected to carry on a provisional service pending installation of the larger units contemplated."[4] Once the company's seven high-power stations were constructed, these stations would also be closed down.

By the time Parliament reassembled in February 1930, however, the prime minister had decided to call an election for the summer. Confronted with more pressing economic problems and reluctant to make broadcasting an election issue, King stalled on presenting the radio legislation.[5] On the grounds that the technical aspects of the bill required study, a special parliamentary committee was named, with J.L. Ilsley the chairman.[6] The committee never met and the House was dissolved without action on broadcasting. The election on 30 July brought King's government down. To the victorious Conservatives was left the decision about what to do with the Aird report.

Ultimately, in May 1932, after the investigation and report of the Special Committee, R.B. Bennett's Conservative government passed a radio broadcasting act that fulfilled in some respects the recommendations of the Aird commission. There were, however, many intriguing and significant differences between the act eventually passed and the bill drafted by Manson. In the two-and-a-half-year interim, a vigorous debate about Canadian broadcasting had occurred and the right of the federal government to legislate in the field had been challenged to the highest level of the courts. Equally important, the context within which Canadian broadcasting existed was markedly altered in these years; not only did the most severe economic depression of the century hit, but considerable growth and change occurred in the North American broadcasting industry.[7] While the aftermath of the Aird report and the debate leading to the Radio Broadcasting Act have been examined in some detail by previous historians, many aspects of this period may be seen in a new light when viewed with greater knowledge of broadcasting's development prior to 1928.

ONCE THEY HAD HANDED IN THEIR REPORT, the three Aird commissioners were given neither funds nor authority to explain or defend it publicly. In the fall of 1929 Aird began a lengthy trip around the world; he did
comment to reporters before leaving that he believed radio was an inappropriate medium for advertising and that the government must maintain
control of broadcasting in order to manage the revolutionary changes soon
to be expected with the introduction of television.[8] Frigon returned to his
other duties and made only a few public comments on the commission's
work, all inside Quebec.[9] Manson was hampered by his employment in the
Department of Marine and Fisheries from openly discussing the report.
Thus, most of the burden of its public defence in late 1929 and 1930 fell on
the shoulders of Charles Bowman; specifically, he produced a series of
editorials in December 1929 (published as a pamphlet the next month)
explicitly replying to criticisms that had been levied in the pages of *La Presse*.
Given the change in government and the preoccupation of both Liberals
and Conservatives with other issues, however, the momentum for the
major transformation in Canadian broadcasting called for by the Aird
commission could not have been sustained in this manner. That the
report was not obliterated under the combined weight of the accelerating
economic difficulties of the early 1930s and the pro-private-enterprise
sentiments dominant in Ottawa and elsewhere was the result, without a
doubt, of the activities of a newly formed pressure group, the Canadian
Radio League.

The Canadian Radio League was conceived by two young Ottawa residents, Alan Plaunt and Graham Spry, in October 1930; after two months of
preliminary organizational work they formally launched the league at a
meeting attended by eight individuals at the Chateau Laurier Hotel on
8 December 1930.[10] Spry later recalled that Bowman's editorials in the
Citizen helped impress on him the importance of radio. "Indirectly," he
wrote, "Mr. Bowman's fear that the new Government would overlook the
Aird Report contributed ... to the idea that someone should take some
action ..."[11] Both Spry and Plaunt were well-educated, well-connected representatives of the new middle class that had emerged in English-speaking
Canada after the First World War. The league was the culmination of a
decade of organization and networking among English-Canadian cultural nationalists striving to foster unity among the different provinces and
peoples of Canada and to strengthen the sense of national identity,
particularly vis-à-vis the United States.[12] Radio, Spry and Plaunt believed,
was "the most powerful of all human agencies of communication." Its
"revolutionary possibilities" and "majestic ... potentialities" made it a crucial
instrument in forming national public opinion in a "sparsely settled,
thinly scattered nation ... like Canada."[13] Because of the economic and

advertising might of the United States and the relative lack of financial resources in Canada, private broadcasters were providing inadequate service in both programming and coverage and were increasingly finding it "more profitable to associate themselves with the American chains and to broadcast American rather than Canadian programmes."[14] As a result, a vital institution of communication that should be a public and a national service was not being utilized for the educational and cultural roles for which it was so brilliantly suited: the sharing of information, ideas, and views among Canadians and the creation of a national public opinion. Instead, Canada had "broadcasting of the advertisers for the advertisers by the advertisers ..."[15] The following passage from a letter Spry wrote to an American broadcasting executive is an eloquent summary of the mixture of nationalist and progressive motivations which in his view lay behind the CRL:

I feel more strongly every day, as I go about this country, that our national problem of creating a distinct nation at once different from either Britain or the United States, based upon two races historically antagonistic – the French and the English – and split up by economically unproductive areas or natural barriers, can be enormously hastened and facilitated by the new weapon science has given us – the radio.

But to trust this weapon to advertising agents and interested corporations, seems the uttermost folly. I would as well hand over our school system to a Manufacturers' Association. Indeed, broadcasting, influencing as it does the adult, the voter, is almost a more dangerous instrument of reaction, and to permit commercial interests to control it is tantamount to abandoning the rash but noble hope of democratic government.

... The strength of the Canadian Radio League is really based upon [a] two-fold foundation, distaste for commercialism, and apprehension of Americanization – an apprehension which has given Canada, I may add, many of the most progressive economic and constitutional changes in our history. Indeed, if the fear of the United States did not exist, it would be necessary, like Voltaire's God, to invent it.

... We fear ... that the broadcasting in the United States, broadcasting which every Canadian listens to and prefers for ninety per cent of the time to listen to, will harmfully alter the character of public opinion. We fear it will make more difficult the none too easy way of the reformer, or even the defender of such publicly controlled institutions as we now possess and which, to some of us, seem to constitute a bulwark against American economic penetration.[16]

In even stronger language, he told the Second Annual Institute for Education by Radio in Columbus, Ohio, in 1931:

To me, the problem is the problem of free public opinion. The issue is freedom. Let the air remain as the prerogative of commercial interests and subject to commercial control, and how free will be the voice, the heart of democracy?

The maintenance, the enlargement of freedom, the progress, the purity of education, the protection, the development of democracy, require the responsibility of broadcasting to the popular will. Commercial interests cannot be chastened. They must be subdued. There can be no liberty complete, no democracy supreme, if the commercial interests dominate the vast, majestic resources of broadcasting.[17]

Given these high ideals for the use of radio, it is not surprising that Spry's summary of the situation as he saw it in the summer of 1931 was gloomy:

The sixty-seven Canadian stations do not ... provide complete Canadian coverage, and some forty percent of the Canadian people cannot regularly receive Canadian programs. Stations operating on an advertising basis have tended to locate near the centers of population and have left remote but important sections inadequately served. Over these stations programs of the greatest difference in quality are broadcast, from the jazz phonograph record to the radio dramas produced by the Canadian National Railways, with the utmost technical efficiency and popular success. But there are not more than ten hours of national broadcasting a week; indeed, the average over a year is only one hour a day. Four of the largest stations – two in Montreal and two in Toronto – are associated with the National and Columbia chains. The result, in brief, is that the American broadcaster has command of the Canadian ear, if not sovereignty over the Canadian air, and most Canadians listen most of the time to American broadcasting.[18]

In making such statements, Spry was dipping into a deep well of Canadian suspicion that the United States – or certain interests within it – was actively intent on direct or indirect domination of Canadian life. Spry himself spent some time in the summer of 1931 consulting with various parties in Washington about the "RCA trust" and came back apparently convinced that RCA and NBC were not content with controlling American radio manufacturing and broadcasting but were aggressively eyeing the Canadian market as well. He made a number of vague and unsubstantiated charges, most particularly in his statements to the 1932 Special Committee, that various representatives of American "interests" were visiting Toronto, Montreal, and Ottawa to lobby for the continuation of a private broadcasting system in Canada that would be open to US expansion.[19] As he wrote to one correspondent: "I have really come to feel that this is a struggle to control our own public opinion, and to keep it free from an American radio monopoly behind which stand the General Electric, J.P. Morgan, United Fruit, United Corporation, Westinghouse, the Motion picture and theatrical group, etc., in a word 'Capitaleesm' with a vengeance."[20] With the help of like-minded American contacts Spry carefully documented the power and control of the "radio trust" in the United States and its links with Canadian broadcasters, advertisers, and manufacturers. Whether any of the rumours on which these charges were based were true or not is essentially immaterial. What mattered was that they provided a powerful weapon for the league to use in its battle for public support.[21] More important, beneath the publicity-seeking rhetoric of conspiracy, Spry was addressing a problem that was very real for those concerned that Canadian airwaves be used primarily to enable Canadians to communicate with one another. Economic imperatives and cultural habits alone were leading Canadian broadcasters and listeners to welcome American network programming, and the commercial goals of the US network owners made them ever-responsive to Canadian market opportunities; no conspiracy theories were needed to explain the Americanization of Canadian radio.

A close reading of Spry's public statements indicates that he had several intertwined concerns. He believed that at its best broadcasting was a public service, preserving and promoting democracy, freedom, and progressive social movements by educating public opinion. Simultaneously, he emphasized its national purposes; Spry believed that one of the major public issues of the 1920s was the desperate need to tie together regions and cultures to create a sense of Canadian national consciousness.[22] The foes were both commercialism and Americanization – because together they made it difficult to utilize Canadian broadcasting for either of the purposes he envisioned.

The only way to combat the combination of commercialism and Americanization, Spry believed, was by concentration of Canadian broadcasting resources. "It may be categorically stated," he told the 1932 Special Committee, "that by the natural limitation of wave lengths and by the enhanced control, efficiency and economy that result from centralized operation, monopoly is the most satisfactory principle on which a national system of broadcasting may be established."[23] But private concentration would not solve the problem; the programming policy of a private monopoly would still be determined by advertising-revenue considerations and consequently remain open to Americanization. Only the creation of a national broadcasting company operated as a public utility would enable the powerful new medium to perform its proper function in the Canadian community. In Spry's most celebrated epigram, there were only two alternatives: "The State or the United States."[24]

Spry and Plaunt effectively used their nation-wide personal connections from the University of Toronto, Oxford, the Association of Canadian Clubs, the Canadian League, the League of Nations Society, and the Canadian Institute for International Affairs, as well as their contacts with men such as Bowman, Vincent Massey, and W.D. Herridge (Bennett's close adviser and as of 1931 his brother-in-law), to orchestrate a vocal, influential, and non-partisan pressure group to back a reform they believed to be in Canada's interest.[25] As the rather less-than-sympathetic T.J. Allard put it:

"The League's activities offer a model for the serious student of political influence, public relations and manipulation of parliamentary opinion. ... Within thirty days the League ... managed to create, in the political world, the impression that implementation of the Aird Report was the most urgent desire of nearly all Canadians – when many of them were drought-stricken, or unemployed, or wondering how soon they would be."[26] For themselves, the young organizers gained the personal satisfaction, status, and sense of purpose that intellectuals so often derive from commitment to nationalist causes.[27] Spry and Plaunt also got some amusement out of it, as their occasional gleeful remarks about the "great fun" they were having with their "luscious intrigue" indicate.[28]

The active members of the Canadian Radio League were Spry, Plaunt, a few close friends such as Brooke Claxton, and a handful of Ottawa contacts including Tom Moore of the Trades and Labour Congress, lawyer Russell Smart, and Father Henri St Denis of the University of Ottawa. This small group coordinated a larger number of supporters across the country who in turn used their connections among the leaders of most of the important church, farm, labour, veteran, university, and women's organizations in Canada to get resolutions advocating some variety of public broadcasting passed. In the business community, the league's major advocates came from the banking, financial, and retail sectors; the names of many prominent lawyers also appeared on the list of national council and executive committee members.[29] Undoubtedly many of the tens of thousands of ordinary Canadians who were members of the various bodies that went on record as supporting the league's cause were indifferent or perhaps even hostile to the notion of public broadcasting.[30] Nevertheless, the league's strategy was well considered. The best way to counteract both political inertia and the lobbying of those who preferred the *status quo* was to attempt to demonstrate that the Aird proposals had widespread public sympathy.

In their publicity campaign, the league activists had considerable help. Spry received backing from Association of Canadian Club executives in Ottawa and elsewhere. Plaunt had worked for Charles Bowman during the summer of 1930 and he had access to Bowman's Aird commission files. From within the Radio Branch, Donald Manson regularly supplied them with information and support, as did Austin Weir from the CNR radio department.[31] This material was used as the basis for a series of pamphlets, articles, and speeches which, along with mailings and personal lobbying of key politicians, were an integral part of the strategy. As Spry summed it up in his manuscript memoirs:

Prime Ministers are not notably accessible to ordinary members of the public and, in lobbying a government to accept a particular policy ... it is paramount ... to gain his attention. Not only to gain his attention, but to nourish it with succinct information – information supporting the case for the objective, and opposed, even politely hostile, to contrary objectives, both reinforced by stalwart information of much public support for the one and little for the other ... There were, then, two approaches in our attempt to influence policy: the rallying of support from national organizations; and the quiet approach to the policy-makers, especially at the highest levels of power and decision.[32]

The league's organizers also utilized, to considerable effect, the Canadian press. The Aird report was supported by many newspapers across the country and the Radio League received favourable publicity in the newspapers owned by the Southams, the Siftons, and Joseph Atkinson, among others.[33] At least in part, these publishers were motivated by a fear that radio was a fast-rising competitor for advertising dollars. In the late 1920s Canadian publishers became increasingly concerned about the inroads of radio on advertising revenues and a special committee was set up by Canadian Press and the Canadian Daily Newspaper Association to look into the question in 1931. Some talk of dropping radio schedules from newspaper pages ensued, but few wished to take a measure that would alienate readers, radio manufacturers, or advertisers who used both media. Nevertheless, some papers did begin to reduce the amount of space they devoted to radio and to drop all mention of sponsors.[34] Thus the CRL struck a responsive chord when it decided actively to seek allies among newspaper publishers. Despite some reservations, in April 1931 the league initiated a very deliberate appeal to the "cupidity" of the press by endorsing a speech Charles Bowman delivered to the convention of the Canadian Daily Newspaper Association and distributing (with Atkinson's help) a pamphlet entitled "Radio Advertising – A Menace to the Newspapers and a Burden to the Public to publishers."[35] These messages cited American statistics to illustrate the threat of private broadcasting to newspaper revenues; the general point was well summed up by a sentence in the pamphlet: "The Canadian Radio League believes the interests of both the public and the newspapers are identical in objecting to turning the home into a billboard and radio sets into advertising agencies."[36] Accusations were made at the time and since that the league was simply a front for certain newspapers; while there is no particular evidence of this, undoubtedly the coincidence and alliance of interests produced considerable free publicity for the league.[37]

From the beginning, the Radio League's organizers maintained that they supported the Aird report in principle but not necessarily in every detail.[38] In keeping with their strategy of gaining the support of as many individuals and groups as possible, they were often vague as to precisely what kind of public broadcasting structure they wished for Canada. Spry made the point explicitly in a letter to Claxton in January 1931: a "draft bill" of the

CRL's proposals "would be fatal," he wrote, because it would "split the League."[39] Even after Spry and Plaunt (it is not clear to what extent other members of the league were consulted) found it necessary to define an organizational plan for the system they favoured, ambiguities remained, the product of both an evolution of views as opponents and circumstances altered and of a desire to be all things to all supporters.[40]

From the first, the league's vision differed from that of the Aird report on several points; by 1932 further significant variations from the report's recommendations had developed. Most crucial was the acceptance of the continuing existence of numerous small local broadcasting stations alongside the high-power chain. While initially the league stated that these stations would be a part of the new Canadian Radio Broadcasting Company monopoly, Spry proposed to the 1932 Special Committee that "permission be given private enterprise, municipal authorities, school board [sic], etc. to erect low-powered stations under licences from the Department of Marine, and subject to the technical control and general supervision of the company."[41] No elaborate justification was given for this significant alteration of the Aird commission's conception except for the suggestion that it was necessary to enable service to local community interests. Some years after the fact, Spry wrote that the position was adopted "partly for tactical reasons to make the government's task easier and to divide the private broadcasters, as well as fear of monopoly itself."[42]

Spry and Plaunt also believed that the organizational structure of the Canadian Radio Broadcasting Company as outlined in the Aird report was flawed; in particular they favoured the creation of the position of a chief executive or general manager. This, it may be recalled, had been suggested in Manson's draft bill; it also paralleled the BBC structure. They also proposed, in keeping with their conviction that the new company must be free from political interference, that it be responsible to a three-member Cabinet subcommittee.[43]

The two league organizers also believed that programming should be more centrally controlled than the Aird report implied. While more sensitive than most English Canadians of their day to the special concerns of French Canada (both Spry and Plaunt came from families with French heritage and considerable effort was made to attract francophone leaders to support the league),[44] and cognizant as well of strong provincialist sentiment in other parts of the country, nevertheless the league's ultimate position was that complete provincial control over programming defeated the nation-building purpose of the proposed broadcasting company. Public pronouncements on this point were as discreetly vague as possible; there was no sense in losing supporters over differences of this kind. But the true position was in fact quite strongly centralist. In November 1930, just as the league was forming, Spry argued in a draft letter to J.W. Dafoe that "the

Aird Report, from a Canadian point of view, indeed, leans too much towards the provinces and it would certainly be desirable that the authority of the federal company be stronger and more assured than indicated in the Report."[45] The first prospectus of the league, written by Plaunt and issued the next month, stated that it recommended that "programmes of provincial utility ... be supervised by a provincial director and advisory council," a hint that *other* kinds of programs need not necessarily be. In a pamphlet issued the following month, in fact, the Aird commission's position was mispresented in this way.[46] Before the 1932 committee the CRL brief recommended "full consultation" with "the provinces," as well as recognition of "the special position" of Quebec, but no mention was made of either provincial advisory committees or directors.[47]

The strongest expressions of this view of centralized national radio came from Spry at the time of the CRL's decision to send legal counsel (Brooke Claxton) to the Supreme Court and Privy Council hearings concerning federal/provincial jurisdiction over radio broadcasting. Spry explained frankly to Gladstone Murray: "We will send Claxton to the Privy council, if necessary, with the twofold purpose of arguing for national radio and for stating the extreme case for federal rights, generally – a combination of radio plotting and another slower, longer plot of Claxton's and mine to fight provincialism."[48] He was even more candid in his diary: "The idea is for a voluntary organization to state the extreme case for federal powers as against the provinces. That is the point that interests me, far more than the radio aspect, itself."[49] Caution and consensus dictated, however, that these interventions not antagonize French-Canadian supporters of the league; they were authorized only after consulting with and receiving the approval of Louis St Laurent and Georges Pelletier of *Le Devoir*.[50] Nevertheless, it is clear that Spry and Claxton at least, and probably other members of the CRL as well, believed that the creation of a national public opinion was so important that it must override provincial authority over radio as far as constitutionally possible. The CRL's leaders believed that radio's greatest potential lay in its use as an educational medium; they struggled, however, to wrest its control from the usual locus of power over education, the provinces. In a sense, for them national radio was just the instrument; the goal was "a nationalized Canada."[51] Thus, while the Aird report had given control over all programming to provincial authorities and had waffled on who should appoint those officials, the CRL not only backed Manson's view that their appointment should be a federal responsibility but strongly implied strict limits on provincial influence over programming. The league assumed, it seems, that the national company would focus on providing national programming and that local or provincial programs for the most part would be left to the local stations owned by other organizations.

The league also differed from the Aird report in its financial proposals. For tactical reasons related to the Depression-induced strain on government resources, but also because of the substantial increase in licences since 1929 and of the desire to keep the new public broadcasting company as independent of Parliament as possible, the league adopted what were considered more realistic financial arrangements. While continuing to advocate that the $3 licence fee comprise a major part of the company's income, the CRL did not (after early 1931) favour even limited-term grants from general tax revenues. The company was to be funded solely from licence fees and advertising.

On the question of advertising, the league fully accepted the Aird commission's argument that Canadian business should have the benefit of access to Canadian consumers "without the huge expense of erecting its own stations."[52] It did maintain, however, that such advertising should be limited to no more than 5 per cent of program time. Although the league insisted that only indirect advertising be allowed on Canadian broadcasting stations, by 1932 its definition of direct was so narrow that the distinction between direct and indirect became trivial. Spry told the 1932 Special Committee that he defined direct advertising as "announcements in excess of 5 per cent of a program exclusive of station call letters, and containing prices, telephone numbers, street addresses," while he defined indirect advertising as "consisting of the name of the sponsor, the products advertised, and reasonable references to the quality of the product."[53] Even given his additional strictures that no patent-medicine advertising be allowed, nor ads on recorded programs, these definitions allowed a lot of leeway. Spry told one correspondent: "We recognize that the definition of indirect advertising cannot be too restrictive as Canadian business must have adequate facilities for competing with American business on the air."[54] The league's support of advertising is in one sense curious, for it ran counter to the interests of the organization's newspaper backers and seemed contrary to its oft-expressed distaste for the overly commercial programming of the prevailing system.[55] In fact, the CRL spokesmen trod a fine and ambivalent line on this question. On the one hand, they asserted that, under private broadcasting, commercialism and advertising were too much in control and they commiserated with publishers who were thereby threatened. On the other, partly because they felt direct public subventions were unrealistic and possibly politically dangerous and partly because they believed Canadian businesses should have access to Canadian consumers, they advocated a public system in which advertising revenue would still comprise a major source of funding.[56]

Finally, and very significantly, Spry and Plaunt recommended a flexible and gradualist timetable for the construction of the key coast-to-coast string of high-power stations. As early as November 1930, before the league was even officially formed, Spry felt that "so large a system must necessarily be an objective rather than an immediate policy" of the company.[57] The three-stage proposal Spry submitted to the 1932 Special Committee posited at least five and possibly seven years before the national chain was constructed, with the interim use of strong private stations as carriers of company-produced network programming. He also urged that all "capital expenditure should be subject to very rigid and effective control by parliament."[58] While again obviously a response to the deepening Depression, one wonders how carefully the league considered the implications of letting powerful private stations continue to exist for some time. As the experience of the CRBC after 1932 was to demonstrate, the "interim" utilization of private stations to broadcast network programs was one of the factors that reinforced the continuing existence of strong private broadcasters side by side (or affiliated) with the public network.[59] Still, it is important to remember that a very real tension has always existed concerning the allocation of ever-scarce dollars for public broadcasting in Canada: should the priority be the expansion of transmission facilities or should it be the improvement of Canadian programming? The CRL's balanced stress on both goals was in marked contrast to the Aird report's emphasis on the first alone.

The CRL was in complete agreement with the Aird commission in two major areas. One concerned the use of American programs. Like the commission, the league envisaged that the new Canadian network would rebroadcast the best American programs and it reassured Canadians that company stations would not hinder direct reception from the United States.[60] Similarly, the league not only accepted but advocated private enterprise and competition in the production of the programs that would be heard on the new company's stations. "The competitive elements in broadcasting are not primarily stations," Spry wrote to one correspondent, "but programmes."[61] To another he elaborated,

We believe also that indirect advertising produces a competitive element not only between the businesses using the radio but between the programmes of business and the programmes of the national company. In this respect we feel that the Canadian proposal has merits which the present British system lacks, namely, the retention of the competitive element in programmes. A national system in our view, would tend to increase rather than decrease competition where competition is most needed, namely, between programmes.[62]

Spry suggested that programming would be arranged by four parties: the national company, provincial broadcasting bodies, private local low-power stations, and sponsors. The question of whether any of them had the funds to produce the high-quality programs necessary to compete with the best American radio does not seem to have concerned him much. Presumably this was because he assumed that, with most of the hard costs of equipment and transmission covered by licence-fee revenue, more resources would be available for program building. Spry wrote to F.R. McKelkan in early 1931: "The way to compete with the $28 millions spent on American programmes is not to spend the money in equipment for competing systems but to keep capital costs low and apply as much money as possible to programmes."[63] To another correspondent in late 1930 he declared: "One of the surprising discoveries we have made is that on a national scale the largest radio advertisers are by no means opposed to a national system; indeed two of the largest [the CNR and Imperial Oil] are in favour of it. This is natural. The capital that might be required for equipment could be saved and money made available for programmes. This would tend to improve programmes, and as well give the indirect advertisers greater coverage."[64] Thus, like the Aird commission, the CRL advocated a system in which the listeners would pay for transmitting stations and lines to carry programs that included both advertising for Canadian businesses and American content.[65] This was the concession apparently necessary in order to ensure that the stations and lines were also available for educational, cultural, and national purposes.

The history of the CRL was not one of consistent optimism and success. Internal divisions and criticism did occur and Spry apparently became disheartened in late 1931 to the point that he not only began to consider but to pursue various major compromises with the original goals of the league. He wrote Hume Blake on 18 December that he had the "definite feeling that financial conditions compel a compromise scheme [and] the temporary abandonment of the idea of a single government company."[66] He then drafted a proposal embodying an acceptable alternative, which (after consultation with other league members) he presented the following month to the Duff Royal Commission on Railways and Transportation. If the Aird plan could not be achieved, Spry suggested to the Duff commission, as a compromise and temporary measure there might instead be created a single broadcasting company formed by the CNR, the CPR, Bell Telephone, and Canadian Marconi interests "under the federal government and with directors appointed by the federal government." This model somewhat approximated the British Broadcasting Company before 1927, although one difference was that the revenues of the company would derive not only from licence fees but also from indirect advertising.[67]

The following month Spry also made an overture to the Canadian Association of Broadcasters, trying to convince them that the CAB and CRL were working for a common cause. He encouraged the CAB to back the proposal for a $3 licence fee by suggesting that, if a national company were not in the end set up, the private broadcasters could use the money to help pay for programs or wire transmission.[68]

While neither overture came to anything, these proposals are interesting in that they reveal where Spry drew his bottom line. As has already been seen, the CRL accepted advertising, it accepted the continued existence of small privately owned stations, it accepted a continuing American broadcasting presence; briefly, before the Duff commission, it even accepted private ownership of the national network. Public ownership *per se*, apparently, was expendable; indeed Spry argued to the 1932 Special Committee that the CRL was not fighting for public ownership as a principle but rather simply for practical reasons because radio was "by nature a monopoly."[69] But two tenets were never conceded: that Canada must make more efficient use of broadcasting resources in order – and this was the real goal – to create more and better Canadian programming.[70]

This point having been made, however, it is nonetheless true that the CRL preferred public ownership of transmitting facilities if possible. This was made very clear in Spry's presentation to the Special Committee, in which he argued that public ownership was necessary in order to guarantee Canadian control of the system and to finance good network service.[71] If the network were left to private enterprise, the tendency to American control would remain and the Canadian people would continue to lack effective recourse. The financial advantage of public ownership was that both licence fees and ad revenues could be utilized to pay for the service, whereas under private ownership advertising income – and therefore advertising priorities – would dominate.[72] By May 1932, before the Special Committee, Spry made the league's central goals crystal clear: "Public ownership of stations, private enterprise and competition in programs, these are the two principles of the Radio League position."[73]

The CRL's organizers, while firm in their advocacy of a national broadcasting company, by 1932 had altered the definition and functions of that company markedly from those proposed by the Aird commission. Primarily for tactical reasons, they had abandoned the notion that the public broadcasting company should have a monopoly of broadcasting in Canada. Given their acceptance from the beginning of private-enterprise program production, this was perhaps not viewed as a major modification of the original goal. Yet it was exactly that, for a monopolistic company and one operating in a competitive environment must necessarily function in very different ways – especially (and this was another of their major assumptions) if it must compete with the commercial stations for advertising revenue. As Frank Peers has said, "This was probably the genesis of the Canadian pattern of a mixed, publicly and privately owned system."[74] In the last chapter it was argued that the Aird report was not quite so "pure" in its advocacy of public broadcasting for Canada as has sometimes been assumed. The same may be said for the Canadian Radio League.

THE OPPONENTS OF THE AIRD REPORT'S recommendations were not united by an umbrella organization such as the CRL. At various times Spry and other league members identified the following groups and individuals as "our friends, the enemy": Ralph Ashcroft, Edward Beatty and the CPR, the American electrical and radio trusts, the Canadian Association of Broadcasters, and the province of Quebec.[75] To that list may be added certain radio manufacturing and advertising interests and a handful of newspapers. While much of the behind-the-scenes lobbying of these groups is not as well recorded as that of the CRL, enough remains of their public statements to discern some of the intricacies of the various anti-nationalization positions.

Most of the opposition to the Aird scheme, both organizational and individual, came from Ontario and Quebec. Ontario, at least the southern part, had satisfactory broadcasting under the *status quo* and there was both scepticism and resentment of a plan that was seen to force Ontarians to subsidize radio service to outlying parts of the country at the same time that it reduced their listening choices. Montreal broadcasters and listeners were also fairly complacent, especially given their access to the US networks. In addition, Quebec opinion was affected by historic suspicion of English-Canadian centralist projects, grave doubts about the efficacy of public ownership, and a lesser fear of Americanization. Some Quebecers were also apprehensive about how much French-language programming a single national broadcasting network would or could provide.[76]

The first strong denunciations of the plan to nationalize Canada's broadcasting system appeared in the pages of Montreal's *La Presse* in October 1929. By the spring, Toronto's *Financial Post*, *Globe*, and *Telegram*, the London *Free Press*, the Calgary *Albertan*, and others had joined the attack. Although these newspapers were in the minority (a summary of press comment prepared by Donald Manson in early 1930 showed that thirty-four newspapers favoured the scheme, sixteen opposed it, and fourteen were non-committal[77]), they were impassioned in their critiques of the Aird plan. Self-interest had much to do with the opposition to public broadcasting from this quarter, for most of the hostile newspapers either owned or were closely affiliated to broadcasting stations, but some genuine concerns were also in evidence. Essentially, the editorialists took a *laissez-faire* stance: private enterprise was in principle always preferable to government ownership. They most strongly criticized those aspects of the Aird report that might reduce profitability for Canadian private enterprise in advertising, broadcasting, and receiver sales: increased licence fees, the ban on direct advertising, and the end of competition in programming. Government-monopoly ownership, they feared, would result in programs being selected by a "dictatorial committee" that would ignore the tastes of the "middle and laboring classes." They also warned that costs would be excessive and that "political misuse of the stations" would be a constant danger.[78] However, while the newspapers critical of the Aird plan kept up an intermittent barrage against it and against the CRL until 1932 and a *La Presse* campaign garnered a 22,000-signature petition that was presented to Parliament, the newspapers did not act in concert and none of them presented briefs to the Special Committee.

The majority of broadcasters also opposed the Aird report, both individually and as members of Canadian Association of Broadcasters. At the time the report was issued, the CAB was a diverse organization representing forty broadcasters big and small, including both private and government-owned (CKY, CNR and CKUA) stations, from all parts of the country but especially Ontario and Quebec. While the majority of CAB members strongly favoured private broadcasting, several of the most active members were quite sympathetic to nationalization. Initially, they were all able to rally around two reforms: an improved regulatory commission and better self-regulation.

The idea of a regulatory commission had been proposed in the CAB's brief to the Aird hearings. Though vaguely worded, it included the notion that such a commission be non-partisan and representative of the whole country and that it be given "broad powers and ample appropriation" and the responsibility to "encourage and supervise Dominion wide broadcasting of national patriotic and educational programs."[79] In February 1931 CAB members adopted a self-regulatory resolution on advertising which they forwarded to the minister of Marine, vowing to allow no advertising on Sunday programs produced in Canada "other than the mention of the sponsor's name, address and nature of the sponsor's business or product" and recommending that no more than 5 per cent of air time be allowed for indirect ads weekdays between 7 and 11 p.m. and no spot ads after 7 p.m.[80] This position was repeated before the 1932 Special Committee, where the president of the CAB, Harry C. Moore of CFRB, informally (and loosely) defined indirect advertising as "the name of the sponsor and the line that he is manufacturing and distributing without going into a great deal of detail."[81] Moore explained to the committee members that the CAB supported these restrictions because some of the smaller advertisers needed to be prevented from crowding out programming completely.

In April 1931 the CAB published a pamphlet outlining its position on the Aird report. According to Spry, the pamphlet was prepared by a CAB subcommittee chaired by J.O. Apps, "General Executive assistant of the C.P.R. and Mr. Beatty's principal lobbyist and handyman."[82] The other members included Ralph Ashcroft of CKGW, over which CPRY broadcast, and J.A. Dupont of *La Presse*'s CKAC. Interestingly, one of the first claims the pamphlet made was that, while in 1928–29 "there was undoubtedly ground for complaint" about Canadian broadcasting, things were quite different in 1931: "Broadcasting has advanced very rapidly in the past two years, not only mechanically, but in the quality and purity of the programmes broadcast as well."[83] One of the principal reasons for this progress, according to the CAB, was the added revenue acquired by the broadcasting of American network programs on Canadian stations. (Later, in 1932, the organization admitted that service in the west and the Maritimes was not up to par, but continued to maintain that all was well elsewhere.[84])

The pamphlet began by endorsing a lengthy section from the Canadian Manufacturers' Association's brief to the Aird commission. One key paragraph read:

So long as the United States stays on the basis of private ownership of broadcasting, open by the turn of a dial to the great majority of Canadian listeners-in, with programmes largely produced by advertisers, surely it is unthinkable that Canadian listeners-in would be deprived of Canadian programmes produced by Canadian advertisers. It will readily be seen that not only would Canadian listeners-in be deprived of programmes from their favorite well-known Canadian stations, but the only goodwill being built up in Canada would be for the products and companies of another country coming freely into Canada from stations in the United States.[85]

The pamphlet argued that competition and choice resulted in superior broadcasting and therefore more employment opportunities; the Aird proposal would increase receiving-licence fees "three-fold" while still generating only enough income to produce mediocre programs unable to hold the attention of Canadian audiences, it declared. Some of the claims of the CRL were also refuted, including the argument that "national integrity" was being threatened by growing American control of Canadian radio. No Americans owned Canadian radio stations, the CAB correctly maintained, and "no programmes originating in the United States are broadcast in Canada, except when sponsored through Canadian organizations ..."[86] The pamphlet concluded with a critique of the BBC for giving the British public not what it wanted but what the BBC "thinks it should have" and with a plea for the continuation of private initiative under a "proper system of Government regulation." "A monopoly," the pamphlet's authors declared, "is not to be desired."[87]

The façade of unity within the CAB fell apart in 1931 and 1932 as the time for decisions approached. In early 1931 the representatives of stations that favoured nationalization (the CNR stations, CKY, and the Calgary *Herald*'s station CFAC) all resigned, as they found their position in an organization dominated by the pro-private lobby impossible. (The Toronto *Star*'s CFCA had pulled out earlier.[88]) Shortly after, Ralph Ashcroft of CKGW also resigned, on the opposite grounds that the CAB had not been tough enough in its defence of private broadcasting. At the meeting of 26 February 1932, what was left of the organization hammered out its proposal for future Canadian broadcasting, the linchpin being a 25-cent tax on radio tubes, the revenue from which (estimated at $750,000) would be used to subsidize network lines so that programs originated by stations in major centres could be picked up by smaller outlying stations at nominal cost. By the time the organization made its presentation to the 1932 Special Committee, however, this proposal had vanished, probably because radio-manufacturing allies objected, to be replaced by the suggestion that any surplus income from receiving-licence fees should be used to subsidize programs in the areas not currently well served.[89] The most important contribution of the CAB to the committee hearings was perhaps its analysis of what it believed would be the true costs of the public broadcasting plan. For a start, the organization claimed (unlike either the Aird report or the CRL) that more than $1 million would have to be paid to the existing stations for goodwill in addition to the amount calculated for expropriation of equipment. While the figures produced by the CAB are not strictly comparable with those of the CRL, generally their estimates of the costs of studio operations, transmission lines, and programs were not substantially different. (This is not surprising, as the CAB apparently asked Graham Spry for help putting them together.[90]) Where they parted company was on income. The CAB assumed *no* advertising income, while the CRL estimated that once the network was in full operation (Stage 3), $900,000 would be earned from sponsors each year.[91] Largely as a consequence, the CAB predicted that receiving-licence fees would have to be at least $5.50 per annum – which it knew would be politically unacceptable.

The CAB was an informal, fluid, loosely organized, and meagrely funded organization in the period between 1928 and 1932. Even after its pro-nationalization members dropped out, the association consisted of an awkward mixture of a few very large urban stations and many small weaker ones. One consequence was that, unlike virtually every other interest group involved, the CAB remained firmly in favour of competitive broadcasting and scorned the commonly accepted idea that radio was a natural monopoly.[92] What scraps remain of internal CAB debates suggest that discord prevailed. This is hardly surprising given the nature of the stations and individuals involved: some were pioneers and entrepreneurs, others were government bodies and bureaucrats, still others were modern profit-oriented firms run by managers and ad salesmen. All had different approaches to the business of radio and therefore different reactions to the idea of a monopolistic national broadcasting company for Canada. The organization lacked a consistent membership or leadership, money, and central direction. As a result, the CAB was unable to rally strongly and decisively against the Aird report and the CRL.

Three other organizations that felt their interests threatened by the Aird proposal were the Radio Manufacturers' Association of Canada (RMA), the Association of Canadian Advertisers (ACA), and the Canadian Manufacturers' Association. All were comprised of a mixture of indigenous and American-owned businesses (branch plants); almost all the members of the RMA were also members of the CMA, and their tactics were coordinated with those of the ACA. Most of their activities are not a matter of public record, except for their briefs to the Aird commission and then later to the parliamentary committee. These presentations reveal an essential similarity of view. All defended radio advertising, advocated the subsidization of broadcasting in areas currently poorly served, and called for an improved regulatory system.[93] Notably, both the RMA and the ACA stated specifically that they had no point of view on the question of who actually *owned* the broadcasting stations in Canada; they were more concerned that the stations be fairly regulated and allow advertising. The CMA, however, believed that private competitive ownership was definitely preferable.[94] The briefs from the CMA and the ACA particularly stressed that there must be no limitations on the type of advertising permitted; both contended that indirect advertising would neither serve Canadian advertisers nor raise enough money to improve Canadian broadcasting. Needless to say, they also argued that Canadian listeners had no objection to radio advertising, although the CMA admitted there might be some problems with spot advertising and the RMA supported the CAB in proposing time limits on ads. The brief from the advertisers claimed that "the weak point in Canadian broadcasting at the present time is *not* the presence of advertising in ... programs. Rather, it is the fact that so few of these well planned advertising programs are carried to distant sections of Canada."[95]

The primary concerns of these three organizations were the expansion of the market for receivers and of the audience for advertising messages. Accordingly, they generally supported both improved programming and better coverage of remote areas and opposed higher licence fees. They believed that the growth of the broadcasting industry would be maximized by a well-regulated system in which the government picked up the costs of audience-acquisition in the parts of the country where it was unprofitable for private enterprise to do so. Mainly, this was to be accomplished by government subsidization of transmission lines, but the RMA also urged that the government erect stations in remote areas until it was profitable for private enterprise to take them over. An exchange between

A.M. Patience of the Radio Manufacturers' Association and E.J. Garland, a United Farmers of Alberta MP on the Special Committee, is instructive:

Mr Garland: You suggested ... that the service should be subsidized?
Mr Patience: Yes.
Mr Garland: Advertisers, in other words, get part of their costs defrayed out of the public treasury?
Mr Patience: No ...
Mr Garland: As I understand it, your suggestion is that the advertisers carry the cost of the programs as far as they can in [Ontario and Quebec].
Mr Patience: Yes ...
Mr Garland: But the government is to step in and help to get their advertising into the west and the east?
Mr Patience: Their advertising or their program?
Mr Garland: That is the same thing, is it not ...[96]

These three organizations thus presented to the Special Committee positions that were based not so much on an ideological dichotomy between public and private broadcasting as on a very practical advocacy of public subsidization of private enterprise to stimulate receiver sales and expand the audience for Canadian (and branch-plant) advertisers.

The most vocal individual opponent of the Aird plan was Ralph W. Ashcroft. Ashcroft was advertising manager of Gooderham and Worts distillery company, the manager of CKGW Toronto, and the general manager of Trans-Canada Broadcasting Company, the most successful Canadian network organization. He had ties with the Association of Canadian Advertisers, the Canadian Association of Broadcasters, the Toronto *Telegram* (which broadcast through CKGW), NBC (CKGW was an NBC affiliate), and the CPR (the CPR's phantom station in Toronto used CKGW facilities). He thus exemplified many of the interconnections linking the various unsympathetic groups.

Ashcroft's criticisms of the Aird proposals ran along familiar lines.[97] The commissioners, he said, had completely underestimated the costs involved in setting up and running a public broadcasting company. Advertisers would not pay for useless indirect ads, and high-quality programming was much more expensive than either the Aird commission or the members of the CRL realized. Either a $15-million annual subsidy would be necessary or a $30 licence fee. If substantial sums were not allotted to creating good programs, Canadian radio listeners would simply turn their dials to American stations, thus defeating the whole purpose of the company. "Art, and beauty, and music, recognize no boundaries nor frontiers ... no nation can be self-contained, and sufficient unto itself, in these respects," he passionately declared.

While most people at the time viewed Ashcroft's position as poles apart from that of the CRL, in fact there were some similarities. For example, although by 1932 Ashcroft loudly scoffed at the league's notion that Canadian stations should carry only indirect advertising, his own definition of acceptable advertising, which repudiated spot ads and defined "direct" as "mentioning the name of the sponsor, [and] also saying something about the products that he makes, and their merits and so on ... [for] not over four to five per cent [of the program time]," corresponded almost exactly with Spry's definition of *in*direct advertising.[98]

Ashcroft also agreed with the CRL that radio was a natural monopoly; the many weak Canadian stations, he said, were "more or less useless" in operating as independent units. What was needed, he told the Association of Canadian Advertisers in 1929, was a concerted effort to weed out the poor stations and "to weld and stabilize the others into one cohesive organization either under government or private ownership."[99] As the debate developed, however, Ashcroft's stance changed somewhat. By 1931, although still advocating the elimination of weak stations, he was also stressing the virtues of competition (competition, he said, "spells progress," while monopoly "predicates lethargy, incompetence and intolerance") and suggesting that a parallel to the national transportation system would be the most effective arrangement: two coast-to-coast networks, one a government-operated system under the direction of the CNR, the second a privately owned organization using the telegraph lines of the CPR. Yet by 1932 he had tacked again. He told the Special Committee: "If you had a national broadcasting system, which allowed Canadian sponsors to use direct advertising on their programs, or to have on the stations in Canada programs containing an equivalent amount of advertising to what the United States stations do, we could operate all right under government ownership."[100] Clearly, Ashcroft's primary concern was the use of radio as an advertising medium – ownership, programming, and other matters were all subsidiary to that priority.

Ashcroft's suggestion that a private CPR-controlled broadcasting chain be set up was not an idle or isolated thought. The CPR had just completed an overhaul of its national telegraph lines, making them suitable for broadcasting use in off-peak hours. A phantom station, CPRY, had been set up in Toronto, using CKGW's facilities, and from these studios programs were sent beginning in the spring of 1930 to a chain of twenty-one private stations.[101] While all the evidence is not available, certainly many have suspected both then and since that the CPR was planning a pre-emptive move to use its influence with the Conservative government to seize at least partial control of Canadian radio. (Edward Beatty, chairman of the CPR, was an old friend of the prime minister's; Bennett had been the CPR's solicitor for many years.[102]) The railway had in fact made an application in early 1930 for eleven licences "to establish the chain of broadcasting stations for a Canada wide system as outlined in the report of the Aird Commission," or alternatively, if the report was not adopted, to set up a chain of commercial stations.[103] However, after being informed that no new licences were being issued, the railway reduced its request to one (to remain on file) for three powerful stations at Montreal, Toronto, and Winnipeg; only the phantom CHRY (later CPRY) was actually licensed in the end. Two months after Ashcroft's suggestion about two national chains appeared in print, the case for a CPR chain was made again in an article by J. Murray Gibbon, a publicity agent of the railway, which appeared in the *Canadian Forum*.[104] Gibbon argued that competition and money were essential to provide the best programs and that they could be acquired only by allowing at least some private broadcasting and by encouraging advertisers to sponsor programs. He agreed that service in the west and the Maritimes was less than it should be but felt that a system of two networks, one owned by the government to provide "uplift" to the 10 per cent of the population that wanted it and the other privately owned and financed by ads, would solve that problem.

It was generally assumed in 1931 that this so-called dual network proposal was the most serious rival to the Aird scheme but by 1932 further economic deterioration had led its proponents to adopt the notion of a single privately owned network, in which the two railway companies along with "other important radio interests" would be involved under the supervision of a government commission. This was the proposal that Edward Beatty, chairman of the CPR, brought to the Special Committee in its closing days.[105] It approximately paralleled both the original British Broadcasting Company and the plan suggested by Spry to the Duff commission in the dark days of late 1931.[106]

Beatty's intervention before the Special Committee was interesting not only for its specific content and potential impact but also for its explicit discussion of some of the issues lying behind the debate. In Beatty's view, "the conflict of opinion arises ... as to the place that commerce should be allowed to have in radio ..." He then went on to make his own position clear:

It has occurred to me that if the advantages of this great invention are as we conceive them to be, it would not be fair or proper to deny the benefits of them to the commerce of this country and to commercial institutions. The divergence of view seems to rest upon a fundamental difference in the conception of radio itself, and those who take an extreme view that the practical advantages of radio should be restricted to education and culture, are, I think, unmindful of the fact that modern industry must keep in step with scientific achievements and should not be deprived of the opportunity of utilizing these achievements in its own development.[107]

He also made clear the reasons for his objections to government ownership in explaining the three advantages his proposal had over that of Aird and the CRL: "The first one was that the costs should be removed from the government and therefore from the taxpayer. The second was the risk of political abuse would not exist, at least to the same extent. The third was that I thought we could secure to the corporation a greater excellence of program through the struggle to satisfy the ... advertisers ... [and] I could never conceive of the idea of a government owned and operated system using advertising."[108] Like Ashcroft, Beatty had a primarily commercial interest in radio. He believed that the interests of Canadian listeners would be best fulfilled by supporting Canadian businesses and advertisers.

For the most part, the historians of Canadian broadcasting have cast the debate about the Aird report in black-and-white terms: pro- and anti-public broadcasting. As the more detailed description above makes clear, however, there were many nuances in the positions of the two "sides," and many points on which they were in accord.[109] All agreed, for example, that there must be governmental regulation (control) of broadcasting and that improvements should be made in the current regulatory system. All agreed that this regulation should be non-political. All agreed that the service in outlying regions was poor and that the government should strive to create an equitable situation in which all Canadians were part of the radio audience. All agreed that advertising would continue to be a major source of funding for Canadian broadcasting; while some advocated direct and others indirect ads, by 1932 the definition of direct was so broad that the distinction was almost meaningless. All agreed that competition in program production was a good thing. All agreed that Canadian listeners must continue to be supplied with American programs, although views varied on the extent to which this was appropriate. They also all (with the exception of the CAB and possibly the CMA) agreed that concentration of resources was necessary for the survival of Canadian radio – and everyone wanted that.

There were, nevertheless, definitely two opposing positions in this debate. Some advocated the creation of a publicly owned broadcasting network which, while not necessarily a monopoly and while still somewhat commercial in its orientation, was nevertheless controlled (at arm's length) by the federal government. Others either opposed the creation of such a broadcasting organization or insisted that it be paralleled by an equally strong privately owned network. Thus, the two camps did differ. They differed first in their assumptions about the role of broadcasting in Canadian society. For those against the Aird report, pleasing "*most* of the listeners, *most* of the time"[110] was the highest priority, because the more satisfied listeners, the more sponsors, the more profits, and the better for Canadian business. For those favouring it, the "national interest," the creation of a progressive Canadian public opinion and the construction of national unity and of a sense of Canadian identity, was more important than profits, or, in fact, than catering to the existing tastes of the largest possible number of listeners. Both groups wished to mould the public but to different ends – the one private profit, the other national consciousness. One side thought of radio listeners primarily as consumers, the other as citizens.

A second difference in emphasis resulted. While the private broadcasters found networking an inexpensive means of providing good and popular programs, they also highlighted the community service their stations provided. Much of their advertising revenue came from local advertisers and much of their programming featured events and news of their own communities. At the bottom line, they were dependent on the loyalty of their local listeners. Before the Special Committee, consequently, the proponents of private broadcasting presented themselves as the defenders of the interests and tastes of ordinary Canadians in their own homes and communities. In contrast, by providing only a single station per province (and, for the Maritimes, only one for all three), the Aird report's major stress was clearly on the national level. Although there were provisions for provincial control of programming, there were none for local stations. In its turn, the CRL recognized more fully the importance of radio as an instrument of community service and advocated the creation of small independent stations as well as the national network. Nevertheless, almost all its rhetoric focused on the national task and, as we have seen, some of its leaders were quite frankly working to use radio to overcome "excessive" provincialism. The Aird/CRL position was therefore vulnerable to attack for being both élitist and nationalist, far out of touch with the everyday lives of listeners.[111]

Specifically, the pro-public ownership forces were open to the accusation that they were attempting to impose their own élitist cultural values on others. In this, to some degree, their opponents were correct. While they had nothing against light entertainment, Spry, Plaunt, and the others believed that radio was wasted if it carried almost nothing else. They wanted to see more balanced programming than that which had evolved in the private market-place, programming that entertained but also educated and enlightened. Canadian pundits and journalists had welcomed broadcasting at the beginning of the 1920s as an agency that would promote communication, civilization, unity, and stability. Insofar as the medium had failed to live up to these ideals and had become instead distraction, diversion, and commercialism, it was a deep disappointment to these essentially middle- and upper-middle-class critics.

To many listeners, however, the content of radio programming in the early 1930s was perfectly satisfactory. They had become accustomed to radio fulfilling a certain function as an in-home source of light entertainment and saw no particular need for change. Manufacturers, broadcasters, and advertisers whose success depended upon pleasing the listening audience were understandably reluctant as a result to do more than tinker with the system they had built up over the previous decade. Because the pro-nationalization forces wanted to divert Canadian broadcasting, even in part, to a very different function from the one it had been performing for a decade, they could be – and were – pilloried for advocating an arbitrary and unnecessary change which few besides themselves cared much about.

To a certain extent, then, the debate pitted an "élite" conception of radio against a "popular" one. Yet the division cannot be accurately characterized as a conflict between a "dominant culture" and "oppositional" forces, as a follower of Raymond Williams might be inclined to argue.[112] The culture the CRL and its supporters advocated was by no means clearly dominant in English Canada – much less French – in the 1920s, and the alternative was so heavily mediated by commercial forces and American influence that it is very difficult to see it as "of the people" in any real sense.

The pro- and anti-nationalization groups also differed in their views of American broadcasting. The nationalists deplored and in some cases actually feared what they perceived to be the growing cultural influence of the United States in Canada. They accepted that they must compromise with the enormous popularity of American radio in this country, but only reluctantly. On the other hand, those opposed to nationalization were more ambivalent about American broadcasting. While both Sir John Aird and Graham Spry promised that the proposed company stations would be located so as not to block reception of American stations, this was not what the private broadcasting interests wanted at all. They wanted Canadians to listen to *Canadian* stations to receive Canadian advertisers' messages. They had no objection to American programs – as long as they were rebroadcast through Canadian facilities, where the listeners and sponsors they attracted would help enrich Canadian broadcasters.[113] It was generally agreed by all that American programming was preferred by most Canadians by 1932. The opponents of the Aird/CRL scheme were convinced that the ironic consequence of government broadcasting would be that Canadians would go back to tuning in directly to American stations. The double irony was that, albeit for different reasons, this was at least as problematic for them than it was for those who supported the public broadcasting plan.

The individuals and groups involved in the broadcasting debate also had significantly different perceptions of how satisfactory the Canadian broadcasting situation was in 1930 and 1931. Partly this was because conditions in different parts of the country varied greatly. It was also, however, because they did not come to their views on broadcasting solely as a result of their experience with that medium. Various long-established assumptions and beliefs tinted the lenses through which they studied the radio question. First, of course, there was a long history of economic development by private enterprise in Canada and of widespread popular belief in the inefficiency of the government as compared to the market-place in virtually all fields. That ingrained belief, combined with the fact that the early development of Canadian broadcasting had occurred in the private sector so that vested interests were in place by 1932, added up to a strong and convincing anti-nationalization position. Moreover, Canadians were firm believers in the liberal principle of freedom of the press and easily persuaded that government ownership of the media was abhorrent and dangerous.[114] The opponents of the Aird report, in expressing their concern about the risk of political manipulation of the proposed company, were well within the mainstream of Canadian opinion. On the other hand, there were also traditions in Canada of anti-Americanism and of government ownership of certain utilities for the public and national good. In addition, there was a longstanding tendency to emphasize, both politically and rhetorically, communications as the key to creating and defending nationhood in a large and disparate country contiguous to such a powerful neighbour. While normally implying differing priorities, these two sets of beliefs had coexisted in Canada for some years prior to 1932. It is perhaps not too surprising, then, that in the end a Conservative government was able to write a radio broadcasting act that *de jure* pleased one side and *de facto* the other.

ONE REASON THE INTERESTED PARTIES had so long to debate the Aird commission's recommendations was the legal challenge posed in the spring of 1931 to the right of the federal government to legislate regarding broadcasting.

From the beginning of wireless telephony in Canada, licensing and other regulatory responsibilities were assumed by the federal government. The provinces do not seem to have disputed this state of affairs until about 1922, when the governments of the three prairie provinces began to show an interest in radio control, primarily because of its implications for their provincially owned telephone systems.[115] As has already been described in Chapter 2, the Manitoba government pursued this interest the farthest, reaching an agreement with Ottawa in 1923 granting the Manitoba Telephone System a monopoly of broadcasting in the province but leaving ultimate regulatory authority in federal hands. The comment of Radio Branch Director C.P. Edwards on the arrangement is significant:

In 1923 the Manitoba Government represented that under the British North

America Act the Province enjoyed authority over broadcasting and they prepared a Bill for the Provincial Legislature giving the Minister of Telephones power to license stations and control radio.

The Dominion Government at that time was not anxious to fight a constitutional case on the relative authorities of the Federal and Provincial administrations, and as the interest of the Manitoba Government appeared to be confined to broadcasting, an amicable arrangement was reached whereby the Provincial Government agreed to accept the jurisdiction of the Dominion over all radio affairs; the Dominion Government on its part agreed not to issue any broadcasting licenses in Manitoba without concurrence of the Minister of Telephones.

The Province desired a government monopoly of radio in Manitoba. The Dominion Government agreed to this, as the experiment of Government broadcasting in Canada was of great interest ...[116]

So the matter rested until the Aird royal commission was formed. The mandate of the commission suggested that one possible future arrangement was provincial control and operation of all Canadian stations. Although this was not the ultimate recommendation, the Aird report nevertheless allocated authority over all *programming* to the provinces. This division of responsibility derived logically from the conception of radio as primarily an educational instrument (education being clearly under provincial jurisdiction) while also allowing the federal government to keep control of transmission, wavelengths, and other matters affecting more than one province.

The Aird commissioners consulted all nine provincial governments during the course of their hearings. Each of these governments pledged cooperation in endeavouring to create a satisfactory Canadian broadcasting system; New Brunswick and Quebec, however, both added statements attesting to their view that the jurisdictional question was by no means yet resolved.

Quebec made the first move. In 1929 the Liberal government of L.-A. Taschereau passed a radio broadcasting act enabling the province to set up its own station or to create programs that could be carried by other stations; CKAC Montreal began carrying "L'Heure Provinciale" in December 1929.[117] Difficulties began when a year later the government tried to make arrangements for time on CKCV in Quebec City for a network tie-in for the program. CKCV did not have, and was not able to obtain, the appropriate time allocation, which apparently so enraged Premier Taschereau (who suspected political interference) that he informed the federal government that he was planning to press Quebec's claim to jurisdiction over broadcasting.[118] On 4 April 1931 Quebec passed a radio act giving its government complete licensing authority within the province.[119]

In the meantime, however, in early February, the federal government informed Taschereau that it planned to submit the jurisdictional question to the Supreme Court for its opinion. (This sort of reference couched in general terms and not relating to a specific legal case was relatively rare at the time.) The fate of Quebec's legislation and the anticipated passage of a new federal broadcasting act would await the outcome of the case, which it was assumed from the beginning would be finally resolved only by the highest court, the Judicial Committee of the Privy Council in London.

The Supreme Court hearings were held on three days in early May 1931. Specifically, the court was asked two questions:

1. Has the Parliament of Canada jurisdiction to regulate and control radio communication, including the transmission and reception of signs, signals, pictures and sounds of all kinds by means of Hertzian waves, and including the right to determine the character, use and location of apparatus employed?
2. If not, in what particular or particulars or to what extent is the jurisdiction of Parliament limited?[120]

Quebec's position was supported by the provinces of Ontario and New Brunswick, while Manitoba, Saskatchewan, and Alberta were represented by counsel but did not take an active part in the case.[121] Counsel for Quebec claimed that radio fell clearly within provincial authority over "property and civil rights" and "matters of a merely local or private nature" according to subsections 13 and 16 of section 92 of the British North America Act.[122] Interestingly, the case was not argued on the basis of education, a content question, but on the more technical grounds of property and technology.[123]

For the federal government, this radio reference was part of a larger campaign to attempt to reverse the historical tendency of the high courts to expand provincial powers. One of the principal arguments its lawyers used was that radio communication, by its nature and uses, clearly fell under the "peace, order and good government" clause of section 91 of the BNA Act, and was therefore a federal responsibility. Counsel for the Dominion "endeavoured to demonstrate the pervasive character of radio waves, the impossibility of limiting their effect within the confines of any province and the necessary association between sending and receiving stations, making in effect, one operation as necessarily extra-provincial in character as a telegraph wire running from one province to another."[124] As to the last point, the federal government also claimed jurisdiction under the exceptions listed in section 92, subsection 10 (a) of the BNA Act, arguing that radio was analogous to "telegraphs and other works and undertakings connecting the province with any other or others of the provinces or extending beyond the limits of the province." The federal case also stressed the international treaty obligations of the Canadian government. This position was backed by a factum presented by Brooke Claxton for the Canadian Radio League, which, as we have seen, had decided to intervene on behalf of "the public" despite some initial hesitation about siding so openly with federal authority.[125] In addition to the arguments made by the Dominion, the league pointed out that the federal government must supervise the powerful impact of broadcasting on national public opinion.

The Supreme Court handed down its decision on 30 June 1931. Chief Justice F.A. Anglin and two of the other judges found in favour of the federal government; two judges, Thibaudeau Rinfret and J.H. Lamont, dissented. According to the majority, the subject at issue was "radio communication" – not the instruments used but "the effects produced by them," which clearly went beyond provincial boundaries. According to the minority, radio was a matter of specific transmitting and receiving instruments which were not physically connected. Therefore it did not fall under section 92 (10) (a) but rather under the property clause, although both dissenting justices admitted that the federal government probably had jurisdiction in some aspects of radio. The decision was not clear-cut, not only because of the split but because the majority carefully noted that their conclusion must be read only "in the light of the present knowledge of Hertzian waves and radio."[126]

As anticipated, Quebec appealed to the JCPC, supported by the government of Ontario. Once again the Canadian Radio League sent Brooke Claxton to support the federal government side. The arguments, similar to those previously made, were heard in December 1931 and the judgment rendered in favour of federal jurisdiction on 9 February 1932.[127] The federal government based its case on three points: its responsibility under the "peace, order and good government" clause of section 91 of the BNA Act; section 92 (10) (a) regarding inter-provincial undertakings; and section 132, the clause giving the federal government treaty-making powers. On the last point, it argued on the basis of its signature on the 1927 (Washington) International Radiotelegraph Convention. The JCPC judges rejected the claim that the Washington Convention was a treaty as defined by section 132, but accepted that "it [came] to the same thing." Because the question of the Dominion making treaties had not been thought of in 1867, they concluded that this fell under the residual "peace, order and good government" clause. They also accepted the federal government's contention that radio communication was an inter-provincial undertaking under section 92 (10) (a). And they rejected Quebec's claim that, while transmitters might be inter-provincial, receiving sets were purely local matters: "Broadcasting as a system cannot exist without both a transmitter and a receiver ... The system cannot be divided into two parts, each independent of the other ... A divided control between transmitter and receiver could only lead to confusion and inefficiency." The decision seemed clear and definitive; subsequently, however, there has been considerable debate about whether the judgment referred only to equipment and technique or whether it also covered program content.[128] It is on the assumption of the former (it may be noted that the reference question indeed seems to relate only to the technical aspects of radio) that the jurisdictional issue has continued to resurface in the broadcasting field.[129] But these were concerns for the future. For the moment, the way was finally cleared for the Bennett government to enact the long-delayed broadcasting legislation.

11 The Radio Broadcasting Act of 1932

Within a month of the Judicial Committee's ruling on 9 February 1932 upholding the federal government's authority over radio, Prime Minister Bennett announced the formation of a parliamentary committee to recommend a course of action. This committee reported on 9 May; the broadcasting bill was introduced on the 16th and passed with one dissenting vote on the 24th. Quickly ratified by the Senate, the act received royal assent on 26 May 1932. The circumstances in which the Bennett government's radio legislation was written in the spring of 1932, however, were very different from those at the time of the Aird report. Before turning to the final chapters of this story, the hearings of the Special Committee and the passage of the Radio Broadcasting Act, a brief review of the Canadian broadcasting situation at the beginning of 1932 will provide the context for that dénouement.

When the Aird commission hearings were held in the spring of 1929 about 300,000 radio receivers were licensed in Canada. By the time the Conservative government was ready to legislate, this number had doubled to just under 600,000. A great part of this increase was attributable to the drop in receiver prices that accompanied the widespread introduction of smaller, electrically operated table models in about 1930; it was also to some extent a product of better broadcasting, including widening access in the Toronto and Montreal areas to American network programs. Despite the onset of the Depression, the percentage of Canadian homes with radios rose from about 15 per cent to over 30 per cent within these three years. Radio-owners remained a minority of the population, however, and were still disproportionately concentrated in urban areas and in

Ontario. The vast majority of the radios purchased as new or replace-ment sets were by 1932 made or assembled in Canada and consequently a more vigorous, if largely branch-plant, manufacturing industry and lobby had come into existence.

At the beginning of April 1928, when the notion of an investigative committee was first bruited, Deputy Minister Alexander Johnston of the Department of Marine and Fisheries sent a form letter to all broadcasting licence applicants: "I am ... directed to inform you that as a result of seemingly unsatisfactory conditions in the matter of Canadian broadcasting services, the Government may at some future day discontinue the present policy and as an alternative adopt a policy of National Broadcasting. It is deemed desirable to give this intimation at this time in order that licensees may govern themselves accordingly."[1] The licences issued in 1929 and 1930 were emblazoned across the top with a warning that they were (as usual) for one year only and that renewal would be "contingent on the report of the Royal Commission on Radio Broadcasting." If that were not explicit enough, stations were routinely warned, as was CKAC Montreal when it received authorization for a new high-power transmitter in September 1928, that "the Department would not in the event of the establishment of a National Broadcasting System, be responsible for any compensation which might be claimed by your Company in respect of cap-ital outlay involved in the proposed new station."[2] As of 1 January 1929, all applicants for new broadcasting licences as well as those requesting increases to more than 100 watts of power were informed that they must wait until the Aird commission's report was dealt with.[3] Later this was loosened and some requests were granted, although the successful appli-cants continued to be warned that they would have no claim on the government in the event of nationalization.[4]

The significance of these provisions was and is controversial; supporters of private broadcasting have blamed government indecisiveness after 1929 for the inadequacies that led Parliament to opt for a radio broad-casting commission in 1932.[5] No doubt many broadcasters did abjure expensive renovations in this period and some artificial lag in development resulted. Nevertheless, Canadian broadcasting did improve greatly between 1929 and 1932; many advocates of private broadcasting not only admitted but boasted of this improvement before the Special Committee.[6] Moreover, it is clear that many broadcasters did undertake new investment, especially in the markets that were already profitable. Returns from a questionnaire sent out by the Special Committee to all Canadian broadcasting stations in March 1932 indicated that the value of the physical plant of the forty-eight stations replying (most of the eighteen that did not answer were small) was $701,000 in March 1928 and had more than doubled to $1,510,000 by March 1932, although equipment prices were falling in this period. The owners of thirteen stations made new investments of more than $20,000 in the period; the owners of five – CKOC Hamilton, CKY Winnipeg, CJRM/CJRW Fleming, Saskatchewan, CKAC Montreal, and CFRB Toronto – spent more than $70,000. It is not surprising that CKAC led the fight against nationalization; *La Presse* had gambled on pouring almost $180,000 into the station in these four years.[7]

Between 1928 and 1932 a large number of stations also filed requests to increase their power and twenty-five were allowed to do so. Five of those received substantial increases, albeit sometimes after considerable delay: CKAC Montreal from 500 to 5000 watts; CFRB Toronto from 1000 to 4000 and then to 10,000 watts; the latter's arch-rival, CKGW Toronto, from 5000 to 10,000 watts; CJGC London from 500 to 5000 watts; and CFCN Calgary from 500 to 10,000 watts. Indeed, these increases, particularly those granted to stations with American network links, have been criticized by historians such as Frank Peers on quite the opposite grounds: that they were inappropriate on the eve of potential nationalization of the principal stations and indicated that "Canadian public authority was most reluctant to interfere with private initiative or with property values."[8]

Up to four hundred firms and individuals (about one hundred of them bona fide, according to Commander Edwards)[9] also applied for new licences in this period, an indication that certainly some businessmen viewed the risk of confiscation as less than the profit potential of broadcasting. Only three new licences were granted, however, in these three years: one to a 50-watt educational station owned by Acadia University, one for a 1000-watt station to a commercial group in Windsor, Ontario, and the third for an amateur broadcasting station in Trail, British Columbia. (As well, VAS, the Canadian Marconi trans-Atlantic transmitter at Louisbourg, was given permission to broadcast at certain times of the day.[10]) The restrictions on new licensing are difficult to fault; even the most ardent advocate of private broadcasting in 1930 or 1931 would have been hard put to argue that Canada needed more little broadcasting stations at that point.

The Canadian Radio League, for its part, used as much influence as it could to persuade the government not to allow power increases or new stations in this period. From the CRL point of view, the more large stations the more costly a takeover would be, and the less necessary, thus discouraging nationalization. The league had to be circumspect about this opposition, however. As Spry explained frankly to one friend with reference to the power increase granted to CFCN Calgary: "The Canadian Radio League cannot very well publicly protest against this action because it would look as if we were trying to deprive the public of improved service."[11]

The net effect of these changes was to skew the inequalities in the system even further; reception of Canadian stations in southern Ontario and Montreal became better, the rest stayed much the same. Canadian broadcasting also remained considerably less developed than American. By 1932 there were thirteen American stations with 50 kilowatts of power, while the strongest Canadian station was at 10 kw. A number of Canadian stations, including CKY, CKGW, CFRB, CFCA, CFCF, CKAC, CNRO, and CNRM, filed requests for 50 kilowatts with the Radio Branch in this period, as did the CPR for two new stations at Toronto and Montreal. Some proponents of private broadcasting indicted the Radio Branch for not granting these applications but that charge was to some extent not justified. For one thing, the branch's hands were tied by the perennial problem of lack of frequencies. Moreover, as we have seen, the branch had always been dilatory about power increases; it was not any worse in this respect after 1929 than before – although this point was an effective argument for a new regulatory body. Also, it is difficult to tell how serious these applications were. All were filed in the full knowledge that they would not be dealt with until the political decisions about broadcasting were made. Some of the applications at least, and probably many, were thus purely tactical and, as far as can be determined, none involved immediate construction plans. CKY's application, for example, was only on condition that no other station on the prairies ever be granted 50 kw, a condition no licensing authority could have met.

As described in Chapter 3, networking became significant in Canadian radio only after 1928. In 1929, 1930, and 1931, national Canadian chain programs were increasingly common and successful, spurred by the installation of the CN and CP carrier lines and growing interest from national advertisers. This improvement ceased abruptly, however, during the 1931–32 season, when few advertisers were apparently willing to pay the expensive line-transmission charges involved in network arrangements to the west and the Maritimes.[12] This fact was seized upon by both sides in the broadcasting debate, the CRL arguing that it proved that a public system was essential, its opponents claiming that all it indicated was the need for governmental assistance with wireline charges. The paring down of the CNR's Radio Department after July 1931 in order to save the beleaguered railway money also led to a severe cut-back in that organization's national network programs.

In August 1931 Austin Weir of the CNR's Radio Department penned a pair of internal memos arguing strongly for negotiations between CN and CP Telegraphs (either cooperatively or competitively with Bell Telephone, then just on the verge of becoming part of a cross-Canada telephone-line system) to work toward arranging cheaper transmission charges and a joint programming organization in order to encourage national broadcasting. He declared that, as a result of geography, demography, and profit-taking, "Canada is the most expensive country in creation in which to conduct chain broadcasting."[13] Because of high wire rates, Weir concluded, "the present tendency is to concentrate on Eastern Canada and particularly in Ontario and Quebec, where the wire-haul is short. That tendency is certain to increase owing to economic conditions."[14] In this same era, as we have already seen, four of the most powerful Canadian stations initiated network ties with NBC and CBS. Between 1929 and 1932, therefore, networking became very much more significant in Canadian broadcasting, but the consequences were mixed. Although it was probable that the decline in national chain programs in Canada was a temporary phenomenon related to the Depression, the fear of individuals such as Weir was that the American network presence would be permanently implanted during the hiatus.

Partly as a result of expanding network programming, the number of hours of service on Canadian stations rose considerably between 1929 and 1932. Once again, however, this was more noticeable on the large urban stations, which now provided all-day service, than on smaller stations in outlying areas. The popularity of American network shows with both listeners and affiliated broadcasters was increasingly evident as well. To the CRL, this demonstrated the growing "danger" of Americanization, but it also suggested that there were limits beyond which the nationalist élite could not push in trying to Canadianize radio. To those against nationalization, it indicated that the Canadian private broadcasting industry was serving the public interest by providing what the listeners wanted and that, once economic conditions returned to normal, the industry would be quite capable of developing good service on a profitable basis at least in the more heavily populated parts of the country.

During this period powerful Mexican and Cuban stations began to cause interference problems on some exclusive Canadian wavelengths. This increased the desire within the Radio Branch to get the North American wavelength arrangements cleared up and to endeavour to erect more Canadian high-power stations.[15] It was also an incentive to get some sort of national radio policy adopted quickly.[16] After the election of the Conservatives, all major decisions about power, wavelengths, station licensing, and regulatory changes were forwarded to the minister of Marine, Alfred Duranleau, and through him to Prime Minister Bennett.[17] Because fundamental decisions were pending, the whole process was overtly political in a way it had not been before. For instance, the Toronto wavelength and power assignments were all readjusted in the fall of 1931 after detailed consultation between Commander Edwards, Duranleau, and Bennett. The result was five wavelengths for the Toronto area, each of the major stations being allowed to broadcast full time if it wished. (The *Star*'s CFCA got the worst assignment at 1120 kHz.[18]) Toronto remained the exception however; in most other markets the old policies forcing time-sharing among stations remained the norm.

Regulatory changes of the post-Aird period included the gradual widening of the definition of direct advertising and a more carefully formulated approach to the use of records and electrical transcriptions, both of which have already been discussed. The government also decided in the spring of 1932 to increase the receiving-licence fee from $1 to $2. While justified as being necessary for revenue purposes, most of the money in fact went not to the Radio Branch but to the consolidated revenue fund. The fee increase, in the context of the deepening Depression, caused a considerable outcry.[19] The reaction likely had a sobering effect on politicians being asked to consider a further hike to $3 to finance the proposed public broadcasting company (not to mention the possibility that the figure might be as high as the $15 to $30 prophesied by the opponents of nationalization).

Bennett announced the formation of the parliamentary committee on 2 March and it began its meetings on the 11th. The mandate of the committee was to consider the Aird report, to "advise and recommend a complete technical scheme for radio broadcasting in Canada, so designed as to ensure from Canadian sources as complete and satisfactory a service as the present development of radio science will permit," and to "investigate and report upon the most satisfactory agency for carrying out such a scheme."[20] Appointed to the Special Committee were five Conservatives (Dr Raymond Morand, J.O. Gagnon, W.A. Beynon, R.K. Smith, and D.M. Wright), three Liberals (P.J.A. Cardin, W.D. Euler, and J.L. Ilsley), and one United Farmers of Alberta member (E.J. Garland). It was assumed by many that all four Opposition members favoured the Aird report and public broadcasting. The views of the Conservative members were not clear; Graham Spry thought that they had "nasty faces" but also claimed to be on good personal terms with most of them.[21]

The hearings of the Special Committee covered parts of twenty-two days and fill (with appendices) over seven hundred pages of text. Much information and many opinions were gathered, representing many different views on the state of Canadian broadcasting and what should be done about it. Little of this need be repeated here, for the essentials of the positions staked out at the hearings have all been described in the previous chapters.

Several authorities have since suggested that the CRL "dominated" the proceedings of the Special Committee. While that is an exaggeration, nonetheless the almost continuous presence of Graham Spry and other CRL leaders and Spry's two presentations on behalf of the league helped keep its option constantly visible. So too did the submissions from a number of other groups supporting the league, such as the National Council of Women, the Trades and Labour Congress, and the British Empire Service League, as well as the CRL-organized mid-hearings barrage of telegrams to committee members.[22]

In his first statement, Spry summed up in "a few and definite words" the league's objects:

1. Canadian operation and ownership of stations.
2. Government regulation and control of broadcasting.
3. Competition and private enterprise in programs.
4. Greater revenue for more and better Canadian programs.
5. Canadian coverage, clearer reception, and fewer and larger stations.
6. The elimination of direct advertising sales appeals, but the continuation of sponsored programs.
7. The development of broadcasting, not only as a means of entertainment, but as "an effective instrument in nation building."
8. The fullest protection of the language and character of the Province of Quebec.
9. Immediate action by Parliament to ensure Canada's interests are safeguarded at the Madrid Radiotelegraph Conference in September, 1932.[23]

Among these demands, the emphasis on Quebec's needs and on the urgency of the international frequency-allocation issue may be particularly noted, as well as the generally minimal and modest nature of the whole package, especially in its complete avoidance of even a suggestion of nationalization. The highlight of Spry's second appearance before the committee was his presentation of a detailed three-stage plan for putting public broadcasting into operation, which did more openly advocate public ownership of a high-power chain to be in operation in five to seven years.[24]

The CRL position was bolstered by the appearance of Gladstone Murray, the Canadian-born director of public relations for the BBC (the league raised the money for his travel expenses and Brooke Claxton briefed him on his presentation).[25] Murray provided the committee members with a brief history of the BBC, reminded them that the initiative for public broadcasting in Britain came originally from Conservatives, and argued eloquently that radio was a natural monopoly too important to society to be left to private ownership. He reassured them that local broadcasting would continue in Canada, that they need not fear political manipulation of the national broadcasting company, and that the system could be self-financing. He also pointed out that the big American radio interests were watching the Canadian situation closely and that criticism of the advertiser-dominated system in the United States was growing. According to newspaper reports shortly after the committee finished its work, Murray's intervention was one of the most effective and influential of the whole session.[26]

Spry also arranged for Dr Joy Elmer Morgan of the American National Committee on Education by Radio to appear before the committee. Morgan was carefully coached to emphasize the power of the "RCA group" and the inability of the Federal Radio Commission to harness the big chains effectively. He was asked to downplay the rhetoric about radio as a medium of education, however, because "private interests are using the argument that the Canadian Radio League wants to have only educational programmes and to abolish Amos'n Andy etc."[27]

There were a few surprises at the committee hearings. One was the appearance of the Ontario Radio League, a listeners' group of mysterious origins (although everyone assumed that Ralph Ashcroft was behind it). The members of the organization were apparently the 50,000 individuals who had sent in postcards in response to a direct appeal opposing government ownership, largely on the grounds that listeners in southern Ontario should not be penalized to pay for service to outlying regions.[28] The government of Nova Scotia presented a brief strongly questioning the need for public ownership and claiming that there was now little support for the Aird report's conclusions in that province.[29] The Nova Scotia brief expressed a view shared by many Maritimers concerned that the plan to erect one powerful station in that region would destroy the local-interest broadcasting that was the only effective counterweight to the appeal of US stations. From the west, radio pioneer W.W. Grant of CFCN Calgary reiterated another well-worn theme in his contention that, given the realities of the continental entertainment market, Canadian stations could hold listeners only by scheduling up to one-third of their airtime with the popular American programs so loved by Canadian radio fans.[30]

The three members of the royal commission appeared before the committee on separate occasions and attempted to explain some of the key elements of their report. There seemed to be considerable confusion among committee members, never really cleared up, as to precisely what "public ownership" meant to Aird, Bowman, and Frigon; most particularly, how independent of the government had they intended the broadcasting company to be?[31] Neither was the crucial question of advertising clarified; Sir John stated that he favoured only indirect advertising but then offered a definition thereof that went beyond the one given in the report three years earlier.[32] Aird also suggested that the financing arrangements recommended by the report should be altered because of the Depression. His new proposals were more in line with the CRL's position: a total expenditure of $2.5 million, of which $1.8 million would come from a $3 licence fee, the rest from indirect ads, and none from parliamentary subsidy. Like the CRL, he also now advocated that small local stations not owned by the company be allowed to continue in existence, possibly financed by indirect ads or voluntary subscriptions.

Perhaps the most telling of Aird's comments to the Special Committee was his clear explanation of why he and his fellow commissioners had rejected the notion that the government subsidize private stations to improve Canadian coverage. Throughout the years of the broadcasting debate, all had agreed (although for different reasons) that as many Canadians as possible should have access to Canadian stations. As we have seen, the private broadcasters and some of their allies had advocated that this could be ensured by government subsidy to private stations or networks; most commonly, they proposed that the government pay some of the rental costs of telegraph- or telephone-transmission lines to remote areas. That Aird, who was by all accounts certainly a believer in private enterprise, rejected this option was crucial. It was the key to his commission's recommendation of the alternative of a national company. The reasons why the Aird commissioners made this choice had never before 1932 been fully elaborated. This is what Aird told the Special Committee:

The possibility of subsidies from the Dominion treasury to private broadcasting stations has been mooted, but the experience of Canada with subsidies during the period of building competitive railways has hardly been so satisfactory as to warrant a proposal that it be repeated in the building of competitive broadcasting stations or chains of stations.

One method of subsidy sometimes proposed for the benefit of private ownership is that the Dominion government should pay the cost of running land lines across Canada between the private stations. Even though this proposed subsidy only applied to broadcasting without advertising, it would be an indirect subsidy to radio advertising. It is well known that radio advertisers are willing to pay more to the private stations for the privilege of coming on the air immediately before, or immediately after, a broadcasting hour of national significance.

Quite apart from the objection to subsidizing radio advertising, the government would be placed in a very difficult position, indeed an impossible position, in having to decide who among private station interests are to be allowed to enjoy the benefit of this proposed subsidy. Under private ownership, the enjoyment of an exclusive wavelength is a special privilege. It would surely be a very special privilege to be subsidized from the Dominion treasury as well as to be granted a wavelength monopoly. Canada's experience in the past has demonstrated that subsidies tend to invite political pressure on the government, as well as to encourage duplication and over-building. It would be a serious error to burden radio broadcasting in Canada with subsidies, whether for land lines or any other form of broadcasting equipment under private ownership.[33]

Since 1923 the federal government had had the power to give a proportion of receiving-licence fees to private broadcasters. For the reasons Aird summed up so well, that right had never been exercised except in the case of the provincially owned Manitoba stations. For the same reasons, it remained a dubious option in 1932 – although, as we shall see, the 1932 act opened the door to a variant of the same idea.

In introducing the special committee's report in the House on 9 May,[34] Dr Morand, the chairman, told the members that the committee had identified four central problems in Canadian broadcasting: the lack of coverage, the lack of trans-Canada or inter-provincial broadcasting, the lack of a body to supervise programs and advertising material, and the danger that a monopoly might be established.[35] While of the opinion that radio constituted a natural monopoly, according to Morand the committee members feared that a private monopoly might fall under American control. They therefore recommended the creation of a radio commission with the power to regulate and control all broadcasting in Canada (including determination of number, location, and power of all stations and issuance of licences), to own and operate stations, to originate and purchase programs, to prohibit privately owned networks, and, "subject to the approval of the Parliament of Canada, to take over all broadcasting in Canada." The commission was to consist of three paid commissioners as well as assistant commissioners from each province (appointed by the federal government "in consultation" with the provincial governments) who would act as chairmen of provincial-advisory program committees. The Special Committee also recommended that a chain of high-power stations be built, supplemented by a number of medium-power stations, the precise locations to be decided after a technical survey. Low-power stations (100 watts and under) were to remain in private hands but be regulated by the commission. While the commission would have the right to prohibit the private stations from establishing chains, under questioning Morand explained that the intention was simply to give regulatory control to the commission: it might prohibit private chains, but it might well not. The committee recommended that no government subsidy be given to finance broadcasting; instead, all receipts from licence fees (the amount of the fees still to be determined by the Governor in Council) and advertising and other business were to accrue to the commission. Specific rules defining direct or indirect advertising were to be worked out by the commission itself, but it was to be limited to 5 per cent of program time. The committee, according to Morand, believed that advertising must be allowed to enable Canadian businesses to compete against American. The commission was to establish a national network service as soon as possible and "eventually" to acquire all necessary stations revenues allowed.

R.B. Bennett was known as a prime minister who kept close control over his caucus. It is highly unlikely that the Conservatives on the Special Committee would have agreed to a report substantially at odds with the views of the prime minister and Cabinet.[36] Within two weeks of the report's issuance, a draft bill of a new radio broadcasting act was ready. As we shall see in a moment, it accepted the broad outlines of the committee's recommendations, although it did weaken them in significant ways. Why had Bennett and the Conservatives opted for this kind of commission over the other options many assumed they would prefer?

The rejection of the *status quo* is not really surprising. The evidence that this system resulted in poor broadcasting unable to serve all parts of the country was overwhelming; Canadian firms simply lacked the resources to build stations competitive with the best American ones either technically or in provision of popular programming. Canadian geography also made national networking too costly for the private sector. For the reasons Aird outlined, direct governmental subsidy of private stations was impossible. Virtually everyone agreed, therefore, that some sort of more centralized, network-oriented system was needed, one that could be funded by licence-fee revenue without political repercussions. Such an arrangement was also necessary because of the limited number of wavelengths available, that is, because radio was a "natural monopoly."

What, then of the alternative presented by Edward Beatty to the Special Committee – a privately owned monopoly controlled primarily by the two national railways? This model was viewed by most as the real threat to the public-broadcasting option; indeed rumors flew in the weeks just before the introduction of the legislation that that would be Bennett's choice.[37] Why was it not?

There are probably several answers to this question. On the positive side, certainly the lobbying activities of the Canadian Radio League cannot be discounted. The league's near-steady pressure over two years not only kept the government-company option alive but gave the impression that many influential and vocal Canadians backed it. The constant reiteration of the argument that private monopoly would lead to control by the "radio trust," as well as the emotional appeals to Canadian nationalism and anti-Americanism, resonated in the hearts of both progressive and conservative Canadians.

In somewhat the same vein, it has been suggested that the pro-British Bennett was personally swayed by a mix-up that prevented the airing of the 1931 Inter-Empire Christmas Broadcast because of problems with the Canadian link.[38] This broadcast necessitated the cooperation of the BBC, Marconi, AT&T, Bell Telephone, and the CNR. The details need not be pursued, but the reluctance of Marconi Wireless and Bell Telephone to give up their lines for forty-five minutes in peak time without recompense was one factor in the brouhaha, cannily fomented by the CRL as revealing Canada's vulnerability to the "alien monopoly influence" headquartered in New York.[39] The message Bennett received was that cooperative broadcasting ventures involving utilization of the lines of large corporations could easily go awry. If one brief broadcast could cause so much unpleasant publicity, what might happen if the government engaged in a permanent arrangement of this type? Brooke Claxton confided to Gladstone Murray: "There is no doubt that the obstruction has done good to the cause of national control in Canada."[40]

The technical adviser to the 1932 Special Committee was Lieutenant-Colonel W.A. Steel of the Department of National Defence. He had also, as director of the Radio Division of the National Research Council, been Bennett's adviser on radio matters for some months previous.[41] In a series of memos written for the prime minister in late 1931 Steel presented a carefully argued case for the public broadcasting model. The first two memos, composed in November and December, summed up the technical requirements of full service for Canadians and the current state of affairs. On the latter point it was Steel's view that Canadian broadcasting had deteriorated since 1929 in the sense that Canadian programs were now heard less and American more than ever, thus making extremely urgent the need for a definitive broadcasting policy.[42] The third memo in the series confronted the question of public versus private ownership of Canadian broadcasting. Here the arguments originally put forward by Charles Bowman in 1928 were reiterated. "Canadian programs are necessary for the entertainment and education of the people, for political purposes, and to tie all parts of Canada together when events of nation wide or empire wide importance are taking place," it began. Unfortunately, no Canadian companies – *including* either of the railways – had the resources necessary to undertake the heavy financial investment involved in erecting the powerful stations Canada needed. The only really wealthy concerns in the electrical or communications field were American subsidiaries. Privately owned broadcasting in Canada thus could only mean "broadcasting ... in the hands of American interests."[43]

The final memo in the series gave a more detailed analysis of the pros and cons of private and public broadcasting, of whether radio should be considered "as a new instrument for promoting the nation's interests, or as a business to be conducted for financial returns."[44] Steel's presentation of the case was hardly objective. Each point raised in defence of the private system was answered with a careful rebuttal. His final sentence summed up his conclusion: "It is difficult to conceive of any government system more inadequate, from the point of view of popular opinion, than the existing one." He added one further politically telling point in an appendix: "The adoption of a private ownership scheme in Canada ... would not only suggest inferentially the condemnation of the British scheme of public ownership, but would ignore the experience of Great Britain, which compelled the change to public ownership, and would also endorse the American scheme of private ownership, now under partial condemnation in the United States." The appendix to the final memo also summarized what Steel considered "the facts" necessary to the final decision Bennett's government must make. First, under the heading "Technical," he argued that only government subsidies would enable private broadcasters to serve the sparsely settled regions of the country and that the United States would never allow Canada enough wavelengths for complete competitive service. Under "Financial," he pointed out that the proposed company would need unlimited advertising revenues, but that even then the government would inevitably have to contribute directly as well, for it would be under an obligation to see that a body it had created "adequately serves the public."[45] Finally, under "Political," Steel offered the most emotional argument against the concept of a private monopoly, namely that it would be susceptible to "foreign influence." "It is idle to suggest," he wrote,

(as has been suggested) that, within the Charter, any provision could be embodied which would offer practical assurance against foreign manipulation or control. Such a corporation, the shares of which would be listed in the market could, of course, be acquired by the representatives of foreign interests. *The substitution, therefore, of one private corporation for the many independent and non-coordinated companies now existing is merely the simplification of the means by which foreign domination could be achieved.* [emphasis added]

As Steel saw it, private-monopoly ownership would mean, even in the short run, "a declaration of alliance with the 'big interests,'" termination of the small stations that could be allowed to continue under public ownership, and public suspicion that rumoured power and private-transportation monopolies were sanctioned by the government. Public ownership, in his view, meant Canadian control; private-monopoly ownership meant, eventually but inevitably, foreign control.

No one memo or one opinion decides a government on a course of action. But Steel presented the most compelling reasons why Bennett should not follow the course toward private monopoly urged by his old friends in the CPR. To A.R. Kaufman, a Kitchener businessman who passionately enunciated the traditional case against public ownership as both inefficient and wasteful, Bennett later wrote: "With much that you have written I think you must know that I am wholly in accord, and nothing but the realization that radio broadcasting is in its very nature a monopoly, and that it would be highly improvident to grant such a monopoly to any private interest at this time, induced the Government to take the action it did."[46] He continued: "We are dealing with an industry that is in its infancy, and about which we know little or nothing." Thus, "I think you will agree with me that it would be a very improvident Government that would part with such an asset at this time."

Bennett, in other words, was persuaded that radio was and would become even more a powerful state instrument. He heartily endorsed a letter that arrived during this crucial decision-making period from

Colonel Ralph Webb of Winnipeg which advocated national ownership of radio to reinforce the loyalty of "new Canadians" to the crown and British institutions as opposed to the "engrossing commercialism of the United States."[47] According to the CRL's reading of the situation, the arguments relating to potential American domination of Canadian radio had the greatest impact on Bennett. Spry quoted the prime minister as saying to him on two different occasions: "We will show the States that Canada is no appendage" and "It may well be, Graham, that you have saved Canada for the British Commonwealth."[48]

For this combination of reasons, it seems that, by the time the Special Committee finished meeting, Bennett had decided that not only could the existing system of under-financed competitive-private ownership not continue but private monopoly was also out. Public ownership it would therefore have to be – but not necessarily "pure" or complete public ownership, and not necessarily immediately. The decision to move toward public ownership thus had largely negative roots; it was not that Bennett believed in this principle but that he believed (to use W.H. Herridge's words) that the "paramount need" was "unimpeded control of radio broadcasting in Canada," and that that could not be assured under either the *status quo* or private monopoly.[49]

One other important point must be added. On 16 May, a week after the Special Committee had reported, one of its Conservative members, D.M. Wright, a furniture manufacturer from Stratford, Ontario, who did business with Rogers-Majestic and was active in the CMA, wrote to Bennett about what he considered "a slight misunderstanding" of the intentions of the committee.[50] He enclosed an editorial from the Ottawa *Journal* (a long-time opponent of nationalization) which he claimed summed up the plan the Conservative members of the committee had had in mind. The *Journal's* scheme involved the following elements: 1) governmental subsidy of wireline rentals (from existing licence fees) to enable sustaining programs from the big Montreal and Toronto stations to go coast to coast, along with some programs created by the government commission; 2) regulations curtailing excessive advertising; and 3) a government department to retain the power to regulate broadcasting and potentially to repossess all channels.[51] Wright elaborated to Bennett:

I might state ... that we were hoping that arrangements could be made with stations that might be designated as part of the National chain, that would ensure their best co-operation; and if this were possible, and these stations were prepared to bring the power of their station up to the required standard, it might eliminate the necessity of the Government purchasing the stations and entering into the broadcasting business.

Personally, I feel that this plan should be thoroughly tested out before the Government should think of trying to operate stations. The owners of several of these large stations have repeatedly stated that they were perfectly satisfied to give the Government one, two, or three hours a day for the broadcasting of any programs they wished to put on ...

In the Committee's judgment, there would be no money available for the purchasing of stations for the next two or three years, as the leasing of land lines connecting up all the stations from coast to coast would cost approximately about $500,000 each; and I deem it advisable, even at the outset, to have at least two such lines ...

Wright then went on to offer his opinion that, politically speaking, the *Journal*'s scheme would attract much favourable comment, whereas actual government ownership would garner mostly criticism. He also suggested that provincial directors of radio should not be appointed for the time being, since they would simply attract trouble. He then concluded:

I have been prompted to write you, in order that it may help to clear up some of the mistaken ideas that are at present abroad; as many people have been led to believe by a perusal of the Committee's Report, that it was the intention of the Government to immediately launch into a national scheme of broadcasting.

The Report itself, while making provision so that the Commission would have ample and adequate power to perform any act that might be deemed necessary to establish a highly efficient national system of broadcasting, did not intend that these powers should be exercised at once, but only as might be required in a slow and gradual development of the system.

I believe it only fair to state that many of our members, and quite a large section of the best people of Canada, view with alarm the consequences of the Government going into the Broadcasting business, hence, if Canada's interests can be protected without the Government assuming this responsibility – and I am positive it can – we will have accomplished a real stroke of good business so far as the Government interests are concerned.

Similar points were made by several committee members interviewed by Wilfrid Eggleston of the Toronto *Star* immediately after it reported.[52] They made abundantly clear that the highest priority was the creation of programs and the leasing of land lines and time on private stations to carry those programs to as many Canadians as possible. For the foreseeable future, existing stations would remain privately owned but would be required to carry commission programs during certain hours. Eventually, those stations that "fit into our scheme" would be acquired by the commission, but even the most enthusiastic member of the committee,

E.J. Garland, contemplated no more than two stations being purchased within the next two years.

So, possibly, the question usually asked, "Why did Bennett and the Conservatives opt for public broadcasting?," is the wrong one. If he understood the situation as Wright and perhaps other committee members did, Bennett endorsed a scheme that resembled what such "opponents" as the Association of Canadian Advertisers, the CMA, and Ralph Ashcroft had advocated all along: a well-regulated system whereby the strongest private stations and the national advertisers were able to flourish by affiliation with a government-organized and listener-financed national network and consequently public ownership was staved off forever.

While the Special Committee had been meeting, it had been announced (as was described in Chapter 7) that the minister to the United States, W.D. Herridge, had negotiated a new wavelength agreement giving Canada the clear frequencies necessary to establish its national network. The new agreement seemed to prove that those who had argued that the adoption of a national radio policy in Canada would improve the bargaining position with the United States were right. From six clear and eleven shared wavelengths under the old Gentleman's Agreement, Canada went to nine clear channels and twenty-seven shared, although of the latter twenty were restricted to power no greater than 100 watts. Canada was better off than it had ever been before, and the new allocation was particularly appropriate for the system being contemplated in the spring of 1932.

The second reading of the Radio Broadcasting Act of 1932 took place on 18 May, introduced by an eloquent, oft-quoted speech from Prime Minister Bennett about the need for Canadian control of Canadian radio so that it could become "a great agency for the communication of matters of national concern and for the diffusion of national thought and ideals," "an agency by which national consciousness may be fostered and sustained and national unity still further strengthened," and "a dependable link in a chain of empire communication by which we may be more closely united one with the other ..."[53] "Public ownership," Bennett asserted, was necessary to ensure greater equality of service among Canadians, so that there would no longer exist discrimination between densely and sparsely populated areas. Finally, it was essential because "the air" was a natural resource whose potentialities were yet unknown; "I cannot think," he stated, "that any government would be warranted in leaving the air to private exploitation and not reserving it for development for the use of the people."

In contrast with Bennett's rhetoric, the act itself contained only prosaic nuts and bolts.[54] The first section set up the Canadian Radio Broadcasting Commission, consisting of a chairman, a vice-chairman, and a third commissioner, with headquarters at Ottawa and such staff as it found necessary to hire under the Civil Service Act. In addition, the act provided that the Governor in Council "may appoint not more than nine Assistant Commissioners" "after consultation with the Government of the province in which the Assistant Commissioner resides." No more than one assistant commissioner was to be appointed from any province and they were not to be salaried but could receive honoraria. Provincial or local advisory committees were to be organized and chaired by these assistant commissioners, the members (also unsalaried) to be selected in consultation with the provincial governments. A general council comprising commissioners, assistant commissioners, and possibly members of advisory councils and representatives of private stations would meet "from time to time." The purpose of this body would also be advisory, particularly with respect to programs.

The commission was to report to Parliament through the minister of Marine. The act reserved to the minister of Marine the (technical) licensing of stations but otherwise the commission was given full power "to regulate and control broadcasting in Canada carried on by any person whatever," including the determination of the number, location, and power of stations, the allotment of channels, and the right to recommend to the minister the issue, suspension, or cancellation of the licences of private stations. It also could set the proportion of time to be devoted by any station to national or local programs or to advertising (although the latter was not to exceed 5 per cent of any program period "unless by permission of the Commission") and prescribe the definition of acceptable advertising. The act also specified that the commission "may prohibit the organization or operation of chains of privately operated stations in Canada" and "may, subject to the approval of the Minister [of Marine], assist and encourage the construction of small private stations."

The commission was also authorized to "carry on the business of broadcasting in Canada," including the acquisition of existing stations by lease or purchase (the latter subject to the approval of Parliament), the construction of new stations (also subject to the acquiescence of Parliament), the operation of stations, and the origination of programs or their purchase from within or without the country. Finally, and again subject to parliamentary approval, the commission was given power to "take over all broadcasting in Canada."

The financial arrangements for the new commission were quite stringent. Its total income was to be allocated by Parliament and was to comprise not more than the revenue from the sale of receiving and broadcasting licences and "the business of the Commission," that is, advertising income and money derived from sale or exchange of programs. In other words, all income from broadcasting would go automatically to the consolidated revenue fund, some but not necessarily all of which would then be appropriated by Parliament for the CRBC on the basis of annual estimates. If at the end of a fiscal year the CRBC had spent less than it had been allocated, Parliament could at its discretion give that to the commission the following year. The commission was granted the right to expropriate property, with compensation equal only to the depreciated value of the equipment. It could acquire and hold real property but could only dispose of it with the approval of the Governor in Council. It could not borrow either on its own credit or by issuing securities.

It was in this latter area that the commission as set up by the 1932 act was most noticeably weaker than the company proposed by Manson's draft legislation back in 1930. Manson's bill had not only guaranteed that *all* licence-fee revenues (minus collection costs) would be handed over to the broadcasting company but had provided for a short-term annual parliamentary subsidy and had given the company the right to borrow money for capital expenditure. Thus the CRBC as it was formed under the 1932 act had considerably less financial autonomy and fewer financial resources than the friends of public broadcasting had advocated. With appropriations determined by Parliament, without a subsidy or the power to borrow, especially in the context of the Depression, the resources of the CRBC would clearly be limited.[55]

In one other main respect the act created a weaker CRBC than the Aird commission had proposed. Virtually all the functions essential to public ownership, including the acquisition and construction of stations and the taking over of all Canadian broadcasting, were subject to the approval of Parliament. Only the leasing of stations could be initiated on the commission's own authority. To put it another way, Parliament reserved for itself the right to decide *later* exactly how many stations would ultimately become government owned.[56] In this sense the legislation set up a tentative, experimental, public broadcasting system, one that might in future become strong and important but also might not. Depending on one's point of view, public ownership was either a threat or a promise; all the 1932 act provided was that it was potential rather than actual.

What the act left unsaid was as important as what it said. There was nothing in it about limiting the power of private stations to 50 or 100 watts, as had been suggested many times between 1929 and 1932 and by the Special Committee. Indeed, nothing was said about these stations being purely "local" in emphasis at all, although they could be prevented from networking if the commission so decided. Neither was the longstanding plan to erect a chain of publicly owned high-power stations made explicit, nor their use for national network programs (again, a weakening from the Special Committee's report). Nothing was said about raising the licence fees; the authority to set the fees was left in the hands of a government vulnerable to pressure to keep them low. The act did not create the position of general manager of the CRBC; it placed all responsibility for both policy-making and day-to-day administration in the hands of the three commissioners. In a significant departure from the Aird report and the Manson bill, the 1932 act did not specify that the provincial assistant commissioners would control programming; because any role they had was purely advisory, and indeed their appointment optional, real authority over program content was clearly centred at the national headquarters.[57] The act did not restrict advertising to the indirect type as had been advocated by Aird and the Radio League; the decision about what was acceptable was to be made later by the commission. Neither was anything said that might limit the right of Canadian stations to continue to affiliate with American networks.

As Frank Peers has pointed out, a major difference between the Aird report, the Manson draft bill, and the final act was the increased regulatory, as distinct from ownership, responsibility given to the commission.[58] During the period of the debate about broadcasting, those in favour of the Aird plan had never discussed regulation in much detail, because for them it was either irrelevant or a minor matter affecting only the few private stations subsidiary to the national broadcasting body they advocated. On the other hand, the opponents of public broadcasting had paid considerable attention to the concept, because for them improved regulation was a readily-agreed-upon alternative to government ownership. Underlying the act's emphasis on the regulatory role of the commission, therefore, lay a key assumption: that private broadcasting stations would continue to exist for the foreseeable future.

Although not recognized by all at the time, it is evident that, like D.M. Wright, the drafters of the act intended that the move toward nationalization would be slow and gradual and perhaps never completed. Arthur Meighen, who introduced the bill for its second reading in the Senate, picked up on this point. "It is apparently the intention to control the radio facilities of this Dominion without at once assuming ownership thereof; possibly in the hope that it will not be necessary to do that at any time," he remarked.[59] W.D. Herridge was even more frank in a memo he prepared for Bennett about the draft bill:

The Bill does not contemplate the automatic expropriation of existing private stations or cancellation of current licenses. It is proposed, rather, to gradually develop government owned stations in collaboration with which, under the rules and regulations of the Commission, private stations may co-operate. At the moment, it would be hazardous to forecast the precise development of this plan, beyond saying that *private ownership will not necessarily suffer from the operation of the Bill. On the contrary, existing stations may participate in the advantages which the scheme implies.*[60]

When read in retrospect, it is obvious that the Radio Broadcasting Act, despite the rhetoric with which it was introduced, was worded in such a way that it could be the instrument to do what everyone from Sir John Aird on had declared absolutely unacceptable: to subsidize private stations and advertisers by using government-administered listener fees for program-creation and networking costs, thereby enabling the private broadcasters and advertisers to cover a larger audience of consumers than they could afford to reach out of their own resources. Several years later, in fact, Graham Spry indicted it in exactly these terms: "The Commission has become an instrument for subsidizing private enterprise," he told an American audience in 1935.[61] It may also be noted that both national railways stood to gain from the more extensive use of their wirelines under the planned system, without having to bear the responsibilities or costs.

In brief, possibly the most striking aspect of the Broadcasting Act of 1932 was that, after years of debate during which virtually everyone agreed that radio was a natural monopoly and many argued that consequently it must be in "public" hands, the act preserved an essentially competitive broadcasting system in which most stations most of the time concentrated on local rather than national needs. Unable to make the stark choice between public or private monopoly, the legislators opted for a compromise which was in its main essentials most similar to the American system: regulated, competitive, local, private broadcasting stations affiliated to a network organization which could more efficiently and centrally produce the kind of programming desired for both national and commercial reasons. In the United States, of course, there were two network organizations and they were privately owned and financed from advertising revenues. In Canada, there was probably only going to be one networking body; because advertising revenues were insufficient it would belong to the government-appointed commission so that licence-fee income could be channelled into broadcasting in a politically neutral manner. While the Canadian legislation made possible the eventual takeover of all broadcasting, in the medium term at least the commission would actually own and operate no more than a few stations – exactly as NBC and CBS did in the United States. Because the federal government was involved and because much of the motivation for the Canadian plan had come from concern about American cultural and economic influence, especially the fear that the American radio "trust" would take over networking in Canada, the national purposes of the Canadian arrangement were stressed more than they were in the United States, where the commercial motive seemed to dominate. But the desire to facilitate national coverage for patriotic and other public service reasons also was a motivating factor in the origination of the American networks – as of course were commercial profits in the Canadian case.

Besides being a program-creating and network-financing organization such as CBS and NBC, the CRBC was also to be the equivalent of the American Federal Radio Commission – the regulator of broadcasting. Various authorities have suggested that regulatory bodies may be perceived as sort of "half-way houses" between the private market-place on the one hand and full government ownership on the other. As such, they are a means by which the government can impose national social objectives on industries deemed for some reason to be of overriding public interest without moving to actual nationalization.[62] Yet numerous scholars have also pointed out that such bodies often are welcomed by those they seek to regulate because they help stabilize markets and reduce risks. In the case of Canadian radio, which had been subject to regulation by a government department since its inception, private interests had been calling for an improved arrangement for some time and had made some moves toward self-regulation as well. Organizations such as the CMA and the CAB hoped that a non-partisan regulatory body at arm's length from the government and representative of a variety of interests would ensure that licence, power, and frequency assignments were more openly and fairly determined. As in many other industries, those most in favour of a competent regulatory board with a well-defined mandate were the private interests who hoped thereby both to avert takeover and to reduce the risks of competitive private entrepreneurship. For them, the replacement of the Department of Marine by the CRBC seemed to be a step in the right direction, and not one that advocates of nationalization could very credibly oppose.

Nevertheless, the CRBC created by the act was not simply an instrument of private interests. The commission's powers were large enough that it could, if it wished, do much more than the Radio Branch had done, especially in the promotion of its own programming and the expansion of the coverage area.[63] As well, because of the personnel-appointment procedures and financial constraints written into the 1932 act, the new commission remained to a considerable degree under governmental rather than industry control. Moreover, the Commission had only the power to recommend to the minister of Marine concerning licensing matters; he retained the final authority. The fact that the CRBC was to be responsible for supervising its own stations and programs as well as those of the privately owned segment of the industry also altered its relationship with the latter – a point of much contention for many years after.[64]

THE CANADIAN ASSOCIATION OF BROADCASTERS does not seem to have responded officially to the 1932 act and the organization became dormant for a few years. From what can be determined, the views of private broadcasters on the act were mixed. Some, anticipating the termination of their jobs, rushed to seek employment with the CRBC. Others appeared brimming with complaints before the 1934 parliamentary committee that studied the first year and a half of CRBC operation. But the main historian of the organization has written that "the Commission was not especially unpopular with the private broadcasters and nearly all of its regulations had been publicly advocated by them prior to adoption."[65]

Some of the other opponents of the Aird scheme were actually very positive about the new regime. The Association of Canadian Advertisers fired off a telegram to Bennett on 12 May, just after the Special Committee had issued its report: "A group of national advertisers who are large users of broadcasting have met today in Toronto and desire to express their appreciation of provision for continued use of radio for advertising purposes ..."[66] This was followed up with a letter praising the restriction of advertising to 5 per cent of program time but suggesting that "determination of details of the number and location of stations be deferred" until the new commission had the time to study all possible needs.[67] The ACA presumably found the resulting act eminently satisfactory.

In fact, the ACA and its ally, the Canadian Manufacturers' Association, were by 1934 committed defenders of the CRBC, and for very good reason. The comments of C.M. Pasmore of the Campbell-Ewald advertising agency (Pasmore had aided in the presentation of the CMA brief to the 1932 committee) are especially interesting in this respect, and worth quoting at length:

When the Canadian Manufacturers Association made representations to the Special Committee on Radio Broadcasting in March, 1932, its principal interest was to ensure the following:

(1) That Canadian manufacturers should not be deprived of the use of broadcast advertising.

(2) That private ownership of stations should not be replaced by public ownership.

(3) That licence fees should not be raised to a point which would restrict the sale of radio sets.

(4) That no tax should be levied on radiotrons (tubes).

(5) That Commission control should not reduce the quality of available broadcast entertainment in such manner as to discourage the purchase of sets.

(6) That there should be no heavy expenditure of public funds in broadcasting. To these, the Association of Canadian Advertisers (which to a large extent duplicates the membership of the Canadian Manufacturers Association) had one additional claim to submit, namely:

(7) That any Commission which might be appointed should seek to reduce the cost of sponsored network broadcasts.

The letter continued:

At the present time, the Commission has been actively in operation for just a little over a year. It is worth noting that

(1) broadcast advertising is still available to the Canadian manufacturer, with only one unreasonable limitation, which I understand is likely to be removed in the near future.

(2) there are more commercially-operated privately-owned stations in operation than there were when the Commission was appointed.

(3) the licence fee of $2.00 per year does not appear high enough to prejudice the sale of radio sets.

(4) there is no tax on radiotrons.

(5) Commission control has not in itself reduced the average quality of radio entertainment available in Eastern Canada; while it has materially improved the quality of entertainment available in the Maritime Provinces and Western Canada.

(6) the million-dollar cost of Commission operation is amazingly low when balanced off against the quantity and quality of entertainment provided.

(7) due to the extensive use of land lines by the Commission, the line companies have been able to reduce line costs very materially for broadcast advertisers.

Pasmore concluded: "If the Canadian Manufacturers Association is considering making further representations to Ottawa, my own opinion is that the Association should back up the Commission along its present lines of development."[68]

The high level of satisfaction expressed by Pasmore should not have surprised anyone. The structures put in place by the 1932 Radio Broadcasting Act suited the needs of his industry very well.

In sum, the system set up in 1932 was much less grand than the term "public broadcasting," used both then and since, might suggest. For the time being, the CRBC was to be a program-creating organization which sent out its products via wirelines and time leased from private stations. It would finance the cost of the programs and of renting wirelines and stations though a combination of fees from listeners and advertising revenue. At the same time, the CRBC would institute "government control" of all Canadian radio through its regulatory functions. The new body, with much higher visibility than the Radio Branch, would make all the rules and regulations for stations, licences, advertising, and so on. In both these roles, the CRBC represented the government's acceptance of responsibility for broadcasting but it did not represent a clear commitment to public ownership. In passing the Radio Broadcasting Act of 1932 the Bennett government acted in the interest of the Canadian state in ensuring control of a vital national

medium, it acted in the interest of Canadian listeners in expanding access
to good programs, and it acted in the interest of Canadian advertisers and
broadcasters and Canadian-based radio manufacturers in instituting
measures to subsidize audience acquisition. "Public" broadcasting to
Bennett meant a broadcasting system that balanced pluralistic interests, it
meant a Canadian and national broadcasting system; it did not necessarily
mean one in which educational, cultural, or public-service priorities
predominated.

Given all the ways in which the act watered down the public-service
aspects of the new system, it is perhaps somewhat surprising that the
Canadian Radio League expressed itself delighted with the legislation. "The
report of the Parliamentary Committee just tabled is eminently satisfactory,"
Graham Spry read in a prepared statement to the press. "It is a complete
victory for the Canadian Radio League. The public has won, won a triumph!"[69] Previous historians have pointed out that this was a response
designed for public consumption and that in private Spry, Claxton, and
others had considerable reservations about a number of aspects of the legislation.[70] This view, however, needs some modification. After an advance
look at the Special Committee's report, Spry confided to his diary, "It is
based on the principles I enunciated. Indeed, there is hardly a line that I
would disagree with," and he and Plaunt cabled Dr Morgan in the United
States with the words "Complete victory ..."[71] Similarly, Claxton wrote
gleefully to Gladstone Murray: "You can see that it is a sweeping victory,
going much further than anything that could have been anticipated."[72]
Even given that the committee's report was stronger than the final act, it
seems odd that the league's activists were so unrestrained in their delight.

Moreover, the private criticisms that league members made of the legislation, while telling, were also few. One of their principal worries concerned the decision to set up a radio broadcasting commission rather than
a company; it would be preferable, they felt (and they were to be proved
right), to have a governing body that was "more of a buffer and less of an
executive," a body that would be both less vulnerable to political pressures
and less preoccupied with details of administration. They also expressed
concern about the fact that commission staff would be appointed under the
Civil Service Act.[73] But about the other major lacunae in the act outlined
above, they wrote – even in private correspondence – not a word.[74]

There are three possible explanations for the initial response of the Radio
League's leaders to the 1932 act, all of which probably contain a grain of
truth. One is that they recognized that it was the best they were going to get
and that compromise was the order of the day. They were receiving
urgent messages from political insiders such as Bill Herridge that no time
could be taken for revisions to the bill in case opposition forces gath-

ered and defeated the whole project.[75] Further, it is clear from his diary that Spry at least had tired of the fight and was ready to move on to other things. (He and Plaunt – mainly the latter – had purchased the farm paper, the *Weekly Sun*, in January and were about to become involved in agrarian and social democratic movements on a wider scale.[76])

Also, as was argued in the previous chapter, the league's position on public ownership was in fact much weaker than has sometimes been perceived. Many of those aspects of the legislation that in retrospect have seriously compromised the ability of the CRBC and later the CBC to fulfil a public-service mandate – such as dependence on advertising revenue, a "mixed" public-private system, strict parliamentary control of capital spending, and very gradual acquisition of stations – were accepted by the CRL well before 1932. The 1932 act, by ensuring the expansion of the Canadian radio audience and creating a centralized national programming body, did fulfil two of the league's highest priorities; its failure to meet the rest apparently faded into insignificance in comparison, at least for the moment. The act gave the CRL its national broadcasting system, if not one committed fully to public service.

Finally, however, and most importantly, it must not be forgotten that the 1932 Radio Broadcasting Act did indeed change the *status quo* considerably. Its most significant contribution was the creation of a strong and powerful regulatory agency to replace the Radio Branch of the Department of Marine. The legislation gave the commission very substantial authority over Canadian broadcasting. For both Bennett and the CRL, as nationalists concerned about the American presence, this was of central importance. "Canadian control of Canadian radio" seemed to be assured, and the Radio League was delighted. Moreover, the act did – even if tentatively – create a publicly owned broadcasting organization which could be utilized for the education and expression of a national public opinion. The Radio League had wanted the CRBC to be the dominant element in the new program structure and the act was disappointing in that it did not clearly make it so. However, the potential was there if Parliament later so willed; in that respect, the future certainly looked much brighter than the past. In the meantime, Canadian programming created for ends beyond the purely commercial would be developed and made widely available.

As well, even if principally a regulator for the time being, the CRBC was stronger in that role than the Federal Radio Commission in the United States, both in its actual powers, including the right to usurp time for its own programming, and because the possibility (or threat) of future full nationalization was written into the act. As Spry put it later, the 1932 act had at least accepted some of the league's ideals "in principle," even if it took further legislation to put them into practice.[77] Moreover, as George

Graham unhappily but perspicaciously remarked to the Senate during the brief debate in that chamber: "True, this Bill is innocuous and tentative, but when the system has been in operation for twelve months a great deal of life will have been infused into it by the members of the commission and those who are interested in taking charge of broadcasting in this country."[78]

The 1932 Radio Broadcasting Act gave the country public broadcasting if necessary but not necessarily public broadcasting. It was not the end but the beginning of the process of deciding just how far the Canadian government would or could go in taking radio broadcasting out of the private market-place within which it had developed during its first decade.

Conclusion

As a child, I was raised on the old joke about the Irishman who, when asked the way to Cork, scratched his head and replied, "If I wanted to go there, I wouldn't start from here." The advocates of public broadcasting for Canada in the early 1930s must have felt like that Irishman. The system they espoused would have been much easier to initiate if the ten years of development in the competitive private marketplace had not occurred. But that was not an option. Canadian broadcasting had reached a certain stage in its evolution by 1932 and the choices made in that year, choices that have affected us ever since, were necessarily made within the limits imposed by that circumstance. As Raymond Williams has written: "The history of broadcasting institutions shows very clearly that the institutions and social policies which get established in a formative, innovative stage – often ad hoc and piecemeal in a confused and seemingly marginal area – have extraordinary persistence into later periods, if only because they accumulate techniques, experience, capital or what come to seem prescriptive rights."[1]

Indeed, even in 1919, when broadcasting was discovered as an exciting new use for the technology of wireless telephony, institutions, habits, and expectations were already in place that constrained and moulded its development.[2] The invention of broadcasting opened up a number of possible paths. Which were chosen in any given country depended on a complex of factors including timing, economic patterns, military influence, and geographical position.[3] In its novelty, broadcasting seemed to represent a sharp break with the past; in fact, many continuities also existed. The form, structures, and content of the medium were a product of the interaction between a new technology and earlier social, economic, political, and cultural norms. Out of the constructive tension created, there emerged a new means of communication whose full potential remained still unclear in 1932.

In Canada, certain very early choices, whether made consciously or not, crucially affected the subsequent direction of radio broadcasting. The most important of these was the decision in early 1922, similar to one made in the United States, to begin granting broadcasting licences to virtually all comers. Whereas the British initially restricted licensing and then structured a monopolistic system first privately and later publicly owned, in North America broadcasting was a matter of competitive private enterprise from the beginning.

Over the course of the decade, however, the problems of competition in broadcasting became more and more evident in both Canada and the United States. Despite the size of the continent, interference among too many stations became a major vexation. Even more serious in a way were the consequent political implications. Lacking clear authority over licensing, the US Department of Commerce had less control than it needed to straighten out clashes. In Canada, the Radio Branch of the Department of Marine and Fisheries had the authority necessary, but its use to determine who should and should not have the right to broadcast left the branch vulnerable to charges of political favouritism. Economic factors also had a large impact; even in the relatively wealthy United States, many early broadcasters dropped out because competitive high-quality service was too expensive to finance, and the situation was even more dire in Canada.

The US Department of Commerce dealt with these problems essentially by allowing a few large manufacturers to create a *de facto* oligopoly through their possession of most of the clear channels and ownership of the major network, which put them in the position of being able to attract the bulk of advertising revenues. Eventually as well, a new regulatory body, the Federal Radio Commission, was set up ostensibly to remove licensing decisions from the hands of politicians; it, however, did little to restrict the sway of the big radio corporations.

In Canada by the end of the 1920s many were arguing that radio was a "natural monopoly," although there were differences of opinion over whether that monopoly should be privately or publicly owned. Of great significance in this country was the fact that the American ownership pattern was not really an option. Because the Canadian radio manufacturing industry was largely American-controlled, granting it dominance in broadcasting was politically out of the question. Moreover, by the time Canada got around to deciding what to do about radio, the only other large organizations interested in financing broadcasting on a semi-monopolistic basis, the CNR and CPR, were suffering from the effects of the Depression. National advertisers were also scarcer than in the United States, at least in part because of Canada's generally weaker and dependent economic position, and costs were higher for geographic and demographic reasons.

A publicly owned monopoly, or near-monopoly, thus became a credible alternative for Canada in the late 1920s, especially after the Aird commission so recommended. A certain segment of the Canadian business and cultural élite was so strongly committed to preservation of the east-west national structure that, despite deep-seated belief in the superiority of private enterprise, it became convinced of the need for some form of government intervention. The British tie undoubtedly helped keep the BBC model in mind as well. Those in favour of government-sponsored public-service broadcasting were also able to draw upon a considerable élite tradition of anti-Americanism rooted in part in suspicion and fear of that country's superior economic strength and its powerful popular culture.

Given the tendency toward monopoly in all three countries, the most interesting thing about the 1932 Radio Broadcasting Act is not its suggestion of possible public takeover of broadcasting sometime in the future but the fact that it did not destroy the competitive private broadcasting system. Rather, it improved its regulation (at the behest of all parties involved) and redirected listeners' licence fees toward national network programming. The majority of stations for the foreseeable future remained in the private sector, the wirelines remained privately owned, and Canadian businesses not only were able to advertise almost as freely as before but potentially gained access to more consumers. The compromise solution of 1932 ensured that local stations would continue to serve their local communities while the federal government could utilize some of the time on the strongest stations to form a network for the type of coast-to-coast programming it believed necessary. A dichotomy between mutually interdependent local private stations and a national public network began to be entrenched in the Canadian broadcasting framework.

Because of geographical contiguity and the advanced technical capacity of the biggest American stations, Canadians were, throughout the 1920s, not only able to listen in to American broadcasting but in some parts of the country could hear nothing else. Although we will never know the precise figures, there is no doubt that large numbers of Canadians regularly tuned in to American stations and that others heard American programs through rebroadcasting or affiliation arrangements on Canadian stations. Thus the Canadian broadcasters, despite their relative poverty, the smaller population base on which they had to draw, and the less developed indigenous culture, had to compete directly with American programming that was, in a technical and professional sense, superior. An exchange between Augustin Frigon of the Aird commission and Special Committee Chairman Raymond Morand at the 1932 hearings made the obvious point:

Dr Frigon: We cannot expect in Montreal or Toronto to have the same quality performances as they have in London or Paris or New York. We have to do with whatever our wealth will permit us to do.

Dr Morand: Unfortunately, doctor, we cannot go to New York, but by turning the dial here we will be able to get New York. That is one of the factors you have to take into consideration.[4]

The brief of the Nova Scotia government to the same committee summed up the consequence nicely: "It is evidently apparent to all that the high excellence of many programs offered by powerful American stations make them now, and will continue to make them, attractive to all radio listeners, and that nothing that this country can do will alter that."[5]

So in the 1920s the expectations and tastes of Canadian listeners were formed not only by their own radio stations but by the programs aired on the powerful transmitters of the world leader in entertaining, commercial broadcasting. By the time the CRBC was formed, with an implicit mandate to present programming that also served more educational and social goals, Canadian listeners had become accustomed to believe that radio was primarily a medium of light entertainment.[6] It was no accident that the opponents of public broadcasting made constant gibes about the BBC's "uplifting" programs; the Canadian Radio League and its friends were only too easily characterized as middle-class do-gooders trying to impose their values on ordinary people who just wanted to enjoy their radios.

Canadian consumers were also exposed to advertising for American products when they listened to American radio. Because it was conceded by all that Canadian businesses must be afforded equal access to domestic consumers, advertising remained integral to Canadian broadcasting even in the proposals of the most ardent advocates of a public system. Indeed this desire to protect local and national advertisers was at least as important as revenue considerations in ensuring that Canadian radio, both the private stations (in full) and the CRBC (in part), remained commercially based after 1932. The attractiveness of the American model created a problem both for those who favoured commercial private broadcasting for Canada and for those who wanted to set up a national system devoted to more informative, educational, and public-service oriented programming. Both groups faced the challenge of direct competition with an external rival with superior economic clout and an addictively appealing product. Whatever Canadian broadcasting system was set up, the "American problem" would remain.

Canadian broadcasting developed under legislation that gave authority to license to the Radio Branch of the Department of Marine and Fisheries. Although the Radiotelegraph Act of 1913 was not very specific about the regulator's role, its terms were wide enough that the branch in fact had considerable discretionary power and its decisions were significant in moulding the direction of the Canadian broadcasting system up to 1932. Because

Radio Branch officials concentrated largely on technical rather than cultural questions, and endeavoured above all to give the listeners what they wanted, some of their decisions hurt rather than helped the development of Canadian broadcasting. Despite this regulatory activity, however, the actual construction of stations and creation of programming were left almost entirely to the private sector, as in the American model. Until it became a matter for public debate in 1928, very little discussion about broadcasting policy occurred outside the branch's offices and the private-enterprise basis of broadcasting was rarely questioned. Radio was therefore both like and unlike previously established mass media. While subject for technical reasons to more regulation than daily newspapers, movies, or mass magazines, it nevertheless developed within the same set of liberal assumptions about the necessity of a free (not state-owned) press in a democratic society.

But the inability of Canadian broadcasters to compete for their own audiences and the unequal distribution of broadcasting services within the country aroused more concern than did similar situations with respect to other media. One reason for this was the idea of frequency scarcity; because of limitations on entry, those who owned broadcasting stations were believed to have much more power than entrepreneurs in other cultural industries. The whole debate about broadcasting from 1928 on was implicitly informed by the assumption that radio was a medium whose power was quite unequalled, a medium that could influence all classes, all regions, and all ages far into an unknowable future. Consequently, despite a deeply rooted belief in freedom of the press, government ownership became a viable option and even those who objected to going that far fully accepted substantial government control.[7]

The measures instituted by the Conservatives in 1932 were designed to ensure that Canadians had a broadcasting system that promoted and protected "the nation's interests."[8] In the short run, the act of 1932 gave the new Radio Broadcasting Commission greater authority to regulate the stations in the private sector, although to what specific ends was not laid out. It also mandated the commission to develop network programming which would more fully utilize radio's nation-building potential. Full public ownership was not instituted, but the provision in the Radio Broadcasting Act for the eventual takeover of all Canadian broadcasting did imply a possibility far different from what had gone before. The 1932 act did not, however, remove commercial imperatives or make the creation of a more informed public and national opinion its sole priority. The mixed messages of the act were the legacy of both the successes and the failures of Canadian broadcasting in its first decade.

Broadcasting was initially greeted with enthusiasm and anticipation. Middle-class journalists and commentators, particularly, viewed radio as a potentially progressive, unifying, and stabilizing force in a country racked by rapid and divisive social change at the end of the First World War. By 1932, although many stations and thousands of manufacturing jobs had been created, although one-third of Canadian homes had sets and the wonders of television were seen on the horizon, Canadian broadcasting was far from perfect. Too many stations were weak and under-financed, the commercial priorities of advertisers seemed to dominate program policy, national networking was rare, and both listeners and broadcasters were increasingly attracted to American programs. There were a number of reasons for this situation, among them Canada's small and scattered population, its geographical contiguity to the United States, its manufacturing dependence on the American electrical corporations, English Canada's longstanding attraction to American popular culture, misguided regulatory decisions, and liberal assumptions that precluded early government intervention. Between 1928 and 1932 a relatively small but influential group of Canadians, distressed that broadcasting had not lived up to its potential, seized the opportunity provided by regulatory gaffes to attempt to convince the government to alter the structural framework of Canadian broadcasting so that it would better serve the social and national purposes they envisioned. They did not succeed completely, for too many habits, expectations, and interests had been implanted in a decade of commercial private broadcasting for that system to be totally dismantled. That they were even partially successful is a measure of the power of the myth and dream of communication in a country ever struggling for self-definition and survival.

Notes

Note: Unless otherwise specified, all archival material is from the National Archives of Canada (NA).

INTRODUCTION

1 Barnouw, *A Tower in Babel*; Briggs, *The Birth of Broadcasting*. A number of more specialized studies of radio in the 1920s have also been published subsequently, especially in the United States. These will appear in endnote references throughout the text.

2 Peers, *The Politics of Canadian Broadcasting*. The emphasis of the other two well-known works on early Canadian broadcasting, Prang's "The Origins of Public Broadcasting in Canada" and Weir's *The Struggle for National Broadcasting in Canada*, is also toward public-policy issues and the CBC. The same is true, at least in formal intent, of the more recent book by Nolan, *Foundations: Alan Plaunt and the Early Days of CBC Radio*, although the latter gives more weight to the views of the private broadcasters than one might anticipate from its title. Nolan has also written several articles that attempt to raise the profile of early private broadcasting, especially "An Infant Industry: Canadian Private Radio, 1919–36." Dewar's "The Origins of Public Broadcasting in Canada in Comparative Perspective," while still primarily concerned with policy decisions, offers a refreshing reinterpretation of the period. The most recent contribution to this literature, covering the 1920s briefly, is Raboy's *Missed Opportunities*.

3 Anecdotal and amateur histories of private broadcasting do exist, however; most comprehensive is Allard's *Straight Up*.

4 The outstanding example I have come across is the following: "The first radio broadcast took place in 1923 under the auspices of the C.N.R., which controlled the medium until 1936 when the C.B.C. was created." Stuart, "Strike Four," 14.

5 See Briggs, "Problems and Possibilities in the Writing of Broadcasting History," 8.

6 Czitrom, *Media and the American Mind*, 184, 186ff.

CHAPTER ONE

1 Montreal *Star*, 20 May 1920, 3, and 21 May 1920, 3, 4.

2 Godfrey, "Canadian Marconi: CFCF, the Forgotten Case"; see also Weir, *The Struggle for National Broadcasting in Canada*, 2 n.2.

3 Rosen, *The Modern Stentors*, 7.

4 Regarding the choice made by the US Congress to pass up the opportunity for government ownership of telegraphs, see Czitrom, *Media and the American Mind*, 22, and DuBoff, "The Rise of Communications Regulation." On Canada's technological and business connections with the United States, see Armstrong and Nelles, *Monopoly's Moment*, 91.

5 Wilkins, *The Emergence of Multinational Enterprise*, 48; Babe, "Emergence and Development of Canadian Communication," 61–4.

6 *Statutes of the Province of Canada*, 16 Vict., chap. 10.

7 *Statutes of Canada*, 44 Vict., chap. 26.

8 For US parallels, see Czitrom, *Media and the American Mind*, 29, and De Fleur and Ball-Rokeach, *Theories of Mass Communication*, 74.

9 *Statutes of Canada*, 38 Vict., chap. 26. According to the British North America Act, telegraph or cable companies could be incorporated either

provincially or federally; federal authority extended over those whose works or undertakings extended beyond the bounds of a single province or those declared by Parliament to be for "the general advantage of Canada." See Lederman, "Divided Authority," 344–82.

10 All the inventions mentioned here – the telegraph, telephone, wired and wireless – were the result of the work of a number of men which in a number of instances culminated almost simultaneously. For simplicity, I have emphasized Morse, Bell, and Marconi as they are the men most usually associated by North Americans with these inventions, primarily because they were the inventors who best managed to raise development capital. I am of course aware that other claims to each of these inventions cannot be dismissed.

11 See Taylor, "Charles F. Sise, Bell Canada, and the Americans"; Armstrong and Nelles, *Monopoly's Moment*, 66ff. AT&T remained the largest single shareholder in Bell Canada, with a minimum of 25 per cent of its stock, until the early 1960s.

12 See Pitt, *The Telecommunications Function in the British Post Office*, 24ff.

13 See *Statutes of Canada*, 45 Vict., chap. 40, s. 1, 18.

14 Ibid., 43 Vict., chap. 67; 45 Vict., chap. 95.

15 Armstrong and Nelles, *Monopoly's Moment*, 164ff.

16 Ibid., 93, 113–4; Babe, *Telecommunications in Canada*, 35–99, 240.

17 Armstrong and Nelles, *Monopoly's Moment*, 186.

18 Sturmey, *The Economic Development of Radio*, 82.

19 Aitken, *Syntony and Spark*, 179ff.

20 Neal, "Development of Radio Communication in Canada," 168.

21 Through the years the Marconi companies were to endeavour to maintain the commercial advantages of their headstart by refusing to allow their stations to communicate with those built by rival firms. See Aitken, *Syntony and Spark*, 233–9.

22 MG 28 III 72, vol. 7, W.H. Hopkins, "History of Canadian Marconi Company: 1901–1959," 1. The other version has William Smith, a Post Office official, as the key intermediary. See Zimmerman, *In the Shadow of the Shield*, 205–7, and Babaian, *Radio Communication in Canada*, 13–15.

23 The Canadian government apparently supported the venture in order to create competition for the cable companies, whose charges were fairly high. See Neal, "Development of Radio Communication in Canada," 165ff, and Sturmey, *The Economic Development of Radio*, 77. The agreement between Marconi and the Canadian government is reprinted in Bird, *Documents*, 10–14.

24 Department of Marine and Fisheries, *Annual Report*, 1922–23, 140.

25 S.J. Douglas, "Exploring Pathways in the Ether," 241.

26 MG 28 III 72, vol. 7, W.H. Hopkins, "History of Canadian Marconi Co.: 1901–1959," 7–8.

27 Ibid., 7; Montreal *Star*, 5 September 1930, 25.

28 United Kingdom, Parliament, Sessional Papers, no. 217, 19 July 1904, "Memorandum Explanatory of the Wireless Telegraph Bill." The first international radiotelegraph conference was held in Berlin in 1903; it dealt solely with questions of ship-to-shore traffic, and was not ratified by the British because they supported the Marconi company's contention that it should not be forced to communicate with the equipment of other companies. In 1906 a further meeting, also in Berlin, resulted in a compromise that in effect destroyed the Marconi monopoly. At Berlin specific wavelengths were also allocated for use by governments, navies, merchant shipping, and commercial communications companies.

29 RG 2, 5, vol. 256, Alfred Lyttelton, secretary of state for colonies, to governor-general of Canada, Lord Minto, 12 October 1904, confidential.

30 *Statutes of Canada*, 4–5 Edward VII, chap. 49; *Revised Statues of Canada 1906*, chap. 126, part IV. The act is reprinted in Bird, *Documents*, 18–19.

31 See Toogood, *Broadcasting in Canada*, 10–11.

32 See Department of Marine and Fisheries, *Annual Report*, 1905–6.

33 Aitken, *The Continuous Wave*, 3–8.

34 Ibid., 217.

35 Reich, "Research, Patents, and the Struggle to Control Radio," 211.

36 Aitken, *The Continuous Wave*, 72–5. Actually, Fessenden had been testing his equipment for at least a month before this dramatic broadcast. Earlier in December he had given a demonstration of voice transmission to news services and technical experts. Fessenden deserves credit for far more than this broadcast as well. It was at his urging that Alexanderson developed his powerful alternator and Fessenden himself invented a heterodyne receiver that was far ahead of its time. Aitken suggests that Fessenden was really the man who demonstrated that a full break with the old spark technology was feasible; by 1911 he had demonstrated the alternative, a complete continuous wave transmitting and receiving system. Ibid., 85.

37 Reich, "Research, Patents, and the Struggle to Control Radio," 212–14.

38 *Statutes of Canada*, 3–4 George V, chap. 43; *Revised Statutes of Canada 1927*, chap. 195. The act is reprinted in Bird, *Documents*, 20–5.

39 RG 97, vol. 91, file 1024–4, part 2, Memorandum, "Bill No. 26: General Explanation of the Bill." See also correspondence between G.J. Desbarats, F.H. Gisborne, and E.L. Newcombe in part 1 of the same file.

40 *Statutes of Canada*, 9–10 Edward VII, chap. 43, section 2. See Canuel, "La Présence de l'imperialisme dans les débuts de la radiophonie au Canada, 1900–1928," 46.

41 Department of the Naval Service, *Annual Report*, 1920–21, 32.

42 See Aitken, *The Continuous Wave*, 190.

43 RG 42, vol. 491, file 209–6–5 and vol. 492, file 209–6–57.

44 This information and that in the following sections comes from the *Annual Reports* of the Department of the Naval Service for the fiscal years ending 31 March 1912 through to 31 March 1921. These reports may be found in the Parliamentary Sessional Papers.

45 RG 12, vol. 603, file 6715–7. See also Sturmey, *The Economic Development of Radio*, 98 and Babaian, *Radio Communication in Canada*, 22–3.

46 HOC, 12th Parliament, 7th Session, Sessional Paper no. 50, 1917, Amendment to Radio-telegraph Regulation no. 88.

47 For further information regarding this early period see the files in RG 42, vol. 491, and RG 97, vol. 85.

48 On the amateurs in the United States see S.J. Douglas, *Inventing American Broadcasting*, 187–215.

49 RG 33, Series 14, vol. 2, file 227–11–6.

50 RG 97, vol. 85, file 6202–30, parts 1–3. The geographical concentration reflected the interest in listening to ships' calls. There also were undoubtedly many amateurs who did not take out licences. See Department of the Naval Service, *Annual Report*, 1913–14, 77.

51 On the use of radio by Canadian flyers in the First World War see Wise, *Canadian Airmen and the First World War*, 256, 543, 545. On wireless use in the army see Kerry and McDill, *The History of The Corps of Royal Canadian Engineers*, vol. 1, chap. 13.

52 Reynolds, "Early Wireless and Radio in Manitoba, 97.

53 See Czitrom, *Media and the American Mind*, 189–90; Pegg, *Broadcasting and Society*, 70–81. One scholar argues that the larger number of amateurs in the United States (because of the shorter wartime ban) created a climate of familiarity with radio that was one of the major reasons for that country's headstart in radio in the early 1920s. See Sturmey, *The Economic Development of Radio*, 137–8.

54 See RG 97, vol. 85, file 6206–30, part 3.

55 RG 42, vol. 492, file 209–7–19.

56 The standard sources on this subject are Archer, *Big Business and Radio*, Maclaurin, *Invention and Innovation in the Radio Industry*, Danelian, *A.T. and T.: The Story of Industrial Conquest*, and Aitken, *The Continuous Wave*.

57 Reich, "Research, Patents, and the Struggle to Control Radio," 215.

58 Aitken, *The Continuous Wave*, 12, 27, 360, 364.

59 Head with Sterling, *Broadcasting in America*, 119.

60 S.J. Douglas, *Inventing American Broadcasting*, 171ff; Head with Sterling, *Broadcasting in America*, 121–2; Sivowitch, "A Technological Survey of Broadcasting's 'Pre-History,'" 16–17.

61 Others include the San Jose station of C.D. "Doc" Herrold, the Detroit *News* station WWJ, and WHA at the University of Wisconsin. See Sterling and Kittross, *Stay Tuned*, 40–2, 58–60; R.F. Smith, "Oldest Station in the

Nation"?, 40–5. The debate, as H.G.J. Aitken points out, centres mainly on semantics and on understanding what was novel about the operation of each station. Aitken, *The Continuous Wave*, 470.

62 This account comes mainly from H.P. Davis, "The Early History of Broadcasting in the United States," 191–4. See also Aitken, *The Continuous Wave*, 470ff.

63 Archer, *History of Radio to 1926*, 199–200.

64 H.P. Davis, "The Early History of Broadcasting in the United States," 194.

65 Aitken, *The Continuous Wave*, 471.

66 My version of these events relies most heavily on Darby Coats's unpublished manuscript "Canada's Fifty Years of Broadcasting." Although written much later and therefore subject to the failures of memory, this account is very precise on such details as demonstrations Coats himself was involved in and modestly vague on other matters that he was not able to confirm. Coats was an Englishman who came to Canada with the Pacific Cable Board before the war. During the war he was the principal instructor at the Canadian Marconi training school for wireless operators in Montreal. See MG 26K, M–1294, D.R.P. Coats to R.H. Webb, 19 February 1930, 366173.

67 Sturmey, *The Economic Development of Radio*, 107.

68 MG 28 III 72, Minutes of Meeting of Executive Committee of Board of Directors, 20 March 1919. Precisely when Canadian Marconi was granted permission to experiment with voice transmission is unclear. It may have been in the fall of 1919. See MG 30 E344, vol. 2, "Draft Article for 25th Anniversary Edition of Radio-TV," 5 October 1961, 1.

69 MG 28 III 72, Minutes of Meetings of Board, 24 September 1919.

70 RG 97, vol. 86, file 6200–1, part 1.

71 Coats, "Canada's Fifty Years of Broadcasting," 32.

72 Coats, "Adventures in Radio, Part 15," 6.

73 Coats, "Canada's Fifty Years of Broadcasting," 25.

74 Bankart, "Putting Canada 'On the Air'", 14; Stewart, "How Radio Got Started ... A Canadian View," 31–4; Godfrey, "Canadian Marconi: CFCF, the Forgotten Case," 64.

75 RG 97, vol. 149, file 6206–72, part 1, W.D. Simpson to C.P. Edwards, 23 March 1928; reply of W.A. Rush to Simpson, 30 March 1928. This file begins in September 1921, so information about earlier activities of the station comes mainly from anecdotal sources. Reference is made at the beginning of the file, however, to permission previously granted the Marconi station in Montreal to broadcast one day each week, and to the Toronto station as early as 31 May 1921 for daily experimental broadcasting. See Manager, Canadian Marconi to deputy minister Naval Service, 6 January 1922.

76 Coats, "Canada's Fifty years of Broadcasting," 34.

77 Montreal *Star*, 5 November 1921, 15.

78 RG 97, vol. 149, file 6206–72, part 1, Marconi company to Radio Branch, 6 January 1922.

79 "Montreal Theatres Install Radio," *Radio News of Canada,* July 1922, 48.

80 Toronto *Globe,* 7 November 1921, 13.

81 *Aviation and Wireless News,* September 1921, 23; November 1921, 28; December 1921, 24.

82 Coats, "Adventures in Radio, Part 14," 13. See also A.H. Morse, "Broadcasting," *Radio,* June 1922, 1; "Will Radio Supplant the Press?," *Radio News of Canada,* November 1922, 10.

83 The central role of newspapers in forming public perceptions of the use of radio is one of the major themes of Susan J. Douglas's *Inventing American Broadcasting.*

84 Jome, *Economics of the Radio Industry,* 70.

85 MTL, Wm. Main Johnson Papers, vol. 17, Diaries, 7 April 1925, 48–50.

86 This first concert was broadcast on the Canadian Independent Telephone station. The *Star* began broadcasting under its own licence with call letters CFCA in June 1922.

87 Toronto *Star,* 29 March 1922, 1.

88 Ibid., 10 April 1922, 4.

89 Charlesworth, "Radio Telephony," 29.

90 Coats, "Canada's Fifty Years of Broadcasting," 16. Details regarding the founding of many Canadian stations may be found in Allard, *Straight Up.*

91 *Wireless and Aviation News,* April 1922, 23.

92 Indirect evidence to this effect may be found in RG 97, vol. 149, file 6206–54, part 1, Marine and Fisheries to R.J. Cromie, Vancouver, 7 March 1922, telegram. See also Peers, *The Politics of Canadian Broadcasting,* 16. For further discussion of this point see Chapter 5.

93 Sturmey, *The Economic Development of Radio,* 138; Briggs, *The Birth of Broadcasting,* 96ff.

94 See advertisement in *Radio News of Canada,* July 1922, cover, for complete sets from England available at Eaton's for prices ranging from $143 to $310.

95 Department of the Naval Service, *Annual Report,* 1921–22; Department of Marine and Fisheries, *Annual Report,* 1922–23.

96 See "Big Opportunities in the Furore over Radio," May 1922, 17. The best-selling radio books in Canada in 1922 were A.H. Verrill, *The Home Radio: How to Make and Use It* and A.C. Lescarboura, *Radio for Everybody.*

97 *Wireless and Aviation News,* April 1922, 9.

98 The Department of the Naval Service was absorbed into the new Department of National Defence.

99 The sudden flowering of broadcasting pushed the pioneers of popular radio, the amateurs, aside. As broadcasting matured throughout the 1920s, the amateurs, having played a very important role in making listening in popular, gradually fell back into the position of being a knowledgeable

but numerically and commercially insignificant group of radio fans. See
G.J. Desbarats, Department of the Naval Service, to editor, *Aviation and
Wireless News*, January 1922, 23; Editorial, "Handwriting on the Wall," *Wireless
and Aviation News*, March 1922, 13; *Radio News of Canada*, April 1924, 7.

100 Charlesworth, "Radio Telephony," 29; "Wondrous Music Winged Thro'
Rain-Laden Air," Toronto *Star*, 29 March 1922, 1; Editorial, "Christmas
Ego," *Radio*, December 1925, 15.

101 "Radio and the Home," 31.

102 "The New Side of Wireless," *Wireless and Aviation News*, March 1922, 16. See
also Charlesworth, "Radio Telephony," 29. On the hopes engendered by the
initiation of broadcasting in the United States, see Koppes, "The Social
Destiny of the Radio." On the imbuing of technological products with
magical qualities and symbolic meanings, see Michael L. Smith, "Selling the
Moon," 179–89.

103 For example, see "CFAC," *Radio News of Canada*, November 1922, 9.

104 Editorial, "Smuggling Must Cease," *Radio News of Canada*, September 1923,
7. See also Toronto *Star*, 27 June 1922, 7.

105 For example, see Robb, "Radio the Newest of Sciences," 14, 58.

106 See Czitrom, *Media and the American Mind*, 10; Susman, "Communication
and Culture," xxii–xxiii; Charland, "Technological Nationalism"; Adams,
"The Nationalism of Communications in Canadian Historiography";
Vipond, *The Mass Media in Canada*, ix–x.

107 "Radio will be a Big Factor in Canada's Future," *Radio News of Canada*,
December 1923, 52; Basil Lake, "Ten Months of Broadcasting," *Radio News
of Canada*, February 1923, 37; A.N. Longstaffe, "Grand Opera in the
Farmer's Backyard," *Radio Bug*, October 1924, 22.

108 "Newspapers and Radio," *Radio*, July 1923, 22.

109 Mrs C. Frederick, "A Real Use for Radio," 77. See also CAVA, Bambrick
Transcripts, Interview with G.R.A. Rice.

110 "Dah-de-de-da-Dad," *Aviation and Wireless News*, December 1921, 21. See also
Editorial, "The Cheapest Pleasure in the World," *Radio News of Canada*, April
1928, 2.

111 *Radio*, April 1923, 30; see also "Radio is Keeping the Family Together,"
Radio, March 1924, 42.

112 Elton Johnson, "Canada's Radio Consciousness," 52.

113 See Mundy, "'Free-Enterprise' or 'Public Service'?," 284, and S.J. Douglas,
Inventing American Broadcasting, 306–13, 321.

114 See for example Kenneth Cooper, "Radio and the Public," *Radio Bug*,
January 1924, 5.

115 Briggs, *The Birth of Broadcasting*, 14. See also Leach, "'Voices Out of the
Night'", 191–209.

116 "The New Side of Wireless," *Wireless and Aviation News*, March 1922, 16.

CHAPTER TWO

1 Editorial, "Canada's National Radio Week," *Radio News of Canada*, January 1925, 2; see also Editorial, "Programmes That Kill Radio Sales," *Radio*, February 1928, 15.

2 Radio manufacturing and patent pooling in the 1920s is discussed in Aitken, *The Continuous Wave*, Maclaurin, *Inventions and Innovation in the Radio Industry*, Danelian, *A.T. and T.: The Story of Industrial Conquest*, Archer, *Big Business and Radio*, Reich, "Research, Patents, and the Struggle to Control Radio," and Schairer, *Patent Policies of Radio Corporation of America*.

3 See Aitken, *The Continuous Wave*, 392–400; MG 28 III 72, vol. 86, file 19–6, Patent Agreements.

4 MG 28 III 72, vol. 151, "History of Radio Valve Company, 1922–5."

5 Wilkins, *The Maturing of Multinational Enterprise*, 71; CGE annual report for year ending 31 December 1923, *Annual Financial Review*, vol. 24.

6 MG 28 III 72, vol. 86, file 19–1, Canadian Radio Licence Agreement, 12 March 1923.

7 Ibid., vol. 19, P.F. Sise, Northern Electric, to F.A. Merrick, Canadian Westinghouse, 5 April 1923, copy.

8 RG 79, vol. 46, file 104, Report of the Auditors, Section IV, Patents, 1.

9 Aitken, *The Continuous Wave*, 497.

10 RG 79, vol. 50, file 104–11, "Rogers-Majestic Corporation Ltd. Statement Under Reference #104 to the Tariff Board." Major James E. Hahn's DeForest Radio Corporation, formed in 1923, also was involved in this arrangement although precisely how is not completely clear. See MG 26K, M–987, Taylor memorandum, 32030.

11 MG 28 III 72, Minutes of Meetings of Board, 15 January 1925.

12 RG 79, vol. 46, file 104, Report of the Auditors, Section IV, 3.

13 Calculated from ibid., Report of the Auditors, Exhibit 13, "Patents: Sales of Radio Sets by Years 1928–1933 Showing Division between Royalty-Paying and Non-Paying Licensees."

14 MG 26K, M–987, Taylor memorandum, 32029, 32032–3.

15 See Sturmey, *The Economic Development of Radio*, 185–6, 263.

16 Canadian Radio Patents Limited, *Patents ... and Radio in Canada*, 15.

17 RG 79, vol. 46, file 104, Report of the Auditors, Exhibit 13, "Patents: Sales of Radio Sets by Years 1928–1933 Showing Divison between Royalty-Paying and Non-Paying Licensees."

18 MG 26K, M–987, Taylor memorandum, 32029.

19 MG 28 III 72, vol. 153, Price, Waterhouse to A.E. Dyment, 2 May 1929, "Comparative Statement of Revenue and Expenses ... 1927 to December 31, 1928." In this period the total expenses of CRPL were $104,447, of which $68,847 went to legal and expert fees.

20 One successful prosecution was by Canadian Westinghouse against W.W. Grant of Calgary, owner of CFCN, for his use of the Armstrong patent in his little manufacturing company. See RG 97, vol. 153, file 6206–164, part 2, W.W. Grant to C.P. Edwards, 2 April 1929; *Canadian Westinghouse v. W.W. Grant, Exchequer Court Reports*, 1926, 165, and *Supreme Court Reports*, 1927, 625. Others included CGE v. *Fada Radio, Exchequer Court Reports*, 1926, 134, *Supreme Court Reports*, 1928, 239, and *Dominion Law Reports*, 1930, 1: 449; *Western Electric v. Elizabeth Bell, Exchequer Court Reports*, 1929, 213, and CRPL v. *Hobbs Hardware, Exchequer Court Reports*, 1929, 238.

21 MG 26K, M–987, Taylor memorandum, 32029.

22 Ibid.

23 AO, RG 4 Series 4–32, file 1932/1899, minister of labour to W.H. Price, 23 June 1932.

24 Ibid., attorney-general to G.H. Riches, 10 November 1934.

25 See Aitken, *The Continuous Wave*, 480–509.

26 Reich, "Research, Patents, and the Struggle to Control Radio," 232–3; Danelian, *A.T. and T.: The Story of Industrial Conquest*, 114–9.

27 It may be noted, however, that RCA apparently had a holding in Canadian Marconi by the end of the 1920s and that the American firm Grigsby-Grunow had a similar stake in Rogers-Majestic after 1929.

28 RG 79, vol. 46, file 104, Report of the Auditors, Appendix III, 2.

29 Canada, Royal Commission on Canada's Economic Prospects, Canadian Business Service Ltd., *The Electronics Industry in Canada*, 4.

30 Taken from RG 79, vol. 46, file 104, Exhibit 25, "Tariff Board Reference No. 104, Set Manufacturers, Number of Sets Sold, Sales Value and Average Prices Per Set, 1928–1937."

31 From Professor Taylor's figures, one may deduce that CGE's sales in 1929 were about 15,000 sets and in 1930 about 11,000. MG 26K, M–987, Taylor memorandum, 32029.

32 DBS, Manufactures of Non-Ferrous Metals in Canada in 1937 and 1938, 81, Table 105. Note, however, that contemporary observers considered DBS figures prior to 1931 to be highly suspect. See RG 79, vol. 49, file 104–4, part 1, "Address Given by Alexander MacKenzie, President ... Radio Manufacturers Association of Canada," 2 June 1931, 6.

33 Special Committee 1932, 177.

34 MG 26K, M987, Taylor memorandum, 32034. (Slight discrepancies in the original.) Concerning Rogers-Majestic, see RG 79, vol. 46, file no. 104, Appendix X, 13.

35 Department of the Naval Service, *Annual Report*, 1921–22; Department of Marine and Fisheries, *Annual Report*, 1922–23, 1929–30, 1930–31; Canada, Royal Commission on Radio Broadcasting, *Report* (1929), Appendix IV, 41; *Canada Year Book*, 1932, 731. There are some discrepancies among the figures found in the annual reports of the department, those reported by

the Dominion Bureau of Statistics, and those reported by the Aird Royal Commission of 1929; these are partially explained by different treatment of free licences issued to the blind after February 1927 and also by varying inclusion of the Yukon and Northwest Territories. The discrepancies are minor.

36 One of the very few bits of surviving evidence comparing licence sales in specific locations over a three-year period shows quite a bit of variability. In Ottawa in 1929–30, 9,528 licences were sold, 12,226 the next year, and 15,073 the next. In London, in contrast, the figures were 8,888, 9,815, and 9,898 respectively, while in Windsor they were 9,447, 10,644, and 9,440. The Toronto sales figures for the three fiscal years in question were 61,863, 81,078, and 83,094. See HOC, *Debates*, 25 May 1932, 3381.

37 See for example, *Canadian Annual Review*, 1927–28, 251; Montreal *Gazette*, 3 January 1929, 1; Weir, *The Struggle for National Broadcasting in Canada*, 90 n. 2. For more on licences and their evasion see Chapter 4.

38 Of course, the rate of non-compliance with licensing requirements probably varied considerably from place to place and time to time, but there is no way to estimate that variance.

39 "Radio Service Now a Necessity," *Radio News of Canada*, June 1925, 31.

40 T.G. Van Alstyne, "The Brilliant Future of Radio," *Radio Bug*, April 1924, 10.

41 Harrison, "Single-Control Tuning." See also G.H. Douglas, *The Early Days of Radio Broadcasting* for a readable description of the technical and manufacturing developments of the 1920s.

42 RG 79, vol. 46, file 104, Report of the Auditors, Exhibit 25, "Set Manufacturers: Number of Sets Sold, Sales Value and Average Prices Per Set, 1928–1937." See also the figures in Weir, *The Struggle for National Broadcasting in Canada*, 23.

43 Calculated from DBS, Manufactures of Non-Ferrous Metals, "Analysis of Radio Sales, Number Sold by Type," 1930 and 1931.

44 DBS, *Seventh Census*, 1931, 5:979–80, Tables 57 and 58; ibid., Bulletin XIX, "Radio Sets in Canada, 1931."

45 Bulletin XIX placed the total at 770,436. The reasons for the difference are not clear.

46 This figure of 22 per cent is a minimum. Presumably some set owners, knowing they were in evasion, did not report their radios to the census takers either. One may also note that 523,100 licences were purchased in the year ending 31 March 1931; two months later an additional 200,000 sets were admitted to – the discrepancy in this case is 31 per cent. To put it another way, the 1931–32 licence total also included sets purchased *after* 1 June 1931, so the difference between that figure and that of the census takers is smaller than it would have been on exactly 1 June, and the percentage evasion rate therefore larger.

47 Based on information in DBS, *Seventh Census*, Bulletin XIX, Table 1.

48 Special Committee 1932, 34.

49 Pegg, *Broadcasting and Society*, 9, 157; Willey and Rice, *Communication Agencies and Social Life*, 211. Fragmentary evidence also suggests that in the United States children of immigrants, especially in the cities, were more likely to own radios. Czitrom, *Media and the American Mind*, 192.

50 To express the figures in another way, over 61 per cent of the households in London, Ontario, reported owning a radio, 60.9 per cent in Toronto, 59.8 per cent in Hamilton, 56.5 per cent in Windsor, and 53 per cent in Brantford. At the other end of the list of twenty Canadian cities with populations over 30,000, only 35.9 per cent of the households in Saint John possessed a set, 32.4 per cent in Trois Rivieres, and 30.3 per cent in Edmonton. See DBS, *Seventh Census*, 5:980, Table 58.

51 Ibid. Bulletin XIX, 7–9, Table 3.

52 For example, see Pegg, *Broadcasting and Society*, 157. Thanks to Carman Miller for asking me this question.

53 Wik, "The Radio in Rural America during the 1920's," 340.

54 See "Radio for the Farmer an Urgent Need," 42.

55 One carefully calculated estimate was that it cost an average $29.55 (US) per year to operate a battery-powered set in 1930 and $35.40 for an electric set. Batson, *Radio Markets of the World, 1930*, 18.

56 DBS, *Seventh Census*, 5:2–3, Table 1.

57 Ibid., 5:4, Table 2.

58 In some of these cities, unusually high unemployment rates affected 1931 wage levels. There may well have been radio owners who had purchased sets during the affluent 1920s who had not yet given them up at the time of the census.

59 Willey and Rice, *Communication Agencies and Social Life*, 212.

60 Allard, *Straight Up*, 38.

61 Willey and Rice, *Communication Agencies and Social Life*, 212. For a similar comment regarding the British case, see Pegg, *Broadcasting and Society*, 24, 157.

62 Allard, *Straight Up*, 9; Weir, *The Struggle for National Broadcasting in Canada*, 19.

63 See, for example, RG 97, vol. 87, file 6040–1, part 1, H, Stewart to director, 21 February 1924; ibid., vol. 151, file 6206–89, N.M. Paterson to P.J.A. Cardin, 10 October 1929; RG 33, Series 14, vol. 2, file 227–12–6, statement read by Mr Nathanson.

64 RG 42, vol. 1076, file 104–1–1, C.P. Edwards, "National Broadcasting in Canada. Tentative Scheme as a Basis of Discussion," 12 May 1928.

65 DBS, *Seventh Census*, 8:1viii, Table 22.

66 Lavoie, "L'Evolution de la radio au Canada français avant 1940," 24–5.

67 Ibid., 40–1. Donald Davis makes a somewhat similar argument about automobile ownership in Quebec. See Davis, "Dependent Motorization," 118–19.

68 CKAC, owned and operated by *La Presse*, apparently broadcast in both languages in order to attract more advertising revenue.

69 A rare example of a listener's complaint about poor French-language service in Montreal may be found in RG 97, vol. 149, file 6206–72, part 2, Frank Jammes to deputy minister, Marine and Fisheries, 24 September 1929. M. Jammes was upset because a regularly scheduled French program had been replaced by a Harry Lauder special, and went so far as to suggest that French listeners should be exempted from the $1 licence fee because of lack of programming in their language.

70 Another factor that may be significant in Quebec's low proportion of broadcasting stations is its relative lack of medium-sized urban centres. For a discussion of this phenomenon see Rudin, "Montreal Banks and the Urban Development of Quebec," 69–70.

71 "Here in Chicoutimi we must limit ourselves to American stations. We get Montreal and Toronto with difficulty." RG 33, Series 14, vol. 2, file 227–10–7, 31 May 1929. See also ibid., vol. 1, file 227–10–5, testimony of Mayor Tetrault, 2; RG 97, vol. 150, file 6206–76, Emile Fontaine to E. Hawken, 23 March 1926; RG 12, vol. 865, file 6206–209.

72 See RG 97, vol. 87, file 6040–1, part 1, T.P. Stewart, Summerside, Prince Edward Island, to director, Radio Branch, 21 February 1924; Special Committee 1932, 399.

73 RG 33, Series 14, vol. 2, file 227–12–6, 18 June 1929, attachment.

74 See RG 42, vol. 1076, file 7–3–1, "Radio," 20 July 1923, 4 and Special Committee 1932, 402. On the refusal of the Department of Commerce to set up a similar classification in the United States, see Bensman, "The Regulation of Radio Broadcasting by the Department of Commerce," 99–101.

75 Special Committee 1932, 28, 37.

76 RG 42 II, vol. 1042, "Official List of Radio Stations in Canada," no. 1, 1 August 1922.

77 RG 97, vol. 149, file 6206–54, part 1, G.A.C. to deputy minister of the Naval Service, 17 March 1922.

78 MTL, Wm. Main Johnson Papers, vol. 17, Diaries, 9 April 1925, 51.

79 RG 12, vol. 862, file 6206–148, J.R. Bone to G.J. Desbarats, deputy minister of the Naval Service, 23 March 1922. See also A.H. Morse, "Broadcasting," Address to the Montreal Publicity Association, *Radio*, June 1922, 1. A.S. Blackburn of the London *Free Press* was apparently similarly motivated. See Nolan, "An Infant Industry," 500.

80 Two, the Hamilton *Spectator* and Quebec City's *Le Soleil*, had licences for phantom stations.

81 In the Canadian case, thi s is particularly emphasized with respect to newspaper support for the public-ownership project after 1928. See, for example, Peers, *The Politics of Canadian Broadcasting*, 50–1.

82 MTL, Wm. Main Johnson Papers, vol. 17, Diaries, 7 April 1925, 55ff; RG 97,

vol. 87, file 6040–1, part 1, A.H.K. Russell to director, 19 February 1924.

83 See, for example, RG 97, vol. 152, file 6202–122, J. Stewart Neill, James S. Neill and Sons, Fredericton, New Brunswick, to deputy minister of Marine and Fisheries, 12 April 1927.

84 Duffy, *Imagine Please*, 22.

85 Black, "The Early Days of Canadian Broadcasting," 27. On the Bell Telephone stations see also Babe, *Telecommunications in Canada*, 202–3.

86 In July 1922 Canadian Marconi officials attempted to interest Northern Electric, Canadian Westinghouse, and Canadian General Electric in a joint broadcasting scheme by which the four companies would share the expense of a service from which they all profited. A meeting in the summer of 1923 reached an agreement in principle; the arrangement foundered for reasons which are unclear, but may have related to patent rights. See MG 28 III 72, Minutes of Meetings of Board, 27 July 1922, 30 November 1922, 13 August 1923.

87 According to the technical experts of the day, the only way to prevent Canadians from receiving American stations (presuming this might ever be politically acceptable) was to reassign all Canadian stations to wavelengths on the spectrum outside the normal broadcast band and then force Canadian manufacturers to produce and sell receivers capable of receiving only signals in this new range. See Special Committee 1932, 60.

88 RG 42, vol. 493, file 290–32–111, part 1, B. Braden, Canadian Westinghouse, to E. Hawken, 23 February 1928. See also Bowman, *Ottawa Editor*, 124.

89 See, for example, MG 26K, M–1315, W. Arthur Steel, "Public Ownership of Broadcasting Facilities," 31 December 1931, 389232.

90 Department of Marine and Fisheries, *Annual Reports*, 1922–23 to 1931–32.

91 See Batson, *Radio Markets of the World, 1926*, 5; Special Committee 1932, 379.

92 These authorized power outputs may not in fact have been fully utilized. In 1931, for example, the London *Free Press* station normally broadcast at only 1700 watts although it was listed at 5000. RG 97, vol. 87, file 6040–1, part 4, D. Manson, "Memorandum to the Director of Radio Re: Review of Broadcasting Situation in Western Ontario," 3 September 1931.

93 Special Committee 1932, 13.

94 The fullest treatment is in Weir, *The Struggle for National Broadcasting in Canada*, but many texts treat Canadian broadcasting in the 1920s as though it were almost the exclusive preserve of the CNR stations.

95 RG 33, Series 14, vol. 1, file 227–1–3, "Memorandum Submitted by the Canadian National Railways to the Royal Commission on Radio Broadcasting in Canada," Montreal, 29 May 1929, 1.

96 For two examples see Special Committee 1932, 3, and Royal Commission on Radio Broadcasting, *Report*, 1929, reprinted in Bird, *Documents*, 43.

97 For example, see "Radio Plans of System Make Transportation History," 7.

98 HOC, *Debates*, 25 April 1933, 4248.

99 MG 30 D67, vol. 19, file 3, "CNR Radio Department, Total Actual Cost of Operation for Year 1929." There is a slight discrepancy between Weir's figures and those given to the Commons in 1933.

100 Weir's book gives a capital expenditure figure of $170,000; the Commons was told it was $132,000. See Weir, *The Struggle for National Broadcasting in Canada*, 94, 22; HOC, *Debates*, 25 April 1933, 4248.

101 Weir, *The Struggle for National Broadcasting in Canada*, 12.

102 For a fuller discussion of CKY, see Vipond, "CKY Winnipeg in the 1920's."

103 PAM, RG 11 A1, Box 3, "Radio Legislation," 4 January 1923; RG 97, vol. 90, file 1024–8, part 1, J.E. Lowry to C.P. Edwards, 10 December 1923.

104 Reynolds, "Early Wireless and Radio in Manitoba," 103–6. According to another version of the story, the initial impetus came from the newspapers. See Babe, *Telecommunications in Canada*, 203.

105 *Canada Gazette*, 16 June 1923; *Statutes of Canada*, 13 & 14 Geo. V, chap. 26.

106 Special Committee 1932, 3.

107 CKX Brandon, set up in December 1928 (and located in the music store of P.A. Kennedy), was also owned by the MTS and was primarily a rebroadcast transmitter for CKY.

108 Winnipeg *Tribune*, 10 February 1927, 8; Winnipeg *Free Press*, 17 February 1933, 2.

109 For a cogent expression of this point, see Editorial, "CKY," Winnipeg *Free Press*, 15 January 1931, 13.

110 RG 97, vol. 154, file 6206–174, part 1, Lowry to A. Johnston, 6 February 1928, and reply of 11 February 1928.

111 RG 12, vol. 864, file 6206–162–3, A. Duranleau, minister of Marine, to T.G. Murphy, 16 March 1932.

CHAPTER THREE

1 HOC, *Debates*, 27 April 1923, 2285.

2 Jome, *Economics of the Radio Industry*, 175–6.

3 See Sterling and Kittross, *Stay Tuned*, 66.

4 Eoyang, *An Economic Study of the Radio Industry*, 179, Table 58; Batson, *Radio Markets of the World, 1930*, 18–19.

5 RG 42, vol. 1076, file 104–1–1, C.P. Edwards, "National Broadcasting in Canada. Tentative Scheme as a Basis of Discussion," 12 May 1928.

6 RG 97, vol. 114, file BX–13, S.J. Ellis to Edwards, 23 March 1928. The same year, CKCL, which had been erected in 1924, estimated its transmitter and studios to be valued at $100,000. Ibid., Ellis to Edwards, 23 March 1928.

7 Special Committee 1932, 13; see also RG 42, vol. 1077, file 227–9–3, R.W. Ashcroft to the Royal Commission on Radio Broadcasting, 17 May 1929.

8 MG 30 A42, vol. 27, file 151, "Valuation of Broadcasting Stations," March

1932. The stations' own submissions suggested higher values: CKAC, for example, claimed its plant, studio, and buildings were worth $207,182 on 31 March 1932 and CFRB reported $161,922.10. Ibid., [7].

9 E.A. Weir claimed that, of the sixty-one stations operating when the CRBC took over on 1 April 1933, only twelve fulfilled its technical standards. Weir, *The Struggle for National Broadcasting in Canada*, 185.

10 See Chapter 6 for more on this subject.

11 "Radio Advertising," 66.

12 MG 30 D67, vol. 19, file 2, "Cost of Toronto Symphony Programmes, 1930–," "Cost of Dramatizations."

13 Ibid., file 3, "Expenses Incurred in Operating the Vancouver Station Since its Erection in Aug. 1925 up to June 1931."

14 PAM, RG 11 A1, Box 3, J.E. Lowry to T.J. Brown, 12 October 1923; ibid., Lowry to Finance Committee, Winnipeg City Council, 4 June 1924; *Winnipeg Tribune*, 10 February 1927, 8; *Winnipeg Free Press*, 17 February 1933, 2.

15 MG 30 A42, vol. 27, file 151, "Valuation of Broadcasting Stations," March 1932. About fifteen stations did not reply in a form suitable for tabulation or at all. Most of them were small, with the exception of CFCN Calgary, CFRB Toronto, CKCL Toronto, and CFCF Montreal. The table as presented here differs slightly from the original in that it eliminates non-commercial stations such as CKUA Edmonton. A brief summary of the highlights of the questionnaire was published in the Special Committee's report, 707.

16 CKAC reported revenues of $178,062.53 in the following year, 1932, and a profit of $38,734. See RG 41, vol. 37, file 2–2–6–9, Phil Lalonde to Canadian Radio Broadcasting Commission, 29 April 1933.

17 See, for example, the claim that CFCF Montreal lost money every year from 1922 to 1928, RG 97, vol. 149, file 6206–72, part 1, H.M. Short, managing Director, Canadian Marconi, to A. Johnston, 28 September 1928; see also ibid., vol. 114, file BX–13, S.J. Ellis to Edwards, 23 March 1928. Other examples are cited in Nolan, "An Infant Industry," 503–4.

18 RG 42, vol. 1076, file 7–3–1, C.P. Edwards, "Radio. Administration: Legislation: Broadcasting: Regulations: Imperial Chain: New Development," 20 July 1923, 1.

19 The first was suggested by David Sarnoff, the second by the influential American radio magazine *Radio Broadcast*. See Archer, *History of Radio to 1926*, 342, and Banning, *Commercial Broadcasting Pioneer*, 191–2. (Voluntary listener contributions were used exclusively to finance broadcasting in Holland after 1930 and are now an important part of the funding of PBS television stations in the United States.) In 1925 *Radio Broadcast* ran a contest on "Who Is To Pay for Broadcasting and How?" According to Susan Smulyan, the many responses indicated the confusion felt by those considering the question in the mid-1920s. The winner advocated a tax on vacuum tubes. See Smulyan, "'And Now A Word From Our Sponsors ...,'" 2. The

winning entry is reprinted in Lichty and Topping, *American Broadcasting*, 207–10.

20 McNeil and Wolfe, *Signing On*, 17.

21 RG 33, Series 14, vol. 1, file 227–9–9, 17 May 1929.

22 See Aylesworth, "The National Magazine of the Air," 229.

23 Briggs, *The Birth of Broadcasting*, 120. A similar scheme was introduced in Canada in the early 1950s to finance television development. In the long term this was a less effective revenue source as the set market became saturated.

24 RG 42, vol. 1076, file 7–3–1, "Radio, 1923–1924," 25 August 1924, 7. See also Alan N. Longstaffe, "The Future of Radio in Canada," *Radio*, February 1923, 1.

25 This aspect will be discussed more fully in Chapter 6.

26 C.P. Edwards suggested in the very early 1920s that possibly provincial governments would be the "proper authorities to undertake radiotelephone broadcasting for the benefit of the communities within their jurisdiction." See RG 97, vol. 90, file 1024–8, part 1, G.J. Desbarats to H.E. Brockwell, 10 May 1922 (drafted by CPE), and ibid., C.P. Edwards, memo to the deputy minister, "Provincial Radio Legislation: Manitoba," 8 March 1923, 5.

27 RG 97, vol. 151, file 6206–108, part 1, A. Johnston to J.N. Cartier, 14 November 1923. See also HOC, *Debates*, 27 April 1923, 2286. In Australia in the early 1920s one class of privately owned stations was funded by public money but the practice was dropped by 1929. Hoover apparently rejected this option in the United States in part because it would lead inevitably to governmental responsibility for program content.

28 RG 33, Series 14, vol. 5, "Report for the British Broadcasting Committee on Radio Broadcasting Situation in Canada," 19 May 1923, 3. See also RG 42, vol. 1076, file 7–3–1, "Radio," 20 July 1923; RG 97, vol. 87, file 6040–1, part 1, C.P. Edwards to E.J. Haughton, 21 November 1924.

29 See Banning, *Commercial Broadcasting Pioneer*, 55–6, Barnouw, *A Tower in Babel*, 106. Some early Canadian government officials made a distinction between this so-called "toll broadcasting" and broadcasting sponsored by direct and indirect advertisements. What distinction they had in mind is not clear, particularly as they used the words "charge a toll" to refer to the latter instance as well. See Department of Marine and Fisheries, *Annual Report*, 1922–23, 141.

30 Smythe, *Dependency Road*.

31 Marchand, *Advertising the American Dream*, 94.

32 More specifically, other stations were prohibited from charging advertisers for airtime; non-telephone-company stations did, however, even before 1924, encourage sponsors to create and pay for programs, thus saving themselves the cost of program production. See Smulyan, "'And Now a Word From Our Sponsors ...,'"80.

33 "Radio Advertising," 66. See also Fourth National Radio Conference, *Proceedings*, 18, in Kittross, *Documents in American Telecommunications Policy*, vol. 1; Head with Sterling, *Broadcasting in America*, 136.

34 RG 97, vol. 87, file 6040–1, part 1, C.N. Valiquet to Edwards, 15 August 1924.

35 RG 42, vol. 1077, file 227–9–3, R.W. Ashcroft to Aird commission (personal communication), 17 May 1929, 3; Special Committee 1932, 332, 339.

36 For more details on the regulation of advertisements, see Chapter 6.

37 See Banning, *Commercial Broadcasting Pioneer*, 152–5. Advertising agencies also apparently feared alienating newspaper customers by moving too enthusiastically to the new medium. See Marchand, *Advertising the American Dream*, 92. The earliest American large-scale radio-audience surveys were conducted in 1929; there was no similar Canadian survey until after 1932.

38 Spalding, "1928: Radio Becomes a Mass Advertising Medium," 32ff.

39 Czitrom, *Media and the American Mind*, 76.

40 Quoted in Marchand, *Advertising the American Dream*, 110.

41 Smulyan, "'And Now a Word From Our Sponsors ...,'" 96; Eoyang, *An Economic Study of the Radio Industry*, 176.

42 Sterling and Kittross, *Stay Tuned*, 112, 114, 516.

43 "The Future of Broadcasting Stations," *Radio News of Canada*, June/July 1927, 28.

44 RG 33 Series 14, vol. 2, file 227–11–6, C.A. Munro to J.B.M. Baxter, 30 May 1929; Winnipeg *Tribune*, 10 February 1927, 8.

45 Special Committee 1932, 35–7. The table published actually distinguished among three types of programs – original talent sponsored, original talent sustaining, and recorded programs. I have used the figures for original talent sponsored as indicative of all advertising-financed programming because recorded programs at that time would very rarely have attracted sponsorship. Sustaining programs were by definition those without sponsors.

46 Ibid., 166.

47 MG 30 D67, vol. 27, file 9, "G and W Case," 10 October 1946.

48 Ibid., vol. 19, file 3, "Total Actual Cost of Operation, Year 1930." The other owned CN stations, however, CNRA and CNRV, had only modest commercial revenues.

49 Special Committee 1932, 9.

50 RG 12, vol. 864, file 6206–162–3, leaflet "Manitoba Telephone System Radio Service," 1 March 1932.

51 Cockfield-Brown, "Radio as an Advertising Medium," Appendix A, 2. This report was probably written by Frank Ryan, a recent economics graduate from Queen's, whose later career in radio culminated in the establishment of CFRA Ottawa. See Zimmerman, *In the Shadow of the Shield*, 367.

52 MG 30 D304, vol. 8, file 8–4, E.L. Bushnell, "Draft Reminiscences," 3–10.

53 RG 42, vol. 494, file 209–32–111, part 3, Caplan to assistant deputy minister

of Marine, 10 May 1932.

54 Cockfield-Brown, "Radio as an Advertising Medium," Appendix A, 4.

55 MG 26K, M–1314, R.W. Ashcroft, "The Fifth Estate," October 1929, 389145–6.

56 Cockfield-Brown, "Radio as an Advertising Medium," 4.

57 Sterling and Kittross, *Stay Tuned*, 161.

58 Smulyan, "'And Now a Word From Our Sponsors ...,'" 15–32.

59 For more on the regulation of electrical transcriptions in Canada, see Chapter 6.

60 MG 30 D67, vol. 19, file 2, "Comparison of Costs of Broadcasting to Various Stations of Canada using Wires as Compared with Records" [memorandum probably written by Austin Weir, 1930–31]. This document argues that 55 per cent of the potential English-speaking listeners in Canada could be reached via stations in Montreal and Ontario for thirty minutes for $411.53 using a wire network, while the cost would be $575.13 using electrical transcriptions. Transcriptions were cheaper to use, however, when the long distances to the west and the Maritimes were involved, and they were not subject to time-zone incompatibilities. Weir, as an employee of the CNR, would not have been completely unbiased on this issue. In the United States the powerful networks sought to influence public opinion and the Federal Radio Commission against transcriptions, with some success. See Smulyan, "'And Now a Word From Our Sponsors ...,'" 168–70.

61 An analysis of programming between 1 December 1931 and 31 January 1932 presented to the 1932 Special Committee indicated that only one station in Canada, CKY Winnipeg, used more than an hour of transcriptions a day; most stations used no more than an hour a week. See Special Committee 1932, 35, 13.

62 It has been argued that RCA promoted super power primarily for tactical reasons relating to its campaign to improve its position within the radio industry as a whole. See Smulyan, "'And Now a Word From Our Sponsor ...,'" 44.

63 Rogers, "The History of the Clear Channel and Super Power Controversy," 70–2.

64 C.M. Adams, "What About the Future of Chain Broadcasting?" *Radio News*, February 1928, in Lichty and Topping, *American Broadcasting*, 181–5. See also Smulyan, "'And Now A Word From Our Sponsors ...,'"53.

65 A somewhat similar system, developed in the United States by General Electric and Westinghouse, was short-wave rebroadcasting. A program originating in one studio would be relayed by short-wave radio to a second broadcasting station, which would then transmit it on its regular frequency. As far as can be determined, no such arrangement was attempted in Canada in the 1920s. One advantage of using a wired system was the familiarity with the technology developed doing out-of-studio broadcasting ("remotes").

66 See Danelian, *A.T. and T.: The Story of Industrial Conquest*, 121ff.
67 Federal Communications Commission, "Early History of Network Broadcasting," in Lichty and Topping, *American Broadcasting*, 166–7; Banning, *Commercial Broadcasting Pioneer*, 164ff, 261.
68 Aitken, *The Continuous Wave*, 486.
69 Eoyang, *An Economic Study of the Radio Industry*, 161.
70 Sterling and Kittross, *Stay Tuned*, 512, 516.
71 Weir, *The Struggle for National Broadcasting in Canada*, 13–14. Station OA used the transmitting facilities of the Department of Marine and Fisheries. .
72 MG 30 D67, vol. 19, file 5, Gordon Olive to Albert Allen, 2 May 1936. See also RG 41, finding aid file, A.J. Black, "Chronology of Network Broadcasting in Canada, 1901–1961."
73 MG 30 D67, vol. 19, file 6, CNR Radio Programme, 1927, 1928.
74 For more details, see Weir, *The Struggle for National Broadcasting in Canada*, 35–9; Kelly, "Developing a Canadian National Feeling: The Diamond Jubilee Celebrations of 1927," 64–7; Diamond Jubilee Broadcast Committee, *A Mari Usque Ad Mare*; RG 33, Series 14, vol. 3.
75 MG 30 D67, vol. 19, file 5, CNR Publicity Department, "Establish New Canadian Record in Nation-Wide Radio Broadcast," 18 December 1928.
76 Ibid., file 6, CNR Radio Programme, 1929.
77 See Weir, *The Struggle for National Broadcasting in Canada*, 43ff.
78 For more examples of private-station networking in the 1920s see Nolan, "An Infant Industry," 507–11.
79 *Radio News of Canada*, November 1928, 3.
80 RG 42, vol. 1077, file 227–9–3, R.W. Ashcroft for Trans-Canada Broadcasting, 15 May 1929.
81 Ibid., vol. 493, file 209–32–111, part 1, E. Hawken to F.W. Hay, 3 October 1928.
82 Nolan, "Canada's Broadcasting Pioneers," 19; Brand, "'The Twentieth Century Bible,'" 119.
83 Weir, *The Struggle for National Broadcasting in Canada*, 46.
84 Special Committee 1932, 677–8. See also MG 26K, M–1289, E.L. Bushnell to A. Duranleau, 17 March 1931 (copy), 360646–7.
85 Nolan, "Canada's Broadcasting Pioneers," 19–20; MG 30 D304, vol. 6, file 6–27, "Victor George: Draft [Reminiscences]," 17.
86 Weir, *The Struggle for National Broadcasting in Canada*, 79–80; RG 97, vol. 151, file 6206–109, part 2, R.W. Ashcroft to deputy minister of Marine, 3 October 1930.
87 Special Committee 1932, 655–7.
88 Ibid., 237, 334.
89 Montigny, "Les Débuts de la Radio à Montréal," 78–9; Nolan, "Canada's Broadcasting Pioneers," 18.
90 MG 30 D67, vol. 19, file 3, "Wire and Station Charges on Networks in the

307 Notes to pages 73–6

U.S.A. – May 1931." The different structural arrangements of CBS and NBC accounts for varying practices with respect to specific stations.

91 "Radio Column," Toronto *Globe*, 9 December 1929, 18.

92 MG 26K, M–1289, M.H. Aylesworth to Bennett, 16 January 1930, 360500.

93 Special Committee 1932, 329. See also RG 42, vol. 493, file 209–32–111, part 2, R.W. Ashcroft to C.P. Edwards, 25 November 1930. J. Arthur Dupont defended CKAC's links with CBS in very similar terms to the Special Committee; see Baulu, *CKAC, une histoire d'amour*, 38–9. The official historian of Canadian Marconi had similar comments about CFCF's relationship with NBC. See MG 28 III 72, vol. 7, W.H. Hopkins, "History of Canadian Marconi Company: 1901–1959," 28.

94 RG 14 D2, vol. 184, file 254, S.H. Henry to radio inspector, Toronto, 23 January 1928 (copy). Similar opinions held even among francophone listeners: "Plusieurs de nos clients se plaignent que le poste CKCV de Québec, les empêche tous les samedis soir d'entendre les concerts de la Symphonie de Boston du poste WBZ," wrote one legal firm to the Radio Branch. (Several of our clients complain that CKCV Quebec prevents them from hearing the Boston Symphony concerts on WBZ on Saturday evenings.) RG 97, vol. 150, file 6206–83, part 1, Robitaille et Fafard, avocats, to Edwards, 29 October 1927.

95 RG 97, vol. 87, file 6040–1, part 1, A. Johnston to J.R. Skelton, 16 March 1925.

96 Toronto *Telegram*, 2 September 1925, 11.

97 RG 97, vol. 151, file 6206–109, part 2, "Crawford-Harris Survey," 9.

98 Special Committee 1932, 126, 209, 224.

99 Initial reaction was not completely positive, however. The author of a study conducted in 1930 suggested that managers at both CKGW and CFRB claimed the hook-ups were unprofitable in themselves, that local programs were their "bread and butter," and that extension of tie-ins to US chains was unlikely. Their alternative, a good strong private Canadian chain, was a possibility that fell afoul of the Depression. See Cockfield-Brown, "Radio as an Advertising Medium," Appendix, 13–14.

100 Special Committee 1932, 330. From another of Ashcroft's statements to the Special Committee, it seems that the sustaining programs given to CKGW were valued at $100,000 per year. Because he claimed that reciprocal payments pretty well cancelled out, this must have meant that the prime time CKGW released to NBC for sponsored shows had an approximately equal value.

101 Ibid., 339.

102 See MG 28 III 72, vol. 7, W.H. Hopkins, "History of Canadian Marconi Company: 1901–1959," 28.

103 Cockfield-Brown, "Radio as an Advertising Medium," 19.

104 Special Committee 1932, 40, 238, 549–50. This trend accelerated during the

1930s. According to Paul Brand's statistics, CFCF Montreal was airing 55 per cent American programs each week by 1939, CKAC 33 per cent, and even on the CBC stations, CBM and CBF, over 30 per cent of time was devoted to US network shows by the end of the 1930s. Brand, "'The Twentieth Century Bible,'" 120–1.

105 MG 26K, M–1314, W. Arthur Steel, Memorandum, "The Broadcasting Situation in Canada To-day," 28 December 1931, 389219.

106 Special Committee 1932, 548, 580.

107 Weir's figures showed that trans-Canadian wireline costs worked out to about 24 cents per mile per hour. Meanwhile, in the United States, wire charges were about 1 cent per mile per hour; this, incidentally, was also the rate charged by Bell for the lines rented to connect Toronto and Montreal stations to the US networks. To put it another way, adding together both wire costs and station rental, an advertiser could have access to a total Canadian population of about 9 million for $1150 for one-half hour. In the United States, an advertiser could rent the NBC Blue Network, a potential audience of 60 million people, for less than $2400 per half hour. MG 30 D67, vol. 19, file 2, [E.A. Weir], "Network Broadcasting Rates in Canada – Some Reasons Why They Should Be Reduced" [August 1931]. Calculations made by others were fairly comparable. C.P. Edwards estimated about $3580 for one evening hour encompassing fourteen cities from Halifax to Victoria in 1932. See Special Committee 1932, 10–11.

108 MG 30 D297, vol. 98, file 98–1, "Memorandum Presented to the Royal Commission on Railways and Transportation by Graham Spry," 14 January 1932, 6.

109 Special Committee 1932, 341, 438; Weir, *The Struggle for National Broadcasting in Canada*, 100

CHAPTER FOUR

1 See Godfrey, "Canadian Marconi: CFCF, The Forgotten Case."

2 "What's Doing in the Ether," *Canadian Wireless*, February 1922, 3.

3 "Canadian Broadcasting Stations," *Radio News of Canada*, October 1922, 24.

4 "Canadian Broadcasting Stations," *Radio News of Canada*, June and July 1923, 30.

5 Montigny, "Les Débuts de la Radio à Montréal," 58.

6 Brand, "'The Twentieth Century Bible,'" 118.

7 RG 97, vol. 87, file 6040–1, part 2, "Radio Broadcasting Schedules," c. February 1927.

8 Vancouver *Sun*, week of 5–12 March 1927.

9 Halifax *Herald*, week of 22–29 November 1927.

10 RG 97, vol. 151, file 6206–103, CFJC "Regular Programme," 8 October 1927,

6 June 1928; RG 12, vol. 230, file 6206–99, vol. 1, CFCY Schedule, 17 May 1927. It is worth noting that Roy Thomson's station, CFCH North Bay, deliberately operated only in the daytime in order to allow the people of the community to listen to the superior big-city stations in the evenings. See Special Committee 1932, 631.

11 "What's Doing in the Ether," *Canadian Wireless*, February 1922, 3; "Program," *Canadian Radio*, 4 April 1924, 10.

12 "Today on Radio," New York *Times*, 24 March 1927, 20; Chicago *Tribune*, week of 1–7 October 1927.

13 George A. Lundberg, "The Content of Radio Programs," *Social Forces*, 7 (1928), reprinted in Lichty and Topping, *American Broadcasting*, 323.

14 See "Toronto CAN be Heard in Montreal," *Radio Bug*, April 1924, 19; Black, "The Early Days of Canadian Broadcasting," 110.

15 Spalding, "1928: Radio Becomes a Mass Advertising Medium," 34.

16 BCA, Radio Station CHYC Log Book, October 1925–January 1927.

17 Ibid., 8 September 1926.

18 Pegg, *Broadcasting and Society*, 255n.11; Scannell and Cardiff, "Serving the Nation," 185.

19 See CAVA, Bambrick Transcripts, Interview with G. Quinney.

20 RG 97, vol. 149, file 6206–72, part 1, "Regular Programme of Broadcasting Station CFCF," 26 May 1928, 11 April 1929; ibid., "Programs to be Broadcast During the Week Commencing Sunday January 24th [1932]."

21 Special Committee 1932, 11.

22 K.M. Swezey, "Quality – not Volume," *Radio News of Canada*, May 1924, 38.

23 Ed Southby of Cycle Supply, quoted in *Radio*, October 1925, 49.

24 See A.N. Goldsmith, "Progress in Radio Receiving 1927," *Radio*, January 1928, 15; Smulyan, "'And Now a Word From Our Sponsors ...,'" 88.

25 *Radio News of Canada*, April 1925, 68.

26 See Elton Johnson, "Canada's Radio Consciousness," 29. For another impressionistic summary of programming in the 1920s see Nolan, "An Infant Industry," 505–17.

27 "Broadcasting," in Kallmann, Potvin, and Winters, *Encyclopedia of Music in Canada*, 117.

28 CAVA, Bambrick Transcripts, Interview with Herb Roberts, 5.

29 Sterling and Kittross, *Stay Tuned*, 72.

30 See Czitrom, *Media and the American Mind*, 191.

31 See Stevens and Garcia, *Communication History*, 140; Williams, *Problems in Materialism and Culture*, 191; G.H. Douglas, *The Early Days of Radio Broadcasting*, 166–7; Coats, "Canada's Fifty Years of Broadcasting," 14.

32 *Radio*, January 1924, 17.

33 *Radio News of Canada*, January 1924, 9. See also MacDonald, *Don't Touch That Dial!*, 10, and, for Britain, Pegg, *Broadcasting and Society*, 203.

34 RG 97 vol. 151, file 6206–109, part 2, Crawford-Harris Survey, 5.

35 Cockfield Brown, "Radio as an Advertising Medium," Toronto question-naire, 19.

36 Special Committee 1932, 632.

37 Ibid., 224.

38 Brand, "'The Twentieth Century Bible,'" 119. See also Elton Johnson, "Canada's Radio Consciousness," 29.

39 Calculated from schedules published in Winnipeg *Free Press*, 22 October 1927, and Toronto *Globe*, 22–28 October 1927. Similarly, in New York City in February 1927, about three-quarters of broadcast time was filled with music. See G.A. Lundberg, "The Content of Radio Programs," in Lichty and Topping, *American Broadcasting*, 323.

40 Kidd, "From a music box to 'The Guess Who,'" 26.

41 "Programmes for Station CKAC," *Radio News of Canada*, March 1924, 36.

42 MTL, Wm. Main Johnson Papers, vol. 17, Diaries, 7 April 1925, 52–5. The part-time Toronto radio inspector agreed with Johnson that the remote broadcasting was "a great improvement." RG 97, vol. 87, file 6040–1, part 1, A.H.K. Russell to C.P. Edwards, 19 February 1924.

43 "Guy Lombardo," in McNeil and Wolfe, *Signing On*, 106.

44 "Jazz," in Kallman, Potvin, and Winters, *Encyclopedia of Music in Canada*, 469.

45 Russel Nye points out that, because loud rhythmic music sounded best on primitive early equipment, record companies tended to produce and promote ragtime and jazz records, with great commercial success. On radio, however, there was a distinct lag in the use of jazz. Nye, *The Unembarrassed Muse* 323; see also G.H. Douglas, *The Early Days of Radio Broadcasting*, 166, 168, 176 and Biocca, "Media and Perceptual Shifts."

46 See, for example, S. Morgan Powell, "Better Music for the Radio," *Radio*, April 1925, 17; RG 42, vol. 1077, file 227–10–8, Aird Hearings, 5 June 1929, 15.

47 Coats, "Canada's Fifty Years of Broadcasting," 261.

48 See MG 26K, M–1314, R.W. Ashcroft, "The Fifth Estate," October 1929, 389147; Smulyan, "'And Now a Word From Our Sponsors ...,'" 87.

49 G.H. Douglas, *The Early Days of Radio Broadcasting*, 158–9.

50 "Broadcasting," in Kallman, Potvin, and Winters, *Encyclopedia of Music in Canada*, 117.

51 RG 97, vol. 88, file 6040–4, part 4, H.N. Stovin to deputy minister, 11 September 1931.

52 Editorial, "Variety in Radio Programs," *Canadian Radio*, 13 June 1924, 8.

53 See Scannell, "Music for the Multitude?," 259 and Scannell and Cardiff, *The Birth of British Broadcasting*, 182, 207.

54 See Pagé, "La radio dans la vie des Québécois," 8.

55 *Statutes of Canada*, 11–12 George V, Chap. 24. See also Claxton, "Protection Against the Unauthorized Use of a Broadcast in Canada."

56 HOC, Special Committee on Bill No. 2 re Copyright Act, 1925, xvii, 79.

57 RG 12, vol. 554, file 1550–6, E.R.E. Chevrier to A. Johnston, 5 March 1925.

58 HOC, Special Committee on Bill No. 2 re Copyright Act, 1925, 91, 180.

59 Ibid., 171.

60 Ibid., 172.

61 Ibid., 171, 180, 246. See also Morse, "Copyright – Opera-Broadcasting by Wireless Telephony – Infringement."

62 This idea had first been proposed to the Radio Branch by Gordon V. Thompson in 1923; see RG 97, vol. 87, file 6040–1, part 1, Thompson to Edwards, 30 May 1923.

63 See especially Allard, *The C.A.B. Story*, 1–4. In the United States as well, it was the copyright issue that inspired the founding of the National Association of Broadcasters. See Sterling and Kittross, *Stay Tuned*, 88.

64 HOC, Special Committee re Bill No. 2 on Copyright Act, 1925, 81, 94, 129; Editorial, "The Proposed Amendment to the Copyright Act," *Radio News of Canada*, April 1925, 11; RG 12, vol. 554, file 1500–6, Open letter from Canadian Radio Trades Association to manufacturers, dealers, and jobbers, 2 March 1925.

65 RG 12, vol. 554, file 1500–6, Herbert Lewis for Canadian Radio Trades Association to members, 2 March 1925.

66 Harkness, *J.E. Atkinson of the Star*, 196.

67 See RG 97, vol. 87, file 6040–1, part 2, A.R. McEwan to Edwards, 10 December 1925.

68 HOC, Special Committee re Bill No. 2 on Copyright Act, 1925, 93.

69 Ibid., 106; RG 12, vol. 554, file 1500–6, Ottawa Amateur Radio Association to E.R.E. Chevrier, MP, 15 March 1925.

70 HOC, Special Committee re Bill No. 2 on Copyright Act, 1925, 145.

71 See *Radio*, April 1926, 29, and RG 42, vol. 1076, file 7–3–1, "Administration of Radio Broadcasting in Canada – Sent to Australian Administration," 13 May 1926.

72 Harkness, *J.E. Atkinson of the Star*, 195.

73 See *Dominion Law Reports*, 1929, 2:1.

74 HOC, *Debates*, 8 June 1931, 2418.

75 MG 30 D304, vol. 22, file 24, "Report of Commission of Inquiry by Hon. Mr. Justice A.F. Ewing," 28 January 1932. Evidence submitted to this inquiry showed that of the musical selections played on three Alberta stations, CKLC, CJCJ, and CFAC, in a sample week, between 49 and 61 per cent were copyright. See also Amey, "Broadcasting and the Performing Rights Societies in Canada," 3–4.

76 See Martin, "Capitalizing on the 'Feminine' Voice"; H. Fink and M. Vipond interview with Lillian Shaw, Winnipeg, June 1989.

77 For example, the Toronto *Globe* had such an arrangement with CFRB by 1931, and the *Mail and Empire* with CKNC. See MG 26K, M–1289,

E.L. Bushnell to the A. Duranleau, 17 March 1931, 360646–7.

78 CAVA, Bambrick Transcripts, Interview with E. Jackson, 4.

79 See Nichols, *(CP): The Story of the Canadian Press*, 258–64.

80 RG 97, vol. 87, file 6040–1, part 2, Canadian Press, "Dominion Election, 1926, circular no. 6," 31 August 1926.

81 See CAVA, Bambrick Transcripts, Interview with G.R.A. Rice, 6; McNaught, *Canada Gets the News*, 250.

82 On Foster Hewitt, hockey broadcasts, and so on see Weir, *The Struggle for National Broadcasting in Canada*, 85.

83 Sterling and Kittross, *Stay Tuned*, 78; Pegg, *Broadcasting and Society*, 213.

84 Nolan, "Canadian Election Broadcasting," 177.

85 BCA, Radio Station CHYC Log Book, 12 September 1926. CKAC in Montreal also aired a notable amount of political programming, beginning as early as 1922, and including in 1925 a regular series of talks by members of the provincial legislature and in 1927 speeches by two leading proponents of female suffrage. See Montigny, "Les Débuts de la Radio à Montréal," 44, 68–9, 101.

86 "Patenaude Howled Down in Riot at St. Mary Meeting," Montreal *Gazette*, 13 September 1926, 2.

87 Coats, "Canada's Fifty years of Broadcasting," 168.

88 Special Committee 1932, 526.

89 MG 30 D67, vol. 19, file 2, "Notes on Political Broadcasting through Canadian National Railways during 1930 Federal Election," n.d.

90 Ibid., vol. 25, file 2, "Memo Showing Amount of Revenue Earned Through Broadcasting Political Speeches During June and July 1930," n.d.

91 See, for example, RG 97, vol. 87, file 6040–1, part 5, E. Hawken to the undersecretary of state for external affairs, 18 February 1932; "French Taught by Radio," *Radio News of Canada*, March 1924, 39; and the descriptions of CKUA programming and of Saskatchewan broadcasting to the Special Committee 1932, 256–62, 709.

92 RG 97, vol. 154, file 6206–176, University of Alberta "Radio Program: Station CKUA," 1 October 1928 to 30 June 1929. The other most active university-owned station, CFRC at Queen's, fulfilled a double purpose: training for electrical-engineering students and university extension work. Its educational programming predated CKUA's but was less extensive. Zimmerman, *In the Shadow of the Shield*, 359, 387.

93 RG 42, vol. 1077, file 227–9–3, A.G. Dorland to Aird commission, 12 February 1929, encl.

94 Montigny, "Les Débuts de la Radio à Montréal," 89–90; Special Committee 1932, 332, 447, 465–7.

95 Special Committee 1932, 382, 391.

96 PAM, RG 11, A1, Box 3, J.E. Lowry to the D.G. McKenzie, 10 October 1929; Schmalz, *On Air*, 83.

97 See, for example, Fink, "The Sponsor's v. the Nation's Choice," 190–2; Esslin, *An Anatomy of Drama.*

98 According to a 1930 analysis, a symphony of 50 pieces cost $550 per hour, a symphonic dance orchestra of 40 pieces $450, and an opera or operetta $650, while dramatic sketches were only $375 per hour. Cockfield-Brown, "Radio as an Advertising Medium," Appendix.

99 MG 30 D67, vol. 19, file 6, "CNR Radio Programmes," December 1924.

100 Montigny, "Les Débuts de la Radio à Montréal," 74.

101 Fink, "The Sponsor's v. the Nation's Choice," 232.

102 *Radio,* June 1926, 28.

103 Fink, "CKUA Radio Drama and Regional Theatre," 224–7.

104 MG 30 D67, vol. 19, file 6, "CNR Radio Programme"; ibid., vol. 8, file 8, "Production List of the CNRV Players," October 1927–October 1931.

105 See Special Committee 1932, 146–7.

106 MacLennan, "'Circumstances Beyond Our Control,'" 67.

107 Special Committee 1932, 238. For an example of a 1931 CFCF program schedule, see Bird, *Documents,* 55–6.

108 Special Committee 1932, 224–5.

109 See Rosen, *The Modern Stentors* 156–8; Smulyan, "'And Now a Word From Our Sponsors,'" 111–28.

110 On the great significance of "Amos 'n' Andy," see G.H. Douglas, *The Early Days of Radio Broadcasting,* 196–205.

111 For example Weir, *The Struggle for National Broadcasting in Canada,* 51–60.

112 Scannell and Cardiff, *The Birth of British Broadcasting,* xiii. See also Langham, "Tuning in," 111.

113 One early listener, when queried in the 1970s, expressed great surprise that Montreal ever had a CNR station. See Brand, "'The Twentieth Century Bible,'" 117. Figures for the months of December 1931 and January 1932 indicate that the three CNR-owned stations, CNRA, CNRO, and CNRV, presented a total of fourteen hours and forty-nine minutes of programming each day (that is, less than five hours each), of which more than one-third was records. Special Committee 1932, 35–6.

114 H.P. Davis, "The Early History of Broadcasting in the United States," 196.

115 Batson, *Radio Markets of the World, 1930,* 3–5.

116 RG 12, vol. 864, file 6206–162–1, "Something to Please Everybody," *Broadcasting,* September 1923, 3. See also MG 30 D67, vol. 19, file 1, W.D. Robb, "Address on CNRT's Second Anniversary," 14 May 1926; C.M. Ripley, "The Invisible Audience," *Canadian Radio,* June 1924, 18; W.H. Easton, "What the Radio Audience Tells Us," *Radio,* May 1923, 27; PAM, RG 11 A1, Box 3, J.G. Hay to Manitoba Telephone System, October 1923.

117 G.H. Douglas, *The Early Days of Radio Broadcasting,* 155; Charlesworth, "Great Artists on Radio," 24.

118 Levine, *Highbrow/Lowbrow.*

119 According to L.D. Batson, this was also true virtually everywhere in the world by 1929. See his *Radio Markets of the World, 1928–29*, 21.

120 Vipond, "Best Sellers in English Canada: 1919–1928."

121 RG 97, vol. 152, file 6206–150, "Radio Fan" to editor, Victoria *Daily Times*, 9 April 1927.

122 Scannell, "Music for the Multitude?," 257.

123 This was not the case in Great Britain, however, where until the end of the 1930s programs were deliberately shuffled about in the schedule to promote more active involvement on the part of listeners. See Scannell and Cardiff, *The Birth of British Broadcasting*, 262.

124 See Lesley Johnson, "Radio and Everyday Life."

125 Batson, *Radio Markets of the World, 1930*, 3–5.

126 Spalding, "1928: Radio Becomes a Mass Advertising Medium," 40. The continuity and regularity of programs, although rarely questioned, is in fact one of the central ways in which radio presents to us a very unreal world. See Abrams, "Radio and Television," 59.

127 Thomas, "A Concept of the Audience," 153–4, 318. See also Stamps, *The Concept of the Mass Audience in American Broadcasting*.

128 RG 97, vol. 151, file 6206–109, part 2, Crawford-Harris Survey, 11.

129 There were no scientifically grounded listener surveys in Canada in the period covered here. In the United States, Daniel Starch, director of research for the American Association of Advertising, conducted a survey of eastern listeners for NBC in 1928 which was updated and made national in 1930; the Crossley organization also began regular surveys for the Association of National Advertisers in 1930. See Smulyan, "'And Now a Word From Our Sponsors ...,'" 123, 132. The only comparable Canadian studies seem to have been the one conducted by an employee of Cockfield-Brown in Toronto in 1930 and the survey of southern Saskatchewan listeners by the Crawford-Harris agency in 1930. While both revealed some interesting data, neither had any scientific validity. Of course, insofar as American advertisers and programmers were influenced by the Starch and Crossley surveys, and Canadian stations either competed with or fed off US stations, the US surveys had an indirect influence on the kinds of programs Canadians heard as well.

130 See Abrams, "Radio and Television," 59–61; Scannell and Cardiff, "Serving the Nation," 187.

131 For a brief survey of this literature, see Vipond, *The Mass Media in Canada*, 99–106.

132 See Cohen, "Encountering Mass Culture at the Grassroots," 17.

133 A lengthy and interesting – if only speculative – contemporaneous list of possible "effects" of radio may be found in Willey and Rice, *Communication Agencies and Social Life*, 153–6.

134 Seldes, *The Great Audience*, 105.

135 Allan Klenman quoted in Duffy, *Imagine Please*, 69.

136 Cantril and Allport, *The Psychology of Radio*, 18.

137 Lesley Johnson, "Radio and Everyday Life," 171–2, 177.

138 Older participatory forms of music such as singing around the piano, however, did go into decline. "Recorded Sound," in Kallman, Potvin, and Winters, *Encyclopedia of Music in Canada*, 796.

CHAPTER FIVE

1 By 1932 the branch was operating twenty-nine coastal stations, twelve direction-finding stations, nineteen radio-beacon stations, four radio-telephone stations, and forty-seven ship stations, as well as supervising all the others. Special Committee 1932, 107.

2 Roberts and Tunnell, *Canadian Who's Who*, 1936–37, 562; Obituary, Toronto *Globe and Mail*, 1 December 1951, 31.

3 RG 42, vol. 723, Department of Marine, Headquarters Staff; Obituary, Ottawa *Journal*, 14 July 1960, 2; Editorial, Ottawa *Journal*, 15 July 1960, 6.

4 RG 42, vol. 723, Department of Marine, Headquarters Staff. On Manson see also MG 30 E344, finding aid.

5 MG 26K, M–1289, A. Johnson to R.B. Bennett, 6 November 1931, and encl., 360910–20.

6 See Vipond, "Nationalism and Nativism: The Native Sons of Canada in the 1920's."

7 No other body openly disputed the federal government's right to regulate in this area until several provinces challenged its authority in the late 1920s; eventually the federal government's power was upheld by the Judicial Committee of the Privy Council of Great Britain. For further details see Chapter 10.

8 RG 97, vol. 88, file 6040–13, Edwards to J.E. Lowry, 17 June 1926.

9 Because the technical regulation of radio has been transferred from one department to another in the intervening years, the files from the 1920s are scattered among the Government Archives' holdings of the Department of Marine and Fisheries, Marine Branch (RG 42), the Department of Transport (RG 12), the Department of Communications (RG 97), and the CBC (RG 41).

10 Apparently such a meeting was considered in late 1925 but it was never called. See RG 97, vol. 87, file 1040–1, part 2, Edwards to A.R. McEwan, 16 December 1925.

11 Department of the Naval Service, *Annual Report*, 1911–12, 66, shows one amateur licence granted for receiving only.

12 RG 42, vol. 1076, file 7–3–1, Radiotelegraph Branch [Bulletin], "Radio Activities in Canada," 11 August 1922.

13 RG 97, vol. 91, file 1024–4, part 5, G.J. Desbarats to F.H. Gisbourne,

31 March 1925, enclosed memorandum (drafted by Edwards).

14 Department of Marine and Fisheries, *Annual Report*, 1924–25, 136.

15 Department of Marine, *Annual Report*, 1931–32, 139.

16 Table created from *Annual Reports* of Department of Marine and Fisheries, 1922–23 to 1931–32, and *Annual Reports* of auditor-general, 1922–23 to 1931–32.

17 Special Committee 1932, 573. The government of Nova Scotia also protested on this point. Ibid., 387.

18 For example see MG 26K, M–1289, Duranleau to A.W. Merriam, 2 June 1931, 360748; ibid., M–1290, Edwards to R.B. Bennett, 15 January 1932, 361113.

19 RG 97, vol. 87, file 6040–1, part 2, "Administration of Radio Broadcasting in Canada," [c. May 1926], 4–5.

20 Special Committee 1932, 4.

21 Alan N. Longstaffe, "The Future of Radio in Canada," *Radio*, February 1923, 20; RG 97, vol. 87, file 6040–1, part 1, J. Macklem to director, 22 February 1924; ibid., RG 12 D–1, vol. 389, file 6500–1, E.J. Haughton to Edwards, 7 May 1924. Other estimates included that of Batson, *Radio Markets of the World, 1932*, 54 (20 per cent unlicensed); of the Montreal *Gazette*, 3 January 1929, 1 ("more than 100,000" unlicensed in addition to the 226,000 with licences in November 1928), and of the president of the Canadian Association of Broadcasters to the Special Committee 1932, 276 (40 per cent unlicensed).

22 A similar suggestion had come from Toronto Radio Inspector S.J. Ellis just a few days earlier. See RG 97, vol. 87, file 6040–1, part 1, Ellis to director, 3 March 1924.

23 RG 12 D–1, vol. 389, file 6500–1, confidential memorandum, "Instructions to Radio Inspectors ... for the Seizure of Radio Apparatus Under Section 8 of the Radio-Telegraph Act" [June 1924]; ibid., draft of letter from Edwards to inspectors in certain cities, 27 June 1924. (On second thought, the search-and-seizure instructions were modified to give owners a forty-eight-hour warning period and inspectors were told to keep the names of those charged confidential.)

24 Ibid., Edwards to Sutherland, 19 November 1924.

25 RG 33, Series 14, vol. 5, "Report to the British Broadcasting Committee," 19 May 1923, 5.

26 Ibid., vol. 2, file 227–12–5, Aird Commission Hearings, 17 June 1929, 16; Editorial, "The Tax on Radio," Ottawa *Journal*, 19 December 1927; Letter to editor, *Radio News of Canada*, June 1924, 40.

27 RG 97, vol. 90, file 1024–8, part 2, A.E. Arsenault to Alexander Johnston, 15 April 1931; RG 33, Series 14, vol. 1, file 227–9–8, Aird Hearings, 12.

28 HOC, *Debates*, 8 April 1932, 1851.

29 MG 26K, M–1289, J. Smith to Bennett, 9 March 1931, 360635.
30 The idea of requiring licences for receiving only was discussed in 1912 and
   again in 1921 in the United States but rejected. Even the licensing of broadcasting stations was accepted with reluctance by some because of the
   freedom of the press issue. The perceived cost and difficulty of enforcement
   also discouraged American authorities from receiving-set licensing. See
   G.A. Johnson, "Secretary of Commerce Herbert C. Hoover," 68; Barnouw,
   "Historical Survey of Communications Breakthroughs," 16; Briggs, *The Birth
   of Broadcasting*, 63.
31 For example, see MG 26K, M–1298, Miss Helena McMeekin to Bennett
   [May 1931], 360724–5.
32 RG 97, vol. 91, file 1024–4, part 6, Johnston to deputy minister of justice,
   1 February 1927, and reply of 2 February 1927.
33 RG 12 D–1, vol. 389, file 6500–1, Donald Manson, "Memo to the Director
   Re: Prosecutions under the Radiotelegraph Act," 14 October 1930.
34 Special Committee 1932, 17–18.
35 Rickwood, "Canadian Broadcasting Policy and the Private Broadcasters,"
   378–9; Weir, *The Struggle for National Broadcasting in Canada*, 263; RG 12 D–1
   vol. 389, files 6300–8 and 6300–12. The licence-fee revenues lost were
   partially recouped in the 1950s by a 15 per cent excise tax on the sale of
   television sets.
36 An example of a broadcasting licence may be found in Bird, *Documents*,
   31–4. The notion of creating a differential fee schedule depending on the
   station's power was discussed but never implemented. See RG 42, vol. 1076,
   file 7–3–1, "Administration of Radio Broadcasting in Canada" [*c.* May 1926],
   1, 4.
37 This period is covered thoroughly in Aitken, *The Continuous Wave*, 250ff.
38 Briggs, *The Birth of Broadcasting*, 40ff.
39 The visit of Post Office official F.J. Brown to the United States in the winter
   and spring of 1921–22 was significant in spreading this perception. See
   ibid., 93.
40 The control exerted in the British case was made possible by three particular factors. First, there was clear 1904 legislation granting the Post Office
   authority over radio licensing. Moreover, the Post Office had established
   a monopoly of domestic telecommunications services (telegraph and
   telephone) more than a decade prior to the introduction of radio, while in
   Canada and the United States both services were almost exclusively in the
   private sector from the beginning. Another distinctive feature of the British
   situation was the previously established success of a relatively compact ruling
   class to define a dominant vision of the national culture – something that
   was certainly lacking, although desperately sought, in Canada in the 1920s.
   See Mundy, "'Free-Enterprise' or 'Public Service'?," 281, 292.

41 RG 97, vol. 87, file 6040–1, part 1, C.P. Edwards, memo to the deputy minister, "Broadcasting licenses," 1 May 1922.

42 RG 12, vol. 864, file 6206–162, part 1, Johnston to Lowry, 14 April 1927.

43 For examples see RG 97, vol. 147, file 6206–1, part 1, E. Hawken to H.R. Reschetrils, 7 December 1926; ibid., vol. 154, file 6206–176, Johnston to H.P. Brown, 10 March 1927.

44 Special Committee 1932, 336.

45 RG 42, vol. 494, file 209–32–116, E. Hawken to E.V. Schreiber, 22 March 1923.

46 This story comes from the CKGW file, RG 42, vol. 493, file 209–32–111, part 1.

47 Ibid., Edwards to deputy minister, 17 August 1926.

48 Millar hastily cabled Senator Murphy for his support. See MG 27 III B8, vol. 14, folder 97, C. Millar to Murphy, 18 August 1926.

49 This story may be found in RG 97, vol. 148, file 6206–51.

50 O.L. Spencer of the *Herald* also alleged in a later letter that Crowe's station was in fact to be used by the International Bible Students Association, but there is no confirmation of this. Ibid., Spencer to Johnston, 15 June 1926.

51 Ibid., Crowe to Johnston, 27 March 1926.

52 Ibid., Ainslie to Edwards, 27 October 1928.

53 MG 26K, M–929, F.W. Hobson to Bennett, 10 April 1928, 28685. CJCJ became CKXL in 1948. Allard, *Straight Up*, 26.

54 For example, see RG 12, vol. 862, file 6206–148, part 1, Edwards to Main Johnson, 12 November 1924, and RG 97, vol. 152, file 6206–110, part 1, G.J. Desbarats to C. Thomas, 21 June 1922, and further correspondence of April-May 1924. See also HOC, *Debates*, 6 June 1929, 3340, and 21 May 1931, 1843. Similarly, in the United States in 1926 a judge ruled in one case that "priority of time creates a superiority in right." See Sivowitch, "A History of Radio Spectrum Allocation in the United States," 42, 125ff.

55 RG 97, vol. 150, file 6206–76, part 1, D. Manson, "Memorandum to the Director Re: Transfer of Private Commercial Broadcasting License," 15 July 1926.

56 Ibid., file 6206–72, part 1, E.J. Haughton to Edwards, 7 July 1926.

57 Ibid., vol. 87, file 6040–1, part 1, W.A. Rush to R. Ainslie, 9 November 1927.

58 Ibid., vol. 153, file 6206–173.

59 RG 12, vol. 2300, file 6206–99, vol. 1, Sutherland to Edwards, 23 December 1927. Not atypically for small stations of the time, the transmitter was in fact in Burke's living room and the studio several blocks away in Rogers's. For the full history of CFCY see Large and Crothers, *Out of Thin Air*.

60 Allard, *Straight Up*, 13; see also Foster, *Broadcasting Policy Development*, 11.

61 See especially Owen, *Economics and Freedom of Expression*, 88–92.

62 For a biting critique of this system, see Hardin, *Closed Circuits*. The CRTC

does discourage licence trafficking and exorbitant profits by commonly requiring purchasers of broadcasting stations to provide a "benefits" package (usually in the form of promises of new programming and capital improvements) and by insisting that value be added while a licence is held.

63 RG 97, vol. 87, file 6040–1, part 2, Rush to Ainslie, 9 November 1927.

64 Ibid., vol. 152, file 6206–150, Telegram, Victoria Radio Club to Edwards, 26 March 1927.

65 RG 12, vol. 2300, file 6206–99, vol. 2, Rogers to Cantley, 15 August 1930; Cantley to Johnston, 18 August 1930; McLure to Radio Branch, 11 November 1930; Johnston to Rogers, 23 January 1931.

66 RG 97, vol. 152, file 6206–133, part 1, Rogers to Malcolm, 31 August 1927, copy.

67 Ibid., vol. 153, file 6206–171, W.A. Rush to E. Hawken, 12 December 1929.

68 Ibid., vol. 151, file 6206–89, C.P. Edwards, "Memo to the Deputy Minister," 17 December 1930.

CHAPTER SIX

1 See for example RG 97, vol. 150, file 6206–76, Radio Branch, "Rules to be Observed in the Operation of Private Commercial Broadcasting Stations in Canada," 24 June 1926; see also Bird, *Documents*, 31–4.

2 In addition to the *Annual Reports* of the Department of Marine and Fisheries, on the inspection service see J.J. Montagnes, "Radio Interference Problems in Canada Solved by Government," *Radio News of Canada*, March 1927, 8, and Raine, "Our Radio Trouble Hunters," 18.

3 RG 33, Series 14, vol. 2, file 227–10–7, Aird Hearings, 6.

4 See for example, the circular Edwards sent to all inspectors on 14 February 1924 asking for information regarding local radio conditions. RG 97, vol. 87, file 6040–1, part 1, "Radio Inspection Circular: Number Nineteen." Ottawa headquarters did not necessarily always follow the advice of its inspectors, as the case of CJCJ Calgary demonstrated.

5 RG 97, vol. 90, file 1024–5, part 1, Edwards to H.E. Willmot, 17 February 1926.

6 "Noise," *Radio*, October 1925, 18.

7 RG 97, vol. 151, file 6206–109, part 2, Crawford-Harris survey.

8 In Britain, 75 per cent of the letters received by the BBC in the 1920s were complaints about interference. Pegg, *Broadcasting and Society*, 40.

9 See *Radio*, May 1925, 49; "Fading Tests Completed – Report Contains Results," *Radio*, September 1923, 29. More specifically, it was realized that interference-free service was possible only in the area where the radio signals were carried by ground waves. MG 26K, M–1314, W.A. Steel, "The Broadcasting Service Required for the Inhabited Belt in Canada," 389222.

10 See *Annual Reports* of Department of Marine and Fisheries.

11 Unless otherwise noted, all information in this section comes from the *Annual Reports* of the Department of Marine and Fisheries.

12 "Annual Report of the Chief of the Radio Division to the Secretary of Commerce for the fiscal year ending June 30, 1931," 3, in Kittross, *Documents in American Telecommunications Policy*, vol. 1.

13 Table created from information in the *Annual Reports* of the Department of Marine and Fisheries, 1926–27 to 1931–32.

14 Department of Marine and Fisheries, *Annual Report*, 1929–30, 153.

15 Royal Commission on Radio Broadcasting, *Report*, 1929, in Bird, *Documents*, 51.

16 RG 97, vol. 108, file 4012–11, "Minutes Taken at the Conference Held at the Toronto Office on October 14, 1929."

17 Department of Marine, *Annual Report*, 1930–31, 136–7.

18 Raymond, "Radio," 101; E.H. Armstrong, "The Story of the Super-heterodyne," *Radio Broadcast*, July 1924, in Lichty and Topping, *American Broadcasting*, 44.

19 Department of the Naval Service, *Annual Report*, 1921–22, 27.

20 RG 97, vol. 108, file 4000–73, Keith Russell to Edwards, 12 February 1925.

21 Sivowitch, "A History of Radio Spectrum Allocations in the United States," 89.

22 RG 12, vol. 608, "Report of Special Radio Conference Held on January 11, 1924." Canadian radio regulations were amended 1 August 1925 to assign all ship stations on the Great Lakes to 715 metres and all others to 600 metres.

23 RG 12, vol. 596; see also RG 97, vol. 87, file 6040–1, part 1, Johnston to undersecretary of state for external affairs, 6 March 1924.

24 Department of Marine and Fisheries, *Annual Report*, 1925–26, 148.

25 Sturmey, *The Economic Development of Radio*, 63.

26 BCA, Radio Station CHYC Logbook, October 1925–January 1927; see also RG 97, vol. 149, file 6206–72, part 1, Edwards to Canadian Marconi, 12 January 1926, which reprimanded CFCF for frequently slipping off its assigned frequency of 730 kHz.

27 RG 97, vol. 87, file 6040–1, part 4, J.W. Bain, "Memorandum to Director of Radio: Reference Frequency Stability of Broadcasting Stations," 22 October 1930. In this memo, Bain recommended and Edwards accepted a rule that stations of more than 500 watts be required to have crystal control to keep them within 300 cycles of their allotted wavelength; the requirement was waived for small 100-watt stations on the grounds that a piezo-electric crystal would increase the total cost of their transmitting apparatus by 40 to 50 per cent.

28 Special Committee 1932, 111.

29 Sivowitch, "A History of Radio Spectrum Allocations in the United States,"

52n.21. By 1926 the Radio Branch was warning broadcasting licence-holders to suppress harmonic radiation. See RG 97, vol. 154, file 6206–174, part 1, "Rules to be Observed in the Operation of Private Commercial Broadcasting Stations in Canada," 24 June 1926; see also RG 12, vol. 864, file 6206–162–3, Edwards to J.E. Lowry, 30 October 1929.

30 H.E. Campbell, "Reradiation Presents Radio's Greatest Problem," *Radio,* November 1923, 17–8; see also RG 97, vol. 87, file 6040–1, part 1, S.J. Ellis to Edwards, 3 March 1924, and A.H.K. Russell to Edwards, 19 February 1924.

31 The expression comes from radio pioneer Vic George; see CAVA, Bambrick Transcripts, Interview with Vic George, 5. A thick file of complaints about regenerative-receiver interference rests in RG 97, vol. 90, file 1024–5, part 1, including a copy of J.S. Grant's letter to the Montreal *Star,* 23 January 1926.

32 RG 97, vol. 90, file 1024–5, part 1, Johnston to deputy minister of Justice, 21 April 1925, and reply of 28 April 1925.

33 Sivowitch, "A History of Radio Spectrum Allocation in the United States," 110.

34 RG 97, vol. 90, file 1024–5, part 1, Edwards to H.E. Willmot, 17 February 1926.

35 Ibid., Edwards to J.A. Blount, 10 February 1926.

36 See *Radio News of Canada,* November 1925, 28–9.

37 Kingston *Daily Standard,* 21 February 1925, cited in Zimmerman, *In the Shadow of the Shield,* 349.

38 RG 97, vol. 90, file 1024–5, part 1, G.J. Malcolm to Radio Branch, 12 November 1925. According to Malcolm, the greatest problems occurred with Westinghouse Radiolas. See also Department of Marine and Fisheries, *Annual Report,* 1925–26, 148; RG 97, vol. 90, file 1024–5, part 1, R.H. Combs to Edwards, 14 January 1926, S.J. Ellis to Edwards, 8 February 1926.

39 "Courtesy of the Air," *Radio,* September 1923, 17.

40 RG 42, vol. 1077, file 227–9–4, C.P. Edwards to W.H. Cross, 8 March 1929, copy.

41 RG 97, vol. 88, file 6040–13, Edwards to Lowry, 17 June 1926; see also ibid., vol. 87, file 6040–1, part 1, Edwards to J.B. Pomey, 25 October 1924.

42 Ibid., vol. 149, file 6026–54, part 3, E.J. Haughton to Edwards, 16 February 1929.

43 Ibid., vol. 152, file 6206–111, part 1, correspondence, 6 June–26 July 1929.

44 See CAVA, Bambrick Transcripts, interview with Les Horton. See also PAM, RG 11, A1, Box 3, J.E. Lowry to D.G. McKenzie, 25 April 1929, encl., "Broadcasting Regulations."

45 RG 97, vol. 131, file 6275–1, part 1, C.P. Edwards, "Memorandum to the Deputy Minister," 18 March 1931.

46 In a somewhat similar case, also in Edmonton, a listener complained about a speaker from the Canadian Labour Party on CJCA who attacked Sir Herbert Holt. The branch also forwarded this to the RCMP for investigation,

but dropped it immediately when the police reported back that the complainant was a well-known crank whose real grievance was that the Bible Students had lost their stations for critical speech of a similar kind. See MG 30 D 304, vol. 8, file 8–3, F.R.F. McKitrick to deputy minister of Marine, 19 January 1932, and subsequent correspondence, copies. In 1931 a question was raised in the House about whether the radio addresses of socialist Dr Lyle Telford on CJWX Vancouver had been censored. It turned out, however, that the branch had had nothing to do with stopping the broadcasts – the station's owner had done so because other listeners complained about them. Ibid., vol. 17, file 7–6, E.J. Haughton to Edwards, 13 July 1931, copy. See also HOC, *Debates*, 13 July 1931, 3945.

47 Special Committee 1932, 332.

48 Strictly speaking, the act gave the Governor in Council power of censorship only in time of war or emergency. However, the section describing the government's authority to determine conditions of licence was worded broadly enough that it could include control over program content – as its use therefor attests.

49 CAVA, Bambrick Transcripts, interview with G. Quinney. Victor introduced an automatic changer in 1927 that obviated this problem. Moogk, *Roll Back the Years*, 110.

50 CAVA, Bambrick Transcripts, interview with T.C. Robertson.

51 The record industry varied in its response to the use of its product on the radio. While some elements saw the advantages in the free publicity, others felt sales would be hurt. Copyright issues were involved as well. Evidence as to the actual effect on record sales is difficult to assess because factors other than the arrival of radio were involved.

52 The file on the regulation of recorded material is to be found in RG 97, vol. 88, file 6040–4, parts 1–5. The rule just cited was one of those listed on the "Special Rules to be observed in the operation of Private Commercial Broadcasting Stations." The exact date on which these regulations were promulgated is not clear but they were in force by August 1925 at the latest. Regulations to the same effect existed in the United States, particularly the relegating of stations that used recordings to less desirable frequencies. Biel, "The Making and Use of Recordings in Broadcasting before 1936," 1:228–33; Rosen, *The Modern Stentors*, 38.

53 Biel, "The Making and Use of Recordings in Broadcasting before 1936," 2:595–7. This ban also harked back to a nineteenth-century tradition – also applicable to radio itself – that anything reproduced mechanically was inferior and unauthentic. See Levine, *Highbrow/Lowbrow*, 163. I have seen no evidence of any concerted attempt by the Canadian record industry to influence the government either way in its decision to ban records at certain times of the day. Neither has any concrete evidence that the musicians'

union was behind the ban on records in the evening come to light, although it did later (when invited) become involved in trying to limit electrical transcriptions.

54 RG 97, vol. 88, file 6040–4, part 1, E. Hawken to D.C. MacLachlan, 14 October 1927.

55 RG 12, vol. 864, file 6206–162–1, D.R.P. Coats to G. Gray, 2 September 1926, copy; see also RG 97 vol. 88, file 6040–4, part 2, Coats to Gray, 29 September 1930, copy.

56 For example, see RG 97, vol. 87, file 6040–1, part 4, J.C. Stephen to director, Radio Branch, 21 and 22 March 1930, enclosures; ibid., vol. 88, file 6040–4, part 4, H.N. Stovin to W.R. Pottle, 10 April 1931 and enclosures.

57 RG 97, vol. 152, file 6206–150, Radio Marine to E.J. Haughton, 29 December 1925; ibid., Victoria Radio Club to E.J. Haughton, 7 January 1926.

58 Ibid., vol. 151, file 6206–109, part 2, Crawford-Harris survey, 12. See also ibid., vol. 88, file 6040–4, part 1, R. Ainslie to Edwards, 13 April 1929.

59 See, for example, ibid., vol. 88, file 6040–4, part 1, A. Johnston to C.W. Deaville, 5 March 1926, Johnston to H.G. Link, 19 June 1928; ibid., vol. 149, file 6206–54, Johnston to Sprott-Shaw Radio, 2 March 1926.

60 For example, RG 12, vol. 864, file 6206–162–2, W.A. Rush to G. Gray, 5 June 1929; ibid., vol. 605, file 6206–50, C.P. Edwards to F.W. Patterson, 8 July 1929; RG 97, vol. 87, file 6040–1, part 3, Edwards to Cyril Edmunds, 12 December 1929; ibid., R. Ainslie to Edwards, 6 February 1930; ibid., vol. 88, file 6040–4, part 1, Edwards to radio inspectors, 26 September 1930, and replies.

61 RG 97, vol. 88, file 6040–4, part 2, Johnston to W. Morris, 20 October 1930.

62 Ibid., part 1, Edwards to radio inspectors, 26 September 1930.

63 Ibid., part 2, "Re: Use of Electrical Transcriptions: Memorandum of a meeting held ... on Wednesday, 8th October 1930."

64 Ibid., Joseph Weatherburn to Duranleau, 10 October 1930, telegram, and G.B. Henderson to Duranleau, 10 October 1930, telegram. There is no evidence that another interested party, the wireline companies, intervened against transcriptions at this time, although they were to do so in 1934.

65 Ibid., part 3, "Re: Use of Electrical Transcriptions: Memorandum of a meeting held ... on Friday, the 21st November 1930."

66 See, for example, MG 30 D304, vol. 12, file 12–5, R.W. Ashcroft to deputy minister of Marine, 3 October 1930, copy.

67 Apparently Dr Ernest MacMillan, principal of the Toronto Conservatory of Music, was the first to formulate this compromise with respect to a series of General Motors transcriptions. RG 97, vol. 88, file 6040–4, part 3, G.B. Henderson to Johnston, 10 January 1931. It may be noted that the regulation eventually adopted was tougher in several minor ways than that recommended by C.P. Edwards to the minister. See ibid., Edwards,

"Memo for the Honourable the Minister: Broadcasting records after
7:30 p.m.," 28 January 1931. See also ibid., part 4, Edwards, "Memo to the
Acting Deputy Minister," 15 April 1931.

68 See RG 97, vol. 88, file 6040–13, H.E. Hawken to J.N. Thivierge, 2 February
1932. The definition of "produced and manufactured in Canada" was strict,
including all preliminary impressions from which the matrix was made as
well as subsequent pressings.

69 Ibid., file 6040–4, part 4, C.P. Edwards, "Memorandum to the Acting Deputy
Minister Re: Use of Electrical Transcriptions by Broadcasting Stations,"
26 March 1931.

70 Ibid., part 5, D.R.P. Coats to H.E. Hawken, 11 February 1932; MG 30 A77,
file 9, Department of Marine, Radio Branch, "Rules to be Observed in the
Operation of Private Commercial Broadcasting Stations in Canada," fiscal
year 1st April 1930–31st March 1931, amendment, rule 8, 10 March 1931.

71 Langham, "Tuning In," 11n.14.

72 RG 97, vol. 88, file 6040–4, part 4, D. Manson, "Memorandum to the
Director," 26 August 1931. It is not clear why the Queen's University station,
CFRC, was not mentioned.

73 Special Committee 1932, 35–9.

74 See RG 42, vol. 1076, vol. 109–1–1, "Radio Broadcasting: An answer to
criticisms appearing in the press re the Radio Commission's report," n.d., 5.

75 "For the Record," 120–1.

76 Most local stations in the United States in fact imitated their betters and
tended to eschew records as well. See Biel, "The Making and Use of
Recordings in Broadcasting before 1936," 1:232–8.

77 RG 97, vol. 87, file 6040–1, part 1, Radio Naval to Basil Lake, 7 June 1922.

78 Apparently Basil Lake of the Toronto *Star* was the first to suggest this
practice. See RG 12, vol. 862, file 6206–148, Lake to Edwards, 21 June 1922,
in which he requested permission for Simons Agnew (stockbrokers) and the
Robert Simpson company to rent the *Star*'s equipment in this way; and
reply, Radio Naval to Lake, 22 June 1922, granting permission pending the
anticipated establishment of toll-broadcasting stations in March 1923.

79 Black, "The Early Days of Canadian Broadcasting," 102. This practice was
not discouraged by Radio Branch officials; in fact, they sometimes recommend it. See RG 97, vol. 152, file 6206–150, E.J. Haughton to Edwards,
15 April 1925, and reply of 15 June 1925; RG 12, vol. 864, file 6206–162–1,
J.E. Lowry to A. Johnston, 3 May 1926, and reply of 8 May 1926.

80 RG 97, vol. 91, file 1924–4, part 5, Edwards to deputy minister, memo,
12 May 1923.

81 The rationale allowing the modification of the meaning of the word
"private" in the term private-commercial broadcasting licence was apparently that the station would still have the right to refuse any message, which
was not the case for the posited public broadcasting stations. See Foster,

Broadcasting Policy Development, 7.

82 A copy of the regulations may be found in Bird, *Documents,* 35–6.

83 RG 97, vol. 154, file 6206–179, Johnston to O.L. Spencer, 10 June 1924.

84 Ibid., vol. 152, file 6206–110, part 1, H.J. Link to Edwards, 6 January 1925, and reply of 14 January 1925.

85 RG 12, vol. 864, file 6206–162–1, Lowry to Johnston, 26 March 1925, and reply.

86 RG 97, vol. 88, file 6040–13, A.R. McEwan to Edwards, 7 May 1926.

87 Ibid., Lowry to Edwards, 9 June 1926.

88 Ibid., Edwards to Lowry, 17 June 1926. In the United States, opposition to direct advertisements in the evening hours continued throughout this period; as late as 1929 the National Association of Broadcasters' code restricted direct ads to the daytime hours, but the expansion of the networks soon weakened that ban considerably. The prohibition of the mention of prices was not lifted until 1932. See Head with Sterling, *Broadcasting in America,* 122–3.

89 See Department of Marine and Fisheries, *Annual Report,* 1925–26, 149.

90 Ibid., 1924–25, 138.

91 See, for example, the letter from a radio salesman who complained that house-to-house radio demonstrations were hurt most by "the persistent advertiser." Letter to editor from R. Adio, *Radio Trade-Builder,* March 1927, 51.

92 RG 97, vol. 87, file 6040–1, part 2, Edwards to Coats, 12 May 1927.

93 RG 12, vol. 2300, file 6206–99, vol. 1, K.S. Rogers to Radio Branch, 23 December 1927, and reply of 30 December 1927.

94 RG 97, vol. 87, file 6206–51, D. Manson, memo to director, 29 November 1928, and Edwards to R. Ainslie, 5 December 1928; ibid., vol. 153, file 6206–166, Johnston to G.R.A. Rice, 21 December 1928.

95 RG 12, vol. 2300, file 1, K.S. Rogers to Johnston, 3 January 1929. See also Large and Crothers, *Out of Thin Air,* 62.

96 RG 97, vol. 88, file 6040–13, Johnston to CKMO, CHGS, CJOR, and CFCY, 16 January 1929.

97 Ibid., Edwards to R.B. Hanson, 14 March 1932.

98 Ibid., D.R.P. Coats to E. Hawken, 29 August 1931, enclosure, and reply of 15 September 1931.

99 Special Committee 1932, 509.

100 RG 97, vol. 151, file 6206–88, Edwards to S.J. Ellis, 10 May 1930; ibid., vol. 88, file 6040–13, Edwards to Ellis, 15 October 1931.

101 Ibid., vol. 88, file 6040–13, Edwards to Ellis, 24 June 1932.

102 Ibid., Edwards to Hanson, 14 March 1932.

103 One direct mention of the price of one product was allowed on each fifteen-minute program on NBC, for example. Ibid., G.W. Payne to Edwards, 4 October 1932.

104 Ibid., R.W. Ashcroft to Edwards, 14 October 1932, telegram; ibid., Edwards to Thivierge, 29 October 1932.

105 Ibid., Edwards, "Memo to the Asst. Deputy Minister," 21 November 1932; H.E. Hawken, "Memo to the Chairman, Canadian Radio Broadcasting Commission," 22 November 1932; Edwards, "Memo to the Chairman, Broadcasting Commission," 1 December 1932.

106 Ibid., Edwards to Valiquet, 21 August 1924.

107 Ibid., vol. 151, file 6206–108, part 1, Johnston to P.R. DuTremblay, 14 May 1923.

CHAPTER SEVEN

1 A good layperson's explanation of the science and technology behind radio transmission may be found in Head with Sterling, *Broadcasting in America,* 35–65.

2 The Americans changed their terminology at the second National Radio Conference in 1923; the Canadian Radio Branch officially began to use frequencies in early 1924. At the International Radio Conference of 1927 the term frequency was agreed upon for international usage but compliance was slow in many countries.

3 One may convert wavelength to frequency by the following formula: wavelength in metres times frequency in kiloHertz equals 300,000.

4 See *Radio Spectrum Conservation, A Report of the Joint Technical Advisory Committee,* IRE-RTMA, 10, in Kittross, *Documents in American Telecommunications Policy,* vol. 2.

5 It has become increasingly clear, for example, that technological innovation can expand spectrum use. A good example is the directional antenna, which can orient signals into preferred patterns. These were not introduced until 1932, however. Another excellent example in the broadcasting field is the introduction of FM service, which has greatly expanded the number of broadcasting stations available to the average listener. For a strong argument against spectrum-scarcity assumptions, see Owen, *Economics and Freedom of Expression.*

6 Barnouw, *A Tower in Babel,* 100, 121–2.

7 RG 12, vol. 862, file 6206–148, part 1, C.P. Edwards to Main Johnson, 12 November 1924.

8 According to the US Radio Act of 1912, the Department of Commerce had the power to license radiotelegraph stations and operators. Certain frequencies were laid out for ship and amateur stations but broadcasting of course was not mentioned. In general, the power of the secretary of commerce was administrative; he had no authority to make new regulations to cope with new conditions. At this point Hoover was also locked in combat with the Navy and the Post Office for control of radio. See L.F. Schmeckebier, *The*

Federal Radio Commission: Its History, Activities and Organization, 1–3, in Kittross, *Documents in American Telecommunications Policy*, vol. 1. See also Rosen, *The Modern Stentors*, 56–8.

9 RG 12, vol. 608, file 5858–8, vol. 1, "Resumé of the Canadian-United States Situation Regarding Broadcasting Wave-lengths," 6 August 1926.

10 Ibid., Johnston to Carson, 29 April 1924.

11 Ibid., Tyrer to Johnston, 15 May 1924.

12 Report of Bureau of Navigation, May 1924, quoted in Bensman, "The Regulation of Radio Broadcasting by the Department of Commerce," 206.

13 RG 12, vol. 608, file 5858–8, vol. 1, resumé, 5. Edwards was accorded the honour of being the first speaker at the conference (after Hoover himself).

14 Ibid., vol. 609, file 5858–8, vol. 3, H.E. Hawken to Laurent Beaudry, 26 March 1930; Department of Marine and Fisheries, *Annual Report*, 1924–25, 137.

15 RG 97, vol. 87, file 6040–1, part 1, Edwards to D.H. Kent, 23 July 1925.

16 Bensman, "The Regulation of Radio Broadcasting by the Department of Commerce," 265.

17 RG 97, vol. 87, file 6040–1, part 1, Edwards to W.D. Terrell, 23 July 1925.

18 RG 12, vol. 608, file 5858–8, vol. 1, Edwards to Carson, 19 February 1925.

19 Ibid., Edwards to Carson, 27 February 1925.

20 Ibid., Edwards to Carson, 5 November 1925, draft.

21 Ibid., vol. 609, file 5858–8, vol. 4, Johnston to O.D. Skelton, 22 December 1930, and reply of 24 December 1930.

22 Ibid., vol. 608, file 5858–8, vol. 1, Edwards to Johnston, 14 November 1925, telegram. It is unclear what type of legislation Edwards meant, whether full-scale US domestic legislation or simply to enable a treaty. A later version of these events had it that Hoover had suggested that the treaty was necessary primarily because of the lack of US radio legislation. See ibid., file 5858–8, vol. 2, "Treaty Negotiations," 1.

23 Ibid., file 5858–8, vol. 1, Carson to Johnston, 18 November 1925, and reply of 15 December 1925.

24 Ibid., C.P. Edwards, "Memo to the Deputy Minister: Broadcasting Wavelength Situation," 27 July 1926.

25 See Rosen, *The Modern Stentors*, 93ff; Bensman, "The Zenith-WJAZ Case and the Chaos of 1926–27."

26 Rosen, *The Modern Stentors*, 93.

27 Davis to attorney-general, 12 January 1926, quoted in Bensman, "The Zenith-WJAZ Case and the Chaos of 1926–27," 428. WJAZ, incidentally, was very popular with Canadian listeners. See RG 97, vol. 87, file 6040–1, part 1, S.J. Ellis to Edwards, 3 March 1924.

28 RG 12, vol. 608, file 5858–8, vol. 1, Statement of the Department of Commerce, "The Opinion of the Attorney-General on Radio," 9 July 1926.

29 Bensman, "The Zenith-WJAZ Case and the Chaos of 1926–27," 436; Rosen,

The Modern Stentors, 103.

30 Rosen, *The Modern Stentors*, 101.

31 Minasian, "The Political Economy of Broadcasting in the 1920's," 402.

32 RG 12, vol. 608, file 5858–8, vol. 1, C.P. Edwards, "Memo to the Deputy Minister: Broadcasting wavelength situation," 27 July 1926.

33 Ibid.

34 Specifically, the Canadians asked for twelve exclusive wavelengths, nine or ten of which would carry more than one station in different parts of the country; twelve wavelengths for 500-watt stations, five in the east, five in the west, and two central; and four wavelengths for low-power stations, mainly for western Ontario. RG 12, vol. 608, file 5858–8, vol. 2, [A. Johnston], "Treaty Negotiations between the Dominion of Canada and the United States of America: Allocation of Channels in the Radio Broadcast Band 500 to 1500 Kilocycles 1927," 28 March 1927.

35 Ibid., 3–4. A similar statement was inserted in the Department of Marine and Fisheries, *Annual Report*, 1926–27, 143.

36 RG 12, vol. 608, file 5858–8, vol. 2, "Treaty Negotiations ...," 4.

37 Massey had presented his letters of credence to President Coolidge on 18 February.

38 RG 12, vol. 608, file 5858–8, vol. 2, "Memorandum of Conversation with Mr. Hoover on February 28th, 1927, Respecting Radio Matters."

39 Ibid., "Treaty Negotiations ...," attached copy, Massey to King, 25 March 1927.

40 Ibid., Wrong to secretary of state for external affairs, 27 September 1928.

41 William Phillips, US minister to Canada, later claimed that he resigned on these grounds. Kottman, "Herbert Hoover and the Smoot-Hawley Tariff," 614.

42 Brandes, *Herbert Hoover and Economic Diplomacy*, 40–60, quote on 41.

43 Rosen, *The Modern Stentors*, 111. Caldwell, the editor of *Radio Retailing*, was not confirmed as a member of the FRC until 30 March 1928.

44 RG 12, vol. 608, file 5858–8, vol. 2, copy of Caldwell speech in New York, 26 March 1927.

45 Ibid., Address of Admiral W.H.G. Bullard to the National Press Club, 30 April 1927, copy.

46 Smead, *Freedom of Speech by Radio and Television*, 140; see also Rogers, "The History of the Clear Channel and Super Power Controversy," 98–101. Caldwell also seems to have been less than consistent on this issue, depending upon which way the domestic political winds were blowing, a point picked up by the alert Hume Wrong at the Canadian embassy. See RG 12, vol. 608, file 5858–8, vol. 2, Wrong to secretary of state for external affairs, 30 June 1927 and 27 September 1928.

47 RG 42, vol. 1076, file 7–1–26, "Memo., re Radio (Short Wave Conference) held in Ottawa 21st January 1929 to 25th January 1929."

48 Weaver, "Imperilled Dreams," 199, 202.

49 Wilkins, *The Maturing of Multinational Enterprise*, 52–3; Brandes, *Herbert Hoover and Economic Diplomacy*, 167.

50 Brandes, *Herbert Hoover and Economic Diplomacy*, xi.

51 Rosen, *The Modern Stentors*, 124.

52 This reservation was confirmed by FRC General Orders 40 and 42 (30 August and 11 September 1928). The number of shared wavelengths was not specified, however, and this was to fluctuate somewhat in the ensuing period.

53 RG 12, vol. 608, file 5858–8, vol. 2, Johnston to O.D. Skelton, undersecretary of state for external affairs, 27 December 1927.

54 Ibid., vol. 609, file 5858–8, vol. 3, Johnston memo to Skelton, 26 May 1928.

55 Ibid., Johnston to Skelton, 2 October 1928.

56 Ibid., M.M. Mahoney for the chargé d'affaires, Canadian legation at Washington, to secretary of state for external affairs, 11 September 1928, encl., copy.

57 Another example may be found in Caldwell, "The Administration of Federal Radio Legislation," 47–8.

58 RG 12, vol. 609, file 5858–8, vol. 3, Hume Wrong to secretary of state for external affairs, 27 September 1928.

59 MG 26J, C–2305, Massey to Skelton, 27 October 1928, copy, 132048.

60 Ibid., Nelson T. Johnson for the secretary of state to Vincent Massey, n.d., copy, 132042–4.

61 See for example, RG 12, vol. 864, file 6206–162–1, Edwards to J.E. Lowry, 22 February 1927 and 15 March 1927; RG 97, vol. 149, file 6206–72, part 1, Edwards to Canadian Marconi, 12 January 1926.

62 MG 26K, M–1289, [W.A. Steel], "Radio situation between Canada and the United States in connection with the broadcast band," 27 January 1931, 360512.

63 RG 12, vol. 609, file 5858–8, vol. 3, Johnston to A.E. Middleton-Hope, 7 January 1929.

64 M. Davis, "International Radiotelegraph Conventions and Traffic Arrangements," 365.

65 RG 12, vol. 609, file 5858–8, vol. 3, Johnston to director, International Telegraph Bureau, 26 December 1928; ibid., vol. 4, Notification No. 80, Berne, 1 February 1929, copy of translation.

66 Leive, *International Telecommunications and International Law*, 47–8.

67 RG 97, vol. 88, file 6040–4, part 4, Edwards to C.B. Jolliffe, 17 April 1931. See also RG 12, vol. 609, file 5858–8, vol. 5, Edwards to Saltzman, 26 January 1931.

68 Special Committee 1932, 7; HOC, *Debates*, 11 May 1932, 2817.

69 RG 97, vol. 86, file 6116–1, part 1, Edwards to L. Beaudry, 21 January 1932.

70 RG 12, vol. 609, file 5858–8, vol. 4, E. Hawken to undersecretary of state for

external affairs, 24 June 1930.

71 Ibid., J.W. Bain, "Report to Director of Radio," 23 January 1931; Alex MacKenzie for Radio Manufacturers Association of Canada to Edwards, 18 December 1930; ibid., vol. 5, Edwards to A.L. Ainsworth, 23 March 1932.

72 Special Committee 1932, 125, 200.

73 RG 12, vol. 609, file 5858–8, vol. 4, M. Mahoney, chargé d'affaires, Washington, to Henry L. Stimson, secretary of state, 16 July 1930. See also testimony of W.A. Steel in HOC, Special Committee on the Operations of the Commission under the Canadian Radio Broadcasting Act, *Proceedings and Evidence*, 1934, 266.

74 Special Committee 1932, 117–8; MG 30 D297, vol. 97, file 97–5, "Distribution of Broadcasting Frequencies in the Band 1500 k/c to 550 k/c Between Countries of North America."

75 MG 30 A42, vol. 31, file 183, Steel to Jolliffe, 22 October 1931.

76 Ibid., vol. 19, file 102, W.A. Steel, "The Division of Broadcast Frequencies Between Canada and the United States," 22 August 1931.

77 More specifically, according to a Steel memo, the breakdown was as follows. Previous arrangement: five clear channels, no power limits; one shared channel, power limited to 4 kw. (this was the channel shared with the US navy station at Arlington); eleven shared channels, power limited to 500 watts. New arrangement: nine clear channels, no power limits; four shared channels, power limited to 1 kw.; three shared channels, power limited to 500 watts; twenty shared channels, power limited to 100 watts. MG30 A42, vol. 29, file 161, "Comparison between 1932 Channel Allotment and Previous Arrangement with U.S.A.," n.d. It may be noted, however, that Canada was actually *using* twenty-three channels by 1932. See MG 26K, M–1289, W.D. Herridge to W.R. Castle, acting secretary of state, 5 May 1932, and reply, 361048–51; HOC, *Debates*, 9 May 1932, 2709, and 11 May 1932, 2817. Some dispute did arise as to differing interpretations of the notes. See RG 12, vol. 609, file 5858–8, vol. 5, Louis G. Caldwell to Brooke Claxton, 28 May 1932, copy.

78 The allocation of 540 kHz to Windsor did arouse some American opposition because of its proximity to Atlantic shipping lanes. US officials chose not to make an issue of it, however, "in order to facilitate negotiations in connection with the proposed [North American Radio] Conference." See RG 12, vol. 609, file 5858–8, vol. 5, William Phillips for the secretary of state to W.D. Herridge, 11 May 1933. The United States itself began to use 540 kHz in 1952. A number of objections to the plan were raised by the American broadcasting industry. The New York *Times* possibly best summarized the situation in an editorial entitled "Canada's Radio Policy" published on 12 May: "Neither Canadians nor Americans will be satisfied with the understanding reached. But this is an indication that it is probably fair."

79 MacKinnon, *Analyzing the Havana Treaty*, 6.

80 MG 26J, C–2305, [L. Beaudry], "Memorandum," 9 November 1928, 13205.

81 Rogers, "The History of the Clear Channel and Super Power Controversy," 113.
82 Wrong, "The Canada-United States Relationship 1927/1951," 537.
83 Special Committee 1932, 113.
84 MG 26K, M–1289, [W.A. Steel], "Radio situation between Canada and the United States in connection with the broadcast band," 27 January 1931, 360512.

CHAPTER EIGHT

1 Archer, *History of Radio to 1926*, 291–4.
2 See for example, RG 97, vol. 152, file 6206–110, part 1, G.J. Desbarats to C. Thomas, 5 May 1922.
3 RG 12, vol. 609, file 5858–8, vol. 4, A. Johnston to O.D. Skelton, 22 December 1930.
4 This estimate came from J.N. Cartier of CKAC Montreal. See HOC, Special Committee on Bill 2 re Copyright Act, 1925, 127.
5 RG 97, vol. 87, file 6040–1, part 1, J. Shannon to Edwards, 25 February 1924.
6 RG 42, vol. 493, file 209–32–97, part 1, A. Johnston to Rev. T. Shields, 15 April 1925. See also ibid., vol. 1076, file 7–3–1, "Administration of Radio Broadcasting in Canada – sent to Australian Administration," 13 May 1926, and RG 12, vol. 2300, file 6206–99, vol. 1, Edwards to F.W. Hyndman, 2 August 1928.
7 RG 97, vol. 151, file 6206–88, W.M. Turnley to Johnston, 28 January 1925; RG 12, vol. 554, file 1500–6, Herbert Lewis, secretary, Canadian Radio Trades Association, to members, 2 March 1925.
8 RG 12, vol. 862, file 6206–148, part 1, J.R. Bone to A. Johnston, 20 January 1925.
9 RG 42, vol. 1076, file 7–1–23, "General Re-allocation."
10 Rogers, "The History of the Clear Channel and Super Power Controversy," 66.
11 RG. 33, Series 14, vol. 5, Department of Marine and Fisheries, "Report for the British Broadcasting Committee on Radio Broadcasting Situation in Canada," 19 May 1923, 1–2.
12 See RG 97, vol. 152, file 6206–110, part 1, correspondence, April–May 1924.
13 RG 12, vol. 2300, file 6206–99, vol. 1, Edwards to R.H. Jenkins, 17 October 1928.
14 RG 97, vol. 152, file 6206–110, part 1, Langford to Edwards, 25 April 1924.
15 Ibid., vol. 151, file 6206–88, Edwards to R.H. Briscoe, 2 March 1925.
16 Ibid., vol. 154, file 6206–179, O.L. Spencer to Johnston, 1 October 1930; see also very similar sentiments expressed by one of Spencer's competitors in ibid., vol. 153, file 6206–174, part 1, W.W. Grant to Edwards, 14 April 1924, and "Dual Broadcasting Inevitable," *Radio News of Canada*, February 1927, 4.
17 MG 26K, M–1289, A. MacKenzie to A. Johnston, 12 March 1928, copy,

360623–4. See also RG 97, vol. 87, file 6040–1, part 4, Charles Shearer to Johnston, 24 September 1930, and Special Committee 1932, 165.

18 MG 26K, M–1289, E.L. Bushnell to A. Duranleau, 17 March 1931, copy, 360646–7. See also "The Broadcaster's Case," *Radio Trade Builder*, April 1927, 29.

19 RG 33, Series 14, vol. 1, file 227–9–9.

20 See, for example, RG 97, vol. 149 file 6206–72, part 1, A. Johnston to J.A. Dupont, 28 September 1928.

21 RG 97, vol. 149, file 6206–72, part 2, Edwards to J.M. Colton, 26 December 1928.

22 Ibid., J.H. Browne *et al.* to Department of Marine and Fisheries, 29 December 1928, and L.L. Sicard to Department of Marine and Fisheries, 1 January 1929.

23 Ibid., Johnston to Canadian Marconi, 6 February 1929.

24 "How to Avoid Radio Interference," *Electrical News*, 15 December 1922, 55. See also Fourth National Radio Conference, *Proceedings*, 21, in Kittross, *Documents in American Telecommunications Policy*, vol. 1.

25 Batson, *Radio Markets of the World, 1930*, 3.

26 See, for example, PAM, RG 11 A1, Box 3, H. Toyer to editor, Winnipeg *Tribune*, 5 August 1927, copy.

27 RG 97, vol. 87, file 6040–1, part 1, R.H. Combs to Edwards, 30 December 1924.

28 Ibid., vol. 153, file 6206–164, part 1, Edwards to J.H. MacLeod, 28 October 1924.

29 Ibid., vol. 151, file 6206–88, W.M. Turnley to Johnston, 17 January 1925. See also the same view expressed in ibid., vol. 87, file 6040–1, part 1, M.K. Pike to Radiotelegraph Branch, 25 February 1924.

30 G.A. Johnson, "Secretary of Commerce Herbert C. Hoover," 176.

31 RG 97, vol. 152, file 6206–133, part 1, correspondence March–August 1926.

32 Ibid., vol. 153, file 6206–164, part 1, W.W. Grant to Edwards, 14 April 1924, and reply of 17 April 1924.

33 Sterling and Kittross, *Stay Tuned*, 85.

34 MG 26K, M–1289, W.W. Grant, "Memo No. Three," 16 February 1931, 369611.

35 Rosen, *The Modern Stentors*, 73.

36 In early 1926, for example, complaints about the power of WJZ Bound Brook from listeners in three neighbouring counties led to a resolution in the New Jersey Senate, ignored by Washington. Sivowitch, "A History of Radio Spectrum Allocation in the United States," 116; see also Archer, *History of Radio to 1926*, 318–9.

37 Eoyang, *An Economic Study of the Radio Industry*, 159.

38 MG 26K, M–1314, W.A. Steel, "The Broadcasting Service Required for the Inhabited Belt in Canada," 15 November 1931, 389221–2.

39 Special Committee 1932, 213–14.

40 Those suburbanites, Edwards regretted, were "simply out of luck," but "'you can't make an omelet without breaking eggs.'" RG 97, vol. 151, file 6206–108, part 2, Edwards to W.D. Terrell, 23 October 1924.

41 RG 42, vol. 493, file 209–32–111, part 1, Edwards to Dr A.N. Goldsmith, 16 July 1927.

42 Ibid., vol. 1075, J.W. Bain, memo, "On the Practical Technical Aspects of the Report of the Royal Commission on Radio Broadcasting," 21 March 1930, 3–6. All the figures cited assumed a five-tube receiver with an appropriate outside aerial.

43 Ibid., 7.

44 RG 97, vol. 152, file 6206–133, part 1, Edwards to S.J. Ellis, 8 November 1928.

45 Ibid., Edwards, "Memo to Deputy Minister," 7 November 1928.

46 MG 26K, M–1289, Edwards, "Memo to the Honourable the Prime Minister," 25 March 1931, 360652.

47 RG 97, vol. 150, file 6206–83, part 2, Edwards, "Memo for File," 19 October 1931.

48 Ibid., vol. 152, file 6206–133, part 2, Duranleau to Bennett, 28 December 1931.

49 Ibid., J.W. Bain, "Memo to Director of Radio," 17 December 1931; Edwards, "Memorandum to the Deputy Minister," 24 December 1931; A. Duranleau to R.B. Bennett, 28 December 1931; Bennett to Duranleau, 31 December 1931; MG 26K, M–1289, Edwards, "Memo to the Honourable the Prime Minister," 25 March 1931, 360652–6; ibid., Edwards to A.W. Merriam, 30 March 1931, copy, 360658–9.

50 RG 97, vol. 152, file 6206–133, part 2, J.W. Bain, "Memo to Director of Radio," 17 December 1931.

51 Ibid., part 1, Edwards to E.S. Rogers, 1 June 1927.

52 Ibid., part 2, Duranleau to Bennett, 28 December 1931.

53 Ibid., file 6206–111, part 1, E. Hawken to J.E. Palmer, 20 April 1927; RG 12, vol. 2300, file 6206–99, vol. 1, Hawken to Island Radio, 26 April 1927.

54 An impassioned but essentially accurate statement of this case written by private broadcaster G.C. Chandler of CJOR Vancouver may be found in MG 26K, M–943, 44361–86.

55 Canada. Task Force on Broadcasting Policy, Report, 171.

56 RG 97, vol. 87, file 6040–1, part 1, Edwards to F.W. Johnson, 9 July 1924.

57 See for example RG 33, Series 14, vol. 5, "Report to British Broadcasting Committee," 19 May 1923, 8, and Special Committee 1932, 111.

58 See Lindblom, "The Science of 'Muddling Through,'" 79–88.

59 Dror, "Muddling Through – 'Science' or Inertia?," 153–7. See also Mosco, Broadcasting in the United States.

60 Aucoin, "Theory and Research in the Study of Policy-Making," 14.

61 Lindblom, "The Science of 'Muddling Through,'" 82; Wilson, Canadian Public Policy and Administration, 150ff.

62 See, for example, RG 97, vol. 149, file 6206–54, part 1, Edwards to
E.J. Haughton, 23 August 1927; ibid., vol. 152, file 6206–150, Johnston to
Victoria Radio Club, 11 April 1927.

63 RG 97, vol. 152, file 6206–150, Edwards to W.T. McGibbon, 10 December
1926.

64 Editorial, "Broadcasting Stations Overlap," *Electrical News*, 1 March 1924, 49;
Department of Marine and Fisheries, *Annual Report*, 1924–25, 138.

65 HOC, *Debates*, 1 June 1928, 3655.

66 See Doern and Phidd, *Canadian Pubic Policy*.

CHAPTER NINE

1 RG 42, vol. 493, file 209–32–97, part 1, C.P. Edwards to S.J. Ellis, 25 February
1925; RG 97, vol. 154, file 6206–176, E. Hawken to H.P. Brown, 20 April
1927. In 1929 the branch refused, despite many importunate letters and
telegrams, to allow a special dual-broadcasting arrangement that would have
brought in a Harry Lauder special from NBC on the grounds that regular
listeners might be upset about interference with the church services
normally heard at that time. The fact that the NBC program was a commercial one, sponsored by the Enna Jettick Shoe Company, also was a factor in
the decision, although Sunday advertising was not formally banned. See
RG 97, vol. 149, file 6206–72, part 2, Edwards to R.W. Ashcroft, 23 July 1929,
and Johnston to R.W. Grimmer, 2 August 1929. See also ibid., vol. 153, file
6206–164, part 2, radio inspector to S.E. Andrews, 23 January 1929.

2 RG 42, vol. 493, file 209–32–111, part 1, A. Johnston to Gooderham and
Worts, 5 January 1928; ibid., Johnston to N.B. Maysmith, 29 June 1928. The
commercial stations do seem to have policed themselves in this respect. For
example, CFCA, the Toronto *Star* station, discontinued the broadcasts of
Rev. G.J. Kirby from St Michael's Cathedral because of complaints that his
sermons were anti-Protestant. See Harkness, *J.E. Atkinson of the Star*, 194. It
may also be noted that, after an "unfortunate" 1925 expression of religious
prejudice during the broadcast of an Orangemen's banquet in Ottawa, the
CNR stations adopted a policy of denying religious or quasi-religious bodies
any airtime whatsoever. See MG 30 D67, vol. 19, file 2, H.W. Thornton to
W.D. Robb, 31 March 1925, copy; Weir, *The Struggle for National Broadcasting
in Canada*, 100–1.

3 See RG 12, vol. 605, file 6206–144, part 1, especially Edwards to E.J.
Haughton, 30 April 1928, and reply of 8 May 1928.

4 RG 97, vol. 152, file 6206–132, Johnston to J.H. Woodward, 31 March 1927.
See also RG 97, vol. 154, file 6206–176, A.E. Ottewell to deputy minister,
13 April 1927, and reply of 25 April 1927; ibid., vol. 153, file 6206–166,
Johnston to A. Yockney, Edmonton *Journal*, 4 May 1927; RG 42, vol. 493, file
209–32–101, Johnston to F.M. Jarrett, 18 December 1925, and RG 97, vol.

138, file 6210–146, part 1, Edwards to E.S. Rogers, 1 February 1927.

5 See Penton, *Jehovah's Witnesses in Canada.* Chapter 5, "The Battles of the Air Waves," covers the issue discussed here.

6 HOC, *Debates,* 12 April 1928, 1951. Cardin also told the House that newspaper clippings on file regarding the Bible Students' pacifist stand during the war (which resulted in the banning of their publications) were a factor in this decision. Ibid., 1 June 1928, 3668.

7 RG 42, vol. 493, file 209–32–101, Edwards to Macklem, 14 May 1924.

8 Ibid., Macklem to Edwards, 20 May 1924, and reply of 27 May 1924. A local Roman Catholic priest claimed that Macklem was favourable to the sect because they had bought their equipment from him and still owed him money. RG 97, vol. 152, file 6206–140, part 1, A. Jan to Minister, 14 April 1925.

9 Unfortunately, perhaps because of file transfers after the treatment of the IBSA stations became a cause célèbre, only the file of the Saskatoon station can be located.

10 MG 26K, M–929, "Statement re Cancellation by the Dominion Government of the Licenses of the International Bible Students Association" [March 1928], 28675.

11 RG 42, vol. 493, file 209–32–101, C.P. Edwards, "Memo to the Deputy Minister: Bible Students' Station – Saskatoon," 7 January 1928, note at bottom signed "A.J." dated 14 January 1928. For the full file of letters of complaint about the IBSA stations, see RG 14 D2, vol. 184, file 254, Second Session of 16th Parliament, 1928, Sessional Paper No. 254 (unpublished), "Return to an order of House of Commons – moved by Mr. Woodsworth for Mr. Heaps May 7, 1928 – for copy of all letters, telegrams and correspondence which caused cancellation of IBSA licenses" (hereafter HOC, S.P. 154, 1928).

12 MG 26K, M–929, Johnston to secretary, Universal Radio of Canada, 8 March 1928, copy, 28758; RG 42, vol. 493, file 209–32–101, Johnston to IBSA, 15 March 1928.

13 CHUC broadcast appeals to its listeners to counter this resolution and four packages of letters, many of them semi-literate, arrived in Ottawa. Many of the letter-writers emphasized that CHUC's "wholesome" programming was much preferable to the "jaz, jaz, jaz" otherwise dominating the airwaves. For Macklem's viewpoint see HOC, S.P. 254, 1928, Macklem to Radio Branch, 18 December 1926.

14 HOC, S.P. 254, 1928, G.M. Hubbard and others to minister of Marine and Fisheries, 2 February 1928. See also RG 97, vol. 149, file 6206–54, part 2, D. Manson, "Memo to Director," 16 March 1928. In a June 1926 letter to J.E. Lowry in which he admitted that the power to issue licences inevitably forced the branch to take some responsibility for the content of what was broadcast, Edwards gave as an example a 2000-signature petition he had

received from radio listeners in Vancouver "praying for the cancellation of a license issued to a religious sect in that city." This could have referred only to the IBSA station but it is puzzling that it was not mentioned in 1928. See RG 97, vol. 88, file 6040–13, Edwards to Lowry, 17 June 1926.

15 A discrepancy may be noted between this summation of the file and the versions presented by W.F. Salter and J.S. Woodsworth at the time and by Penton later. Salter and Woodsworth both had an axe to grind, however, and Penton did not look at the original file but took Woodsworth's word for its contents.

16 Editorial, "Visiting Orators Take Notice," 1. See also Penton, *Jehovah's Witnesses in Canada*, 89.

17 HOC, S.P. 254, 1928, Ellis to director, 22 March 1928. This recommendation arrived after the non-renewal decision had already been taken; it was probably simply a written confirmation of advice Ellis had already communicated orally to his Ottawa superiors.

18 Penton, *Jehovah's Witnesses in Canada*, 95; see also MG 26K, M–929, document that begins "In the Statement Delivered in the House of Commons ..." [March 1928], 28926, and HOC, *Debates*, 1 June 1928, 3658. Another version is that the prime mover was J.H. Cranston of the *Star* (an interested party because the paper owned a competing station and because he was an adherent of Bloor Street Baptist), who contacted Mackenzie King on the subject. See MG 30 D304, vol. 8, file 8–4, E.L. Bushnell, "Draft Reminiscences," 16.

19 HOC, S.P. 254, 1928, A.C. Crews to Radio Branch, 22 July 1927, copy.

20 Ibid., Crews to E. Hawken, 6 February 1928, copy.

21 Petitions were presented to Parliament from some 133,000 individuals from Ontario and the four western provinces. A petition with 458,026 signatures (of whom 82,468 were radio listeners) was also mentioned in the House. A mass meeting attended by "thousands" was also held at the Pantages Theatre in Toronto. See HOC, *Debates*, 23 May 1928, 3294–5; 25 May, 3348; 31 May, 3644. See also MG 26K, M–934, 35080–200 for the forty letters R.B. Bennett received between March and May 1928 on the subject; all but three were opposed to the licence cancellation. Regina inspector W.R. Pottle reported a door-to-door canvass in his city and the gathering of a thousand signatures at a Ku Klux Klan meeting conducted by J.J. Maloney. RG 42, vol. 493, file 209–32–101, Pottle to director, 2 April 1928.

22 See HOC *Debates*, 31 May 1928, 3648. Inspector Ellis suspected that CKCX was using a power higher than that authorized, for it seemed to blanket WJZ and WEAF more than CFRB did, but there is no confirmation of this. See HOC, S.P. 254, 1928, Ellis to director, 19 November 1926.

23 MG 26K, M–929, "A Further Statement Regarding the Cancellation by the Government of the International Bible Students Association's Licenses to Broadcast" [April 1928], 28719. See also ibid., W.F. Salter to W.L.M. King,

19 March 1928, copy, 28721.

24 Ibid., W.F. Salter to R.B. Bennett, 10 April 1928, 28729; ibid., "Statement re Cancellation of the License of the Universal Radio of Canada Ltd by the Dominion Government" [April 1928], 28756–60; ibid., Universal Radio to P.J.A. Cardin, 24 March 1928, copy, 28694–5; HOC, *Debates*, 1 June 1928, 3659–63; "Closing of Station CJYC Is Rank Party Patronage," Toronto *Telegram*, 31 March 1928, 33.

25 MG 26K, M–929, document beginning "In the Statement Delivered in the House of Commons ..." [March 1928], 28724–5. A unique factor in the controversy over the Bible Students' expression of their beliefs over the air was that there was no written or taped record of precisely what was said in any given broadcast; thus there was no concrete evidence upon which to base an opinion as to whether their views were offensive or not. Among the MPs who debated the issue, for example, probably only a minority had ever heard an IBSA station broadcast; others may have read some of the sect's literature, but the radio broadcasts may have been quite different in tone from the published material. See HOC, *Debates*, 1 June 1928, 3666.

26 MG 26K M–929, "Statement Re Cancellation ..." [March 1928], 28680.

27 James Simpson, vice-president of the Trades and Labour Congress, addressed a mass meeting in Toronto; editorial support was also obtained from such farm organs as the *Western Producer*. See RG 42, vol. 1076, file 227–2–6, copy of *The Messenger*, 3, no. 1 (n.d.). In Saskatoon, the Ministerial Association sponsored a protest meeting and petitions were passed around in every Protestant church, in defence both of free speech and of the licensing of religious broadcasting stations. Even Macklem, the inspector, rallied to the cause of free speech. RG 42, vol. 493, file 209–32–101, Macklem to Edwards, 17 April 1928; MG 26K, M–929, Macklem to W.F. Crawford, 16 April 1928, copy, 28773. See also HOC, *Debates*, 31 May 1928, 3619–20 (Woodsworth), 3649–50, and ibid., 1 June 1928, 3669–70 (Bird).

28 HOC, *Debates*, 1 June 1928, 3622.

29 PAM, RG 11 A1, Box 3, J.E. Lowry to J. Bracken, 31 January 1928, encl., and F.E. Rutland to Lowry, 13 May 1931; RG 97, vol. 152, file 6206–110, part 1, C. Thomas to Edwards, 13 April 1928; RG 12, vol. 864, file 6206–16–22, Radio Marine to C. Gray, telegram, 27 April 1928; RG 97, vol. 153, file 6206–164, part 2, radio inspector to S.E. Andrews, 23 January 1929; RG 97, vol. 87, file 6040–1, part 3, D. Manson "Memorandum to the Director: Re Broadcasting," 15 November 1928, 5. See also Schmalz, *On Air*, 41. Some stations, of course, may have been frightened away from accepting Bible Students' programs by the fuss in 1928. See, for example, RG 97, vol. 153, file 6206–172, part 1, E.J. Haughton to Edwards, 31 July 1928. Broadcasting of Jehovah's Witnesses' messages continued to be controversial into the 1930s. See Weir, *The Struggle for National Broadcasting in Canada*, 187–8.

30 See MG 26K M–929, F.W. Hobson to R.B. Bennett, 10 April 1928, 28685–6.

See also HOC, *Debates*, 31 May 1928, 3747, and 1 June 1928, 3668.

31 Similarly, when a number of complaints came in to the branch in 1929 about the radio broadcasts of William "Bible Bill" Aberhart on CFCN Calgary, no action was taken on the traditional grounds that the branch did not censor program content. For example, see RG 97, vol. 153, file 6206–164, part 2, Johnston to J.C. Buckley, 8 February 1929. It is perhaps significant that Aberhart did not attack political and clerical authority in the IBSA manner; indeed, the only other religious groups he apparently criticized explicitly were the Bible Students and Christian Scientists.

32 Perhaps the closest the branch came to taking similar action with another station involved CFDC Vancouver, which was notified that its licence would not be renewed after 31 March 1926 "unless department considers such action in interest bcls." While the licence was renewed, a year later in a most unusual action the station's 1927–28 licence was made subject to cancellation on one month's notice. See RG 97, vol. 153, file 6206–172, part 1, Radio Marine to E.J. Haughton, 5 October 1925, telegram. No comparable warnings were given to the IBSA stations.

33 MG 26K, M–929, "Statement Re Cancellation ..." [March 1928], 28677–8. Cardin tried to argue that the IBSA must have known there were some problems, because after the 1927 Saskatoon Board of Trade resolution recommending that CHUC be allowed to broadcast on Sundays only, a petition with 20,000 signatures in favour of the station was gathered. He was forced to admit, however, that no special warning, formal or informal, was ever given to any of the IBSA stations that their licences might be non-renewed. HOC, *Debates*, 1 June 1928, 3656.

34 RG 42, vol. 493, file 209–32–101, W.F. Salter to Johnston, 18 January 1928.

35 A meeting was also apparently held with Prime Minister King, but not until 19 March 1928, after the licences had been cancelled. See MG 26K, M–929, "A Further Statement ...," 28720; ibid., document beginning "In The Statement Delivered in the House of Commons ...," 28722–3.

36 MG 26K, M–929, "This letter sent to the Prime Minister over Heyd, Heyd, & Shorey Signature," 28696.

37 HOC, *Debates*, 1 June 1928, 3663–4.

38 CHIC (Northern Electric) also broadcast briefly in this period.

39 RG 97, vol. 152, file 6206–133, part 1, J. Malcolm to Edwards, 9 December 1927.

40 RG 42, vol. 493, file 209–32–111, part 1; RG 97, vol. 152, file 6206–133, part 1. This decision was justified on the grounds that CKGW's transmitter was forty miles from the city centre.

41 RG 12, vol. 862, file 6206–148, part 2, M. Johnson to A. Johnston, 13 February 1928.

42 MG 26K, M–929, "Memo for I.E.R[obertson]," 10 April 1928, copy, 28710. See also ibid., M–1289, R.W. Ashcroft to R.A. Stapells, 27 January 1931, copy,

360554. Later Irving Robertson claimed that "Edwards acted as a lackey for WLMK." Ibid., Robertson to Bennett, 31 October 1931, 360897. See also editorial, "Keep Radio Out of Politics," Toronto *Telegram*, 29 March 1928, 45. King recorded a "pleasant" lunch with Atkinson and his son Joe on 17 February in his diary. *The Mackenzie King Diaries*, transcript. There are no documents in the surviving CFCA file revealing any political intervention in the spring of 1928.

43 See RG 12, vol. 862, file 6206–148, W.A. Rush for director to S.J. Ellis, 10 March 1928.

44 See, for example, MG 26K, M–929, "Memo for Mr. I.E. Robertson," copy, 28699–700; Toronto *Globe*, 17 March 1928, 13; HOC, *Debates*, 1 June 1928, 3661–4, 3672. For a good summary of CKGW's case, see RG 42, vol. 493, file 209–32–111, part 1, R.W. Ashcroft to F.W. Hay, 28 September 1928, copy. No one denied that CFCA had a weaker, less modern transmitter than either CFRB or CKGW nor that it had been using little of its available broadcasting time in recent years.

45 HOC, *Debates*, 1 June 1928, 3662.

46 Ibid., 2 June 1928, 3708.

47 *The Mackenzie King Diaries*, transcript. The major biography of King, Neatby's *William Lyon Mackenzie King: The Lonely Heights, 1924–1932*, makes no mention whatsoever of the Aird commission.

48 See Vipond, "Canadian Nationalism and the Plight of Canadian Magazines in the 1920's"; Vipond, "The Nationalist Network"; Trofimenkoff, *Action Française*, 76.

49 Elton Johnson, "Canada's Radio Consciousness," 53.

50 MG 30 D297, vol. 108, file 108–12, Typescript History, 1961, 6.

51 CAVA, CBC Program Archives, Allan Thomas interview with Charles A. Bowman, 18 February 1960, tape.

52 Bowman, *Ottawa Editor*, 121; Peers, *The Politics of Canadian Broadcasting* 35–6. The system Bowman so admired in 1926, however, was in fact the earlier, private-monopoly arrangement. It has been suggested that Bowman's first notion for Canada was a similar company owned by the major newspapers, but he soon dropped that in favour of a public monopoly. See Allard, *Straight Up*, 62.

53 Editorial, "For National Broadcasting," Ottawa *Citizen*, 16 April 1928, 24.

54 "National Radio Influence," Ottawa *Citizen*, 3 April 1928, 26; "Canadian Radio Channels," ibid., 7 April 1928, 25; "Please Stand By," ibid., 10 April 1928, 24.

55 RG 12, vol. 608, file 5858–8, vol. 2, "Treaty Negotiations between the Dominion of Canada and the United States of America: Allocation of Channels in the Radio Broadcast Band 500 to 1500 Kilocycles 1927," Massey to King, 25 March 1927, copy.

56 MG 26J, C–2305, Massey to Skelton, 27 October 1928, copy, 132048.

57 See also Ellis, *Evolution of the Canadian Broadcasting System,* 1; Peers, *The Politics of Canadian Broadcasting,* 34.

58 J.W. Dafoe turned down an invitation to serve and apparently no other appropriate westerner could be found. Prang, "The Origins of Public Broadcasting in Canada," 6 n. 12.

59 Bowman, *Ottawa Editor,* 123; Special Committee 1932, 499.

60 Bowman, *Ottawa Editor,* 123; Peers, *The Politics of Canadian Broadcasting,* 37.

61 See Clement, *The Canadian Corporate Elite,* 45ff.

62 See CAVA, Bambrick Transcripts, interview with R.T. Bowman. In later interviews Bowman himself tended to downplay the amount of advertising on the radio in 1928 and the extent to which fear of this competition motivated him. See ibid., CBC Program Archives, Allan Thomas interview with C.A. Bowman; also Special Committee 1932, 74.

63 See Resnick, *The Land of Cain.*

64 Massey, *What's Past is Prologue,* 454; Bissell, *The Young Vincent Massey,* 195 n. 37; O'Brien, "A History of the Canadian Radio League," 53.

65 See Bowman, *Ottawa Editor,* 123; Peers, *The Politics of Canadian Broadcasting,* 37.

66 CAVA, CBC Program Archives, Allan Thomas interview with C.A. Bowman. On Johnston see MG 30 D297, vol. 108, file 108–38, Spry's notes on Margaret Prang's article; for an example of Edwards's negative view of the BBC, see RG 97, vol. 87, vol. 6040–1, part 2, Edwards to A.R. Burrows, 23 December 1926. One may speculate that Edwards in particular was less than happy with the implied criticism of his handling of broadcasting since its inception.

67 RG 97, vol. 87, file 6040–1, part 3, D. Manson, "Memorandum to the Director: Re Broadcasting," 15 November 1928, 6–7.

68 Graham Spry attested to Manson's influence on the three commissioners in a memorandum he prepared for Margaret Prang in 1964. See Prang, "The Origins of Public Broadcasting in Canada," 7 n. 15.

69 *Canada Gazette,* 62 (19 January 1929), 2306.

70 A copy may be found in Bird, *Documents,* 37–9.

71 A discussion document prepared on 12 May 1928 by C.P. Edwards of the Radio Branch posited five somewhat different possible methods of operation. They were "direct operation by Dominion Government under an existing department," "operation by a public utility company owned by the Dominion Government (something along the same lines as the Canadian National Ry. Company)," "direct operation by provincial governments under subsidy from the Dominion government," "operation by public utility companies owned by provincial governments," and "operation by private enterprise under contract with the Dominion Government." RG 42, vol. 1076, file 104–1–1, "National Broadcasting in Canada: Tentative Scheme as

a Basis of Discussion."

72 Dr Frigon made this point in his appearance berfore the 1932 Special Committee, 66–7.

73 Bowman, *Ottawa Editor*, 124, 126; Peers, *The Politics of Canadian Broadcasting*, 38 n. 5.

74 RG 33, Series 14, vol. 1, file 227–9–10; Royal Commission on Radio Broadcasting, *Report*, in Bird, *Documents*, 42.

75 RG 33, Series 14, vol. 1, file 227–9–9.

76 Ibid., Canadian Manufacturers Association, "Brief Respecting Radio Broadcasting," 17 May 1929. See also ibid., "Brief of the Representatives of the Radio Trades," and file 227–10–3, *La Presse* brief, 29 May 1929.

77 For example, see RG 42, vol. 1077, file 227–9–3, R.W. Ashcroft to Royal Commission on Radio Broadcasting, 17 May 1929; ibid., file 227–9–3, CAB to royal commission, 19 July 1929.

78 RG 33, Series 14, vol. 1, file 227–9–9, 6. The submission from two small private stations in Vancouver also argued that already they were facing unfair competition from a government-subsidized station, CNRV. RG 41, vol. 303, file 14–2–1, part 1, F.G.T. Lucas, "Submission of CKMO and CJOR Vancouver to Royal Commission," 24 April 1929.

79 RG 33, Series 14, vol. 1, file 227–9–10, "Views of the Canadian Legion of the B.E.S.L. on Radio Broadcasting in Canada."

80 Ibid., vol. 2, file 227–12–6, brief from station CJCB read by Mr Nathanson; ibid., file 227–13–5, supplementary statement of Mr J.L. Holman; ibid., file 227–11–6.

81 Editorial, "CKY," Winnipeg *Free Press*, 13 May 1929, 13; Editorial, "CKY," ibid., 15 January 1931, 13.

82 Canada, Royal Commission on Radio Broadcasting, *Report*, Appendix III, 38–40.

83 RG 42, vol. 1076, file 227–2–4, D. Manson, "Memorandum to the Deputy Minister," 11 June 1929.

84 One contemporary observer pointed out that there was both a higher turn-out and more criticism of the prevailing system at the western hearings than at the eastern. Despite the somewhat controversial fact that none of the commissioners was a westerner, they seemed to pay greater heed to western opinion. See Edwards, "Does Canada Want Government Radio?: No," 8. On the other hand, Schmalz (*On Air*, 47) says that virtually all spokesmen at the four Saskatchewan hearings opposed nationalization in favour of local service.

85 RG 33, Series 14, vol. 1, file 227–9–5, 8 May 1929, 5; ibid., 14 May 1929, 12; ibid., file 227–9–6, 13 May 1929, 9; ibid., file 227–9–9, 7; RG 42, vol. 1077, file 227–10–8, 12.

86 RG 33, Series 14, vol. 1, file 227–9–5, 8; ibid., vol. 2, files 227–11–6 and

227–13–5, 12.

87 Ibid., file 227–9–8, 14–15.

88 Ibid., vol. 2, file 227–13–5, 1–15. Over thirty years later Bowman was still using this encounter as an example of some of the ridiculous statements made by private broadcasters to the commission. CAVA, CBC Program Archives, Allan Thomas interview with C.A. Bowman.

89 Canada, Royal Commission on Radio Broadcasting, *Report*, in Bird, *Documents*, 43–4.

90 This last point was a compromise reached between Bowman and Frigon. Only on the general issue of relative federal/provincial jurisdiction was there any disagreement between the views of the two men. Aird agreed to sign whatever document the other two could mutually draft. See Peers, *The Politics of Canadian Broadcasting*, 42; Bowman, *Ottawa Editor*, 131; RG 33, Series 14, vol. 2, file 227–14–1, Aird Commission, General Correspondence, Frigon to Bowman, 19 August 1929, Bowman to Frigon, 20 August, Frigon to Bowman, 30 August. See also MG 30 D79, M–826, drafts by Bowman and Frigon.

91 Although by 1932 the commissioners and other supporters of the CRBC favoured allowing private ownership of small supplementary stations, this was not the intention in 1928, as the overall recommendation that "the stations providing [broadcasting service] should be owned and operated by one national company" makes clear. This point is misinterpreted in Blakley, "Canadian Private Broadcasters and the Reestablishment of a Private Broadcasting Network," 42.

92 In contrast, the initial discussion document prepared by Commander Edwards in May 1928 had envisaged twelve stations (six of 20,000 watts, one of 1000, five of 500 watts) which would serve all the settled parts of the country at night but not in the daytime. Edwards estimated capital costs of $3.4 million, of which just over $1 million was to compensate owners of the existing stations. He assumed that programs would cost $662,500 per year, station operations $777,500, and headquarters administration $300,000. The necessary annual revenues of $1.7 million would come from a $2.50 licence fee (for a total of about $800,000), a tax of 25¢ on each radio tube (total income $225,000), and "rental of broadcasting station time for advertising programmes, approximately two hours per station per day, six days per week" (bringing in $662,500). RG 42, vol. 1076, file 104–1–1, "National Broadcasting in Canada. Tentative Scheme as a Basis for Discussion."

93 Edwards, "Does Canada Want Government Radio?: No," 36.

94 MG 30 D79, M–826, "Report," 6; RG 42, vol. 1076, file 105–1–1, C.A. Bowman, "Radio Public Service for Canada," 8–10.

95 RG 42, vol. 1076, file 105–1–1, Bowman, "Radio Public Service for Canada,"

9. Over the years the CBC has produced most of its own programs; a move to a system approximating Bowman's notion was recommended by the Applebaum-Hébert Report in 1982.

96 My thanks to Mike McConkey for helping me to see the Aird report in this light. See McConkey, "Monopoly Capitalist Communications in Canada."

97 As Peers points out, however, the commissioners were assuming that without any alternative private stations to turn to, advertisers would have had to use the CRBC stations whatever restrictions they imposed. Peers, *The Politics of Canadian Broadcasting*, 131.

98 See especially Charland, "Technological Nationalism."

99 In retrospect, Charles Bowman claimed that this whole unwieldy bureaucratic structure was adopted only at Frigon's insistence and that he was happy it never became operative. CAVA, CBC Program Archives, Allan Thomas interview with C.A. Bowman; see also Peers, *The Politics of Canadian Broadcasting*, 50.

100 Royal Commission on Radio Broadcasting, *Report*, in Bird, *Documents*, 46; see also RG 42, vol. 1075, J.W. Bain, "On the Practical Technical Aspects of the Report of the Royal Commission on Radio Broadcasting," 21 March 1930, 7.

101 Special Committee 1932, 64–5, 79–80. See also Nolan, *Foundations*, 59–60.

102 Special Committee 1932, 330.

CHAPTER TEN

1 *The Mackenzie King Diaries*, transcript, 11 September 1929.

2 RG 12, vol. 404, file 5558–1, vol. 1, "An Act to incorporate the Canadian Radio Broadcasting Company," 1930 (draft).

3 RG 33, Series 14, vol. 2, file 227–13–5, "Explanatory Remarks re Bill: An Act to incorporate the Canadian Radio Broadcasting Company," n.d.

4 RG 12, vol. 404, file 5558–1, vol. 1, D. M[anson], "Memorandum," 2 April 1930.

5 King had received intimations that not only were some important newspapers and broadcasters opposed to the bill, but so were other sectors of the electorate. A PEI member of Parliament reported to him that opposition in his riding was intense: "Some people have gone so far as to suggest that this is the one thing that might wreck the Liberal Party in Canada." MG 26J, C–2320, A.E. MacLean to King, 10 February 1930, 151066.

6 HOC, *Debates*, 9 April 1930, 1399.

7 On this period see especially Peers, *The Politics of Canadian Broadcasting*, 63–107; Weir, *The Struggle for National Broadcasting in Canada* 117–136; Prang, "The Origins of Public Broadcasting in Canada"; O'Brien, "A History of the Canadian Radio League"; and Nolan, *Foundations*.

8 "Radio Commission Prepared to Back Published Report," Montreal *Gazette*,

13 September 1929, 12.

9 For example, Frigon, "The Organization of Radio Broadcasting in Canada," a speech given to the Engineering Institute of Canada.

10 For complete details about the league's membership and activities, see the works by O'Brien and Nolan cited in note 7.

11 MG 30 D297, vol. 108, file 108–12, G. Spry, Typescript History, 8.

12 Vipond, "The Nationalist Network"; Vipond, "National Consciousness in English-speaking Canada in the 1920's: Seven Studies," Chapter 4.

13 Special Committee 1932, 545; Spry, "The Canadian Broadcasting Issue," 246.

14 Spry, "A Case for Nationalized Broadcasting," 157.

15 Spry, "Should Radio Be Nationalized in Canada?," 2.

16 MG 30 D297, vol. 95, file 95–4, Spry to G.W. Alexander, 12 May 1931.

17 MG 32 B5, vol. 5, CRL file, G. Spry, "The Canadian Radio Situation," *Education by Radio*, 2 July 1931, 85. For an earlier example of Spry's concern about the education of Canadian public opinion, see editorial "Public Opinion," 11.

18 MG 32 B5, vol. 5, CRL file, Spry, "The Canadian Radio Situation," 83.

19 Special Committee 1932, 554–65. In the United States at approximately the same time, educational and religious groups, reformers, and newspaper publishers were also banding together – less successfully – to fight the commercialization of broadcasting there. The Radio League was in touch with some of these organizations. See Smulyan, "'And Now a Word From Our Sponsors ...,'" 183ff.

20 MG 30 D297, vol. 94, file 94–11, Spry to D.B. McRae, 2 March 1931; see also MG 30 D67, vol. 2, file 11, E.A. Weir to Frank England, 1 February 1932.

21 On this tangled subject, see Prang, "The Origins of Public Broadcasting in Canada," 28; MG 30 D297, vol. 108, file 108–33, "Canadian Radio League: The American Radio Trust"; MG 32 B5, CRL 1932 file, Spry to Claxton, 8 March 1932.

22 Different viewpoints exist about whether the "national unity" or the "public service" motive predominated in the thought of Spry, Plaunt, and the CRL. In a recent work Marc Raboy stresses the latter but I would argue that that became true only after 1932. See Raboy, *Missed Opportunities*, 36–8; see also Spry, "Radio Broadcasting and Aspects of Canadian-American Relations," 107–8. While another interesting recent analysis, that of Richard Collins, does not examine the CRL in any depth, it does make a careful distinction between these two goals and indeed suggests that they are contradictory. Collins, *Culture, Communication and National Identity*, 335.

23 Special Committee 1932, 547.

24 Spry, "The Canadian Broadcasting Issue," 247. A number of generally sympathetic individuals, for example J.W. Dafoe and King Gordon, wrote to Spry concerned about the use which governments such as those of the

"prejudiced and autocratic" Howard Ferguson would make of radio if they could control it. While Spry recognized that governments too could be reactionary, he argued for full government control on two grounds: because politicians were more subject to public opinion and because there really was no other alternative to control by big business. He also repeatedly argued that much would depend on the quality of the people appointed to the directorate. See MG 30 D297, vol. 94, file 94–7, J.W. Dafoe to Spry, 3 November 1930, and draft reply; ibid., vol. 95, file 95–2, Spry to King Gordon, 11 April 1931; ibid., vol 97, file 97–8, Spry's comments on memo of F. Chalmers to Mr Hunter, c. November 1930.

25 Herridge was Massey's successor as Canadian ambassador to the United States; he and Bowman were old friends and Spry had known him through the Canadian League since the latter 1920s. Bowman gave Herridge much credit for lobbying for public broadcasting in the inner circles of the Conservative Party. CAVA, CBC Program Archives, Allan Thomas interview with C.A. Bowman. While both Spry and Plaunt had more ties with the Liberal Party than with the Conservative, they deliberately attempted to find allies on both sides of the House.

26 Allard, *Straight Up*, 68.

27 Hayes, "The Propagation of Nationalism," in *Essays on Nationalism*, 77.

28 MG 30 D297, vol. 94, file 94–11, Spry to D.B. McRae, 2 March 1931; ibid., Spry to Hume Blake, 19 March 1931; MG 30 D67, vol. 5, file 6, Plaunt to E.A. Weir, 10 January 1933.

29 See O'Brien, "A History of the Canadian Radio League," 115–16 and 149–51, and Prang, "The Origins of Public Broadcasting in Canada," 9ff. A list of supporters was also presented to the Special Committee 1932, 594–8.

30 At the 1932 Special Committee hearings, representatives from the National Council of Education and from the universities, while supporting "regulation in the public interest," did not necessarily believe that government ownership was absolutely necessary. See 447, 614.

31 See Prang, "The Origins of Public Broadcasting in Canada," 27.

32 MG 30 D297, vol. 84, file 84–13, Spry, Manuscript Memoirs, 4/1, 4/15. Spry had access to Prime Minister Bennett through Herridge and Bennett's personal assistant R.K. Finlayson, and because Spry's father and Bennett had been friendly years earlier in Calgary. See Prang, "The Origins of Public Broadcasting in Canada," 26.

33 Spry commented later that he felt the supportive newspapers were not nearly as "vehement or persistent" as the opposition of *La Presse* or the Toronto *Telegram*. While Atkinson, for example, was personally pro-CRL, the *Star*'s support was muted by the reality that the Aird position was so unpopular in the Toronto area. MG 30 D297, vol. 108, file 108–38, Spry's notes on Margaret Prang's article, 10–11.

34 [W.A. Craick], *A History of Canadian Journalism*, 2:207–9; MG 30 D297, vol. 97,

file 97–10, "Report of the Joint Radio Committee," n.d.

35 MG 30 D297, vol. 95, file 95–4, Spry to Gladstone Murray, 14 May 1931; UBC, Plaunt Papers, vol. 1, file 2, Atkinson to Plaunt, 17 April 1931.

36 Ibid., vol. 97, file 97–10, "Radio Advertising," [6]. Bowman had information that broadcast advertising revenues in Canada and the United States had risen 74 per cent in 1930 while newspaper ad revenues had dropped almost 12 per cent. Ibid., vol. 95, Arthur Partridge to C.A. Bowman, 20 April 1931, copy. For the concern expressed by Claxton and Philip Fisher about this tactic, see MG 32 B5, vol. 5, CRL 1930–31 file, Claxton to Plaunt, 23 June 1931.

37 For example, R.W. Ashcroft told minister of Marine Alfred Duranleau: "So far as we know Graham Spry merely represents a group of Canadian newspapers headed by Charles Bowman ... masquerading under the title Canadian Radio League." RG 12, vol. 609, file 5858–8, part 4, Ashcroft to Duranleau, 18 June 1931, telegram; MG 26K, M–1314, R.W. Ashcroft, "Government vs. Private Ownership of Canadian Radio," 389171; Allard, *Straight Up*, 69.

38 O'Brien, "A History of the Canadian Radio League," 99.

39 MG 32 B5, vol. 5, CRL 1930–31 file, Spry to Claxton, 21 January 1931.

40 Nolan, *Foundations*, 91.

41 G. Spry, "Should Radio Be Nationalized In Canada?," 2; Special Committee 1932, 569.

42 Spry, "Public Policy and Private Pressures," 26; see also Spry, "The Origins of Public Broadcasting in Canada: A Comment," 139 n. 12.

43 Spry, "A Case for Nationalized Broadcasting," 165.

44 Spry also suggested that a separate French-Canadian chain with its own advisory committee could be created out of the company's French-language stations. See Spry, "The Origins of Public Broadcasting in Canada: A Comment," 139, and Special Committee 1932, 570. For further evidence of Spry's empathy with French Canada, see Spry, "One Nation, Two Cultures," 21.

45 MG 30 D297, vol. 94, file 94–7, Spry to Dafoe, draft reply to letter of 3 November 1930.

46 [Alan Plaunt], *The Canadian Radio League*, 14. Spry argued in a private letter to league supporter F.R. McKelcan that the Aird commission's report was in fact very ambiguous on the subject of the power of the provinces and that despite a couple of statements apparently granting provincial directors full control over broadcasting, when read in the context of the whole report and with access to certain "authoritative knowledge" which he possessed, it was clear that "it was the full intention of the framers of the report to give the Dominion control in all but *specifically* educational and provincial broadcasts." MG 30 D297, vol. 94, file 94–5, Spry to McKelcan, 9 October 1931.

47 Special Committee 1932, 571; see also UBC, Plaunt Papers, vol. 1, file 1, Eugène L'Heureux to Plaunt, 29 mars 1932.

48 MG 30 D297, vol. 95, file 95–4, Spry to Murray, 14 May 1931; see also ibid., file 95–7, Spry to Hume Blake, 26 August 1931.

49 Ibid., vol. 21, file 21–3, Diaries and Journals, 5 November 1931.

50 MG 32 B5, CRL File, Spry to Claxton, 21 January 1931.

51 MG 30 D297, vol. 95, file 95–2, Spry to R.K. Finlayson, 11 April 1931.

52 [Alan Plaunt], *The Canadian Radio League*, 13; see also MG 30 D297, vol. 94, file 94–6, Spry to C.O. Smith, 30 October 1930, in which Spry urges Smith to interest Bennett in "a system which would do something to give Canadian business men the same broadcasting opportunities through sponsored programmes over a government controlled system, that Americans have over a largely monopolistic private system." See also ibid., file 94–3, Spry to H.W. McManus, 18 December 1930.

53 Special Committee 1932, 567.

54 MG 30 D297, vol. 94, file 94–11, Spry to W.J. Stewart, 17 March 1931; see also ibid., file 94–10, Spry to G.B. Fisher, 17 February 1931.

55 O'Brien, "A History of the Canadian Radio League," 102–3.

56 See Allard, *Straight Up*, 87–9.

57 MG 30 D297, vol. 94, file 94–7, Spry to J.W. Dafoe, draft reply to letter of 3 November 1930.

58 Special Committee 1932, 566–9, 583.

59 Spry would have defended himself by arguing that the main reason the CRBC remained dependent on the private stations was the failure to raise the licence fee to $3, thereby substantially delaying the commission in building its own stations. See MG 30 D297, vol. 108, file 108–38, Spry's notes on Margaret Prang's article, 13. My point, however, is that his scheme opened the door – more than just a crack – to the possibility of the entrenchment of strong private stations. Spry did not at the time criticize the 1932 Radio Broadcasting Act for its lack of revenue guarantees for the CRBC; indeed, he advocated strict parliamentary control of the company's capital expenditures.

60 MG 30 D297, vol. 94, file 94–4, Alan Plaunt to Radio Clubs, 26 February 1931; ibid., file 94–10, Spry to G.B. Fisher, 17 February 1931; see also Spry, "The Canadian Broadcasting Issue," 248; Special Committee 1932, 571, 580.

61 MG 30 D297, vol. 94, file 94–10, Spry to F.D.L. Smith, 20 February 1930.

62 Ibid., Spry to G.B. Fisher, 17 February 1931.

63 Ibid., file 94–5, Spry to McKelkan, 9 January 1931.

64 Ibid., file 94–3, Spry to H.W. McManus, 18 December 1930.

65 When challenged, Spry denied this charge in a rather obfuscating manner: "We are not subsidizing advertising programs, we are selling service at cost." See Special Committee 1932, 588.

66 MG 30 D297, vol. 95, file 95–11, Spry to Blake, 18 December 1931.

67 Ibid., vol. 98, file 98–1, "Memorandum Presented to the Royal Commission on Railways and Transportation by Graham Spry," 14 January 1932, 7. This possibility had also been mentioned as a "rumour" in Spry's article in the *Canadian Forum* in April 1931, 247. Approximately this same idea was advocated by both Austin Weir and Brooke Claxton also; see MG 30 D67, vol. 19, file 2, "Centralization of Canadian Wire Services," 14 August 1931, and MG 32 B5, vol. 5, file CRL 1932–36, Claxton to Gladstone Murray, 26 January 1932.

68 RG 12, vol. 403, file 5550–1, part 1, Spry to H.S. Moore, 23 February 1932, copy.

69 Special Committee 1932, 562.

70 Ibid., 565.

71 Ibid., 581, 584. See also MG 30 D297, vol. 94, file 94–5, Spry to F.R. McKelkan, 9 January 1931, 4–5.

72 Although he did not say so explicitly, Spry apparently assumed for the reasons discussed in Chapter 3 that licence-fee revenues could not be allocated to private enterprises.

73 Special Committee 1932, 565.

74 Peers, *The Politics of Canadian Broadcasting*, 418.

75 MG 30 D297, vol. 95, file 95–4, Spry to E.A. Corbett, 6 May 1931; ibid., vol. 94, file 94–10, Spry to Canon R. Chartier, 10 February 1931; ibid., file 94–7, Spry to Rod Finlayson, 6 November 1930. Many years later Spry wrote: "In fact, in 1930/32 ... we had far better connections and knew our way about the Government far better than our opponents, the rather small town boys from Toronto and Montreal who were seeking their fortunes in private broadcasting." See ibid., vol. 108, file 108–38, Spry's notes on Margaret Prang's article, 15.

76 J.A. Dupont to Special Committee 1932, 651; see also telegram of Premier Taschereau to committee, 519–20. Even *Le Devoir*, which favoured nationalization, worried about this aspect. See Prang, "The Origins of Public Broadcasting in Canada," 19. Raboy argues throughout his book that integration of Quebec into the pan-Canadian nation was one of the primary motives of those who advocated a public broadcasting system. While, as my previous argument makes clear, I agree that the CRL was definitely pan-Canadian in intent, my reading of the evidence is that its executive members were more sensitive to Quebec's different needs than they were to those of other regions. The amount of French-language programming on the national network did indeed become a point of contention in the CRBC years, but mainly for the opposite reason, as most of the complaints were about too much French programming and came from the prairies. Peers, *The Politics of Canadian Broadcasting*, 128–30, 140.

77 RG 42, vol. 1076, file 109–1–1, D. Manson, "Memorandum Re: Comment on Report of the Royal Commission on Radio Broadcasting," 31 March 1930.

78 See, for example, ibid., vol. 1079, file 105–1–1, *La Presse*, "The Aird Report Menaces the Trade and Commerce of Radio," n.d.; ibid., vol. 1076, file 109–1–1, D. Manson, "Report of the Royal Commission on Radio Broadcasting: Digest of Press Comment," 10 April 1930, 1; Toronto *Telegram*, 13 January 1931, 5 and 19 January 1931, 4; Toronto *Globe*, 22 March 1930, 4. Nolan, *Foundations*, 78–9, elaborates a bit further on the positions taken by newspaper owners.

79 RG 42, vol. 1077, file 227–9–3, Executive Committee of the CAB to Royal Commission on Broadcasting, 19 July 1929.

80 Allard, *The C.A.B. Story*, 11. This altered the regulations then in effect in only two ways: the direct advertising allowed on Sundays before 7 p.m. was now to be indirect, and for the first time a time limit on ads was proposed.

81 Special Committee 1932, 277.

82 MG 30 D297, vol. 95, file 95–4, Spry to Gladstone Murray, 14 May 1931; see also O'Brien, "A History of the Canadian Radio League," 201, Peers, *The Politics of Canadian Broadcasting*, 74.

83 MG 26K, M–1289, 360665–74, Canadian Association of Broadcasters, "Facts Respecting Radio Broadcasting Under Private Ownership," n.d. [*c.* April 1931], 3, 6–8.

84 Special Committee 1932, 271.

85 MG 26K, M–1289, 360665–74, CAB, "Facts Respecting Radio Broadcasting Under Private Ownership," 5–6.

86 Ibid., 12.

87 Ibid., 15, 8.

88 While J.E. Lowry of CKY favoured public broadcasting, he did not agree with the national emphasis of the Aird report and advocated instead a network of provincially owned stations. See Special Committee 1932, 251–6. Joseph Atkinson announced at the CAB meeting of 17 February 1930 that he favoured continuing the private-enterprise system in broadcasting only if he could be guaranteed that no new competitors would be allowed to enter the field. As this was clearly not feasible, the *Star* came out in favour of the Aird report shortly after. CFCA closed in September 1933. See Allard, *The C.A.B. Story*, 12 (whose dates are incorrect); Nolan, *Foundations*, 79; O'Brien, "A History of the Canadian Radio League," 201–2; Harkness, *J.E. Atkinson of the Star*, 198–9.

89 Allard, *The C.A.B. Story*, 12; Special Committee 1932, 271.

90 MG 30 D297, vol. 84, file 84–13, Spry, Manuscript Memoirs, 4/27, 4/28.

91 See Special Committee 1932, 572–3, 684–6.

92 Ibid., 279–80.

93 See ibid., 172–6, 124–52, 169–70.

94 RG 33, Series 14, vol. 1, file 227–9–9, Canadian Manufacturers' Association, "Brief Respecting Radio Broadcasting," 17 May 1929, 11. Officials of Canadian General Electric apparently believed that the interests of radio

manufacturers would be maximized by government creation of the national network rather than under private monopoly or competition. See Prang, "The Origins of Public Broadcasting in Canada," 17.

95 See Special Committee 1932, 169–77, 271–2.

96 Ibid., 176. Another difficulty was also pointed out here: that advertisers on one medium (radio) would be subsidized while those on others would not be.

97 Ashcroft, "Should Radio Be Nationalized in Canada?," 2. Substantially the same article was later published as a separate pamphlet, *Government vs. Private Ownership of Canadian Radio*, a copy of which may be found in MG 26K, M–1314, 389168–76. See also Special Committee 1932, 330–41.

98 Special Committee 1932, 336.

99 MG 26K, M–1314, R.W. Ashcroft, "The Fifth Estate," 389142; see also Special Committee 1932, 337.

100 Special Committee 1932, 336. It was perhaps this remark that led other private broadcasters to believe that Ashcroft's "wild, sweeping and unsupported statements" "damaged their case." This, at any rate, was how league supporter J.F. Garrett remembered the hearings. MG 27 III c7, c–9160, Garrett to J.S. Woodsworth, 18 March 1936, 866a.

101 For details see Special Committee, 1932, 655–7.

102 Weir, *The Struggle for National Broadcasting in Canada*, 123–4.

103 HOC, Fourth Session, 16th Parliament, 1930, Sessional Paper No. 202, J. McMillan, general manager of Telegraphs, CPR, to A. Johnston, 17 January 1930 and 2 April 1930.

104 Gibbon, "Radio as a Fine Art," 212–4. This article, and Graham Spry's reply to it, are reprinted in Bird, *Documents*, 58–69.

105 For the specifics of Beatty's plan, see Special Committee 1932, 655–76. Representatives of the two railway companies had at least one meeting to discuss cooperative ventures prior to May 1932. See MG 30 D67, vol. 19, file 2, "Meeting of Special Committee Representing Canadian Pacific and Canadian National Communication, Telegraph and Publicity Departments," n.d. Spry believed that the CPR wished to become involved in radio because it wanted to block the CNR and the public-ownership idea, because it would gain revenue from the rental of its telegraph lines, and because it could use the medium to advertise its other services. He also speculated that the CPR's increasing tendency to look to the United States "both for traffic and for capital" was tying it in closer to the "great banking groups, or group, which are behind the General Electric and the Radio Corporation of America." MG 30 D297, vol. 94, file 94–11, Spry to D.B. McRae, 2 March 1931.

106 Indeed, Spry made a point not to come out too aggressively against Beatty because he wanted to leave the door open to compromise. See MG 30 D297, vol. 95, file 95–11, Spry to Hume Blake, 18 December 1931.

107 Special Committee 1932, 656.

108 Ibid., 668.

109 Nolan, *Foundations*, 77, also makes this point. See also editorial, "Canada Can Do Better," Ottawa *Citizen*, 19 February 1932, 20.

110 MG 26K M–1314, R.W. Ashcroft, "Government vs. Private Ownership," 389170.

111 This difference in emphasis, just perceptible in 1932, was to become much more evident later. As Marc Raboy puts it, by 1938 "the public/private dichotomy ... came to be framed in terms of 'public' versus 'community,' where 'public' meant national and publicly owned, and 'community' meant local and privately owned." See Raboy, *Missed Opportunities*, 63.

112 See, for example, an interesting analysis of Australian broadcasting along these lines, in Lesley Johnson, "Radio and Everyday Life." A good brief summary of Williams's ideas may be found in his "Base and Superstructure in Marxist Cultural Theory."

113 This statement must be modified with an example of one Canadian radio-advertising bureau executive who feared that the import of American programs would squeeze out domestic shows and advertisers during the best hours. MG 26K, M–934, P.H. Dorte to R.B. Bennett, 1 May 1929, 35285.

114 For more extensive discussion of the issues from this angle, see Vipond, *The Mass Media in Canada*, especially x–xi.

115 See correspondence in RG 97, vol. 90, file 1024–8, part 1. As early as April 1922 the Department of Justice gave its opinion that radiotelegraphy was under federal jurisdiction because of its interprovincial and international implications. See ibid., E.L. Newcombe to deputy minister, Marine and Fisheries, 7 April 1922. Nevertheless, in the absence of a firm decision, the Radio Branch's approach to the provinces during the 1920s was one of negotiation rather than confrontation.

116 RG 12, vol. 864, file 6206–162–3, C.P. Edwards, "Memo to the Minister: Manitoba Broadcasting situation to be discussed with the Hon. T.G. Murphy," 26 April 1932.

117 *Statuts refondus du Québec*, 1941, chap. 254; Peers, *The Politics of Canadian Broadcasting*, 69.

118 This version of the story comes from the testimony of R.W. Ashcroft in HOC, Special Committee on the Canadian Radio Commission, 1936, *Minutes of Proceedings and Evidence*, 647–8. See also RG 97, vol. 150, file 6206–83, parts 1 and 2, for the correspondence between CKCV and the Radio Branch in 1930 and 1931.

119 *Statuts de Québec*, 21 Geo. V, chap. 36, repealed in 1936 without being proclaimed operative.

120 Bird, *Documents*, 75.

121 Claxton, "Legislative Control of Radio in Canada," 441.

122 See Robinette, "Radio Legislation," 294–5, for a statement of this case.

123 See Raboy, *Missed Opportunities*, 36; Atkey, "The Provincial Interest in Broadcasting under the Canadian Constitution," 217.

124 Claxton, "Legislative Control of Radio in Canada," 447.
125 MG 32 B5, vol. 5, CRL 1930–31 file, Spry to Claxton, 18 March 1931.
126 The full text of the judgment may be found in Bird, *Documents*, 70–104.
127 The full text may be found in ibid., 105–10.
128 See Mullan and Beaman, "The Constitutional Implications of the Regulation of Telecommunications," 69ff; Wilkie, "*The Radio Reference* and Onward," 49.
129 Mullan and Beaman, "The Constitutional Implications of the Regulation of Telecommunications," 72ff.

CHAPTER ELEVEN

1 For example, RG 97, vol. 149, file 6206–72, part 1, Johnston to Canadian Marconi, 1 April 1928.
2 Ibid., Johnston to J.A. Dupont, 28 September 1928.
3 HOC, *Debates*, 28 April 1930, 1503.
4 Ibid., 30 May 1930, 2918; Special Committee 1932, 105.
5 See, for example, Special Committee 1932, 129, 169–70, 399; Nolan, *Foundations*, 78; Allard, *Straight Up*, 84–5. It has also been argued that lack of expansion in this period severely and permanently reduced our wavelength allocation within North America. See MacKinnon, *Analyzing the Havana Treaty*, 9.
6 Special Committee 1932, 592, 659. See also Nolan, "An Infant Industry," 517. Graham Spry also pointed out that while the threat of nationalization might possibly be blamed for a slowdown in building new physical facilities after 1929, it could not explain the poor programming offered in the period; indeed, with money freed up, there should have been even more resources available to devote to improving programs. Special Committee 1932, 551.
7 Special Committee 1932, 706–7, 547; MG 30 A42, vol. 27, file 151, "Valuation of Broadcasting Stations," March 1932. The only major stations not replying were CFCA, CFCF, CJCJ, and CFCN.
8 Peers, *The Politics of Canadian Broadcasting*, 116. Soon after the Special Committee reported, Gooderham and Worts withdrew its application for a power increase and CKGW stayed at 5000 watts. For a list of all stations that requested power increases in this period, see RG 97, vol. 147, file 6201–1, part 1, E. Hawken, "Memo to the Chairman, CRBC," 12 January 1933, encl.
9 Special Committee 1932, 6.
10 Ibid., 5; Department of Marine, *Annual Report*, 1931–32, 137. The Windsor station created controversy because it was aimed at American listeners and involved CBS affiliation. See HOC, *Debates*, 24 May 1932, 3346–7; MG 30 A42, vol. 19, file 102, W.A. Steel to R.B. Bennett, c. June 1932. For a list of all applications for private-commercial stations that had not been granted as

of January 1933, broken down by year and province, see RG 97, vol. 147, file 6206–1, part 1, E. Hawken, "Memo to the Chairman, CRBC," 12 January 1933, encl.

11 MG 30 D297, vol. 95, file 95–4, Spry to E.A. Corbett, 6 May 1931, and reply of 11 May 1931; see also ibid., Spry to John F. Garrett, 21 May 1931.

12 Special Committee 1932, 341, 438, 657.

13 CN Telegraphs had had, he claimed, a net income from broadcast transmissions of over $100,000 between 1929 and May 1931. MG 30 D67, vol. 19, file 2, [E.A. Weir], "Network Broadcasting Rates in Canada – Some Reasons Why They Should Be Reduced" [August 1931], and [E.A. Weir], "Centralization of Canadian Wire Services for the Development of Canadian Broadcasting," 14 August 1931.

14 Ibid., [E.A. Weir], "Network Broadcasting Rates in Canada – Some Reasons Why They Should Be Reduced," 4.

15 For example, CKAC Montreal at 730 kHz was bothered by XER, a Mexican station, and by CMK Havana.

16 MG 26K, M–1289, [W.A. Steel], "Radio situation between Canada and the United States in connection with the broadcast band," 27 January 1931, 360512.

17 The CRL claimed credit for this; one of Spry and Plaunt's first endeavours in late October 1930 was to get through to Bennett (who was in Britain) to persuade him to take personal charge of all licence and power changes pending the decision on broadcasting. See MG 30 D297, vol. 94, file 94–7, Spry to J.W. Dafoe, 5 November 1930.

18 RG 42, vol. 493, file 209–32–111, part 2, Edwards, "Memo for the Information of the Minister: Application CKGW Toronto for 840 K/C channel," 5 December 1930 and encl.; MG 26K, M–1289, Duranleau to Bennett, 28 December 1931, and reply, 360959–61; ibid., M–1290, Toronto *Star* to Radio Branch, 19 April 1932, copy, 361499ff; RG 97, vol. 152, file 6206–133, part 2, correspondence between CFRB and Radio Branch, October-December 1931; RG 42, vol. 494, file 209–32–111, part 3, correspondence between CKGW and Radio Branch, December 1931–May 1932.

19 See, for example, MG 26K, M–1294, C. Knowles, Toronto *Telegram,* to Bennett, 19 May 1934, 366174: "The raising of the license fee from $1.00 to $2.00, while apparently a trifle, was very unpopular ..." See also HOC, *Debates,* 8 April 1932, 1846.

20 Special Committee 1932, ii.

21 MG 32 B5, vol. 5, CRL 1932 file, Spry to Claxton, 8 March 1932. In a later version, Spry described Morand as helpful, Ilsley, Garland, Gagnon, and Cardin as allies, Euler as tough but "on our side," and R.K. Smith as "a little cool." MG 30 D297, vol. 108, file 108–38, Spry's notes on Margaret Prang's article.

22 See, for example, UBC, Plaunt Papers, vol. 1, file 12, A. Partridge, Canadian Daily Newspapers Association, to Plaunt, 28 March 1932 and 31 March 1932.

23 Special Committee 1932, 42.

24 In preparing the three-stage plan the league had the help of an unused presentation prepared for the committee by E.A. Weir of the CNR. MG 30 D67, vol. 19, file 1, Weir to W.D. Herridge, 26 May 1932.

25 MG 32 B5, vol. 5, file CRL 1932–36, Brooke Claxton to Murray, 29 March 1932; UBC, Plaunt Papers, vol. 1, file 19, Claxton to Plaunt, 24 March 1932.

26 Special Committee 1932, 295–323; Wilfrid Eggleston, "Won't Give Present Surplus To New System of Radio," Toronto Star, 12 May 1932, 1.

27 MG 30 D297, vol. 95, file 95–4, Spry to Morgan, 16 March 1932, 7 April 1932; Special Committee 1932, 469–90.

28 Special Committee 1932, 347–50.

29 Ibid., 384–8.

30 Ibid., 369–74.

31 Ibid., 407–8, 502.

32 Ibid., 508–9.

33 Ibid., 494.

34 HOC, Debates, 9 May 1932, 2709–11; Special Committee 1932, 729–31.

35 HOC, Debates, 11 May 1932, 2816ff.

36 Indeed, some years later Charles Bowman claimed that it was only the prime minister's "direct intervention" that prevented the committee from presenting a report adverse to the Aird recommendations. RG 41, vol. 303, file 14–2–1, part 1, Bowman to D. Manson, 10 January 1949.

37 The Montreal Gazette headlined a front-page story from its Ottawa correspondent on 23 April: "Radio Question Will Be Solved This Session: Beatty Plan is Likely to Be Adopted." After a quick denial from Bennett, the story was changed in the next issue to a more correct prediction that a compromise solution had been found involving a regulatory commission and the continued existence of private-enterprise stations. Montreal Gazette, 25 April 1932, 1.

38 See Special Committee 1932, 321, 703; Weir, The Struggle for National Broadcasting in Canada, 141–2; Spry, "Public Policy and Private Pressures," 31–3; MG 30 D67, vol. 2, file 11, and vol. 25, file 5.

39 MG 26K, M–1289, "Memorandum for the Prime Minister: B.B.C. Inter-Empire Christmas Broadcasting," 22 December 1931, 360953. Years later, Spry boasted, "We didn't spare the issue at all. We kept telephoning, seeing powerful people, shaking our heads with horror and so on." MG 30 D297, vol. 84, file 84–13, Spry, "Manuscript Memoirs," 4/56–7. See also MG 30 D67, vol. 6, file 4, Spry to E.A. Weir, 11 May 1962, and editorial, "Alien Monopoly Influence," Ottawa Citizen (23 December 1931), 20.

40 MG 32 B5, vol. 5, CRL 1932–36 file, Claxton to Murray, 26 January 1932.

41 W.D. Herridge also privately asked Steel to prepare background memos for the government's use. See MG 30 A42, vol. 32, file 183, Herridge to Steel, 6 February 1932, private and confidential.

42 MG 26K, M–1314, W.A. Steel, "The Broadcasting Service Required for the Inhabited Belt in Canada," 15 November 1931, 389221–28; ibid., W.A. Steel, "The Broadcasting Situation in Canada To-day," 28 December 1931, 389219–20.

43 Ibid., W.A. Steel, "Public Ownership of Broadcasting Facilities," 31 December 1931, 389232–3.

44 Ibid., M–1315, "Memorandum: Some aspects of the questions involved in the determination of the merits of public as against private ownership of radio broadcasting in Canada," 389236–47. While this memo is neither signed nor dated, internal evidence suggests fairly clearly that it was written by Steel.

45 Steel had written elsewhere that direct advertising would have to be allowed in order to raise sufficient revenues for the new broadcasting organization and to allow Canadian advertisers fair competition with American. See MG 30 A42, vol. 31, file 183, W.A. Steel to W.D. Herridge, "Memorandum" [April 1932].

46 MG 26K, M–1290, Bennett to Kaufman, 4 June 1932, 361663. The Ottawa *Citizen* had also made the same point after Beatty's testimony to the Special Committee. See editorial, "Radio Issue Defined," 21 April 1932, 28.

47 MG 26K, M–1290, Webb to Bennett, 28 March 1932, and reply of 1 April 1932, 361332–3.

48 MG 30 D297, vol. 21, file 21–3, "Diaries and Journals," 7 April 1932, 9 July 1932.

49 MG 26K M–1314, W.D. Herridge, "Preliminary Notes to be read in conjunction with the draft bill," n.d., 389210.

50 MG 26K M–1292, D.M. Wright to Bennett, 16 May 1932, 363763–7.

51 Editorial, "That Radio Report," Ottawa *Journal*, 10 May 1932, 6.

52 Wilfrid Eggleston, "Won't Give Present Surplus to New System of Radio," Toronto *Star*, 12 May 1932, 2.

53 HOC, *Debates*, 18 May 1932, 3035–6, reprinted in Bird, *Documents*, 111–14. Years later, Spry told Austin Weir: "Incidentally, my memory is that I supplied notes through Bill Harridge [*sic*], or Rod Finlayson, for the Prime Minister's statement, but this is not a thing I can ever prove; perhaps just as well." MG 30 D67, vol. 6, file 4, Spry to Weir, 28 August 1961.

54 *Statutes of Canada*, 22 & 23 Geo. V, chap. 51, reprinted in Bird, *Documents*, 115–23.

55 Indirect evidence suggests that the original draft of the bill did enable the CRBC to borrow but that this provision was removed after checking with the Department of Finance, which was ultra-cautious about ensuring that the commission not be allowed to go into debt. See MG 26K, M–1290, W. Sellar,

"Memorandum for Mr. Rhodes: Re Bill 94 (Radio Broadcasting)," 18 May 1932, 361617.

56 In amendments to the Radio Broadcasting Act introduced one year later, in May 1933, the sections giving Parliament final say in the purchase and construction of stations were altered to read "Governor in Council." While removing these powers from Parliament loosened the ties slightly, the commission's ability to act in this area remained subject to political will. See *Statutes of Canada*, 23 & 24 Geo. V, chap. 35.

57 Cardin suggested in the debate in the House that the word "may" be strengthened to ensure that the provinces really did get a say in programming, but he was put off by Bennett with legalisms and a promise that "action will be taken." HOC, *Debates*, 18 May 1932, 3037.

58 Peers, *The Politics of Canadian Broadcasting*, 105–6.

59 Senate, *Debates*, 25 May 1932, 484.

60 MG 26K, M–1314, W.D. Herridge, "Preliminary Notes," 389214. Emphasis added.

61 Spry, "Radio Broadcasting and Aspects of Canadian-American Relations," 115.

62 See Schultz, "Regulatory Agencies in the Canadian Political System," 336; Hodgetts, "The Public Corporation in Canada," 184–211; Baggaley, *The Emergence of the Regulatory State in Canada*, 8–15.

63 Canadian scholars emphasize that the regulatory tradition in this country tends to be somewhat different from that in the United States. Canadian regulatory agencies not only police the economic activity of private enterprises but also are often empowered to plan and promote the public interest. They also are often asked to regulate mixed public/private systems. See Cairns, *Rationales for Regulation*, 2–6.

64 The CRBC was not created in a vacuum. The issue of regulation and/or public ownership had been debated – and variously resolved – with respect to a number of public utilities in the previous hundred years. As with broadcasting, the solutions arrived at depended less on ideology than on the circumstances of the case. See Armstrong and Nelles, *Monopoly's Moment*, especially 321–8.

65 Allard, *Straight Up*, 97.

66 MG 26K, M–1290, Association of Canadian Advertisers to Bennett, telegram, 12 May 1932, 361539–40.

67 Ibid., Association of Canadian Advertisers to Bennett, 13 May 1932, 361572–3. The Advertising and Sales Roundtable of Toronto reported to Bennett that a mail ballot of its members indicated that 50 per cent favoured government control of private stations, 38 per cent the continuation of the present system, and 15 per cent government ownership. Ibid., 12 May 1932, 361565.

68 MG 28 I230, vol. 149, file "Radio Broadcasting, 1929–55," C.M. Pasmore to T.M. Kerruish, 13 March 1934. See also ibid., Alex MacKenzie, Canadian National Carbon, to T.M. Kerruish, 9 March 1934, and W.S. Campbell, CGE, to Canadian Manufacturers' Association, 9 March 1934. My thanks to Mike McConkey for bringing these letters to my attention. See also the favourable report on the act to the CMA in Marshall, "Report of the Commercial Intelligence Committee," 158.

69 MG 30 D297 vol. 95, file 95–18, "Statement by Graham Spry, Chairman, Canadian Radio League" [May 1932].

70 For example, Peers, *The Politics of Canadian Broadcasting*, 100.

71 MG 30 D297, vol. 21, file 21–4, Diaries and Journals, 8 May 1932; ibid., vol. 95, file 95–17, Spry and Plaunt to Morgan, telegram, 9 May 1932.

72 MG 32 B5, vol. 5, file CRL, Claxton to Murray, 14 May 1932.

73 Ibid., Claxton to Gladstone Murray, 14 May 1932; ibid., Spry to Claxton, 19 May 1932; MG 30 D297, vol. 95, file 95–17, Spry to W.D. Herridge, 14 May 1932. The last restriction was in fact removed in amendments to the act in 1933.

74 Weir, *The Struggle for National Broadcasting in Canada*, 135, says that the league also felt the $2 licence fee was a serious problem.

75 MG 32 B35, vol. 5, file CRL, Spry to Claxton, 19 May 1932.

76 Nolan, *Foundations*, 97–9.

77 MG 30 D297, vol. 108, file 108–38, Spry's notes on Margaret Prang's article.

78 Canada, Parliament, Senate, *Debates*, 25 May 1932, 485.

CONCLUSION

1 Williams, *Television*, 147.

2 For an eloquent discussion of this idea, taking it back to the late nineteenth century, see Marvin, *When Old Technologies Were New*, especially Introduction and Epilogue.

3 See Dewar, "The Origins of Public Broadcasting in Canada."

4 Special Committee 1932, 91.

5 Ibid., 386.

6 See Raboy, *Missed Opportunities*, 61.

7 In the United States, in contrast, the free-enterprise models (metaphors) of newspapers and railways dominated the debate about broadcasting in the 1920s and the public-utility concept was relegated to the sidelines. See Mander, "The Public Debate About Broadcasting in the Twenties." In Canada, of course, railways have also sometimes been conceived as public utilities under public ownership.

8 MG 26K, M–1315, [W.A. Steel], "Memorandum: Some aspects of the questions involved in the determination of the merits of public as against private ownership of radio broadcasting in Canada," 389236.

Bibliography

ARCHIVAL SOURCES

ARCHIVES OF ONTARIO (AO)
Records of Department of Attorney General. RG 4

BELL CANADA ARCHIVES (BCA)
Radio Station CHYC Log Book, October 1925–January 1927

METRO TORONTO LIBRARY, BALDWIN ROOM (MTL)
Johnson, Wm. Main. Papers

NATIONAL ARCHIVES OF CANADA (NA)
Allard, T.J. Papers. MG 30 D304
Bennett, Richard B. Papers. MG 26K
Bowman, Charles A. Papers. MG 30 D79
Bushnell, Ernest. Papers. MG 30 E250
Canadian Manufacturers' Association. Papers. MG 28 I 230
Canadian Marconi Papers. MG 28 III 72
Claxton, Brooke. Papers. MG 32 B5
King, W.L.M. Papers. MG 26J
Manson, Donald. Papers. MG 30 E344
Murphy, Charles. Papers. MG 27 III B8
Records of the Canadian Broadcasting Corporation. RG 41
Records of the Department of Communications. RG 97
Records of the Department of Transport. RG 12

Records of the Marine Branch. RG 42
Records of Parliament. RG 14
Records of the Privy Council Office. RG 2
Records of Royal Commissions. RG 33
Records of the Tariff Board. RG 79
Spencer, Leonard. Papers. MG 30 A77
Spry, Graham. Papers. MG 30 D297
Steel, W.A. Papers. MG 30 A42
Weir, E. Austin. Papers. MG 30 D67
Woodsworth, J.S. Papers. MG 27 III C7

NATIONAL ARCHIVES OF CANADA, CARTOGRAPHIC AND VISUAL
ARCHIVES (CAVA)
Bambrick, Kenneth. Interview Transcripts
CBC Program Archives Collection

PROVINCIAL ARCHIVES OF MANITOBA (PAM)
Public Utilities Records. Minister's Office. RG 11

UNIVERSITY OF BRITISH COLUMBIA LIBRARY, MANUSCRIPT
COLLECTIONS (UBC)
Plaunt, Alan B. Papers

PRINT SOURCES

Abrams, Philip. "Radio and Television." In *Discrimination and Popular Culture*,
    edited by Denys Thompson. Harmondsworth: Penguin 1964.
Adams, D.J. "The Nationalism of Communications in Canadian
    Historiography: A Survey of Sources." *Canadian Review of Studies in Nationalism*,
    7 (1980): 151–71.
Aitken, H.G.J. *The Continuous Wave: Technology and American Radio, 1900–1932.*
    Princeton, NJ: Princeton University Press 1985.
– *Syntony and Spark: The Origins of Radio.* New York: John Wiley and Sons 1976.
Allard, T.J. *The C.A.B. Story, 1926–1976: Private Broadcasting in Canada.* Ottawa:
    Canadian Association of Broadcasters 1976.
– *Straight Up: Private Broadcasting in Canada, 1918–1958.* Ottawa: Canadian
    Communications Foundation 1979.
Amey, P.D. "Broadcasting and the Performing Rights Societies in Canada. "
    Canadian Communications Law Review 2 (1970): 3–7.
Annual Financial Review. Toronto: William Briggs 1923.
Archer, G.L. *Big Business and Radio.* New York: Arno Press 1971; first published
    1939.
– *History of Radio to 1926.* New York: Arno Press 1971; first published 1938.

Armstrong, C., and H.V. Nelles. *Monopoly's Moment: The Organization and Regulation of Canadian Utilities, 1830– 1930*. Philadelphia: Temple University Press 1986.

Ashcroft, R.W. "Should Radio Be Nationalized in Canada?" *Saturday Night*, 24 January 1931:2.

Atkey, R. "The Provincial Interest in Broadcasting under the Canadian Constitution." *Canadian Communications Law Review*, 1 (1969): 212–74.

Aucoin, P. "Theory and Research in the Study of Policy-Making." In *The Structures of Policy-Making in Canada*, edited by G.B. Doern and P. Aucoin. Toronto: Macmillan 1971.

Aviation and Wireless News. May 1921–February 1922.

Aylesworth, Merlin. "The National Magazine of the Air." In T*he Radio Industry: The Story of its Development*. New York: Arno Press 1974; first published 1928.

Babaian, Sharon. *Radio Communication in Canada: An Historical and Technological Survey*. Ottawa: National Museum of Science and Technology 1992.

Babe, R.E. "Emergence and Development of Canadian Communication: Dispelling the Myths." In *Communication Canada: Issues in Broadcasting and New Technologies*, edited by R. Lorimer and D. Wilson. Toronto: Kagan and Woo 1988.

– *Telecommunications in Canada*. Toronto: University of Toronto Press 1990.

Baggaley, Carman D. *The Emergence of the Regulatory State in Canada, 1867–1939*. N.p.: Economic Council of Canada Technical Report 1981.

Bankart, D. "Putting Canada 'On the Air.'" *MacLean's*, 15 November 1926.

Banning, W.P. *Commercial Broadcasting Pioneer: The WEAF Experiment, 1922–1926*. Cambridge, Mass.: Harvard University Press 1946.

Barnouw, Erik. "Historical Survey of Communications Breakthroughs." *Proceedings of The Academy of Political Science*, 34, no. 4 (1982): 13–23.

– *A Tower in Babel: A History of Broadcasting in the United States* (vol. 1, to 1933). New York: Oxford University Press 1966.

Batson, L.D. *Radio Markets of the World*. Washington: Government Printing Office, 1926 to 1932.

Baulu, Roger. *CKAC, une histoire d'amour*. Montréal: Stanké 1982.

Bensman, M.R. "The Regulation of Radio Broadcasting by the Department of Commerce, 1921–1927." Ph.D. dissertation, University of Wisconsin 1969.

– "The Zenith-WJAZ Case and the Chaos of 1926–27." *Journal of Broadcasting*, 14 (1970):423–41.

Biel, Michael J. "The Making and Use of Recordings in Broadcasting before 1936." Ph.D. dissertation, Northwestern University 1977, 2 vols.

"Big Opportunities in the Furore over Radio." *Bookseller and Stationer*, May 1922:17.

Biocca, Frank. "Media and Perceptual Shifts: Early Radio and the Clash of Musical Cultures." *Journal of Popular Culture*, 24 (1990):1–15.

Bird, Roger, ed. *Documents of Canadian Broadcasting.* Ottawa: Carleton University Press 1988.

Bissell, Claude. *The Young Vincent Massey.* Toronto: University of Toronto Press 1981.

Black, R.H. "The Early Days of Canadian Broadcasting." M.Sc. thesis, Boston University 1968.

Blakley, S.W. "Canadian Private Broadcasters and the Reestablishment of a Private Broadcasting Network." Ph.D. dissertation, University of Michigan 1979.

Bowman, C.A. *Ottawa Editor: The Memoirs of Charles A. Bowman.* Sidney, BC: Gray's 1966.

Brand, Paul. "'The Twentieth Century Bible': Listening to the Radio in Montreal, 1924–1939." *The Register* 1, no. 2 (1980): 108–30.

Brandes, J. *Herbert Hoover and Economic Diplomacy: Department of Commerce Policy, 1921–1928.* Pittsburgh: University of Pittsburgh Press 1962.

Briggs, Asa. *The Birth of Broadcasting, The History of Broadcasting in the United Kingdom,* vol. 1. London: Oxford University Press 1961.

– "Problems and Possibilities in the Writing of Broadcasting History." *Media, Culture and Society,* 2 (1980):5–13.

Cairns, Robert D. *Rationales for Regulation.* Technical Report No. 2, Centre for the Study of Regulated Industries. Montreal: McGill University 1980.

Caldwell, O.H. "The Administration of Federal Radio Legislation." In American Academy of Political and Social Science, *Radio.* New York: Arno Press 1971; first published 1929.

Canada. Department of the Auditor-General. *Annual Reports.* 1921–22 to 1931–32.

– Department of Marine and Fisheries. *Annual Reports.* 1922–23 to 1931–32.

– Department of the Naval Service. *Annual Reports.* 1911–1912 to 1920–21.

– Dominion Bureau of Statistics. *Seventh Census of Canada, 1931.*

– Parliament. House of Commons. *Debates.*

– Parliament. House of Commons. Special Committee on Bill No. 2 re Copyright Act, 1925.

– Parliament. House of Commons. Special Committee on the Canadian Radio Commission, *Minutes of Proceedings and Evidence,* 1936.

– Parliament. House of Commons. Special Committee on the Operations of the Commission under the Canadian Radio Broadcasting Act, 1932, *Minutes of Proceedings and Evidence,* 1934.

– Parliament. House of Commons. Special Committee on Radio Broadcasting. *Proceedings and Report,* 1932.

– Parliament. Senate. *Debates.*

– Royal Commission on Canada's Economic Prospects. Canadian Business Service Limited. *The Electronics Industry in Canada.* Ottawa: Queen's Printer 1956.

– Royal Commission on Radio Broadcasting. *Report*. Ottawa: King's Printer 1929.

– *Statutes of Canada.*

– *Statutes of the Province of Canada*

– Task Force on Broadcasting Policy. *Report*. Ottawa: Minister of Supply and Services 1986.

Canada Gazette.

Canada Year Book.

Canadian Annual Review. Toronto: Canadian Review 1921 to 1932.

Canadian Radio. April–August 1924.

Canadian Radio Patents Limited. *Patents ... and Radio in Canada.* N.p.: 1937.

Canadian Wireless. October 1921–August 1922.

Cantril, H., and G. Allport. *The Psychology of Radio.* New York: Arno Press 1971; first published 1935.

Canuel, Alain. "La Présence de l'imperialisme dans les débuts de la radiophonie au Canada, 1900–1928." *Journal of Canadian Studies,* 20, no. 4 (1986):45–59.

Charland, Maurice. "Technological Nationalism." *Canadian Journal of Social and Political Theory,* 10, nos. 1–2 (1986):196–220.

Charlesworth, H. "Great Artists on Radio." *Canadian Home Journal,* December 1929.

– "Radio Telephony." *Canadian Home Journal,* June 1922.

Claxton, Brooke. "Legislative Control of Radio in Canada." *Air Law Review,* 2, no. 4 (1931):439–54.

– "Protection Against the Unauthorized Use of a Broadcast in Canada." *Canadian Bar Review,* 10 (1932):1–19.

Clement, Wallace. *The Canadian Corporate Elite: An Analysis of Economic Power.* Toronto: McClelland and Stewart 1975.

Coats, D.R.P. "Adventures in Radio," parts 14 and 15. *Manitoba Calling,* 4 (November and December 1940).

– "Canada's Fifty Years of Broadcasting and Stories Stations Tell: Featuring the Pioneer Station XWA, later given the call letters CFCF: 1919–1969." Canadian Marconi Library, Montreal, n.d.

Cockfield-Brown Ltd. "Radio as an Advertising Medium" [1930–31]. Copy in author's possession, thanks to John Twomey.

Cohen, Lizabeth. "Encountering Mass Culture at the Grassroots: The Experience of Chicago Workers in the 1920s." *American Quarterly,* 41, no. 1 (1989):6–33.

Collins, Richard. *Culture, Communication and National Identity: The Case of Canadian Television.* Toronto: University of Toronto Press 1990.

[Craick, W.A.]. *A History of Canadian Journalism.* Vol. 2. Toronto: Ontario Publishing Company 1959.

Czitrom, D.J. *Media and the American Mind: From Morse to McLuhan.* Chapel Hill, NC: University of North Carolina Press 1982.

Danelian, N.R. *A.T. and T.: The Story of Industrial Conquest.* New York: Arno Press 1974; first published 1939.

Davis, H.P. "The Early History of Broadcasting in the United States." In *The Radio Industry: The Story of its Development.* New York: Arno Press 1974; first published 1928.

Davis, D.F. "Dependent Motorization: Canada and the Automobile." *Journal of Canadian Studies,* 21, no. 3 (1986):106–32.

Davis, M. "International Radiotelegraph Conventions and Traffic Arrangements." *Air Law Review,* 1, no. 3 (1930):349–73.

De Fleur, M.L. and S.J. Ball-Rokeach. *Theories of Mass Communication,* 4th ed. New York: Longman 1982.

Dewar, K.C. "The Origins of Public Broadcasting in Canada in Comparative Perspective." *Canadian Journal of Communication,* 8 (1982):26–45.

Diamond Jubilee Broadcast Committee. *A Mari Usque Ad Mare.* N.p.: 1927.

Doern, G.B., and R.W. Phidd. *Canadian Public Policy: Ideas, Structure, Process.* Toronto: Methuen 1983.

Dominion Law Reports. 1929, 1930.

Douglas, George H. *The Early Days of Radio Broadcasting.* Jefferson, NC: McFarland 1987.

Douglas, Susan J. "Exploring Pathways in the Ether: The Formative Years of Radio in America, 1896-1912." Ph.D. dissertation, Brown University 1980.

– *Inventing American Broadcasting, 1899–1922.* Baltimore: Johns Hopkins University Press 1987.

Dror, Y. "Muddling Through – 'Science' or Inertia?" *Public Administration Review,* 24 (1964):153–7.

DuBoff, R.G. "The Rise of Communications Regulation: The Telegraph Industry, 1844–1880." *Journal of Communication* 34, no. 3 (1984):52–66.

Duffy, Dennis. *Imagine Please: Early Radio Broadcasting in British Columbia.* Victoria: Public Archives of British Columbia 1983.

Editorial. "Public Opinion." *Canadian Nation,* 1 (February 1929):11.

Editorial. "Visiting Orators Take Notice." *Saturday Night,* August 1927:1

Edwards, Frederick. "Does Canada Want Government Radio?: No." *MacLean's,* 1 May 1930.

Electrical News. 1922 to 1924.

Ellis, David. *Evolution of the Canadian Broadcasting System.* Ottawa: Department of Communications 1979.

Eoyang, T. *An Economic Study of the Radio Industry in the United States of America.* New York: Arno Press 1974; copyright 1937.

Esslin, Martin. *An Anatomy of Drama.* London: T. Smith 1976.

Fink, Howard. "CKUA Radio Drama and Regional Theatre." *Theatre History in Canada,* 8, no. 2 (1987):221–33.

– "The Sponsor's v. the Nation's Choice: North American Radio Drama." In *Radio Drama,* edited by Peter Lewis. Toronto: Academic Press 1981.

"For the Record: A Brief Historical Note on the Mechanical Reproduction Announcement Requirement." *Journal of Broadcasting*, 4, no. 2 (1960):119–22.

Foster, Frank. *Broadcasting Policy Development.* Ottawa: Franfrost Communications 1982.

Frederick, Mrs C. "A Real Use for Radio." *Good Housekeeping* July 1922.

Frigon, A. "The Organization of Radio Broadcasting in Canada." *Revue Trimestrielle Canadienne* (1929):395–410.

Gibbon, J.M. "Radio as a Fine Art." *Canadian Forum*, 11 (1931): 212–14.

Godfrey, D. "Canadian Marconi: CFCF, the Forgotten Case." *Canadian Journal of Communication*, 8, no. 4 (1982): 56–71.

Hardin, Herschel. *Closed Circuits: The Sellout of Canadian Television.* Vancouver: Douglas and McIntyre 1985.

Harkness, Ross. *J.E. Atkinson of the Star.* Toronto: University of Toronto Press 1968.

Harrison, A.P. Jr. "Single-Control Tuning: An Analysis of an Innovation." *Technology and Culture*, 20, no. 2 (1979):296–321.

Hayes, C.J.H. *Essays on Nationalism.* New York: Macmillan 1926.

Head, Sydney W. with C.H. Sterling. *Broadcasting in America: A Survey of Television, Radio, and New Technologies*, 4th ed. Boston: Houghton Mifflin 1982.

Hodgetts, J.E. "The Public Corporation in Canada." In *Canadian Public Administration*, edited by J.E. Hodgetts and D.C. Corbett. Toronto: Macmillan 1960.

Johnson, Elton. "Canada's Radio Consciousness." *MacLean's*, 15 October 1924.

Johnson, G.A. "Secretary of Commerce Herbert C. Hoover: The First Regulator of American Broadcasting, 1921–1928." Ph.D. dissertation, University of Iowa 1970.

Johnson, Lesley. "Radio and Everyday Life: The Early Years of Broadcasting in Australia, 1922–1945." *Media, Culture and Society*, 3 (1981):167–78.

Jome, Hiram. *Economics of the Radio Industry.* New York: Arno Press 1971; first published 1925.

Kallman, H., G. Potvin, and K. Winters, eds. *Encyclopedia of Music in Canada.* Toronto: University of Toronto Press 1981.

Kelly, G. "Developing a Canadian National Feeling: The Diamond Jubilee Celebrations of 1927." M.A. thesis, McGill University 1985.

Kerry, A.J., and W.A. McDill. *The History of The Corps of Royal Canadian Engineers.* 2 vols. Ottawa: Military Engineers Association of Canada 1962.

Kidd, J. "From a Music Box to 'The Guess Who'." *Broadcaster* (October 1969).

King, W.L.M. *The Mackenzie King Diaries, 1893-1931.* Toronto: University of Toronto Press 1973, transcription.

Kittross, J., ed. *Documents in American Telecommunications Policy.* 2 vols. New York: Arno Press 1977.

Koppes, C.R. "The Social Destiny of Radio: Hope and Disillusionment in the 1920's." *South Atlantic Quarterly*, 68 (1969):364–76.

Kottman, R.N. "Herbert Hoover and the Smoot-Hawley Tariff: Canada, a Case Study." *Journal of American History,* 62 (1975):609–35.

Langham, J. "Tuning in: Canadian Radio Resources." *Archivaria,* 9 (1979–80):105–24.

Large, Betty and T. Crothers. *Out of Thin Air: The Story of CFCY "The Friendly Voice of the Maritimes".* Charlottetown, PEI: Applecross Press 1989.

Lavoie, E. "L'Evolution de la radio au Canada français avant 1940." *Recherches sociographiques,* 12, no. 1 (1971):17–49.

Law Reports of Canada: Exchequer Court of Canada. 1926, 1929.

– *Supreme Court of Canada.* 1927, 1929.

Leach, E.E. "'Voices Out of the Night': Radio Research and Ideas About Mass Behavior in the United States, 1920–1950." *Canadian Review of American Studies,* 20, no. 2 (1989):191–209.

Lederman, W.R. "Divided Authority in Canada to Incorporate Companies and to Regulate the Telecommunications Industry." In *Telecommunications in Canada: An Interface of Business and Government,* edited by H.E. English. Toronto: Methuen 1973.

Leive, D.M. *International Telecommunications and International Law: The Regulation of the Radio Spectrum.* Leyden: A.W. Sijthoff 1970.

Levine, Lawrence. *Highbrow/Lowbrow: The Emergence of Cultural Hierarchy in America.* Cambridge, Mass.: Harvard University Press 1988.

Lichty, L.W., and M.C. Topping, eds., *American Broadcasting.* New York: Hastings House 1975.

Lindblom, C.E. "The Science of 'Muddling Through'." *Public Administration Review,* 19 (1959):79–88.

MacDonald, J.F. *Don't Touch That Dial!: Radio Programming in American Life, 1920–1960.* Chicago: Nelson-Hall 1979.

MacKinnon, Keith A. *Analyzing the Havana Treaty.* N.p.: CBC 1944.

Maclaurin, W.R. *Invention and Innovation in the Radio Industry.* New York: Macmillan 1949.

MacLennan, Anne. "'Circumstances Beyond Our Control': A Portrait of Canadian Radio during the 1930's." Seminar paper, Concordia University 1986.

Mander, Mary S. "The Public Debate About Broadcasting in the Twenties: An Interpretive History." *Journal of Broadcasting* 28, no. 2 (1984):167–85.

Marchard, Roland. *Advertising the American Dream: Making Way for Modernity, 1920–1940.* Berkeley and Los Angeles: University of California Press 1985.

Marshall, Alex. "Report of the Commercial Intelligence Committee." *Industrial Canada,* 33, no. 3 (1932), 158.

Martin, Michèlle. "Capitalizing on the 'Feminine' Voice." *Canadian Journal of Communication,* 14, no. 3 (1989):42–62.

Marvin, Carolyn. *When Old Technologies Were New: Thinking About Electric Communication in the Late Nineteenth Century.* New York: Oxford University Press 1988.

Massey, Vincent. *What's Past is Prologue.* Toronto: Macmillan 1963.

McConkey, M. "Monopoly Capitalist Communications in Canada, 1879–1932: Critical and Empirical Inquiries Toward a Cultural-Economy of Communications History." MA original essay, Concordia University 1986.

McNaught, Carlton. *Canada Gets the News.* Toronto: Ryerson Press 1940.

McNeil, Bill, and M. Wolfe. *Signing On: The Birth of Radio in Canada.* Toronto: Doubleday 1982.

Minasian, J.R. "The Political Economy of Broadcasting in the 1920's." *Journal of Law and Economics,* 12 (1969):391–403.

Montigny, B. "Les Débuts de la Radio à Montréal et le Poste C.K.A.C." Mémoire de MA, Université de Montréal 1979.

Moogk, E.B. *Roll Back the Years: History of Canadian Recorded Sound and its Legacy.* Ottawa: National Library of Canada 1975.

Morse, C. "Copyright – Opera – Broadcasting by Wireless Telephony – Infringement." *Canadian Bar Review,* 5 (1927):623–6.

Mosco, Vincent. *Broadcasting in the United States: Innovative Challenge and Organizational Control.* Norwood, NJ: Ablex Publishing 1979.

Mullan, David, and R. Beaman. "The Constitutional Implications of the Regulation of Telecommunications." *Queen's Law Journal,* 1, no. 4 (1973):67–78.

Mundy, G. "'Free-Enterprise' or 'Public Service'? The Origins of Broadcasting in the US, UK and Australia." *Australian and New Zealand Journal of Sociology,* 18, no. 3 (1982):279–301.

Neal, A.L. "Development of Radio Communication in Canada." *Canadian Geographical Journal,* 22 (1941):164–91.

Neatby, H.B. *William Lyon Mackenzie King: The Lonely Heights, 1924–1932.* Toronto: University of Toronto Press 1963.

Nichols, M.E. *(CP): The Story of the Canadian Press.* Toronto: Ryerson Press 1948.

Nolan, Michael. "Canada's Broadcasting Pioneers, 1918–1932." *Canadian Journal of Communication,* 10, no. 3 (1984):1–26.

– "Canadian Election Broadcasting: Political Practices and Radio Regulation 1919–1939." *Journal of Broadcasting and Electronic Media,* 29, no. 2 (1985):175–88.

– *Foundations: Alan Plaunt and the Early Days of CBC Radio.* Toronto: CBC Enterprises 1986.

– "An Infant Industry: Canadian Private Radio, 1919–36." *Canadian Historical Review,* 70 (1989):496–518.

Nye, Russel. *The Unembarrassed Muse.* New York: Dial Press 1970.

O'Brien, J.E. "A History of the Canadian Radio League, 1930–1936." Ph.D. dissertation, University of Southern California 1964.

Owen, Bruce. *Economics and Freedom of Expression: Media Structure and the First Amendment.* Cambridge, Mass.: Ballinger 1975.

Pagé, Pierre. "La radio dans la vie des Québécois." ASCRT/AERTC *Bulletin,* 3 (1978):8.

Peers, Frank W. *The Politics of Canadian Broadcasting 1920–1951*. Toronto: University of Toronto Press 1969.

Pegg, Mark. *Broadcasting and Society, 1918–1939*. London: Croom Helm 1983.

Penton, M. James. *Jehovah's Witnesses in Canada: Champions of Freedom of Speech and Worship*. Toronto: Macmillan 1976.

Pitt, Douglas C. *The Telecommunications Function in the British Post Office*. Farnborough, UK: Saxon House 1980.

[Plaunt, Alan.] *The Canadian Radio League*. N.p.: January 1931.

Prang, Margaret. "The Origins of Public Broadcasting in Canada." *Canadian Historical Review*, 46 (1965):1–31.

Québec. *Statuts de Québec.*

Raboy, Marc. *Missed Opportunities: The Story of Canada's Broadcasting Policy*. Montreal and Kingston: McGill-Queen's University Press 1990.

Radio. May 1922–January 1929.

"Radio Advertising." *Fortune*, 1 (December 1930):66.

"Radio and the Home." *Canadian Home Journal* May 1927.

Radio Bug. August 1923–November 1924.

"Radio for the Farmer an Urgent Need." *Canadian Magazine*, August 1929.

Radio News of Canada. July 1922–August 1930.

"Radio Plans of System Make Transportation History." CNR *Magazine*, 10, no. 1 (January 1924).

Radio Trade Builder. September 1926–December 1928.

Raine, N.R. "Our Radio Trouble Hunters." *MacLean's*, 1 November 1927.

Raymond, B. "Radio." In *Mass Media in Canada*, edited by J.A. Irving. Toronto: Ryerson Press 1962.

Reich, L.S. "Research, Patents, and the Struggle to Control Radio: A Study of Big Business and the Uses of Industrial Research." *Business History Review*, 51, no. 2 (1977):208–35.

Resnick, P. *The Land of Cain: Class and Nationalism in English Canada 1945–1975*. Vancouver: New Star Books 1977.

Reynolds, G.F. "Early Wireless and Radio in Manitoba, 1909–1924." Historical and Scientific Society of Manitoba *Transactions*, Series III, 34–5 (1977–79):89–113.

Rickwood, Roger. "Canadian Broadcasting Policy and the Private Broadcasters 1936–1968." Ph.D. dissertation, University of Toronto 1976.

Robb, W.D. "Radio the Newest of Sciences." *CNR Magazine*, 10, no. 12 (1924).

Robinette, J.J. "Radio Legislation: Can It Be Enacted by the Dominion Parliament?" *Canadian Forum*, 11 (1931):294–5.

Rogers, G.H. "The History of the Clear Channel and Super Power Controversy in the Management of the Standard Broadcast Allocation Plan." Ph.D. dissertation, University of Utah 1972.

Rosen, Philip T. *The Modern Stentors: Radio Broadcasters and the Federal Government, 1920–1934*. Westport, Conn.: Greenwood Press 1980.

Rudin, R. "Montreal Banks and the Urban Development of Quebec, 1840–1914." In *Shaping the Urban Landscape*, edited by G. Stelter and A. Artibise. Ottawa: Carleton University Press 1982.

Scannell, P. "Music for the Multitude? The Dilemmas of the BBC's Music Policy, 1923–1946." *Media, Culture and Society* 3 (1981):243–60.

Scannell, P. and D. Cardiff. *The Birth of British Broadcasting: Volume One 1922–1939 Serving the Nation*. Oxford: Basil Blackwell 1991.

– "Serving the Nation." In *Popular Culture: Past and Present*, edited by B. Waites *et al*. London: Croom Helm 1982.

Schairer, O.S. *Patent Policies of Radio Corporation of America*. New York: RCA Institutes Technical Press 1939.

Schmalz, Wayne. *On Air: Radio in Saskatchewan*. Regina: Coteau Books 1990.

Schultz, R. "Regulatory Agencies in the Canadian Political System." In *Public Administration in Canada: Selected Readings*, 3rd ed., edited by K. Kernaghan. Toronto: Methuen 1977.

Seldes, Gilbert, *The Great Audience*. New York: Viking Press 1950.

Sivowitch, Elliot. "A History of Radio Spectrum Allocation in the United States, 1912–1926." MA thesis, Syracuse University 1957.

– "A Technological Survey of Broadcasting's 'Pre-History,' 1876–1920." *Journal of Broadcasting*, 15 (1970–71):1–20.

Smead, Elmer. *Freedom of Speech by Radio and Television*. Washington: Public Affairs Press 1959.

Smith, Michael L. "Selling the Moon." In *The Culture of Consumption: Critical Essays in American History*, edited by R.W. Fox and T.J.J. Lears. New York: Pantheon 1983.

Smith, R.F. "Oldest Station in the Nation"? *Journal of Broadcasting*, 4, no. 1 (1959–60):40–55.

Smulyan, Susan. "'And Now a Word From Our Sponsors ...': Commercialization of American Broadcast Radio, 1920–1934." Ph.D. dissertation, Yale University 1985.

Smythe, Dallas. *Dependency Road: Communications, Capitalism, Consciousness and Canada*. Norwood, NJ: Ablex 1981.

Spalding, J.W. "1928: Radio Becomes a Mass Advertising Medium." *Journal of Broadcasting*, 8, no. 1 (1963–64):31–44.

Spry, Graham. "The Canadian Broadcasting Issue." *Canadian Forum*, 11 (1931):246–9.

– "The Case for Nationalized Broadcasting." *Queen's Quarterly* 38 (1931):151–69.

– "One Nation, Two Cultures." *Canadian Nation*, 1 (February 1929):21.

– "The Origins of Public Broadcasting in Canada: A Comment." *Canadian Historical Review*, 46 (1965):134–41.

– "Public Policy and Private Pressures: The Canadian Radio League 1930–6 and Countervailing Power." In *On Canada: Essays in Honour of Frank H. Underhill*, edited by N. Penlington. Toronto: University of Toronto Press 1971.

– "Radio Broadcasting and Aspects of Canadian-American Relations." In Conference on Canadian-American Affairs Held at the St Lawrence University, Canton, New York, June 17–22, 1935, *Proceedings*, edited by W.W. McLaren *et al.*

– "Should Radio Be Nationalized in Canada?" *Saturday Night*, 24 January 1931.

Stamps, C.H. *The Concept of the Mass Audience in American Broadcasting: An Historical-Descriptive Study.* New York: Arno Press 1979; copyright 1957.

Sterling, C.H., and J.M. Kittross. *Stay Tuned: A Concise History of American Broadcasting.* Belmont, CA Wadsworth 1978.

Stevens, J.D., and H.D. Garcia. *Communication History.* Beverly Hills, CA: Sage 1980.

Stewart, Sandy. *From Coast to Coast: A Personal History of Radio in Canada.* Toronto: CBC Enterprises 1985.

–"How Radio Got Started ... A Canadian View." *AudioScene Canada*, 17, no. 5 (1980):31–4.

Stuart, Ross. "Strike Four: The Story of Canada's Cultural Sellout." *Atkinson Review of Canadian Studies*, 1, no. 1 (1983):13–20.

Sturmey, S.G. *The Economic Development of Radio.* London: Duckworth 1958.

Susman, Warren. "Communication and Culture." In *Mass Media Between the Wars: Perceptions of Cultural Tension, 1918–1941*, edited by C.L. Covert and J.D. Stevens. Syracuse: Syracuse University Press 1984.

Taylor, Graham. "Charles F. Sise, Bell Canada, and the Americans: A Study of Managerial Autonomy, 1880–1905." *Historical Papers*, 1982:11–30.

Thomas, Alan M. "A Concept of the Audience: An Examination of the Work of Harold A. Innis with Respect to its Application to the Development of Broadcasting." Ph.D. dissertation, Columbia University 1964.

Toogood, Alexander. *Broadcasting in Canada: Aspects of Regulation and Control.* Ottawa: Canadian Association of Broadcasters 1969.

Trofimenkoff, S.M. *Action Française: French Canadian Nationalism in the Twenties.* Toronto: University of Toronto Press 1975.

Vipond, Mary. "Best Sellers in English Canada: 1919–1928." *Journal of Canadian Fiction*, 35–6 (1986):73–105.

– "Canadian Nationalism and the Plight of Canadian Magazines in the 1920's." *Canadian Historical Review*, 58 (1977):43–63.

– "CKY Winnipeg in the 1920's: Canada's Only Experiment in Government Monopoly Broadcasting." *Manitoba History*, 12 (1986):2–13.

– *The Mass Media in Canada.* Toronto: James Lorimer 1989.

– "National Consciousness in English-speaking Canada in the 1920's: Seven Studies." Ph.D. dissertation, University of Toronto 1974.

– "Nationalism and Nativism: The Native Sons of Canada in the 1920's." *Canadian Review of Studies in Nationalism*, 9 (1982):81–95.

- "The Nationalist Network: English Canada's Intellectuals and Artists in the 1920's." *Canadian Review of Studies in Nationalism,* 7 (1980):32–52.

Weaver, John. "Imperilled Dreams: Canadian Opposition to the American Empire, 1918–1930." Ph.D. dissertation, Duke University 1973.

Weir, E.Austin. *The Struggle for National Broadcasting in Canada.* Toronto: McClelland and Stewart 1965.

Wik, R.M. "The Radio in Rural America during the 1920's." *Agricultural History,* 55, no. 4 (1981):339–50.

Wilkie, J. Scott. "*The Radio Reference* and Onward: Exclusive Federal Jurisdiction over General Content in Broadcasting?" *Osgoode Hall Law Journal,* 18 (1980):49–86.

Wilkins, Mira. *The Emergence of Multinational Enterprises: American Business Abroad from the Colonial Era to 1914.* Cambridge, Mass.: Harvard University Press 1970.

- *The Maturing of Multinational Enterprise: American Business Abroad from 1914 to 1970.* Cambridge, Mass.: Harvard University Press 1974.

Willey, M.M., and S.A. Rice. *Communication Agencies and Social Life.* President's Monographs on Recent Social Trends. New York: McGraw-Hill 1933.

Williams, Raymond. "Base and Superstructure in Marxist Cultural Theory." *New Left Review,* 82 (1973):3–10.

- *Problems in Materialism and Culture: Selected Essays.* London: NLB 1980.

- *Television: Technology and Cultural Form.* New York: Schocken Books 1975.

Wilson, V. Seymour. *Canadian Public Policy and Administration: Theory and Environment.* Toronto: McGraw-Hill Ryerson 1981.

Wireless and Aviation News. March–April 1922.

Wise, S.F. *Canadian Airmen and the First World War.* Toronto: University of Toronto Press 1980.

Wrong, Hume. "The Canada-United States Relationship 1927/1951." *International Journal,* 31, no. 3 (1975):529–45.

Zimmerman, Arthur E. *In the Shadow of the Shield: The Development of Wireless Telegraphy and Radio Broadcasting in Kingston and at Queen's University: An Oral and Documentary History, 1902–1957.* Kingston: the author 1991.

Index